EMBEDDED GENERATIONS

Embedded Generations

FAMILY LIFE AND SOCIAL CHANGE IN CONTEMPORARY CHINA

LIU JIEYU

PRINCETON UNIVERSITY PRESS

PRINCETON & OXFORD

Published by Princeton University Press
41 William Street, Princeton, New Jersey 08540
99 Banbury Road, Oxford OX2 6JX

press.princeton.edu

GPSR Authorized Representative: Easy Access System Europe - Mustamäe tee 50, 10621 Tallinn, Estonia, gpsr.requests@easproject.com

ISBN 978-0-691-25839-3
ISBN (pbk.) 978-0-691-25840-9
ISBN (e-book) 978-0-691-25841-6

British Library Cataloging-in-Publication Data is available

Editorial: Rebecca Brennan and Rebecca Binnie
Production Editorial: Jenny Wolkowicki
Cover design: Katie Osborne
Production: Lauren Reese
Publicity: William Pagdatoon and Kathryn Stevens

Copyeditor: Lachlan Brooks

Cover images *clockwise from top left*: author visiting Tiananmen Square with her family as a tourist at the age of 13, author's mother visiting Tiananmen Square with her urban peers at the age of 13 to participate in the Cultural Revolution, author's grandparents' wedding photo, author's parents' wedding photo. All photos courtesy of the author.

This book has been composed in Arno

10 9 8 7 6 5 4 3 2 1

This book is dedicated to all Chinese families I encountered during my fieldwork as well as my own family who supported me as I researched and wrote up this book.

CONTENTS

ACKNOWLEDGEMENTS

I WOULD like to thank all the people who participated in the research under-pinning this book. The willingness of these individuals to sacrifice their time and tell me their life stories made all of this possible.

I would like to thank the following academics based in China: Fan Ke, Lin Ka, Wu Zongjie, Wu Chongqing, Zhang Dayong, Wei Liqun, Zhao Wei, Yin Luanyu, Zhao Qiuyan, Yan Yu, and Zhang Shiyong. They helped me assemble a local team of Chinese research assistants including Feng Bochen, Zhou Fang, Ma Fangfang, Chen Huiping, Li Jia, Yu Jiaqing, Liu Jinbo, Li Jingchun, Huang Jinghui, Shen Keyu, Chen Peier, Li Qin, Liu Rongxiong, Wang Ruixue, Lin Xiaolan, Wang Yingqi, Xiong Yiyi, Zhang Yuchi, Yan Yuping, Li Yunqiu, and Cui Zhinan. I am indebted to all of these Chinese scholars for helping to in-troduce families to participate and their ongoing support of the project.

Some of the project findings have been presented previously in workshops and symposia and on these occasions I have benefited greatly from the advice and support of many scholars, including Hongwei Bao, Kwok Shing Chan, Susanne Choi, James Cummings, Sarah Dauncey, Sara Friedman, Jacqui Gabb, Xiaorong Gu, Colette Harris, Henrietta Harrison, Derek Hird, Travis Kong, Pei-Chia Lan, Chen Mei-Hua, Rachel Murphy, Emiko Ochiai, Merrill Silverstein, Dorothy J. Solinger, Rachel Thomson, Fan Xin, Brenda S. A. Yeoh, and Jean Yeung. In particular, I would like to thank Stevi Jackson, Ellen Judd, William Jankowiak, Charlotte Ikels, Deborah Davis and Brian Heaphy for their sharp insight on the project findings. I would also like to thank Martin King Whyte who has provided detailed comments on the first draft of the manu-script, not only correcting any factual errors but also helping me to sharpen my arguments. At SOAS University of London, I would like to thank many colleagues including but not exclusively Lindiwe Dovey, Colette Harris, Kha-lid Hasan, Xiaoning Lu, Shirin Rai, Li-Sa Whittington, and Bob Ash. In par-ticular, I am grateful to Bob—not only a mentor, who reviewed several drafts of the manuscript, but also a great friend.

I am very grateful for the support from my editor, Rebecca Brennan who provided invaluable advice and helped me to construct a stronger academic / empirical narrative. I have also benefited greatly from the editorial support of

Chloe Coy who provided detailed comments, especially how to make it more engaging and accessible. Rebecca Binnie also kindly and patiently dealt with all administrative matters. I would also like to thank two anonymous reviewers who provided insightful suggestions on the full manuscript to enable me to sharpen my arguments. Finally, I would like to thank my copyeditor Lachlan Brooks who carefully read through my manuscript and offered beautiful language editing.

I am very grateful for the financial support received from the UK Economic and Social Research Council and the European Research Council who funded my two fieldwork trips to the region.

Finally I would like to thank my family, John, Elizabeth, and Alfie for their love and support.

A small part of chapter 1 appeared in Jieyu Liu, "Childhood in Urban China: A Three-Generation Portrait," *Current Sociology* 70, no. 4 (2022): 598–617.

A small part of chapter 5 appeared in Jieyu Liu, "Filial Piety, Love or Money: Foundation of Old Age Support in Urban China," *Journal of Aging Studies* 64 (2023):101–4, and Jieyu Liu, "Ageing and Familial Support: A Three-Generation Portrait from Urban China," *Ageing and Society* 44 (2024): 1204–1230.

EMBEDDED GENERATIONS

Introduction

The Chen Family (Urban Household from Tianjin)

In 1962, after the completion of her primary school education, Grandma Chen (grandparent generation labeled as G1, born in 1943, one elder brother and two younger sisters) was assigned to a state-owned manufacturing work unit. It was here where she met the love of her life—the late Grandpa Chen.[1] She recalled the evolution of their courtship:

> He was my workmate. We had been courting for a week when my family set up a matchmaking meeting for me with someone else. They described the man they had selected as a tall good looking military officer. But I declined this offer and stuck with my workmate. To be honest, I pursued my husband to some extent. When we were apprentices, I really liked him and I asked one of his friends if he already had a girlfriend. His friend passed on my message and he wrote me a poem in return. He was very talented. From then on, we started courting. . . . At that time, I was an activist studying Mao Zedong's thoughts and was keen to join the party; as my father was a party member, the work unit also wanted to enlist me in the party. But his father was classi-fied as a small business owner,[2] and the party secretary of my work unit warned me that if I wanted to join the party I'd have to break up with him. I couldn't agree to this and as a result I was unable to join the party.

Explaining why she chose him, Grandma Chen sweetly recalled: "He was very good looking and honest. He also had a very nice temperament. When we were young, as soon as I saw him my heart always started to thud." When asked if she would choose him again in her next life, Grandma Chen replied firmly: "Yes, he'd still be the one. He treated me very well, and he was very kind to our children and my family. Even now I still dream about him—especially the years when we were courting and when we just got married."

In 1988, Daughter Chen (middle generation labeled as G2, born in 1968, one younger brother) had started to work in a state-owned clothing factory after completing her senior middle school education. At the time it was the fashion among young urbanites to visit dance halls after work. It was there she met her future husband. Daughter Chen explained why she chose him as her spouse:

> At the time I was very young. I just felt that he knew how to have a good time, and was good at singing, dancing and playing music. I was impressed that he could do so many things well. But he also deceived me on a very important matter. He told me that his father was Head of the Railway Bureau and would be able to arrange for my brother to get a good job there after finishing at vocational school. In the end, it turned out that only his brother-in-law worked there. He'd been bluffing all along. I was so young that I was deceived into marrying him.

When asked if in a future life she would choose the same spouse again, she replied with a firm disavowal: "No. Certainly not. I would definitely not marry that sort of person. I would want to find someone who really cares about me." She admitted that when they quarreled, she had occasionally thought about divorce. But she said with a sigh, "After all, we've been through so much over so many years together. Like the left hand touching the right hand, we've got used to each other. We just make do [*cehuo*] and treat each other as companions."

In 2016 Grandson Chen (grandchild generation labeled as G3, only child, born in 1991), a white-collar employee in a state-owned company, was married to a friend he had known since they were teenagers. He described how they had come together: "We had already known each other since our teenage years. She was the former classmate of my middle school mate. We dated for a few months, but I broke up with her as she was quite ugly when she was a teenager."

Thanks to his handsome looks he was popular with girls and had at least ten different girlfriends. But in 2014 he and his original girlfriend started dating again. He explained why in the end he chose her as his wife:

> She had been persistently pursuing me for many years. I also knew that she was a good person and not one of those women with a scheming mind. Just imagine how tiring it would be if you had to live with someone who was always scheming. We dated for less than two years and she kept pressing me to get married. I personally didn't want to get married, but she was keen. And when all is said and done, we are from compatible families [*mengdan-ghudui*, "matching households"], and we've been comfortable with each other. So I was happy when we eventually got married.

But although insisting that he would choose the same wife if he had to relive his life, Grandson Chen remained skeptical about the role of "love" in marriage: "As time goes by, for sure it eventually disappears. I have no doubt at all that after 20 or 30 years of living together, most married couples stay together for the sake of their children. After all, China is unlike other countries. It's impossible for couples to still be deeply in love in their 50s and 60s. In my whole life I've never met such a couple."

The Li Family (Rural Household from Shandong)

After having served in the army for four years, in the 1960s Grandpa Li (G1, born in 1942, with four younger brothers) returned to his Shandong village and worked in the local production brigade. Through a village matchmaker, he was married in 1968. He explained how this came about: "My wife and I were from the same village. I often went to her side of the village to play when I was a child, so I'd known her from childhood." He recalled the marriage introduction as follows: "At the time parents tended to make the final decision, although they also discussed it with us children. I had seen her before, and in my eyes although she was a bit short, there was nothing dumb about her. With no many brothers and a poor family background, it wasn't easy for me to find a wife so I had no objection to this marriage proposal."

After living together for nearly fifty years, his assessment of his wife was simple and direct: "She is not a bad wife. Her nature is simple and straightforward. She treated my parents well and didn't fuss about things. She also gets on well with her sisters-in-law. I'd have chosen her again if I had the chance."

Son Li (G2, born in 1969, with a younger brother and a younger sister) was married in 1989 through an arranged marriage. The marriage was initiated by the bride's mother who lived in the same village and, having known Son Li as a very handsome and smart child, had engineered his engagement to her daughter when he was just twelve years old. Son Li recalled his early impressions of his wife: "When we became engaged I was too young to understand anything and only interested in playing. Only after we got married did I get to know her better and realize what a good temperament she had."

For the first few years of marriage, they worked together in the fields. But with the birth of their two children and the need to earn more cash income, Son Li followed the example of fellow villagers and worked on urban construction sites, leaving his wife to look after the children and tend the fields. Commenting on their marital journey, his wife confided, "I had a crush on him when I was young because he was good looking. In the initial years of our marriage, his temperament wasn't good. But life became much better as he grew older and became more accommodating."

In 2012 Granddaughter Li (G3, born in 1990 and with one younger brother), married a man from a neighboring village through an introduced marriage. After failing to complete her senior middle school education, she joined other village dropouts to work in clothing factories in China's coastal region. After working for six years in various cities, she was summoned back to her village to attend matchmaking meetings: "I'd dated someone when I was working away from my village, but my family didn't approve of me marrying someone from a different region. My mother said that if I were to marry someone living far away, it wouldn't be easy for me to visit home, whereas if I married someone from my own region, I would be able to visit home every two or three days. So in the face of my parents' disapproval I stopped dating until I was introduced to my husband back home."

When asked why she had chosen her husband, she shyly explained:

> I didn't think very much. At the time, several of my relatives all said that he was a good person and hard-working. They also emphasized that my parents-in-law were good people. So I gave in. We got to know each other through phone calls for nearly two years before we finally got married. During this period, I also felt that he seemed to have a good temperament. After we were married I joined him in the place to which he had migrated and looked for work. But after giving birth to my son, I stayed at home while he continued to go out to work.

These examples provide a snapshot of the mate selection processes of various members of two of the three-generational families studied in this book. Do they demonstrate, as the existing literature would argue, a clear trend toward increasing autonomy among the younger generation?[3] Has Chinese marital life experienced a shift from a language of duty to a language of love?[4] The picture emerging from both the Chens' and Lis' narratives and the other families interviewed resists such linear generalizations, instead suggesting complex and sometimes paradoxical changes and continuities across three generations.

In the urban Chen family, Grandma Chen's narrative from the Mao era depicted a passionate and romantic love story in which she defied the matchmaking efforts of her family and the meddling of her workplace superiors in order to pursue the love of her life. In these regards her approach toward marriage was distinctly "modern" and contrasted with that of Grandson Chen, who grew up in the market reform era of the 1990s. Paradoxically, despite his greater experience of dating, his embrace of the Chinese idiom of "matching households" as a basis of spousal choice and his skepticism toward the role of "love" in marriage indicated a more "traditional" attitude toward marriage than that of his grandmother. Yet notwithstanding the very different degrees of intensity that characterized their courtship experiences, both retained the same understanding of marriage as a partnership of shared responsibilities. As for the middle generation, Daughter Chen's experience offers a vivid example of how personal desire and family duty can go hand in hand in the selection of a partner. In her case, she fell for her husband for two main reasons: on the one hand, she was attracted by her future husband's personal charm; on the other hand, she was swayed by the belief that his supposedly powerful family could facilitate her brother's career advancement.

In the rural Li family, a distinctly nonlinear trajectory seems to have characterized the mate selection process across three generations. Both Grandfather Li, bound by the conventions of the Mao era, and Granddaughter Li, who was more representative of the period of widespread migration, found their partners through "introduced marriages"; by contrast, middle-generation Son Li, who reached marriageable age in the early post-1978 reform years, entered an *arranged* marriage—albeit one regarded by his wife-to-be as desirable. Adult children's ability to veto the proposal could be interpreted as conferring a greater degree of autonomy than in arranged marriages. However, this autonomy is positional and relational. Thanks to his family's impoverished circumstances at the time, for example, Grandpa Li did not enjoy the luxury of choice. In the case of Granddaughter Li, her mother set the parameters within which she could exercise her autonomy, defined in such a way as to prevent her from marrying someone who lived far from her natal home—a principle which Granddaughter Li, like many other women of the grandchild generation, had internalized as her own preference in the search for a spouse.

The experiences of siblings add a further dimension to the complexity of the three-generational picture. In the Chen family, for example, while Grandma Chen exercised "free will" in choosing her husband, she also played a critical role alongside her older siblings in persuading her youngest sister to marry someone who lived very close to the natal family in order to provide support for their parents in old age. In the Li family, while Son Li quietly agreed to an arranged marriage, his younger brother's termination of two village engagements to which he had already agreed caused anguish to his parents, even though they eventually had to bow to his recalcitrance and "let him be." However, in the case of their disabled daughter who lacked the ability to speak, Grandpa Li took direct control of the process and prudently selected as her marriage partner a young man from a smaller and less influential lineage group in order to protect her against discrimination within her marital family. As for the grandchildren, while Granddaughter Li's spouse selection was carefully orchestrated, Son Li and his wife were more accommodating toward their son, allowing him total freedom and discretion in choosing a wife in the belief that as a college graduate that he would choose a wife from a "superior" background to that of their own acquaintances. As it turned out, Granddaughter

Li's brother, a white-collar employee in a fourth-tier city, married a kindergarten teacher also from a rural family background.

Concealed in this mosaic pattern of spouse selection, some shared characteristics also emerge from the experiences of all three generations. As illustrated in the spouse appraisals of both the Chen and Li families, it is evident that marriage in China is still not only a matter of two individuals coming together, but is also viewed as the union of two extended families. As such, it embodies a mixture of emotions embracing the expression of the couple's personal feelings for each other as well as the fulfilment of mutual responsibilities and obligations toward their respective families. It is clear too that in the Chinese context love is not blind. Rather, there is a strong tendency to marry someone from a "compatible" family background, as evidenced, for example, in the persistent urban-rural segregation across three generations in both the Chen and Li families. Finally, far from indicating a linear shift from declining parental authority to increasing youth autonomy, my findings suggest that the outcome of intergenerational negotiations depends on a wide range of factors, including institutional context, demographic family profile, material conditions, gender, and life stage. Indeed, it is precisely the nonlinear nature of change, the continuity and diversity of Chinese family practices, and the hidden forces that shape the dynamics of intimate practices within such families that this book seeks to capture.

In contrast with the existing literature, which mainly uses cross-sectional data or focuses on a single urban or rural site, this book provides the first comprehensive and in-depth examination of family life across three successive generations in multiple urban and rural locations in China between 1949 and the 2010s. Grounded in life history narratives, it describes and analyses the whole gamut of family practices over the entire course of life, including childhood experiences, courtship and marriage decisions, marital life, sex and intimacy, and aging and old age support. Through intersecting analytical lenses of generation, location (urban-rural) and gender (son-daughter, husband-wife), it shows how family members have negotiated changing socioeconomic and cultural conditions in order to forge their own distinctive and varied family life trajectories.

Theorizing Family Life and Social Change

Notwithstanding the importance of its empirical content, this book is more than an empirical study. No less significant, its arguments are theoretically framed as a means of adding to and sometimes challenging the academic debate on family life and social change. As an early influential modernization theorist representative of Western sociology, William Goode argued that there existed a "fit" between industrialization and the conjugal family.[5] The essence of his thesis was that the forces of industrialization and urbanization had facilitated a shift from vertical family and extended kinship obligations toward the "modern" nuclear family centered on the conjugal relationship between husband and wife. Goode's implicit prediction was that as industrialization spread, family patterns throughout the world would converge to the Western conjugal family model. His thesis attracted widespread criticism on the grounds that it was rooted in an ethnocentric developmental paradigm and failed to capture the empirical reality of family life in Western societies. Nevertheless, two of his subsidiary hypotheses have continued to gain purchase among academic scholars:[6] first, that parents' control over their children would diminish as industrialization proceeded; second, that the ideology of the Western conjugal family, with its emphasis on companionate and romantic love, would spread widely throughout the world.

In response to more recent developments affecting family life in the United States and Western Europe since the second half of the twentieth century—for example, later marriages, a sharp rise in divorce, declining fertility rates, and an increasing proportion of children born out of wedlock—the theorizing of family life and social change has entered a new phase that delineates the deinstitutionalization of marriage. In the United States, Cherlin argued that from the 1950s there was a shift from companionate marriage to individualistic marriage that emphasized personal fulfilment and self-development.[7] Similarly, across the Atlantic, the British sociologist, Anthony Giddens[8] depicted a transformation of intimacy from romantic love to a "pure relationship" encapsulating the late modern condition, whereby couples stayed together for only as long as their relationship remained mutually satisfying. Again, German sociologists Beck and Beck-Gernsheim[9] argued that individualization, closely associated with de-traditionalization and de-normalization of roles, had led to increasing emphasis on negotiation and contingency in intimate relationships and the weakening of gender and class factors. A variant of the deinstitutionalization narrative was evident in the framework of a second demographic transition, proposed by Belgium demographer Lesthaeghe and his colleagues. This contrasted the first demographic transition, comprising a shift from a pattern of high fertility and high mortality to one of low fertility and low mortality (completed in most Western countries before the 1950s), with the second, post-1950s transition characterized in those same countries by "sustained subreplacement fertility, a multitude of living arrangements other than marriage, the disconnection between marriage and procreation, and no stationary population."[10] The primary driver of this supposedly evolutionary process was a cultural shift toward postmodern values and norms (i.e., those stressing individuality and self-actualization).[11]

Such grand theorizing is grounded in five major assumptions. First, the self / individual under discussion reflects a particular liberal notion of an autonomous self and individual. Second, it follows the logic of an unilinear historical progression model, exemplified in the evolution from traditional through modern to postmodern family practices. Third, in the absence of kin and extended families, the nuclearized family has become the default condition in the new theorization. Fourth, the nation-state is the basic unit of analysis. Fifth, although the theorizing of much of the new literature derives from the context of Western Europe and North America, an implicit assumption is that as modernization proceeds, the rest of the world will eventually embrace the Western model.

However, contrary empirical evidence and alternative conceptualization have emerged in a number of countries in which these supposedly universalizing theories originated. For example, among British sociologists there has been a robust debate since the late 1990s on the extent to which Giddens' transformation of intimacy and Beck and Beck-Gernsheim's individualization theses have taken place.[12] Empirical evidence from Britain has indicated that while commitment may no longer be embodied in traditional forms such as marriage, notions of family, partnership, and kinship remain central to people's lives.[13] Nor has there been a significant weakening of pre-existing social structures: for example, class and gender remain important in shaping intimate practices.[14] Indeed, frustrated by the fixation of many commentators on the supposed decline of commitment and the weakening of family life, British sociologist Carol Smart proposed the "connectedness thesis" in antithesis to the Beck and Beck-Gernsheim individualization thesis in order to highlight the continuing importance of notions of connectedness, relationality and embeddedness in personal choice-making and family formation.[15]

In the United States, Bengston and colleagues[16] drew on a longitudinal quantitative study of four generations in Southern California to debunk what they regarded as the myth of the decline of the American extended family. Instead, they sought to show how parents across a wide range of family types had continued to play a central role in shaping the life orientations and achievements of younger family members and how intergenerational bonds had remained resilient against the background of massive social changes since the 1960s. In contrast to the de-traditionalization / deinstitutionalization narrative, they employed the concept of "linked lives"[17] to capture the process of intergenerational transmission and continuity. In more recent decades, empirical research has also pointed to a growing class divergence in family practices within the United States. Thus, while well-educated and securely employed Americans brought up their children within stable marriages, their less well-educated counterparts whose employment status was more vulnerable eschewed marriage in favor of bringing up their children in short-term cohabitating relationships.[18]

Thanks to the asymmetrical nature of global academic exchange, however, such critiques and alternative theorizations are seldom translated and made known in societies beyond the English-speaking world.[19] Consequently, both Goode's modernization theory and the new modernity writers' work (e.g., Giddens and Beck / Beck-Gernsheim) have continued to exert a strong influence on academic studies focusing on developing countries (including China) and undertaken by scholars in these countries.

The China Context

Throughout much of premodern history the core principle of social governance adopted by the rulers of China was Confucianism—above all, its hierarchical precept that everyone should be aware of and behave in accordance with their position in society to achieve a harmonious social order. Out of this precept emerged a highly structured family organization whose members' conduct was governed by a set of ethical guidelines—aligning with age, gender, and generation—in which respect and obligation were central to building harmonious family relationships. Filial piety was the defining principle ordering relations between adult children and older parents. In the words of Confucius himself, "In serving his parents, a filial son reveres them in daily life; he makes them happy while he nourishes them; he takes anxious care of them in sickness; he shows great sorrow over their death; and he sacrifices to them with solemnity."[20] Filial piety emphasized submission of the will of adult children to that of the senior generations, and also stressed the continuity and maintenance of familial lineage.

Within this system, marriage and sexuality were mainly directed toward building future generations, with love and sexual pleasure taking a secondary role. Parents played a prominent role in making marriage decisions for their children. Confucian familism was also fundamentally gendered with the ultimate objective of perpetuating the patrilineal descent line.[21] Daughters were located at the bottom of the kinship hierarchy and property was transmitted through males.[22] The notion of *nanzun nübei* ("women are inferior to men") effectively defined women's conduct in society, exemplified by prescriptions such as the *sancong* ("Three Obediences"), which dictated that women were subject to the authority of their father when young, their husband when married, and their son when widowed.

In the early twentieth century, reformist intellectuals condemned Confucian protocols of hierarchical family relations, arguing that they had caused China's defeat in the Opium War and were a barrier to its modernization and development. Their demands for greater freedom from family control for women and young people led to some modifications to family practices, although the impact was largely limited to urban educated circles.[23] However, the Communist Revolution of 1949 transformed China's political landscape. In the years that followed, the Communist Party launched a series of campaigns designed to radically reform the traditional Confucian family organization by advocating freedom of mate choice and redirecting citizens' loyalty from the family elders to the state. Individuals were assigned work either in state-run urban work units or in rural village production brigades, thereby reducing their material dependence on family and kinship networks.[24] Not least important, the party's advocacy of women's liberation for the first time mobilized able-bodied women into paid work outside the home, enabling female work participation to become a normative feature of women's lives in the Mao era. Yet notwithstanding these onslaughts on the power and authority of family elders, countervailing forces—material necessity, lack of labor mobility under the constraints of the household registration scheme (see below), and political chaos during the Cultural Revolution—simultaneously served to strengthen family ties.[25]

Following Mao's death in 1976 and Deng Xiaoping's accession to supreme power in 1978, implementation of China's watershed "open-door" policy symbolized a reorientation of China's economic development trajectory, paving the way for decentralization and other reformist economic initiatives.[26] In the countryside, collective farming was displaced by a return to family farming, while at the same time restrictions on rural-urban migration were relaxed. Rural family members became a source of cheap labor for China's burgeoning manufacturing sector, as a result of which millions of children and aging grandparents were left in villages as the middle generation migrated to cities in search of higher wages. In cities, the economic restructuring of state enterprises eliminated de facto permanent employment associated with the "iron rice bowl" and removed other welfare benefits such as subsidized public housing allocation, generating mass redundancy toward the end of the 1990s[27] and plunging citizens into a market economy in which employment precarity became the norm. Meanwhile, China's opening-up to the outside world and the forces of globalization exposed its citizens to Western ideologies and values, including consumerism and more liberal attitudes toward marriage and sexuality. In the face of so many potentially subversive forces, Chinese Communist Party officials sought to reinstate the family at the center of social life in order to strengthen stability and uphold moral rectitude[28]—a process that has continued into the twenty-first century, enabling the family to regain its central position in state governance.[29] The last decade has witnessed a resurgence of Confucian ideologies in state propaganda and mainstream media at the same time alongside the continuation of a neoliberal discourse centering on personal choice and responsibility.[30]

China has also undergone rapid demographic change. Before 1949 the Confucian emphasis on lineage encouraged families to have relatively large numbers of children. In the 1950s the party-state made a limited attempt to alter traditional marital fertility patterns.[31] After 1960, official policy began a shift toward the promotion of birth control in cities, which gradually evolved into the "later marriage, longer birth spacing, and fewer children" (*wan-xi-shao*) campaign—the main driver of rapid fertility decline in the 1970s.[32] In 1979 the government introduced the one-child policy: while modifications were permitted in rural areas, where couples were allowed to have a second child if the first was a girl, in cities the policy was strictly implemented through the use of workplace fines and other punitive measures. China's economic boom since the 1980s further accelerated a sharp decline in fertility, which has generated a new set of demographic challenges. Of these the most acute has been the aging of China's population. The first generation born under the one-child policy have now become parents themselves, burdening them with the responsibility of supporting two parents and four grandparents.[33] In an effort to address China's inverse population pyramid, in 2015 the state abandoned the one-child policy, introducing first a national two-child policy and, in 2021, a three-child policy. However, no more than 5–6 percent of couples have responded by opting to have a second child, citing inadequate childcare facilities and the high cost of child-rearing as the main reasons, especially in big cities like Beijing and Shanghai.[34] For the first time since 1961, in 2022 the rate of natural increase was negative (-0.6 percent), as a result of which the total population declined by 0.85 million. In 2023 China suffered an even greater contraction of almost 2.1 million, with the rate of natural increase falling by -1.48 percent.[35] In short, China has now entered a new long-term demographic trajectory of negative population. Despite the shrinking population, the state continues to fulfill its residual default role in welfare provision, while Chinese families remain the main providers of funding and services for their dependent members.[36]

Understanding Chinese Families

Assessing the impact of rapid social change on family life since 1949 has been a central theme of scholars investigating the dynamics of families in China.[37] Early research drawing on fieldwork in the Mao era[38] focused on the nature and scale of changes in traditional patterns of family life in early post-1949 China. Research findings highlighted paradoxical changes as well as continuities in family life, shaped by multiple complex and often contradictory forces. For example, in her investigation of old age support, Davis-Friedmann found that alongside efforts to eliminate values that threatened to subvert the collective economy, Chinese Communist Party cadres "simultaneously legitimated traditional obligations of mutual support and long-term reciprocal care," as a result of which the elderly "benefited from a basic continuity between the pre- and post-1949 definitions of filial behavior."[39] Similarly, drawing upon systematic studies of both urban and rural Chinese families,[40] Whyte and Parish found that while the most egregious practices, such as minor marriage and concubinage, had quickly disappeared, core elements of traditional Chinese familism, such as intergenerational solidarity and marriage stability, had survived. They also highlighted differences in the pace of change between urban and rural China, illustrated, for example, in the greater success of state efforts to eliminate bride price and parental control of mate choice in cities, compared with the countryside. After 1978, as de-collectivization and other reforms propelled China toward a more market-based economic system, a new literature emerged, grounded in data collected in the 1980s and early 1990s and focusing on the impact of such changes on Chinese family life.[41] The findings highlighted the return of some pre-1949 traditions, such as the revival of teenage marriages and child betrothals, but also revealed significant variations in family composition and dynamics associated with diverse regional cultural traditions and differences in the impact of reform initiatives on local economies.

Prior to the 1990s the theoretical thrust of scholarly research on Chinese families was mainly embedded in Goode's modernization proposition, albeit with various revisions dictated by the use of Chinese data. Accordingly, this "revisionist" literature painted a counternarrative to the linear transition model implicit in Goode's theory: the paradoxical changes and continuities captured in China's experience suggesting that any simple "traditional versus revolutionary, socialist versus post-socialist" dichotomies were a misleading representation of reality. It also underlined the crucial importance of the state in shaping Chinese family life—an agency overlooked in Goode's model—even allowing for the partial nature of changes inherent in adaptive family practices that emerged out of state-directed policies. Finally, in contrast to Goode's emphasis on industrialization and urbanization as the main drivers of family change, the "China narrative" showed that socialist institutions—sometimes eschewing traditional customs, and at other times reinforcing them—often affected family life in contradictory ways, resulting in the complex and nonlinear pattern of family change documented in the China-based studies.[42]

US-based anthropologist Yan Yunxiang's study on private life and family change in rural China[43] marked a departure from these early lines of inquiry. Drawing upon extensive field research conducted between 1989 and 1999 in Xiajia village in the northeastern province of Heilongjiang, Yan argued that a decline of patriarchal power had given way to the rise of youth autonomy in everything from the choosing of spouses to the control of resources. He noted that following its intrusion into village society and family life after 1949, the state's subsequent withdrawal after de-collectivization had left "a moral and ideological vacuum," which alongside the impact of marketization and consumerism, had encouraged the emergence of "ultra-utilitarian individualism" and the rise of "the uncivil individual."[44]

Reusing the ethnographic data from Xiajia village as well as adding two new chapters focusing on urban China, in his 2009 book Yan examined how the Beck and Beck-Gernsheim individualization thesis might be applied to Chinese society. He argued that the rise of individual agency since the 1970s has led to an individualization of Chinese society. In more recent work,[45] Yan followed the Beck/Beck-Gernsheim's emphasis on individualization as a macro-sociological phenomenon and argued that the state's withdrawal of welfare support alongside increasing risk and distrust in post-Mao economic reforms has dis-embedded individuals from former institutions and re-embedded them in a framework of familism. However, in order to distinguish this from traditional familism grounded in generational and gender hierarchy, Yan conceptualizes it as "descending familism," characterized by a downward flow of resources and care within Chinese families from the older generation to the youngest generation of children. Building upon this, Yan subsequently formulated another term—"neo-familism"—to capture the "emergent centrality of the family and the associated new changes since the 1990s,"[46] including descending familism, emergent intergenerational intimacy, the impact of materialism, and tensions between individual and family interests. In his 2021 edited volume, Yan outlined an inverted generational hierarchy in the rise of neo-familism, which he termed "the inverted family," the essence of which he characterized as "the constant decline of parental authority and power and the parallel increase in youth autonomy and freedom in both urban and rural Chinese families."[47] He credits "the gradual yet constant development of self-awareness and individual desires" since the 1980s to "the much stronger yet still ongoing trend of individualization at the turn of the twenty-first century" as the most important factor contributing to the inversion of generational relations.[48]

Three key issues can be identified in Yan's framework of individualization[49] and Chinese family change. First—and here there is a parallel with the conceptual weakness in Becks' work—Yan's conflation of the notion of individualization as a state-initiated social process with individualization as personal motivation reflecting individual choice runs the risk of romanticizing agency.[50] Second, Yan's strong emphasis on *change*[51] set a narrative tone that has tended to spotlight change while obscuring continuities. Third, through its portrayal of a unidirectional intergenerational power shift, the "descending familism" / "inverted family" framework runs the risk—which it shares with any model of linear change—of overgeneralization and fails to acknowledge the impact on intergenerational negotiation in a variety of material circumstances. As Whyte has noted, given the unevenness of development and scale of China, "any single predictive theory or set of hypotheses specifying comprehensive changes in a particular direction is not likely to do justice to the complexities of evolving family life in the PRC."[52]

There are other studies that also do not neatly accord with the individualization narrative. Drawing upon urban case studies in China, Taiwan, and Hong Kong, Davis and Friedman engage with the deinstitutionalization of marriage and the "second demographic transition" theory.[53] They find that in the new millennium all three Chinese societies have experienced a higher average age at first marriage, fewer barriers to divorce, declining marital fertility, and greater social acceptance of premarital, extramarital, and same-sex intimate relationships. However, they have not experienced another key indicator of the "second demographic transition"—namely, the delinking of procreation from marriage. Instead, the authors identify "strong continuities in the 'rules of the games' for family formation, especially in the insistence that marriage precede childbearing and in broad support for the norm of lifelong reciprocity between generations."[54] Other recent scholarship embracing a wider range of case studies also highlights the diversity and complexity of contemporary family life. Santos and Harrell, whose edited volume focuses on "patriarchal configurations" concludes that "with all the changes in the classic patriarchal nexus, China remains a heavily male-dominated or andrarchical society, even though women continue to have significant power both inside and outside the family."[55] In terms of generational hierarchies, several of the volume's contributors question and complicate Yan's individualization thesis, revealing the persistence of filial values and patrilineal thinking alongside significant familial adaptations. Finally, drawing upon Illouz's[56] theorization of relations between emotion and capitalism, Sun's[57] study of rural migrant workers' experiences of love, romance, and intimate relationships argues that the socioeconomic hardships that they face have made these migrants an emotional precariat.

The quantitative analysis of Chinese Family Panel Studies, the Family Module of the Chinese General Social Surveys and census data undertaken by Xie Yu and his colleagues lend further support to a narrative of nonlinear family change, characterized by both continuities and diversity in the post-Mao era. For example, their finding that cohabitation before marriage has increased nationally from less than 2 percent in the 1980s to 32.6 percent after 2000 is qualified by their assessment that this usually represents a transitional phase for couples who go on to marry—and by their finding that in any case cohabitation is still stigmatized in many parts of Chinese society.[58] As for marriage,[59] their investigation of trends during the period between 1990 and 2010 shows a delay in first marriage age and a decline in marital fertility, but also reveals that childlessness remains rare among married couples while nonmarital childbearing is still virtually nonexistent in China. Another group of demographers[60] has sought to build on Bengston, Biblarz, and Roberts' suggestion of "linked lives" and their intergenerational solidarity model. Based on an analysis of national and / or regional survey data, the consensus from these studies is that intergenerational bonds remain solid even in the face of the emergence of new trends. At the same time, however, there are variations within each generation, shaped by a variety of factors such as location (urban or rural), education, gender, and socioeconomic status. In light of the complex picture of familial relations, Ji has used terms such as "mosaic temporality" and "mosaic familism" to capture post-Mao social transformational processes in which "tradition and modernity, the resurgence of Confucianism, the socialist version of modernity, the capitalist version of modernity, and the socialist heritage" all have their part to play.[61] Nevertheless, none of these alternative approaches has as much attention among Chinese scholars as Yan's individualization thesis. With translation of Yan's work, as one of the recent review articles highlights, the individualization model has replaced Goode's work as the dominant theoretical framework in studying family life within China.[62]

There are several deficiencies in the existing studies of Chinese families. First, they make an implicit assumption that there is a break in continuity between the Mao and post-Mao eras. This reflects the absence of any single work examining urban and rural family behavior that embraces both eras. Earlier book-length studies charting changes in Chinese family relationships derive mainly from fieldwork data from the 1970s to 1990s and therefore focus on the Mao and early reform periods. The focus of more recent publications has been the post-1980s generation, whose experiences have often been viewed as marking a "breakthrough" from those of previous generations. This book is the first to examine the extent to which their family dynamics differ from those of their parents and grandparents.

Second, the existing literature places great emphasis on the ways in which—both directly and indirectly—the institutional framework created by the state has shaped family behavior. However, this may obscure other forces that are at work. The principle of "linked lives" is a reminder that an individual's life is embedded within the lives of other family members, including those of different generations.[63] A major contribution of this book is its attempt to incorporate the ways in which families transmit values and behavior[64] across generations into an analysis of family life and social change in China.

Third, there is the question of which criteria to use in appraising change. Early studies of Mao era used pre-1949 conditions as a comparative basis while investigations of the post-Mao era have tended to make "tradition" the implicit yardstick for comparison. There is, however, an epistemological risk in comparing contemporary practices with traditional Confucian discourse, which serves as a rhetoric on what family relations ought to be. Empirically, such an approach threatens to exaggerate change and obscure continuities.

Consider, for example, the following three statements, each of which seeks to capture the nature of intergenerational relationships in a particular era. Based on empirical data from the 2010s, Zhang[65] concluded that "the new formulation of filial piety" emphasizes "both generational interdependence and independence" and "underscores a parent-child relationship that is reciprocal rather than hierarchical." Again, commenting on his findings from Xiajia village in the 1990s, Yan[66] argued that "unconditional filial piety, which was based on the sacredness of parenthood, no longer exists. For younger villagers, intergenerational reciprocity, like other types of reciprocity, has to be balanced and maintained through consistent exchange." Finally, analysis of data from the Mao era led Davis-Friedmann to conclude that ordinary people relied on "deliberate calculations of reciprocal exchanges between young and old" and that "interdependence is the dominant characteristic of the ties between elderly parents and adult children. But families vary in their degree of solidarity. . . . One reason for this variation is the difference in the quality of parents' earlier efforts to meet the needs of their children." When compared with the discourse of Confucian familism, Zhang's findings were labeled as a "new formulation of filial piety," while Yan's were viewed as signaling a "crisis of filial piety." However, when compared with Davis-Friedmann's findings of the Mao era, it becomes clear that intergenerational reciprocity, grounded in mutual support and exchange, remained central in shaping Chinese intergenerational relations and had hardly changed over the previous seventy years.[67] In an effort to minimize such potential confusion and inconsistency, I have deliberately employed a generation-sequence design in order to compare the life experiences and perspectives of successive generations.

Fourth, while the individualization thesis has been strongly criticized in British family studies, it has, perhaps ironically, become the dominant model used in such studies within China. As I have already noted, findings from the existing empirical literature are not consistent with the individualization narrative. Hence there is the urgency of formulating an alternative framework to analyze and explain family life and social change.

An Alternative Analytical Framework

INTIMACY

As part of responses to and critiques of new modernity theorists' work on modernity and intimacy, sociological work on family life in the West (especially in the United Kingdom) has generated a growing corpus of literature focusing on the emotional quality of family relationships and ways in which different acts of intimacy sustain relational ties.[68] Chinese family research also reflects this theoretical shift, as seen in increasing research emphasis on the place of affection and emotions within Chinese families.[69] In order to facilitate analysis of the findings presented in this book, I highlight here two aspects that demand greater attention in the "intimate turn" of research on Chinese families.

The first relates to a tendency to privilege certain forms of intimacy. For example, notwithstanding Yan's presentation of a variety of ways in which Xiajia villagers demonstrated intimacy, he defines "intergenerational intimacy" as "a new kind of mutual knowing, understanding, and emotional sharing across generational lines,"[70] an approach that seemingly accords with Giddens' notion of intimacy (viz., "opening oneself to the other"[71] in "a process of mutual disclosure").[72] Jamieson refers to this as "disclosing intimacy"—"a process of two people mutually sustaining deep knowing and understanding, through talking and listening, sharing thoughts, showing feelings."[73] However, empirical research drawing on British and Chinese data[74] reveals that while disclosing intimacy may be more evident in modern relationships, it is not the key organizing principle of people's personal lives. For this reason, I have adopted Jamieson's concept of "practices of intimacy,"[75] which she defines as "practices which enable, generate and sustain a subjective sense of closeness and being attuned and special to each other" so to be open to other practices people adopt to build and sustain their intimacy. For example, in her analysis of empirical data from the United States, Zelizer[76] reveals the intertwining of intimacy and money: "Every relationship of coupling, caring, and household membership repeatedly mingles economic transactions and intimacy, usually without contamination." Throughout my own book, "intimacy" is not conceptually confined to the communicative or emotional, but also embraces the material, practical, and other formats. Boundaries between different ways of enabling intimacy are blurred rather than rigidly demarcated.

The second aspect is captured in Giddens' suggestion that personal life brings about social change by spreading democracy through the search for more intimate and equal relationships.[77] The problem here is that much empirical research indicates that intimacy does *not* automatically democratize personal relationships. On couple relationships, for example, Jamieson has documented extensive evidence that reveals the complexity of the relationship between practices of intimacy and the reproduction of male privilege. On parent-child relations, Western studies have shown that parental vocabulary viewed by parents as primarily as a means of conveying intimacy is considered by their children to be a surveillance device.[78] Practices of intimacy have also been blamed for contributing to class inequalities. For example, Lareau[79] has shown how middle-class parents in the United States use words of praise to communicate a sense of privilege to their children, while disadvantaged parents communicate the virtues of helpfulness and accommodation in preference to those of independence and self-reliance, which might expose their children to being victimized or thought troublesome. In the Chinese context, such considerations have largely been ignored, Sun's investigation of migrant workers being one of the few studies that touch on the reproduction of inequalities in intimate domains. In any case, there remains an implicit assumption that intimacy is likely to lead to equality.[80] With such considerations in mind, this book views intimacy as a social domain in which existing social structures can be revivified.

INDIVIDUAL

The theoretical construct of new modernity writers (for example, Giddens and Beck and Beck-Geinsheim) is underlined by a notion of the individual as someone who is autonomous. In contrast, Smart argues that relationality remains central to late modern selves. Drawing upon Mead's[81] conceptualization of the self as social and reflexive Smart proposes a notion of relational self: "To live a personal life is to have agency and to make choices, but the personhood implicit in the concept requires the presence of others to respond to and to contextualize those actions and choices. Personal life is a reflexive state, but it is not private and it is lived out in relation to one's class position, ethnicity, gender and so on."[82] Jackson further argues that "reflexivity is found in self-other relationships, the ability to reflect on oneself from the perspective of another and, in turn, reflexivity enables co-operation with others."[83]

The notion of relational self is not alien to scholars of China, the individual in Chinese personal relationships having long been viewed as not sharing a Western liberal notion of an autonomous self. Commenting on personal relationships in Republican China, Fei Xiaotong[84] put forward the concept of a "differential mode of association" (chaxugeju). According to Fei, personal relations are circles of networks with the self at the center and relationships become increasingly distant as one moves further from this core; rather than being guided within a common structure, a person can be predicted to engage differently with those whom s/he encounters, depending on their positions within these circles. Fei's conceptualization has striking similarities with those of contemporary British sociologists, both of which highlight the relational as well as the adaptive nature of interactions between individual and others.

Grounded in these theorizations, I propose the concept of "elastic individuality" in order to capture the flexible and fluid processes in which a person's agency and relationality is embedded. The concept has two main features. First, the elastic individual is relational. As suggested by Fei's concept of the "*differential* mode of association" (my emphasis), the individual can have different interactions with different people. Thus, s/he is more likely to display more individualistic attitudes or behavior toward those who are located more distantly from the self, while exhibiting a greater degree of loyalty toward those considered closer to the self. Such differentiation also varies according to temporal rhythms. Second, the elastic individual is also positional and social, the malleability of elasticity being shaped and constrained by one's position in various structures (for example, family, local community, workplace, village, and wider society). Conceptualizing "individual" in this manner, I hope to obviate a fundamental dichotomy that permeates the existing literature on Chinese family relations—parental authority and individual autonomy—and reveal the much more nuanced and dialectical nature of relations between individuals and their family members over the life course.

THE NARRATIVE OF CHANGE

Critics have frequently noted that a linear narrative of change, mobilized by both classic and new modernity writers, relies on a binary conceptual distinction between tradition and modernity, and is grounded in the oppositional thought convention of the enlightenment, with a present defined and differentiated from a fixed "othered" past.[85] During the last two decades this narrative has also helped shape Chinese family research, in which "tradition" tends to be used as the implicit comparative yardstick. For example, Yan's latest concepts—"neo-familism" and "the inverted family"—are coined in relation to "traditional familism" / "patriarchal family in traditional Chinese culture."[86] While Yan acknowledges the mixture of traditional, socialist, and neoliberal values in post-Mao China, interactions between tradition and modernity and their impact upon family relations have largely been omitted in the literature.

Opposition between tradition and modernity, as noted by Jackson and Ho,[87] is often "based on essentialist notions of indigenous culture and ignores the evolution, reshaping and (re)invention of tradition." Moreover, we are reminded by scholars that tradition is not always invented: values and ways of life are passed down from one generation to another and persist through time.[88] Thus, Jackson and Ho[89] argue in favor of striking a balance between acknowledgement of the ways in which tradition is constructed and reshaped and recognition of the persistence of histories and cultural ideals. Going one step further, Carter and Duncan[90] argue that "tradition" may feature strongly in people's improvisation of family practices in new or changing circumstances because of our tendency to make do with what we have at hand—a process they refer to as "bricolage." Duncan argues that "bricolage" provides a better analytical tool with which to capture the relationship between agency and structure through action.[91] Although it shares with the individualization thesis an emphasis on do-it-yourself practices, bricolage is also different in the sense that individuals are not completely free agents, but make sense of *existing materials and knowledge* to create something new. Duncan summarizes, "People try to both conserve social energy and seek social legitimation in this adaption process, a process which can lead to a 're-serving' of tradition even as institutional leakage transfers meanings from past to present, and vice versa."

Using British data, embracing personal life in the 1950s, as well as young women's attitudes toward marriage, and the rise of cohabitation and living apart in the twentieth-first century, Carter and Duncan reveal how people build their lives through an assemblage of "tradition" and "modern." Rather than experiencing a radical break with a traditional past in late modern Britain, people constantly adapt and revivify traditions to accommodate new and changing situations. As a result, change may be "more gradual and partial than often claimed, or even act to reinforce continuity."[92]

EMBEDDED GENERATIONS

Building on these various theoretical constructs, in this book I introduce an "embedded generations" framework to depict a nonlinear process of generational change, continuity, and diversity in family life. The concept of "embedded generations" refers to the ongoing, multifaceted, relational, and institutional configuration of family life in which each generation is anchored and entails three interrelated processes. Firstly, "generation" is an important social structural factor, producing a particular set of formative and sociohistorical experiences.[93] Generational divides matter particularly in the Chinese context thanks to the country having witnessed a number of major state-engineered political, economic, and demographic mass movements in the second half of the twentieth century, each of which disproportionately impacted a specific generation. The family dynamics of each generation therefore reflect the institutional markers of the era with which its members are associated. Secondly, generation is also relational in the sense that a familial generation does not stand on its own, like the "elastic individual." Children's, parents', and grandparents' lives are intricately and dependently intertwined across each generation's life course. Each generation is connected to other generations and serves as a bridge for intergenerational transmission and negotiation at the everyday level. Finally, individuals are diverse in their resource endowments and knowledge in materializing their agency. This generates uneven processes of intergenerational configuration (how individuals relate to other family members during intergenerational negotiations) as well as of institutional configuration (how individuals respond to the broader institutional context). In short, there are variations and contestations of family practices within a generation and between generations.

Noteworthy also are two structural factors that may contribute to these uneven processes. *Gender* is a key structural factor in family life: maintenance of family welfare and preservation of intergenerational relations are premised on an implicit gender contract.[94] In China traditionally patrilineal culture cultivated a strong son preference, since sons were looked to as sources of old age support in contrast to married daughters who were transferred into the filial landscape of their in-laws. Although women's liberation has been a core component of the Chinese Communist Party's rhetoric since 1949, gender inequalities have persisted in both public and private spheres, and care and domestic work has remained a woman's responsibility.[95] In post-Mao China, gender ideology became even more entrenched with the rise of a public discourse promoting a "natural" gender order with women's family duties emphasized (as a wife and mother).[96] In the new millennium, a "resurgence of Confucian patriarchal tradition" has gone hand in hand with the "neoliberal rhetoric of individual responsibility," emphasizing the traditional virtues of womanhood while simultaneously presenting "women's sacrifices as their own personal choice."[97]

Western sociologists have often viewed class as another structuring factor. Despite government efforts, starting in the Mao era, to address class inequalities, actions of the party-state have paradoxically generated an urban-rural divide that persists as the most fundamental form of stratification within China. The *urban-rural divide* is not merely a geographic division, but is systemic, differentiating people's access to opportunities, livelihood, and welfare benefits. Since 1958 a strict household registration system (*hukou*) has existed, serving to segregate China's entire population into these two residential categories. In Mao era, it effectively prevented rural-urban migration in order to control consumption and finance capital-intensive heavy industrialization in urban centers. Although subsequent economic reforms removed the ban on rural-urban migration, urban-rural segregation has remained intact. Here the crucial institutional feature is that the benefits to which someone and his or her family are entitled are tied to where their *hukou* is located. Previously, rural families were far less likely than urban families to have health insurance and access to pensions. Due to the systematic extension of various social benefit programs over the last two decades, most rural families are now covered by health insurance and may also have access to pensions. However, thanks to the very uneven administrative structures of welfare benefits in China, the level of benefits, and reimbursement rates available to rural citizens are much inferior to those of urban *hukou* holders. Thus, migrants with a rural *hukou* have to rely on health insurance and pension provisions back in their native villages, not those provided to urbanites who may be employed alongside them. As a result of unequal access to the benefits of China's modernization, urban and rural families possess profoundly different financial and discursive capacities to practice family life and intimacy. The interaction of many other factors, including sibling structure and the enactment of life courses, generate further compound effects. By incorporating such factors into my analysis, I reveal how individuals, in a multitude of ways, have imagined, negotiated, and lived out their family lives.

Central to my argument is the belief that these multifaceted, interacting, and uneven processes—institutional and intergenerational—have contributed to a nonlinear transition from the past to the present and brought about complex shifts and continuities in family practices across several generations in China. The "embedded generations" model makes no preconceived assumptions about the direction of generational change and offers a dynamism that is absent from the linear historical progressions implied in the modernization theorizing or the neo-familism / "inverted family" model.

Fieldwork

This book draws on life history interviews collected during two phases of fieldwork, which I conducted in China as part of two research projects. In 2011 I spent four months in two villages (in Shandong and Hunan), collecting sixty life history interviews with seventeen multigenerational families in order to investigate the impact of rural-urban migration on familial support in rural China. Since I lived with local families in each village, I was involved on a daily basis in various family life routines, such as cooking, washing, cleaning, shopping, eating meals, and playing with children, as well as joining in frequent informal discussions with villagers from all walks of life. These experiences provided me with rich ethnographic data that further contextualized the life history narratives. Although my focus at the time was on intergenerational relations and old age support, I also collected detailed information about other aspects of family life, including child-rearing, mate selection and marital relations across different generations. This first phase of fieldwork sparked my interest in undertaking a much larger-scale study that would show how Chinese family life has shifted across multiple generations. Thanks to funding made available by the European Research Council, in 2016 I was able to assemble a research team, which, under my leadership, embarked on a three-year intensive program of fieldwork in China. In this second phase, I applied the same research methods—life history interviews and ethnographic observations—but broadened the geographical scope of fieldwork sites by adding a village in Fujian and three major Chinese cities.

THE SITES

All three rural fieldwork sites were villages located far away from urban centers (*yuanjiaocun*)[98] with a relatively high proportion (at least 70 percent) of households that had experienced migration. However, each was characterized by its own distinctive migration history and trajectory. The village in Shandong was located in the interior of the northern Chinese province. From the 1990s male villagers—initially in small numbers—began to migrate in search of work in Beijing and other provincial cities in North China. As they became aware of the significantly higher wages earned by these pioneers, others followed and from the year 2000 migration increased markedly. The gender composition of migrants aged between sixteen and twenty-five was quite even, and most of them—some having completed, others having curtailed their middle school education—sought work in urban factories. After returning to the village to marry, most husbands maintained their migrant status, usually leaving their wives in the village, although in a small number of cases returning to the urban sector with their new wives. As a result, except during the Chinese New Year holiday, when most migrants returned to their villages, the majority of permanent village residents comprised older people, married women, and children. However, when I revisited the region in the second phase of my fieldwork, a new trend was observable whereby following the marriage of their adult children many middle-generation male migrants returned to their village and become wage-earning local workers.

The village in Hunan (South-Central China) was located in the interior of the province. Its relatively hilly terrain made arable farming more difficult than in the Shandong Village (which was located on a plain), but its closeness to Guangdong—the site of one of China's first Special Economic Zones—meant that it had a longer history of outward migration. Starting in the 1980s, young men who had dropped out of school began to leave the village to work on urban construction sites, mainly in Guangdong. Most of them subsequently returned to the village to get married, after which their wives stayed behind to look after the young children. When these children reached school age, however, most married women followed their husband in search of urban work, supporting their husbands as street vendors or working as cleaners in factories. As a result, from the year 2000—earlier than in Shandong—the permanent population of the Hunan village mostly comprised older people and their grandchildren.

The Fujian village was in Southern Fujian province (southeast China). Being close to Nan'an, a city with a manufacturing base for plumbing appliances, it had experienced outward migration since the 1980s. However, unlike the other two villages, a local tradition of entrepreneurship[99] meant that most village migrants found their first jobs as self-employed traders, buying appliances and parts from Nan'an factories and selling them to customers in major cities in western China. As in rural Shandong and Hunan, male migrants returned to their village to marry, subsequently returning to cities with their wives who supported their business activities as well as seeing to household tasks. When they became pregnant, the wives went back to the village to give birth, but several months later they returned to the city with their babies. As part of this migration trajectory, many grandchildren born in the village grew up in a city, while those who remained in the village were mainly older grandparents and members of the middle generation who worked as casual wage laborers in nearby township enterprises.

My urban fieldwork sites were the three cities of Tianjin, Guangzhou, and Xi'an. In the nineteenth century Tianjin, in northern coastal China, was an important port (including for Beijing) and housed the site of foreign-controlled concessions. After 1949 it grew into one of the most important industrial and commercial centers in China, with a population of 13.8 million and per capita GDP of $14,726 (2023). Guangzhou (south China), once known to the Western world as Canton, was for centuries a commercial melting pot, where China met the rest of the world. Today it is the capital of Guangdong province, and remains one of the largest (with a population of 18.6 million) and most economically advanced Chinese cities (with a per capita GDP of $19,422 in 2020). Xi'an (in central inland China) was one of China's ancient capital cities. It is now the provincial capital of Shaanxi province, with a population of 12.9 million and per capita GDP of $11,216 (2020). All three cities now comprise rapidly aging urban societies. According to the latest National Census, in 2020 the share of total population aged sixty-five and over was 7.82 percent in Guangzhou, 10.9 percent in Xi'an, and 14.75 percent in Tianjin.

The choice of these sites was strongly influenced by previous anthropological investigations of spatial variations in China. The renowned anthropologist William Skinner[100] identified nine regions of China—each possessing its own distinctive economic and natural resource endowments, environmental conditions, and cultural traditions—based on the drainage basins of major rivers and other geomorphological features affecting communications.[101] Others also have emphasized north-south divides, highlighting, for example, the strong lineage tradition of southern provinces, such as Guangdong and Fujian, in contrast to the absence of such a tradition in the northern half of the country.[102] With the benefit of hindsight, it has become clear that differences between my fieldwork sites in cities and their impact on family dynamics and behavior proved to be of minor importance, thanks to the nature of China's state-led urban-oriented economic development and engineering. By contrast,

differences between conditions in the three villages, especially divergent migration and livelihood trajectories, generated varied and distinctive patterns
of family formation and dynamics (see chapter 1 and chapter 5). In the end,
however, the most significant divide of all was and remains the contrasting
circumstances between the urban and rural fieldwork sites and the divergent
family life trajectories to which they have given rise.

SAMPLING AND INTERVIEWEES CHARACTERISTICS

Purposive nonrandom sampling techniques were utilized in the recruitment
of interviewees.[103] Four key criteria were employed to target specific groups
within the population: namely, location (urban, rural and semi-rural / semi-
urban—the last comprising suburban counties and villages), socioeconomic
background, age, and gender. In total, this book draws upon 130 urban interviews with 43 urban families, and 130 rural interviews with 37 rural families.[104]
Private interviews were conducted with members of two or three generations
in each family unit.[105] Each interviewee was first asked to recall his or her
childhood and then encouraged to take the lead in narrating their life stories.
Further questions relating to relationships with family members were raised
if these had not been covered during previous conversations. Particular care
was taken to assure each interviewee that their responses would be treated in
total confidence and not revealed to other members of their family.[106]

The life history approach proved fruitful for several reasons. First, people's
life histories provided a captivating way of linking the past and present, bringing individual lives and wider social processes together and offering rare insights into changes and continuities. In doing so, they also exemplified Mills'
idea of the sociological imagination and its ability to link history, biography,
and society. Second, in a family setting, the life history approach helped to
map out the relationships and dynamics between family members. Third, it
provided overlaps between the chronologies of different family members,
making it possible to cross-reference narratives, testing their credibility and
identifying discrepancies between them. In addition to the life history interviews, through repeated physical visits and frequent communications via
social media I was able to follow closely[107] the lives of a significant number—
about one-third—of the interviewees during the second phase of fieldwork
(2016–19). In 2023, after the end of the COVID-19 pandemic, I also revisited
some of the interviewees.

Members of the grandparent generation (G1) were born between the early
1930s and early 1950s. Those of the middle generation (G2) were born in the
1950s and the early 1970s. The generation of grandchildren (G3) were born
between the 1980s and 2000s. I use the generation of grandparents to define a

multigenerational family as either urban or rural, which means that among rural G2 and rural G3 members, some may be resident in cities as a result of rural-urban migration. The interviewees' characteristics are listed in Appendix A. They represent a mixed gender distribution within each generation and include interviewees from different socioeconomic backgrounds. Among urban families, the proportion of interviewees engaged in working-class occupations (factory workers, self-employed vendors, and low-paid service workers) fell sharply across the three generations: from 76 percent (G1), to 53 percent (G2), to just 8 percent (G3). Among rural families, the proportion of interviewees who were farmers in each generation declined from 76 percent (G1), to 20 percent (G2), to 0 percent (G3). These occupational shifts across the three generations reflect the broader process of socioeconomic transformation that has taken place in China since the 1980s, including the expansion of higher education, growth of the service sector, and accelerated rural-to-urban migration.

The household sample includes a small number of elite families in the G1 generation, but the overwhelming majority are "ordinary" families. Prompted by Carter and Duncan's warning[108] against the disproportionate "marking" and exaggeration of the unusual and extraordinary at the cost of neglecting the ordinary and mundane that constitutes the bulk of social life, I have excluded new family formations that have emerged in post-Mao China, such as homosexual couples and transnational families, and focused on heteronormative, domestic families such as those of Chen and Li (see above). In other words, my book does not claim to be exhaustive in the sense of embracing all family formations in every generation. Rather, through the multi-sited and generational-sequence design it seeks to identify and capture the common features of generational change and continuity as well as diversity within families across different sites. In doing so, it fills a major gap in the scholarly literature on the dynamics and behavior of Chinese families.

Structure of the Book

Grounded in a careful analysis of life history interviews, the chapters that follow trace how family practices—childhood experiences, courtship, marriage decisions, marital life, sex and intimacy, and aging and old age support—shift throughout the life course. Except for the discussion of sexual relationships (where it was impossible get all members of one family unit to talk openly about sex),[109] each chapter comprises a small number of multigenerational urban and rural family case studies that are indicative of patterns of family behavior in chosen settings. In order to avoid repeating similar quotes, I provide a detailed description of these cases by way of contextualizing lived experiences and family history. Discussion of these cases is supplemented by other family data in order to capture variance and diversity within each generation.

Chapter 1 examines the changes and continuities in childhood experiences across three generations. While the economic value of children as family helpers has dramatically declined, their potential value as a source of security in old age has remained an important adjunct to the emotional value that they command. In cities, overseen by their parents and driven by both neoliberal market and post-socialist state forces, the one-child generation has experienced an increasingly regimentalized childhood. By contrast, while facing the same pressure to study hard as their urban counterparts, the childhood of the younger rural generation has been profoundly shaped by multilayered institutionalized inequalities, including urban-rural segregation and patrilineal gender ideology.

Chapter 2 examines marital experiences across three generations. Rather than a universalizing triumph of conjugal intimacy, the picture that emerges reveals an embeddedness of conjugal intimacy within extended family ties. Chinese parents continue to matter greatly in children's lives, whether in terms of choosing a spouse, getting married, or managing conjugal life. As the life course evolves, the configuration of conjugal intimacy and intergenerational intimacy fluctuates. Whether or not vertical ties are managed well can have a major impact on the quality of conjugal intimacy. It also emerges from the analysis that intimacy is not automatically emancipatory and that inequalities, such as gender and urban-rural divides, are reproduced in the intimate domain.

Chapter 3 examines premarital sex, conjugal sex, and extramarital affairs. In contrast to Western sociology's progressive narrative of the impact of rapid social change on sexual lives during the last half century, the Chinese narrative reveals paradoxical changes and continuities across three generations of men and women. Despite a widening repertoire of sexual practices and increasing emphasis on "pleasure" among members of the youngest generation, gender transcends both the urban-rural and generational divides. In premarital and conjugal sex, male privilege in sexual agency and discourse permeates activities behind closed doors, where consent can be manufactured and women are more likely to be pressured into having sex. Only extramarital affairs offer a momentary glimpse of the "pure relationship" and "plastic sexuality" described by new modernity writers.

Chapter 4 focuses on grandparenting and shows how it has morphed into a familial responsibility. The three-generation comparison suggests that while grandparenthood has traditionally been honored in Chinese families, grandparenting is not embedded in Chinese culture. Rather, it is a reinvented "tradition" in response to the challenges presented by China's socioeconomic and demographic transformations. The chapter also emphasizes gender and urban-rural differences. As a general rule, grandmothers throughout China bear the main responsibility for everyday tasks in raising grandchildren. However, thanks to their more advantageous economic status, *urban* grandparents are much more favorably placed than their rural counterparts in negotiating inter-generational dynamics.

Chapter 5 examines shifts and continuities in old age support practices across the three generations. While generational comparisons reveal a decline in everyday financial and instrumental support by adult children for their parents, crisis-induced intergenerational solidarity (arrangements for hospitalization and terminal care) remain intact. Concurrently, as the market economy has developed, differences in aging experience have widened between urban and rural families as well as between working-class and affluent families. The chapter further examines how filial morality, material considerations, and affection toward parents figure together in driving children's old age support. Against a backdrop of commercialized housing and the rapid development of the real estate market, the increasing financial importance of urban parental property has become a powerful weapon to prevent children straying from the filial path. However, for rural parents who lack significant material leverage, reliance on the weight of affective and moral imperatives in turning adult sons' filial obligations into solid care practices can carry risks.

The concluding chapter summarizes the main findings and returns to the framework of the "embedded generations." The diversity within Chinese families, along with the coexistence of continuity and change, shaped by the multifaceted and uneven processes underlying institutional and intergenerational configurations, do not support arguments based on a linear, unidirectional theory of family change. Rather than a transition from tradition to modern / postmodern, ideas and practices deemed "traditional" have constantly been reapplied and adapted to family life in different eras. As family life is embedded in local sociocultural and material conditions, while the youngest generation exhibits superficially similar trends (e.g., nuclear family lifestyles, falling fertility) to Western societies, the meaning or consequences of these practices are profoundly different. Chinese families continue to honor "traditional" intergenerational life-long reciprocity, and conjugal intimacy continues to be firmly anchored within the interdependent web of family and kin relations.

1

Growing Up

FROM CHILD LABORERS
TO ACADEMIC ASPIRERS

THE SCHEDULE shown in Table 1 sets out the plan for the first few days of Ms. Wang's seven-year-old daughter during her 2022 winter school holiday. The rest of the holiday followed the same pattern until the eve of the new school term. The only major additional activity was "tidying up own bedroom," which was scheduled once a week. Throughout the thirty-day school holiday, only the first day and last day were study-free. Ms. Wang was apparently sufficiently pleased with her careful planning that she publicized the schedule on WeChat (a popular Chinese messaging app) for her circle of friends and acquaintances.

Ms. Wang (rural G3) was born in 1990 and grew up in a farmer's family in Shandong. From her primary school days, her father followed the example of other male villagers and found work on urban construction sites. She stayed with her mother and her younger brother in the village. In contrast to her daughter's childhood, which involves a mixture of study and play, the rhythm of her own childhood was one of having to help her mother with housework as well as attending to her school work. Her mother was largely illiterate, and she received no home support for her studies. But she still vividly remembered her mother frequently telling her that "for kids in the countryside, the only way to go outside [that is, achieve social mobility] is to study hard to enter university." She did not disappoint her parents and navigated her education successfully, eventually entering a university in Beijing. However, despite gaining BA and MA degrees from a reputable Beijing university, her rural family background failed to provide the cultural and social capital she needed to settle in Beijing. Instead, she returned to the fourth-tier city near her home village, where she worked as a teacher in a vocational school. She married a former schoolmate who had settled in the same city as a white-collar professional. Having benefited herself from a university education and driven by a

TABLE 1. Ms. Wang's Sample Study Schedule for Her Daughter

Wednesday	Thursday	Friday	Saturday	Sunday
January 12	January 13	January 14	January 15	January 16
End of term	Start of school holiday	Chinese: Learning Poem 1 Describing a picture Math: 10 practice questions Reading: Comprehension Physical exercise: 30 minutes	Chinese: Learning Poem 2 Describing a picture: memorizing Memorizing text of "Four seasons" Math: 10 practice questions 5 applied questions Reading: Comprehension Physical exercise: 30 minutes	Chinese: Learning Poem 3 Memorizing poem 1, poem 2, and "Four seasons" Math: Learning currency and practicing related questions Reading: Comprehension Physical exercise: 30 minutes

desire to provide a good start for her daughter among her urban peers, she went to great pains to maximize her daughter's educational opportunities. The winter holiday schedule was one example of her efforts in this regard.

While Ms. Wang did her best to give her daughter a good start in the urban environment, her family lagged behind in the national educational race and could not compete with affluent urban families.[1] A new trend that has emerged among affluent urban G3s is to send their child to elite private schools[2] that follow international educational curricula. Ms. Guang (urban G3, one-child generation) thirteen-year old daughter was enrolled in a bilingual private middle school in Guangzhou. Ms. Guang explained why, despite it costing her and her husband 140,000 yuan (approximately $19,300) a year, she had decided to follow the private school route instead of taking advantage of free tuition[3] in a state school. First, she felt that access to various clubs in the private school would save her time and energy that she would have to spend in order to organize such activities in a state school. Thus, her daughter had been engaged in a wide range of extracurricular activities—math, English, Chinese poetry, debating, carpentry, choir, canoeing, sailing, skiing, triathlon, horse-riding—either at school or through the school's recommendations. Second, she felt that her daughter was not "naturally" academically oriented and therefore might not otherwise have survived the fierce competition to secure a place in a good state secondary school and thereafter in a top Chinese university. Since the private school followed the International Baccalaureate curriculum, she hoped that her daughter would obtain a university place in an English-speaking country such as the United Kingdom or the United States. She sighed: "Times have changed. When we were children, we only needed to study hard. But nowadays children have to acquire all kinds of skills in order to get ahead of others in the competition. For example, when we were in schools, there was probably only one or two children learning a musical instrument. Today it has become a standard part of children's lives. The pressure on the children is so high." Despite her grievances, she was an active participant in this system, and frequently showed off her daughter's achievements, such as her Piano Grade 8 Distinction certificate, on WeChat.

The depiction of childhood in twenty-first-century China shown here is far removed from the upbringing of previous generations. Grandma Wang (rural G1) endured hunger and poverty as she grew up in the 1940s, and from a very early age had to help with her parents' daily struggle to survive. Mother Wang (rural G2), who grew up in the 1960s in Mao's China, needed to help her parents with housework, but the more rigid organization of collective agricultural labor during her childhood meant that from a young age she was left alone to wander. While the material conditions of Ms. Wang's (rural G3) childhood as a "left-behind child"[4] contrasted considerably with those of Ms. Guang (urban G3 and in the first cohort of urban "little empresses")—they shared the academic aspirations that had become so prominent in post-Mao China. Now their children's upbringing displayed features associated with the pattern of "concerted cultivation"[5] emerging in many urban settings throughout the world.

This chapter first examines the transformation in the experiences of growing up across three generations[6] through two case studies—those of the Yuans (a rural family in Shandong, the Wang family's neighbor) and the Qins (an urban family in Xi'an). Generational and urban-rural comparisons reveal the "divergent destinies"[7] of Chinese children. While there is a convergence in terms of educational aspirations among younger generations, the growing disparity in parental resources between urban and rural families has generated an even more complex nexus of compound inequalities. Further, this chapter disputes a modernization of childhood narrative that points to a shift from a family's economic valuation of a child to an emphasis on the child's needs.

Instead it reveals that while the economic value of children as family helpers and coworkers has dramatically diminished across three generations, the potential economic benefit of children as a form of old age security goes hand in hand with the emotional value of children, shaped by the cultural tradition of filial piety, the social welfare context, and demographic structure. Thirdly, while it confirms the child-rearing tensions documented in the existing literature, my analysis deconstructs dualities such as obedience versus autonomy and throws fresh new light upon the fluid dynamics that characterize child-parent interactions. Finally, in contrast to existing scholarly studies of children and child-rearing in China, most of which focus on the G3 generation or their children,[8] this chapter provides additional valuable perspectives by drawing on the memories of childhood of *three* generations of adults.

Childhood

Survival

The grandparent generation (G1) recalled a childhood that took place within a large family and was marked by poverty and privation. Grandpa Yuan (rural G1), born in 1930, was the middle child of a farmer's family, which comprised himself, two elder sisters, and two younger brothers. He recaptured the hardship of his childhood in his village: "Life then was quite a struggle. We were very poor and there were so many children. We often didn't have enough to eat and wear. My clearest memory of childhood was going out to collect tree branches [as fuel] to facilitate my mother's cooking. During the winter, it was snowing and so cold, I was only wearing cloth shoes but I had to go out to collect the branches."

There was little difference between the lives of urban and rural citizens, and urban families also faced financial constraints. Grandma Qin (born in 1939, urban G1) recalled her childhood in Xi'an: "I was very poor when I was a child and had nothing to eat. My father was a manual worker and my mother a housewife. The eight of us [two parents, six children] really struggled. The meals were mostly made from wheat bran. It tasted horrible! Life then was just miserable."

Despite material deprivation, both Grandpa Yuan and Grandma Qin's siblings survived into adulthood. However, tragic reports of siblings dying at a young age were commonplace among as many as a third of my G1 interviewees. For example, three sisters of Grandpa Gao (rural Shandong, see chapter 5) and four brothers of Grandma Jing (Tianjin) died when they were children. The exception to this normative picture of hardship and survival were children from a small group of elite families who recalled a comfortable childhood. The

daughter (urban G1) of a public servant in the Guangzhou government, recalled that in the early 1950s "in contrast to other workers' families who rarely
ate a full meal, we never went hungry. We always had food and clothes to wear
and received education."

Free-Range Childhood

The majority of the middle generation (G2) grew up in a period of political
chaos when class privilege was reversed, causing enormous upheavals for elite
families. During the Cultural Revolution (1966–76) the Guangzhou public
servant (see above) was tortured and died in jail, while his daughter was sent
to work in a chemical factory despite being a university graduate (a qualification that would have otherwise guaranteed her a government bureau job).
Unlike elite families, interviewees born in ordinary workers' or farmers'
families described their childhood in this period as relatively stable and carefree (albeit poor). Son Qin (urban G2), born in 1960, was the eldest child of
Grandma Qin (a former factory worker): "At that time, parents were so busy
that we were just left on our own. I played with our neighbors' children a lot.
We were roaming around, just like sheep herds . . . I was quite naughty when
I was a child and often got into fights. When the neighbors came to complain,
since my dad was very busy, he gave me a good beating without asking what
was going on."

Due to the mobilization of female labor, unlike the preceding generation,
almost all G2s' mothers were engaged in paid work, generally leaving older
siblings to look after younger ones. The heavy emphasis on socialist production during the Mao era limited the time available for family interaction and
parental involvement in their children's education was minimal or nonexistent.
Son Qin explained, "In our generation, no parents had enough energy to be
able to help with our studies. Everybody was the same."

Daughter Yuan (rural G2, born in 1959) was the sixth child of Grandpa Yuan
in rural Shandong. Her remarks echo those made by Son Qin: "My mother
died when I was only six years old. . . . My father was a party member, so he
was at production team meetings most of the time, hardly at home at all. My
two elder sisters got married when I was eight. For my everyday living, I completely relied upon my third sister. She was like a mother. My father didn't pay
any attention to us. He spent most of his time with the production team."

However, the considerable freedom that children enjoyed at the time was
sometimes accompanied by abuse through child neglect.[9] One woman from
Daughter Yuan's village recalled an "unpleasant" incident when she was about
seven or eight years old: she was forced to join in a children's game in which,
as part of the play, older boys touched her genital area in a deserted courtyard.

This was a very uncomfortable—bordering on painful—experience, but she felt compelled to keep "playing" until one of the villagers stopped and intervened.

In the Mao era the party-state adopted an industrialization strategy that prioritized the development of cities over the countryside, as a result of which the urban sector benefited disproportionately from allocations of capital and other resources. While the Maoist class struggle reduced social stratification within urban and rural sectors in the 1960s and 1970s, gaps in household income and living standards between the urban and rural sectors actually widened. For example, when both Son Qin and Daughter Yuan described their families' living conditions as "poor," there was a subtle difference in their depictions of poverty: viewed through his urban prism, Son Qin spoke of not being able to access "good food" (*haochi de*) or "new clothes," whereas for Daughter Yuan poverty meant not having enough food to eat (*bugou chi*). Further, while it was commonplace for urban and rural children to help with housework and childcare, older rural children carried the additional burden of having to participate in collective production to earn work points[10] for the household. One consequence of this is that rural children tended to experience a much shorter period of schooling compared with their urban counterparts, despite the disruption of education during the Cultural Revolution: Son Qin and his siblings (including his sister) were all educated up to junior middle school level. In contrast, only the youngest brother of Daughter Yuan continued education up to junior middle school, while Daughter Yuan and her eldest sisters—the former receiving just three years of primary schooling, and the latter no schooling at all—were left largely illiterate. Finally, a small minority of rural families (10 percent) in the middle generation still reported child deaths. Such tragic events most often occurred in households with a large number of young children and reflected the tension inherent in trying to balance the daily needs of physical reproduction and the maximization of work points (which placed a premium on mobilizing as many family laborers as possible into work).

Academic Cultivation

Members of the grandchild generation (G3) were born in an era when China had embraced a strategy of economic reform, which—in stark contrast to the Maoist emphasis on egalitarianism—promoted a discourse of "competition" and "efficiency." It was also an era characterized by strict official nationwide adherence to the one-child policy (albeit with urban-rural variations), marked by a dramatic reduction in the average number of children per family. Improved living standards, smaller family size, and structural changes associated with the transition to a market economy—for example, the removal of state allocation of urban jobs, agricultural de-collectivization in the farm sector, and the promotion of a knowledge economy[11] that equated good educational qualifications with rising incomes and improved living standards[12]—have placed a premium on maximizing the educational opportunities of children growing up during these years. However, such commonalities apart, there have been pronounced differences between urban and rural trajectories of children's academic study.

Granddaughter Qin (urban G3, born in 1984) was the only child of Son Qin. She recalled a childhood where improvement in urban living standards was taking place. For example, her parents were particularly indulgent in letting her sample the various kinds of food that were becoming available:[13] "My parents were ordinary workers so I didn't have many fancy toys as I grew up. However, they were particularly generous when it came to food—they bought lots of nice things for me to eat. I remember vividly that when KFC first came to the city in the 1990s, my parents took me all the way to the restaurant to try it."

Parental generosity in terms of the range of food offered to children undoubtedly reflects the shortages of food experienced by previous generations: when economic reform revived the role of households as the primary locus of consumption,[14] making available a better and more diverse diet was the most potent way in which parents could enhance the childhood experiences of their children.

Alongside their success in raising their daughter's material aspirations, Granddaughter Qin's parents became much more demanding in setting academic goals: "Every day when I went home, I had to study. If my mother saw me watching TV or playing, she would scold me badly [xiong]. If I had poor exam scores, I became very nervous, knowing that this would make my parents very unhappy with me."

Granddaughter Qin did not learn a musical instrument[15] as she grew up, but her parents subscribed to children's magazines in the hope of fostering a favorable study environment for her. During Spring Festivals, the amount of money she received in the red envelopes[16] given by her parents was closely correlated with her academic ranking in class. Thanks to these multilayered processes of academic nurturing, she was consistently in the top quarter of her class throughout her schooling.

Chinese media coined the terms "little empress" and "little emperor" to capture the spoiled nature of the urban only-child generation. Indeed, like Granddaughter Qin, this cohort was usually not required to help with household chores nor did it experience the hunger and hardship faced by previous generations. However, the more indulgent material environment also gave way to an increasingly routinized and regimented childhood in which academic study was the priority and everything else was secondary and designed to help fulfill this ultimate goal.[17]

In contrast to Granddaughter Qin, Granddaughter Yuan (rural G3, born in 1983) grew up in a farming household. In order to maximize cash income to cover family expenditures, her father joined Ms. Wang's (at the start of this chapter) father to work in construction sites when she was in primary school. Unlike Granddaughter Qin whose after-school activities focused primarily on academic study, as the eldest sibling[18] Granddaughter Yuan undertook various household tasks: "When I was little, as soon as I finished school, I went home to work [*ganhuo*]. I did the cooking. I also fed the cows, pigs and pigeons." Her mother took a conscious decision not to ask her children to work in the fields in order not to encroach on their time, but her wishes were not entirely fulfilled: "I didn't ask them to do agricultural work. But of their own accord they came to help by cutting the grass. Perhaps they saw that working on my own left too much work unfinished." Like Ms. Wang's mother and other rural peers, Daughter Yuan (rural G2) was largely illiterate. Apart from urging her children to study hard, she was unable to offer practical support and was reliant on schools to foster her children's academic talents.

Unfortunately, rural-urban segregation is built into China's education system, and poor-quality teaching and inadequate physical infrastructure are common in rural schools.[19] A growing body of literature has shown a sharply increasing gap in educational attainment between rural and urban youths. Efforts to close the gap have mostly involved diverting rural youths into vocational schools, rather than enhancing their chance of getting into an academic senior middle school and then college.[20] As a consequence, the massive post-1998 university expansion has overwhelmingly favored urban youths rather than rural youths. Against this institutional backdrop, Granddaughter Yuan struggled academically and failed to progress beyond junior middle school. She recalled: "In the countryside most people are like me and end their education when they leave junior middle school. People like Wang who went to university were a minority. So when I saw that my second sister was good at studying, I really wanted to help her to continue her education."[21] Granddaughter Yuan started to work as a migrant laborer in a coastal factory at the age of seventeen and sent 80 percent of her income back home to support her family—in particular to help further educate her second sister.

Granddaughter Yuan was one of the early cohort of "left-behind children"[22] to whom journalists and researchers in China have given much attention in recent years, not least through the publication of sensational reports and alarming scholarly articles. Thus, rural left-behind children have been reported to suffer low self-esteem, depression, and lack of motivation at school, as well as being susceptible in the absence of proper adult supervision to sexual and physical abuse.[23] Alongside the perception of the urban one-child generation as spoiled "little emperors," rural migrant children have become subjects of pity. The public discourse on "left-behind children" has placed a dispropor-tionate burden of blame on parental separation and its impact on children, but has downplayed and masked the institutionalized inequalities to which rural families are exposed—such inequalities constituting a more fundamental cause of the difficulties experienced by so many rural children.

Since the mid-1980s urban households' disposable incomes and living stan-dards have risen more quickly than those of their rural counterparts, giving rise to a steady widening of the urban-rural income gap. Granddaughter Yuan recalled that when she was a small child there were sometimes not enough white buns to share and that in winter there were shortages of warm clothes. Deprivation of this kind was unknown in cities. The widening urban-rural income gap and the burden of covering increasing social reproduction expenditure[24] led many villagers, including Granddaughter Yuan's father and herself, to migrate to cities in search of higher-paid employment. However, urban-rural segregation means that rural migrants have been overwhelmingly concentrated in low-paid manual jobs. While outmigration helped to lift rural households out of subsistence farming, until recently at least the additional income made available from migrant work did little to narrow the gap between urban and rural living standards.[25] The consensus among rural families is that "The only way for rural children to escape from the countryside is to enter university." Children's education has become an all-consuming familial project for the fulfilment of which all family members make sacrifices: parents migrate to the cities in search of work to pay for the children's education; mothers and grandparents act as carers; and children themselves are expected to study hard.[26] Lareau described a contrast in parenting styles between "concerted cultivation" (middle-class families) and "the accomplishment of natural growth" (working-class families) in the United States.[27] The Chinese rural parents in my sample lay somewhere in between: they were strongly motivated to push their children to excel academically, but the limited resources and cultural capital they possessed inhibited them from investing intensively, consequently ending in the "natural growth" of their children.

"Compound Inequalities"

Rural families' efforts in pushing children to do well academically can be viewed as a family reproductive strategy to escape from entrenched urban-rural inequalities. However, as Granddaughter Yuan's childhood experiences show, those very inequalities have dramatically constrained rural families' capacities to nurture educational competencies in their children. Trapped in a cycle of vulnerability, rural families are falling further and further behind their urban counterparts in the race for educational and social mobility. Existing inequalities have been reproduced and aggravated in the childhood experiences of future generations.

Under her parents' continuous monitoring, Granddaughter Qin (urban G3) successfully enrolled at a university in her home city of Xi'an and after graduating she became a white-collar professional in a company. Three years later through contacts at work, she got to know and subsequently married a high-flying company manager, and in 2011 she gave birth to a daughter (urban G4). In order to give her the best possible start, when her daughter was three she enrolled her in a bilingual kindergarten and then paid a high premium to send her to a private school that offered academic provision from primary to senior middle school level in preparation for a university education overseas. All these educational opportunities were made possible through access to resources owned by her nuclear family. As evidence of the scale of these resources, from time to time she posted on her social media photographs of her family enjoying a luxury holiday and staying in a hotel that cost more than 3,000 yuan per night, which is the monthly wage of Granddaughter Yuan as a migrant worker.[28]

In sharp contrast, Granddaughter Yuan (rural G3) met her husband—who was born in a neighboring village, but worked as a migrant—at the age of twenty-two when her parents arranged a date for them in the village. After her marriage, she initially joined her husband and worked in the city, but then returned home to give birth to her first child (a daughter, rural G4) in 2007. When her daughter was one year old, she returned to the city for three years, leaving her baby to be cared for by her parents and in-laws. When her daughter was four, Granddaughter Yuan's brother-in-law had a son, whom he expected her in-laws also to look after. Concerned that her own daughter might not receive sufficient care, Granddaughter Yuan decided to return to the village and find work nearby. In 2018 she gave birth to a second child (a son, rural G4), which ruled out the possibility of once more returning to the city to work: "I need to look after the baby. My elder child is nearly ready for junior middle school and now that I need to pay careful attention to her education, I won't migrate again. Wages in the village are too low for my husband to stay behind, so he has to remain in the city. There's no other option open to us." When Granddaughter Yuan returned to the village, the nuclear family's monthly income fell from 6,000 yuan to 4,000 yuan. Given the limitations of her family resources and the tendency of parents to prioritize the interests of their sons, there was a danger that, as in so many other rural families, her daughter's long-term educational development might be jeopardized.

The comparison of Family Yuan and Family Qin not only serves to demonstrate the wide gap in childhood opportunities available to urban and rural
families, but is also illustrative of the intergenerational reproduction of urban-
rural inequalities in Chinese families—a process termed "compound inequalities."[29] Drawing on Bourdieu's key concepts of habitus and capital in the
micro-processes of reproduction,[30] as well as feminist political economy
scholarship relating to social reproduction, Nunn and Tepe-Belfrage propose
the concept of "compound inequality" to capture the way in which preexisting
structural inequalities impact household strategies to reproduce inequalities
over time. In analyzing educational inequalities in Britain, Nunn and Tepe-
Belfrage explain how the agency of households, located at different positions
in the class hierarchy, tends to reinforce compound inequalities into the future,
through inequalities of the income and the different educational strategies
they adopt.

In a way similar to that of privileged middle-class British families, Granddaughter Qin carefully positioned her daughter, from a young age, in a well-
connected network that provided access to resources (financial as well as
social). In the private school, her daughter's classmates came from a wide
range of economically and politically influential families, whose connections
in a variety of socioeconomic domains promised to be beneficial for her
daughter and her family. Their family income having made possible the choice
of an elite private school, Granddaughter Qin's daughter was destined for a
university education abroad and a global career trajectory. Over three generations, Qin's family educational strategies had successfully transformed their
socioeconomic status from that of an urban working-class family (Son Qin,
urban G2) to that of a global professional class (Granddaughter Qin's daughter,
urban G4). In contrast, from her rural working class background, Granddaughter Yuan had been forced to reenact the child-rearing pattern adopted
by her parents in which mother and children stayed behind in the village while
the father migrated to a city. The likely consequence was that with a failing
rural school system and limited family resources, like her mother, Granddaughter Yuan's daughter would end up as a low-paid migrant worker. In short,
despite the Yuan family's educational aspirations for their children, their disadvantaged social position was reproduced over three generations. It is worth
highlighting that US and UK studies document class inequalities, particularly
between children raised by well-educated parents and less-well educated ones.
In China, there are socioeconomic differences within urban families (for example, an affluent urban family might send their child to private school); however, the different developmental trajectory between urban and rural schooling and infrastructure overrides economic differences within the urban sector,

driving the major social cleavage in childhood experience between rural and urban families in China.

Ms. Wang (at the start of this chapter) was among seven of the thirty-four rural G3 individuals to have broken through the urban-rural hierarchical divide to obtain a university education and enter white-collar professions. In so doing, she disrupted the intergenerational reproduction of urban-rural inequalities. However, due to the constraints of her rural extended family network, she lacked the opportunity to settle in a first-tier city (as Granddaughter Qin had done), and instead returned to the fourth-tier city in which her home village was administratively located. Compared with Granddaughter Yuan, as well as her own parents and grandparents, Ms. Wang had achieved upward social mobility by settling in an urban setting and following a professional career trajectory. In order for her family to maintain this position into subsequent generations, she strove hard to monitor her daughter's educational attainment, investing time and energy into designing a strict regime of educational activities for her young daughter. Nevertheless, constrained by family resources and regional inequalities between first-tier cities and fourth-tier cities, her daughter's educational and career prospects were far removed from those of Granddaughter Qin's daughter. That is, Ms. Wang's horizon was limited to domestic and local (regional) competitive opportunities, while Granddaughter Qin's eyes were set firmly on the global horizon. As a result of "compound inequalities," the stratification of families from a variety of socioeconomic backgrounds became entrenched and was even exacerbated over time. While Ms. Wang and Granddaughter Qin had both managed to achieve social mobility by securing a university qualification, it would be hard for Granddaughter Yuan's children to catch up with Ms. Wang's children and even harder to catch up with Granddaughter Qin's children.

The Value of Children

Zelizer[31] traced the social construction of the economically "worthless" but emotionally "priceless" American child across a sixty-year period from 1870 to 1930. She explained how the changing value of children was related to middle-range changes in the occupational and family structures wrought by the Industrial Revolution. This narrative has been implicated in China research; for example, some scholars argue that Chinese urban children have become emotionally precious, but economically useless to parents with whom they enjoy—or at least seek to enjoy—democratic relationships and expressive intimacy.[32] I employ Kagitcibasi's[33] analytical model to examine three value types—economic / utilitarian, psychological, and social values—to discuss whether the linear modernization narrative captures the changing role of children in Chinese families.

Utilitarian Value

Utilitarian values derive from the economic / material benefits of having children, not only while they are young, but also when they become adults. In the case of China, the economic role of young children diminished dramatically over the three generations, albeit at a different pace between urban and rural families. The narrative of the older generation (G1) highlighted a variety of tasks undertaken by children from the age of five, such as helping with household chores, providing care for younger siblings / relatives and assisting with parents' work. From the middle generation (G2) onward, the urban-rural divide becomes more visible. In urban families, children cooked and helped care for younger siblings, but were largely relieved from assisting their parents in labor outside the home thanks to paid employment being allocated by the state work unit. In contrast, in the countryside older siblings were still required to help their parents in the production team in order to earn work points. In the case of the youngest generation (G3), urban parents and other carers (mostly grandparents) assumed responsibility for household chores in order to maximize children's study time: young children no longer possessed an immediate utilitarian value to their families, but instead were an investment for the future. However, in rural households, older siblings (mostly girls) were still required to assist in housework and occasionally undertake farm work (for example, during harvesting). When rural children failed to continue their education, most of them found work as migrants as young as thirteen and sent home remittances to provide economic support for the family—especially siblings who offered the promise of significant financial returns for the family from educational investment. Thus, Granddaughter Yuan recalled that before getting married she had sent home 80 percent of her migrant wage income.

The shifting yet varied role of young children in Chinese families strongly reflects the uneven and unbalanced nature of economic development and infrastructural modernization in China since 1949. A dominant theme in this narrative has been the disproportionate benefits from modernization that have accrued to urban families, transforming the burden of housework. In the 1950s and 1960s homes lacked sinks and family members had to fetch water from a local well. Most urban residents did not have access to a gas or electric cooker until the 1980s; instead, whenever they cooked they had to light a beehive coal fire.[34] The installation of modern facilities, such as mains-connected water and electricity and gas greatly reduced the time needed for basic household tasks and made it possible to relieve children from having to help with them. The use of refrigerators, washing machines, modern heating, and even air conditioning has become commonplace in urban households in China. However, infrastructure development in rural regions has remained sadly lacking. During my fieldwork visits to villages in 2011, a considerable number of households (60 percent) continued to fetch water from a local well and still used firewood for cooking. When I revisited the villages during 2016–19, the supply of water through taps had become more common (80 percent). Yet because the provision of other basic modern infrastructure—for example, for heating, cooking, and sanitary facilities[35]—is still wholly dependent on the economic status of individual families, only some economically well-off families have benefited (20 percent). In most rural families, stay-behind carers (mothers and / or grandparents) still have to rely on children for assistance in housework.

While the economic value placed on young children diminished across the three generations, the economic value placed on adult children in China followed a nonlinear and far more complex trajectory—this aspect is distinctive from the transformation of US childhood described by Zelizer. Among urban families, most of the G1 generation had access to pensions from their Mao era work unit that were sufficient to cover the costs of food and daily living expenses. However, when they fell ill or became immobile, they were still mainly reliant on instrumental support and care from their children—the middle generation (G2, see chapter 5). In the context of a "socialist market economy", such care and support was only available at a price. Thus, the economic value of adult children was defined in terms of unpaid familial care activities in parents' old age.

When asked about their expectations for old age, the middle generation (G2) expressed contradictory desires that oscillated between wanting and not wanting to rely on their children:[36]

> I've been wondering what I should do about my old age. Although I feel that I shouldn't rely on my child, I still need to do so. This is her obligation. If there's an old age care home that suits me, I can go there. But I'll miss my child. I once told my daughter that I would follow her wherever she went. She said that she wanted me to live with her so that I could keep her home clean and tidy while her dad helped her out with other chores. (Urban G2 mother, born in Xi'an)

Several themes emerge from this woman's reflections. First, they reveal that the traditional cultural norm of filial obligation required of adult children still played a role in formulating plans for old age care. Second, they highlight the lifelong interdependence between adult children and aged parents, which has remained a dominant feature in Chinese families. Elderly parents were not only expected to do housework for their adult children, but also assumed an important role as carers for grandchildren (see chapter 4). Both parent and adult children interviewees agreed that the embeddedness of reciprocity in Chinese culture generated an expectation that adult children should, when needed, provide support and care for their aging parents (see chapter 5). Third, the woman's comments hint at the low level of access to socialized care that has persisted in China. Notwithstanding reports of elite families (former government officials) having access to high quality institutional care, ordinary families find it difficult to access or afford old age care homes of similar quality. Further, there is still a general distrust of care services—both for children and the elderly—provided outside the family, and being looked after by family members remains elderly people's preferred care option.

Thanks to the gap in welfare provision between cities and countryside in China, among rural families, the emphasis on children as the providers of old age security has persisted across the three generations. Unlike urban families who were entitled to pensions during the Mao era, it is only since 2009 that rural pensions have gradually been introduced. This initiative was universally welcomed by rural interviewees, but the wide gap between rural and urban pension levels has endured. In 2019, for example, a retired urban factory worker's monthly pension was around 2,000 yuan, while the state monthly pension for a rural resident was a mere 5 percent of this figure (about 100 yuan). As a result, aging rural parents are still reliant on their adult children for every kind of assistance, including financial support.

Against the background of parents' increased investment in the education of both sons and daughters in younger rural generations, traditional patrilineal expectations have been extended from sons to daughters. In effect, expectations about children's financial contribution toward old age care has become firmly anchored in a quasi cost-benefit framework in which parents seek to calculate an appropriate return, in terms of anticipated care in old age, on investment in their children's education. A rural G2 man who had three daughters and a son commented: "Without a shadow of doubt, it's right that my children should behave in a filial manner. It cost us a fortune to send them to universities. How could they not return their gratitude? If I can, I'd prefer to live with my wife when we become old. Even so, every child ought to send some money back."

Psychological Value

The psychological value placed on children derives from the joy, pride, love and companionship that children provide to their parents.[37] Both the older and middle generations of urban and rural families tended to have many children whom they brought up in straitened material circumstances, which affected parents' psychological attachment to their children. One urban G1 recalled: "There were so many of us children that we were no longer precious. Sometimes in summer we slept outside, and if parents couldn't find us, they took no notice. The fact was that parents didn't want to keep all their children."

With parents of the older generation (G1) primarily concerned with simply getting by, and those of the middle generation (G2) caught up in state-run or collective production activities, children's memories were of their parents always seeming to be under great pressure. In these contexts, children became their parents' emotional outlets—not for parental love and affection, but for stress and anger. Many interviewees recalled that when they were under pressure or became irritated, parents would vent their anger at their children and beat them—even over very trivial matters: "Children were the 'Chuqi Tong' [an anger release mechanism] for their parents."

Given the large family size among the early generations, parents tended to have favorites among their children. The favored child developed a very close emotional attachment toward his or her parent(s) that was not shared by the other siblings. For example, when asked about their relationships with their parents, Grandma Jing and her youngest sister (urban G1, Tianjin) gave contrasting responses. Grandma Jing recalled: "Every day I was concerned about my parents and how they were. My heart tightened when I thought about them." On several occasions she wept as she recalled those early times spent with her parents. By contrast, her youngest sister commented: "I don't feel particularly close to them. Ever since childhood, my mother liked my younger brother best, whereas my father's favorite was my second sister [Grandma Jing]." The gender structure of the family was partly responsible for this. If parents had sons and daughters, thanks to the patrilineal tradition it was the boys, like Grandma Jing's younger brother, who were more likely to be favored. But where there was a preponderance of boys in a family, the birth of a girl would often lead to a strong emotional attachment to her.

The weak psychological attachment to children was reversed in the younger generation (G3) following the introduction of the one-child policy. A G2 Guangzhou mother recalled: "When my son was a baby, he and I slept in the same bed . . . I often looked at him while he was asleep. Moments like that were just so special. Perhaps this kind of emotional attachment towards him was a compensation for the lack of it when I was a child."

Part of the psychological value of children lies in the pride their parents derive from them. In the Chinese context, such pride is closely associated with the concept of "face"[38] (*mianzi*) and the most obvious way in which children confer face upon their parents in post-Mao China is academic success. Academic achievement generates good job prospects and promises substantial future economic returns (see Granddaughter Qin's example above). Thus, the psychological value placed on children has become inextricably linked to their economic value. As a G2 father put it, "The child has become the object of competition [*panbi*]."

The changing nature of the psychological value of Chinese children is closely linked to the demographic transition. Alongside rapid economic growth, increasing incomes, rising urbanization, and enhanced educational attainment, as well the state-engineered population control, changes in Chinese family demographics have taken place within a remarkably short period of time and much more rapidly than other societies. The number of children in Chinese families has fallen dramatically, from between two[39] and six in the first two generations, to one (urban) and two or three (rural) in the younger generation, contributing to the rise of emotionally "priceless" children. In the words of a traditional Chinese saying, "When things become rare, they become precious."

Social Value

The social value of children is captured in the public affirmation conferred on married adults when they have children.[40] When asked "Why did you have children?," the consensus of all three generations was that "after marriage, the next step in life is to have children." If a couple did not have a child within a few years of marriage their relatives, friends, and colleagues would gossip and speculate about whether they had problems conceiving. According to traditional Chinese cultural norms, being childless has long been considered unfilial,[41] and the social value of having children was consistently high across the three generations, albeit with clear generational differences in the value of boys and girls.

Chinese families have traditionally placed a premium on sons, and son preference was unambiguously expressed in the rural older generation.[42] This sentiment was well captured in a saying from rural Shandong, which a G1 interviewee quoted to me: "A single crippled son is worth more than ten beautiful daughters." Daughters were regarded as "split water" when they married; parents focused only upon investment in their sons. As Grandpa Yuan (rural G1) recalled, "At that time the norm was for boys to go to school. The only girls who did so were those from wealthy families." Among the middle generation, son preference persisted. During the Mao era, except during the Cultural Revolution when it was seriously disrupted, the campaign to reduce illiteracy made schooling more accessible to girls, although it was still the girls—especially the eldest daughters—who assumed a disproportionate share of the care work and domestic chores to the detriment of their education.

Among the youngest rural generation (G3), gender preference has become more ambiguous. The value placed on rural daughters noticeably increased in the pairs between G2 parents and G3 children, due to a combination of factors such as shrinking family demographic profiles, an increasing role in old age care of their own parents, and growing economic capacity (due to working as migrants rather than farmers).[43] Nevertheless, in terms of their symbolic function in the patrilineal system, daughters are still considered secondary to sons. As a rural G3 mother succinctly put it, "After all, if we only have daughters and no son, there is always a sadness in our heart. In reality, daughters are better than sons in looking after us in old age—for example, they wash clothes and do other things that sons are no good at. But sons have a role in the village that daughters cannot fulfil. Now that I've had a son, I'd be happy to have a daughter."

This paradox generated further contradictions. On the one hand, members of Granddaughter Yuan's (rural G3) and her daughter's generations (rural G4) received far more educational investment than that available to Daughter Yuan's (rural G2) generation. On the other hand, in young rural households the most common sibling structure was that of elder sisters living alongside a younger brother—a pattern that reflected the persistent and widespread practice of trying to have a son. Echoing Johnson,[44] in late twentieth-century China rapidly changing culture hastened a positive revaluation of daughters, but policies limiting births undercut girls' status in the family and reinforced the "traditional" preference for boys generating disproportionate rates of female child abandonment, infanticide, and sex-selective abortions especially in rural areas.

In urban families of the older generation, son preference was widespread, and most G1 (men and women) accepted it as the norm. Among the middle generation, daughters also recalled that parents saved better food for their brothers and that boys' education was prioritized. However, despite the culturally conditioned bias, thanks to higher urban wages and increased spending on educational infrastructure, educational access significantly improved for urban G1 and G2 daughters, most of whom at least completed junior middle school. Further, compared with rural families, the social value of urban daughters has gradually increased since G1 days as their role—both financial and practical—in providing care for their elderly parents has come to match that of their brothers (see chapter 5).[45]

The introduction of the one-child policy has further increased parental investment in urban only-child daughters, as seen in the absence of evidence pointing to gender differences in educational achievement between single-girl and single-boy families.[46] Among my interviewees, most urban only-child girls had university degrees and held professional jobs.[47] More than 95 percent of them, like their male counterparts, did no housework during childhood. After marriage, they remained close to natal parents for both emotional and practical reasons (e.g., their parents regularly assisted with cooking and everyday chores). Among married interviewees from the one-child (G3) generation, men and women generally displayed no gender preference for their as yet unborn only child. Following the introduction of a two-child policy in 2015, many urban interviewees (70 percent of urban G3) commented that the best family structure was one boy and one girl, somewhat converging with rural G3s' aspirations. Whether the reversal of one-child policy will lead to the revival of son preference in urban China remains to be seen.

Obedience versus Autonomy

The increase in the emotional value placed on children is associated with the democratization thesis of parent-child relationships, which points to more egalitarian interactions between parents and children in Euro-American societies since the 1960s.[48] Critics have, however, pointed out that alongside the child-centeredness of family dynamics, parental control over and surveillance of children has intensified,[49] epitomized in the notion of "intensive parenting,"[50] increasingly characteristic of many urban settings throughout the world. Likewise, children's autonomy has become a particularly contentious area of investigation in scholarly work on China because of its deeply rooted cultural tradition of Confucianism, which dictated a rigid and hierarchical family structure. From a very young age, children were expected to be obedient and respectful toward their seniors, indebted to their parents throughout their lives.[51] The May Fourth Movement (roughly 1919–23) comprehensively targeted Confucianist families and called for their reform. Chen Duxiu, Lu Xun, and other leading thinkers of the time believed that nurturing individuality was essential to China's modernization. However, their impact was minimal, and it was not until the Communist revolution in 1949 that major political and social campaigns were launched to reform family life in China. The goal of the post-1949 government was to reduce parental power and increase children's autonomy to facilitate their role as political actors,[52] although some have argued that political upheavals and lack of mobility in the Mao era may have served to strengthen ties between parents and their children.[53]

The introduction of the one-child policy and market reforms in post-Mao China brought a new emphasis on scientific parenting (in particular, scientific *mothering*), designed to raise the "quality" (*suzhi*) of the population by producing a new generation of well-educated and enterprising youths.[54] In 1999 the Chinese government introduced a wide-ranging program of reform to promote "education for quality"[55] in schools in order to prepare Chinese children to be able to compete in global labor markets. Viewed from the perspective of this wider institutional context, Naftali suggests that a new mode of speaking and thinking about children's rights is emerging, in which children are cast as "independent" persons rather than mere "appendages" to their families, society, and even the state, looking to parents and carers to adapt their child-rearing methods to cultivate children's autonomy.[56] The conflicts and tensions in raising and educating the one-child generation inherent in competing ideologies have been documented in various ethnographic studies.[57] My focus here is on parent-child interactions revealed through the prism of adult memories of childhood. The temporal dimension of the narrative that emerges makes available new perspectives by revealing how the tension between obedience and autonomy has been managed and resolved over time. An important finding is that the dynamics between them are far more fluid than other studies have suggested and that they are not necessarily mutually exclusive.

Parameters of Obedience and Autonomy

The childhood of each generation embodies features associated with both obedience and autonomy. The parameters of obedience and autonomy fluctuate across generations, and are shaped by the prevailing institutional context. As shown above, parents from the early two generations were preoccupied with the demands of making ends meet or fulfilling their roles in socialist production activities. The areas that required children to demonstrate their obedience were mostly related to the fulfilment of prescribed tasks such as housework, farm work, and so on. Failure to comply with parents' instructions most frequently led to corporal punishment in order to ensure future obedience. Verbal communication between parents and children was very limited not only because of busy work schedules, but also because of the reverence for age embodied in the Confucian family behavioral code. Thus, a female member of the G1 generation reported, "We were expected not to talk too much in front of parents. We were the junior generation, and parents were the senior generation." Nevertheless, outside these parameters, children enjoyed considerable freedom in terms of managing the rest of their everyday lives.

In the grandchild generation—especially the urban only-child generation—the parameters of obedience and autonomy were somewhat reversed. Compliance with parental requests was now focused on academic excellence, to which all other activities were subordinated. By contrast, they now enjoyed considerable autonomy in decisions relating to food and other kinds of material consumption. At the same time and in accordance with the traditional Confucian code of filial piety inculcated into the previous two generations, urban G3 interviewees were expected to be respectful toward the senior generations. As Granddaughter Qin recalled, in addition to lax academic discipline a behavioral lapse that frequently led to the urban G3 being punished was "answering back" (*huizui*): "My parents didn't ask me to do any housework so that I could concentrate on my study. However, they were strict with me if they caught me answering back to them or my grandparents—something that was considered very bad behavior."

Rural children had very limited autonomy in terms of making material decisions, but those who were forced by the state centralization of rural schooling to become boarders in middle schools enjoyed a greater degree of autonomy than their urban counterparts who continued to be closely monitored by their parents until going to university. Mr. Wei (rural G3) recalled his excitement at becoming a boarder: "At last there was nobody who could control me anymore. I know life in the past hadn't been easy for my mother, so I didn't want to be disobedient towards her. But because I had to go home as soon as I'd finished school, I felt that I didn't have much freedom to do whatever I wanted to. So the prospect of becoming a boarder made me extremely happy."

These comments highlight several points of interest. First, like many other interviewees, Mr. Wei internalized the feeling that children should show gratitude to parents who had made sacrifices for their children's futures. His parental family was not well off, and his mother, who had remained in the village when her husband went off to work in a city, took on whatever odd jobs were available in addition to her farm work in order to maximize her cash income. Mr. Wei was grateful for his mother's efforts, the main aim of which was to help pay for his and his sister's educational expenses. Second, Mr. Wei recognized the tension between obedience and autonomy: he felt that he owed it to his mother to be obedient, but at the same time he bemoaned the lack of autonomy to do what he wanted. Leaving home to become a boarder offered a convenient solution, his new status enabling him to continue to display obedience toward his mother when they were together while giving him greater autonomy when he was at school and they were apart.

The scholarly literature has documented the tension parents raising the one-child generation felt in their efforts to reconcile the desire that children be obedient with the need to foster children's individuality, creativity, and resourcefulness in order that they might succeed in the fiercely competitive market environment—also reflecting the emergence of new economic values among children. By the time they had joined the work force and become parents, the first cohort of the one-child generation no longer recognized such challenges as a significant issue. Mr. Jin (urban G3) explained: "These are no longer problems for us because we Chinese treat family members and outsiders differently. We're capable of making sacrifices for those who belong to our family, but when it comes to non-family members we can be very self-centered."

Mr. Jin's explanation describes an operational model of individuality in Chinese social relationships that aligns neither with the model of "individuality" promoted by May Fourth intellectuals nor that of post-Mao policymakers (since both are grounded in a Western liberal notion of autonomous self). Instead, what Mr. Jin describes maps onto the relational selfhood in Fei's concept of the "differential mode of association" (see the Introduction).[58] Thus, the "elastic individual" is able simultaneously to display more individualistic attitudes or behavior toward those who are located more distantly from the self, while also exhibiting a high level of loyalty toward those considered to be closer to the self. As Mr. Jin's comment illustrates, there is a clear demarcation between family members (via consanguineal and affinal ties) and nonfamily members. This distinction is also reflected in the responses of many interviewees, which starkly contrast the self-centered and competitive attitudes they display in their work and the mutual support and obligations that characterize their family lives. The weakening of social trust and development of a highly competitive market economy in post-Mao China have further contributed to increasingly widespread distrust of nonfamily members.[59] In short, regardless of intra-family differences and conflicts, family members are considered by default to be more trustworthy than nonfamily members, thereby encouraging the projection of different forms of individuality toward family members and outsiders.

Gender also shapes the dynamic boundaries between obedience and autonomy. Social construction of masculinities and femininities locate sons and daughters differently in parents' search for an appropriate balance between obedience and autonomy. As younger children, the one-child generation was expected to display obedience toward parents and grandparents. However, as adulthood approached, sons' parents became more concerned to inculcate independence and strength into a boy, deeming such traits to be appropriate for manhood and essential if he was to fulfill his expected role in a future marital household. One G3 mother explained such paradoxical expectations upon raising sons: "I normally manage the household, but I try to avoid being too controlling in the family as that would impact badly upon children, especially boys. For example, my son [born in 2007] is indecisive and has to ask for my opinion about everything. But his merit is that he is very obedient and always does everything we ask him. . . . Because he's quite weak, I hope in future he finds a girl who is very gentle. Otherwise, if he chooses someone very domineering, he'll be in real trouble."

Such care in balancing autonomy and obedience in parents' interactions with their sons is less evident where daughters are concerned. Parents urge girls to excel academically but also try to inculcate feminine traits into their daughters, such as being "soft" and "gentle." A number of city women from the one-child generation (20 percent) mentioned that when they found it difficult to find a boyfriend, their mothers blamed them for "having a strong temper," which jeopardized their marriage prospects. Since obedience is essential to filial piety but is also regarded as a feminine trait, parents have tended to demand and expect a greater degree of obedience from a daughter than from a son.

The Art of Communication (Goutong)

Within G1 and G2 generations beating was widely used and accepted as a means of ensuring a child's obedience.[60] Physical punishment continued to be a normative disciplinary method of control when the G3 generation was growing up.[61] However, as part of the effort to transform traditional authoritarian methods of child-rearing into a more loving and democratic process, during the post-Mao era educational experts advocated the importance of "communication" (goutong) and the verbal articulation of emotional needs and desires between parents and children.[62] Ms. Ning was one of a very small minority of urban G3 (less than 5 percent) who benefited from greater communicative intimacy: "My interactions with my mother were mostly positive and amiable. She wasn't 'harsh' [xiong] like other mothers. Instead, she had a tender way of speaking. I can't remember any conflicts with her as I grew up. Instead, I thought of my mother as a sister or a friend."[63]

But Ning also admitted that two additional factors had helped generate the affectionate nature of her interactions: "My family was unusual in that from my childhood until senior middle school, we always had a nanny at home who saw to all the housework [her mother did no cooking as she grew up]. My parents are also doctors—both specializing in psychological health."[64]

As living standards improved and families had fewer children, mothers found more time to communicate with their children. However, despite their desire to modify a communicative style which their children often considered excessively harsh (xiong), the end result, more often than not, was to reproduce the child-rearing habitus[65] from which they (the mothers) had been formed. The following reflections by a mother and her son capture these contradictory impulses. Son Zhong (urban G3) recalled the way his mother talked to him: "When I was in primary school, my mother was in charge of checking my homework. She could be very brutal: if I got anything wrong, she tore the paper up and asked me to redo it. And she also tagged a question to her comments, such as 'how could you get this wrong?' or 'how could you not understand this?' The tone of her voice on these occasions was quite hurtful. My counter-strategy was to start crying, and then she would stop."

Mother Zhong recalled the treatment she had received from her mother as a child as well as how she treated her son:

My mother was very "harsh" [xiong], and whenever I had a disagreement with her, she would start hitting me as she spoke. Whenever that happened, I told myself that when I became a parent, I would be much more consultative with my children and explain my point of view. But when I did become a parent, I turned into another dictator: when my son was little, whenever he didn't do what I told him, I always wanted to give him a good scolding. This experience made me understand much more clearly the difficulties my mother had faced when she was bringing me up as a child.

Mother Zhong's comment reveals the contradictory forces bearing on her behavior. On the one hand, she was at pains to reconstruct her family child-rearing habitus by making a conscious effort to remedy the negative aspects of her mother's behavior to her as a child. One significant benefit of this, as her son acknowledged, was that Mother Zhong never hit him so that physical punishment was eradicated from the child-rearing process. On the other hand, the authoritarian underpinnings of child-rearing persisted and were reproduced, through Mother Zhong's scolding communicative style, indicating the tenacity with which the habitus survived.

The propensity to scold tended to subside as children reached the end of their schooling, when it gave way to a more intimate communicative style. Even so, this did not necessarily presage the attainment of a truly democratic relationship; rather, parents still consciously used communication opportunities to inculcate their own ways of thinking into their children. Like forms of discipline,[66] the ultimate aim of these communications was the molding and shaping of children.[67] A key area in which parents sought to influence their children was in the choice of a marriage partner. Mother Zhong told me of a conversation she had had with her son when he was at university:

> I said to him, "You decide on your own criteria in finding a girlfriend. But I'd like to share with you my own criteria of what makes a good daughter-in-law. I'd like a girl who is from a good family, sensible [*tongqing dali*] and understanding [*dongshi*]." He replied, "Mum, you can relax. You don't need to worry—I can guarantee that any girl I bring home will be someone you like." When he said this, I told him, "I believe you and I won't worry."[68]

Through the contrasting styles that she used to communicate with her son when he was little and when he had grown up, Mother Zhong's words capture the flexibility and changing dynamics of parent-child interactions over time. Yet it would be misleading to suggest that she had acceded to her son's complete autonomy in selecting a partner. Rather, as shown below, she strategically pointed him in the direction she herself favored—the cultivation of "obedient autonomy." Similarly, Granddaughter Yuan recalled that as a result of the many phone calls she had had with her mother when she was working as a migrant worker in a coastal city in Shandong, she had internalized and eventually endorsed her mother's view that a daughter should not get married far away from her natal family. The outcome was that she returned home and married someone born in a neighboring village.

Finally, echoing Evans,[69] public advocacy of and emphasis on "communication" as a means of making family relationships more intimate and democratic conceals a strong gender bias that reaffirms women's responsibilities in the domestic sphere. Across three generations, childcare has symbolically remained a woman's duty. The evidence that emerges from my fieldwork is overwhelmingly that as they grew up, interviewees spent far more time with their mothers than with their fathers. As a result, in addition to their full-time work, mothers[70] assumed multiple roles in child-rearing—as carers, disciplinarians, educators, and so on. The pressure and anxiety from having to carry so many responsibilities sometimes hindered their ability to be more open and relaxed in their interactions with their children. Son Zhong recalled that his mother seemed very "impatient" (*bu naifan*) when he was little. His mother attributed this to the time-poverty she had experienced when bringing him up. If, like Ning's family, her family had been able to employ someone to do the housework, her relationship with Son Zhong might have been more "tender" (*wenrou*) and less "brutal" (*cubao*). However, the evidence suggests that the gender-biased ideology whereby mothers were expected to assume the main responsibility for raising and educating their children transcended differences in families' socioeconomic backgrounds.

The more recent emphasis on expressive intimacy had added additional pressure and anxiety to women who were currently engaged in bringing up their children. Ms. Guang (urban G3, at the beginning of this chapter) was torn between trying simultaneously to fulfill the disciplinarian role expected of her as her daughter's educator and the more outwardly loving role expected of her by offering greater communicative intimacy. In practice, she found it impossible to fulfill both roles. In what she saw as the interests of her daughter's future development—but to the resentment of Daughter Guang—cultivating a more loving relationship took second place to acting as disciplinarian. Adding to Ms. Guang's frustrations, her husband paid little attention to their daughter's education and care, but during the few interactions they had together, he pampered their daughter with gifts, which led her to regard him as her favorite parent.

In recent years Chinese media have coined a special phrase—"child-rearing as a widow" (*sangoushi yuer*)—to capture the practice whereby mothers assume overwhelming responsibility for child-rearing. The phrase is at once both a depiction and a critique of the gender-biased methods now practiced by many families in bringing up and educating their children in China.[71] To what extent this emergent critique of absent fathers in child-rearing will prompt future changes in policy and family behavior remains to be seen. Ms. Guang fatalistically commented,

> On the surface, there seems to have been a lot of improvement in women's status in China. But fundamentally the quality of their lives hasn't really changed. In Chinese society men still dominate in so many spheres. In particular, after childbirth, the chasm between men and women remains very visible. Now the government is advocating a two-child policy. But this is really detrimental to us women because not only do we have to carry the baby for 10 months, but we also carry the burden of meeting all the child's future educational needs. For men, one more baby means just one more person to call them daddy. But for women, it isn't that simple.

Cultivating Obedient Autonomy

> My father explained to me that there are three tiers of people. A person from the top tier responds to a meaningful glance. For example, if the family has a visitor, parents will give a glance without saying anything and a clever child will respond by pouring the tea and serving the guest. A second tier person responds to verbal orders. But someone in the bottom tier only responds to hands [corporal punishment]. This is what my father taught me. When I started to educate my son, I copied him. If he did something wrong, I pulled a sulky face. He could tell that I was unhappy and realized that he'd behaved in a way that he shouldn't behave again. (Son Yan, urban G2, Xi'an)

The now deceased Father Yan had been born in the early 1930s. He was illiterate and throughout his life was a manual worker in a transportation work unit. However, he strongly embodied the strategies and aspirations many Chinese parents harbored in bringing up their children. First, Father Yan's three-tier system highlights two modalities of power to which parents resorted in raising children. Central to the first modality is the enacting of verbal or physical punishment in order to exert control over children's lives. It resembles the forces of domination and control encapsulated in the Foucauldian notion of "sovereign power," which exists in its most unadorned fashion in a monarchy where a king and / or queen possesses ultimate authority over their subjects' lives.[72] The second modality of power in Father Yan's three-tier system is exercised through the inculcation of a parental ideology that effectively makes children self-governing subjects. This process conveys the Foucauldian notion of "disciplinary power," which people exercise over themselves in response to messages received—often through surveillance and knowledge systems—from society about how they are supposed to behave.[73] The meaningful glance referred to by Father Yan serves as a form of surveillance to let children know that they are being watched. The metaphor itself is also part of the knowledge system to incentivize his son to become a self-governing subject, albeit within the confines of a trajectory defined by parental values. While Father Yan lauded the second modality of power, in practice he used both modalities as Yan recalled being frequently beaten. The same priorities were evident in the ways in which Son Yan raised his own son.

Second, Father Yan made clear his view that the ultimate goal of child-rearing is to mold children into parentally guided self-governing subjects. Other parents, including educated G3s, have subscribed to the same broad objective. For example, Granddaughter Qin proudly told me of her daughter's improved "self-awareness" (*ziwo renzhi*) and quoted her as saying, "I am doing this and that myself now, Mum. So you relax [*fangxin*]." In her study of Chinese archaeologists and the ways in which they dealt with authority, Evasdottir[74] coined the term "obedient autonomy" to describe how intellectuals seek to preserve and maintain rules and order as the best means of fulfilling their personal needs and aspirations. I find that the concept is equally applicable to the form of autonomy with which Chinese parents seek to inculcate their children. In liberal democracies the notion of autonomy frequently conveys a sense of freedom—a self-controlled state of being unfettered by the constraints of rules or obligations to others. By contrast, the notion of "obedient autonomy" recognizes that such rules and obligations (on the one hand) and individual personal needs and space (on the other hand) are intertwined and not mutually exclusive.

Stated differently, fostering "obedient autonomy" offers a way of resolving negotiations between parents and children as they seek to navigate the tensions between "modern" and "traditional" methods of child-rearing in the post-Mao public discourse of scientific parenting.[75] From the perspective of parents, the rules and obligations that they seem to impose provide the parameters for children's self-governed development. From that of children, complying with the rules and obligations facilitates their pursuit of greater freedom. There is a widespread perception that once a child has met the parents' aspirations for him or her—the ultimate goal being to secure a university place—he or she will have been rewarded with attainment of a significant degree of freedom.

Viewed from a child's perspective, an arguably more creative way of exercising "obedient autonomy" might be to interpret the rule metaphorically by "displaying obedience." Ms. Feng (urban G2) explained how she had become her father's favorite child:

Why did my father love me most? It was because he felt that I was particularly perceptive in avoiding putting myself at a disadvantage [*buchikui*].

One winter I had a fight with my brother. I was wearing a padded jacket and while we were fighting, my jacket touched the kerosene lamp and caught fire. We both realized that we'd be in deep trouble with our parents. My brother was so scared that he ran away. Instead of following him, I ran to my dad and apologized: "Dad, it was my fault. It was my fault. I shouldn't have got into a fight with my brother." In the end my dad didn't beat me and instead repaired the jacket for me.

Ms. Feng mentioned other examples of misbehavior during her childhood, but said that she had never "answered back," instead conforming to the generational hierarchy by displaying the obedient demeanor expected of the junior generation. In so doing, she strategically negotiated the hierarchical system and carved out space in which she could fulfill her own goals as a playful child growing up.

Conclusion

There has been a profound and rapid transformation in the experience of growing up in China. The role of children in the family has transitioned from one of laborers and domestic helpers to that of aspirant academic achievers. While parents and children of the "grandchild generation" communicate more readily than their counterparts of the middle generation, the authoritarian nature of parental guidance and teaching has persisted across all three generations. Today, China has become a child-centered society even if the younger generation has not morphed into the kind of autonomous individuals hoped for by May Fourth intellectuals and post-Mao policymakers. Rather, young people in China are expected to become parentally guided self-governing subjects. Overwhelmingly oriented toward the fulfilment of academic goals conditioned by the combined pressures of state, market, and family forces, far from becoming more individualized, the childhood of the grandchild generation is now increasingly regimented—while G3s have access to a more substantial resource base and to a greater range of care practices, they are also subject to different kinds of restrictions and limitations. In general, childrearing practices in evidence today have by no means abandoned "traditional" expectations of obedience by the younger generation in the face of parental authority; rather, they have redefined and recast traditional childhood in new ways, epitomized by the cultivation of "obedient autonomy." Recognizing these continuities and discontinuities is essential to understanding recent changes that have taken place in the valuation of children in China.

This chapter has challenged the Eurocentric modernization of childhood narrative that predicts a shift from a family's economic valuation of a child to a primary emphasis on the child's needs. Central factors in differentiating Chinese families from those in the West are that current institutions and welfare constraints affecting intergenerational relations in China remain quite different from those in Western societies. For example, many young Chinese people live close by their parents after marriage, the hectic work schedules of most parents make dependence upon grandparents for childcare and even shopping, cooking, and laundry very common (see chapter 4), and still the majority of China's elders (those in the countryside) depend centrally on financial and other support from a grown child or children (see chapter 5). This is in contrast with Western societies, where many more elderly citizens live independently and often far away from grown children, giving rise to a booming economy for retirement communities and elderly health care. The Chinese institutional context has therefore continued to foster conditions for intergenerational lifetime interdependence—a central tenet in filial piety. As a consequence, while the economic value of children as family helpers has dramatically diminished across three generations, a new emphasis on the increasing *emotional* value of children has been tempered by recognition of their continuing economic and practical role as a source of support in old age.

Despite diverging from the preconfigured trajectory of the modernization framework, Chinese childhood experiences still exhibit features that have characterized development elsewhere in the world. Two of these are particularly noteworthy. The first feature is the entrenchment of inequality shaped by wide gaps in the levels of family resources. While this is mostly epitomized in class inequalities, particularly between children raised by well-educated parents and less well-educated ones in developed societies (for example, in the United States and United Kingdom), the key social cleavage behind diverging childhood experiences in China is between urban and rural families. As levels of parental income and economic assets have widened between urban and rural households, the divergence between urban and rural childhood experiences has worsened and become more entrenched over time, revealing a process of widening compound inequalities. The second feature is captured in the persistent gender inequality in the domestic domain. This is evidenced most starkly in the process of intensive mothering articulated in my interviews with G3 women, who have come to typify a new generation of exhausted and anxious mothers.

2

Getting Married

"CHINESE MARRIAGE IS NOT ONLY THE UNION
OF TWO INDIVIDUALS, BUT ALSO THE
UNION OF TWO FAMILIES"

Let me start with a quote from the Confucian Book of Rites: "The ceremony of marriage aims to unite two families, paying respect to the ancestral temples of the past and ensuring the continuation of generations in the future. Therefore, it is highly esteemed by noble individuals." What does this sentence mean? Its main thrust is that marriage has the function of inheriting the past and opening the future [*chengqian qihou, jiwaingkailai*], carrying on the bloodline of one's ancestors as well as educating future generations. We are gathered here today to celebrate the wedding ceremony between Mr. Gao and Miss Yin. Let us applaud and warmly welcome the couple to the stage!

Mr. Gao, dressed in a dark blue Western lounge suit, held hands with Miss Yin, dressed in a red Chinese-style bridal gown with a red veil over her face. They were waiting anxiously at the entrance of Mr. Gao's family courtyard, which had been decorated into a wedding venue with at least fifty relatives and villagers seated rather haphazardly inside. At a sign from the chair, Mr. Gao led Miss Yin slowly toward the central stage and the ceremony started. The couple first bowed down to pay respect to the deities representing Heaven and Earth (*bai tiandi*), second bowed down toward the paternal grandfather of Mr. Gao, third bowed down to the parents of Mr. Gao, and finally bowed toward each other.[1] After a thirty-minute interval, during which the stage was changed from that of a shrine to a romantic setting with flowers and plants, the chair announced the start of the second phase of the ceremony. For this, Mr. Gao, still in his lounge suit, came onto the stage alone, while Miss Yin, who had changed into a Western-style white wedding gown, stood at the entrance of the courtyard with her father.

At the instruction of the chair, Miss Yin's father led his daughter to the stage and handed her over to Mr. Gao, who proceeded to reenact his marriage proposal and publicly declare his love for his bride. Under the guide of the chair, they exchanged their rings and kissed. The parents of Mr. Gao and Miss Yin were then invited onto the stage to be served tea by the married couple. The chair gave a final congratulatory speech, this time on behalf of the entire audience:

> You have fallen in love "under the flowers and beneath the moon" [*huaqian yuexia*]. From today onwards, as you deal with pots and pans, firewood, rice, oil and salt, please remember that your love toward each other is one of mutual support rather than of control and demand, and one of mutual communication rather than of reporting everything [*fanshi jiaodai*]. If your love is to be long lasting, you must be considerate as well as accommodating to each other. Let us congratulate you two once more![2]

The groom made the closing speech:

> Distinguished guests, friends and relatives: today is the most important day in my life. First, I'd like to thank my hard-working parents for bringing me up; from now on, I will be more filial towards you. I would also like to thank my parents-in-law for raising such a lovely daughter and for trusting me to take over caring for her; I will care for her as you have done, and I will also be filial towards you as she has been. I would also like to thank my wife for her trust and belief in me; I will look after you well all my life. Finally, I would like to thank all of you here as guests and wish you a healthy and prosperous life!

Such was the scene on the wedding day of Mr. Gao and Miss Yin in May 2021.[3] Mr. Gao was born into a rural Shandong family (see chapter 5) in 1992. His father had been a migrant construction worker for many years while his mother had stayed in the village, tending the fields and looking after their children. Following his graduation from a third-tier university in Ji'nan (the capital of Shandong province), Mr. Gao now worked in real estate. Conscious of his family's limited resources, he had delayed his marriage in order first to accumulate some savings. By the time he got married, Mr. Gao had already purchased a car and flat in a fourth-tier city (albeit with his parents covering the deposit and a mortgage). Following a relative's introduction, he met Miss Yin who was also from a rural family but had successfully trained as a nurse and settled in the same city.

Mr. Gao's wedding crafted a discourse of Chinese marriage rich in meaning and imaginary. It portrayed a spatial image with the couple at center stage but—through their filial declarations and actions (serving tea and bowing)— they were intricately embedded in close-knit kinship networks including the bride's and groom's parents. The wedding also evoked a temporal message that indicated an evolution from "romantic love" during dating to "conjugal love"[4] when faced with the day-to-day practicalities of married life. Finally, it epitomized an assemblage of traditional and modern elements, not least the style of dress Mr. Gao and Miss Yin wore. Although the speeches made by the chair and groom seemed to project an egalitarian ideal of marriage that emphasized mutual support, understanding, and trust, the wedding itself performed a version of patriarchy in which the bride was ceremonially incorporated into her husband's family.[5] The theme of "love" featured heavily in the proceedings, while the wedding itself involved overt materialism and status symbols,[6] not to mention a bride price of 160,000 yuan paid by Mr. Gao's parents (accumulated through nearly thirty years of hard work and saving).[7]

These observations and reflections are an existing focus of inquiry in literature on family and marriage in China. Influenced by Goode's two subsidiary hypotheses (the decline of parental control and the spread of the companionate marriage ideal), existing scholarship has, for example, investigated whether conjugal ties supersede vertical ties as social modernization takes place, and whether Chinese marriage has evolved from a duty-bound institution to an emotionally involved partnership. But the focus of these studies is a single location or a single generation of one era,[8] while this chapter revisits these debates and offers a more nuanced picture of changes and continuities. I start by introducing two case studies—those of the Zhao family (a rural family in Fujian) and the Mu family (an urban family in Xi'an), followed by examinations of marriage decisions, marital dynamics (including division of labor and women's indirect power), and how practices of intimacy have evolved over time. I reveal how parental involvement both in mate selection and later marital relations continues to be very important and how, as a result, Chinese marriages today are still distinctive. Moreover, with the growing consumerism and materialism of the post-Mao era, existing material inequalities—for example, the urban-rural divide—can be reproduced in the intimate domain.

The Zhao Family in Rural Fujian

Grandma Zhao was born in 1943 in Singapore to a migrant couple from Fujian. However, her time in Singapore was abruptly curtailed by the arrival of a letter from her paternal grandfather, requesting that her father return to his homeland and fulfill his filial duties. As the only surviving son, he felt compelled to heed his father's call and relocated his family back to China in 1947. Tragically, the challenging circumstances of the era led to the successive passing of both her grandparents, and then her mother when she was eleven, followed by her father when she was seventeen. Her half-brother (from her father's first marriage), harboring resentment toward his father's new family, did not extend any kindness to Grandma Zhao. Within two years of her father's passing and unbeknownst to her, he accepted a marriage proposal from Grandfather Zhao—a blacksmith, nine years her senior, who lived in a neighboring village. Learning of her nuptials just twenty days beforehand, in 1962 she found herself unhappily wedded into the Zhao family at the age of nineteen.

After three grueling years living with her in-laws—especially her abusive mother-in-law, Grandma Zhao and her husband moved into their own marital home. Unfortunately, however, their marriage remained an unhappy one. She frequently recalled her husband telling her that, "If he wanted me to die, I would die; if he wanted me to live, I would live." It was not until she was in her fifties that the relationship with her husband began to mend, coinciding with his growing appreciation for her contribution to the household's financial stability and with his physical decline. In old age, with all children except the eldest daughter living away from the village, Grandma Zhao looked after her husband until he passed away in 2015. When asked if she would choose the same spouse in another life, Grandma Zhao laughed bitterly and said, "If I were to marry the same person again in the next life, I would truly be exceedingly unfortunate."

In contrast with Grandma Zhao, Elder Daughter Zhao reported a satisfactory conjugal life. Born in 1965, as the eldest among six siblings, from the age of five, she assisted with the care of her younger brothers and sisters. She only had one year of formal education, and by the time she reached twelve years of age, she had already joined her parents in the village production brigade. Agricultural de-collectivization in the early 1980s saw Elder Daughter Zhao take charge of her family's fields, enabling her parents to shift their focus to nonagricultural pursuits, in particular their blacksmith workshop. When she was twenty-two, at the strong encouragement of her mother, Elder Daughter Zhao was introduced to a young man from their village and they were married soon after. Fortunately, she was welcomed by a supportive and caring mother-in-law who later assisted with the childcare of her three children (two daughters and a son). Economically, Elder Daughter Zhao was the least affluent among her siblings. She was a farmer her entire life but took on various odd jobs to supplement her income (the most recent being a cleaner). Initially employed in a local brick factory, her husband now worked as a construction site driver earning 200 yuan per day.[9] Asked whether she would choose her husband again, she responded with a smile: "A definite yes. He was hard-working and a good person. I would marry him again."

Unlike her sister, Younger Daughter Zhao resented her husband. She likened her life to what she termed the *jiangjiu* marriage pattern—"making do with each day, even if two people don't get along"—a phrase also used by

Grandma Zhao. Younger Daughter Zhao (born in 1969) had received a few years of primary school education before her parents arranged for her to learn tailoring. (This decision was part of her parents' strategy to diversify the family income as a form of insurance against the high educational expenses of their two sons.) Blessed with fair skin and a tall stature inherited from her mother and being a capable village tailor, Younger Daughter Zhao was considered a desirable potential wife in her youth. She caught the eye of the patriarch from the village's largest lineage, who engaged a matchmaker to facilitate an introduction with his third son, a migrant worker in Chengdu (provincial capital of Sichuan province in southwest China). Grandma Zhao and her husband agreed to this proposal, believing that a union with the dominant lineage group in the village would aid their much smaller family.[10] As a result, they discouraged other suitors, and eventually, swayed by his handsome features and honest demeanor, Younger Daughter Zhao went along with the proposal.

Younger Daughter Zhao experienced an initial period of happiness following her marriage in 1991. However, her husband soon returned to Chengdu while she remained a village tailor under the watchful eye of her parents-in-law who consistently berated and demeaned her. The breaking point arrived when Younger Daughter Zhao gave birth to a daughter in 1992. Her husband was absent from the birth and her in-laws provided no support. When her husband finally returned to see the baby six months after the birth, at the encouragement of her own mother to distance herself from her unsupportive in-laws, Younger Daughter Zhao followed her husband when he returned to Chengdu. The city expanded her horizons but also exposed her to a harsh environment hostile toward rural migrant families. A son arrived in 1994, but the weight of poverty and her husband's uncaring nature meant Younger Daughter Zhao's discontent with him grew steadily and she considered divorce on numerous occasions. Yet, Grandma Zhao implored her to abandon the idea for the sake of her children's future and reputation of her natal family. When asked if she would choose him again, she replied firmly with "a definite no."

In the third generation, Granddaughter Zhao, the middle child of Elder Daughter Zhao, shone as an example of contented marriage. Born in 1989, she had completed her education up to junior middle school but did not pass the exam to continue. She therefore followed her elder sister to the nearby city of Quanzhou where she received training in touch-typing and basic computer skills, and was introduced to a series of sales positions, all arranged through connections with her bilateral extended family. In contrast to her elder sister, who had since returned to work in a factory near where she grew up, Granddaughter Zhao found the allure of city life irresistible and remained in Quanzhou for six years until, through an online school reunion, she met her first (and only) boyfriend. The boyfriend had migrated with his family to Wuhan,[11] the provincial capital of Hubei in central China, where their bathroom appliance business now thrived and he had become a "wealthy second generation" (*fu erdai*).[12]

Granddaughter Zhao left Quanzhou and married into her husband's family in Wuhan in 2010. Initially, she resided and worked in the family business, operating out of a rented three-floor house alongside her husband and her brother-in-law's family. Her father-in-law managed the operations, and her mother-in-law cooked for the extended family. As the business expanded, her father-in-law purchased three flats in a residential compound—one for each son's family while retaining one for him and his wife. In 2013, after giving birth to her daughter, Granddaughter Zhao launched an online retail business (*weishang*). This change was partly motivated by a fear that, if she outsourced her daughter's care to her illiterate mother-in-law, it might hinder her educational development. Her online retail venture flourished, leading to Granddaughter Zhao purchasing a flat in her home county,[13] an achievement that solidified her position within her husband's family as a capable earner. While she and her husband initially did not feel compelled to have more children, her mother pestered her to try for a son, to ensure her "small family" an inheritance of the "big family" business, especially since her brother-in-law already had a son. Granddaughter Zhao gave birth to another daughter in 2017 and, in 2023, eventually welcomed a son. Reflecting on her relationship with her husband, she took immense pride in her "model" husband: not only did he fulfill his role as an economic provider, but he also shared domestic responsibilities— for example, by assisting in the kitchen and with childcare. She felt she would choose to marry him again.

The Mu Family in Xi'an

Grandma Mu was born in 1942 into the family of a Nationalist (Kuomintang) officer. Her mother, a concubine, was eighteen years her father's junior. After the Communist Party seized power in 1949, her father moved into business, but his past affiliations made him a target of political campaigns in the 1950s and Grandma Mu's mother felt compelled to divorce him for her own safety. Deeply indoctrinated by the party-state's propaganda of the time, Grandma Mu actively engaged in school activities and joined the Communist Youth League at the age of fourteen. After completing senior middle school, she was assigned to work at a local hospital and train as a medical doctor.

Despite her mother's divorce, her father's death in 1959, and embracing the ideology of the time, her father's history affected Grandma Mu's life course. Introduced by a former school teacher to a classmate who had gone on to become a military officer, they became close through letters, but the specter of her father's past as a member of Kuomintang cast a shadow over her boy-friend's prospects and promotion in the army, and she chose to end the relationship to safeguard his future. During her recovery from this emotional loss, Grandma Mu's line manager at work introduced her to the man who would become her husband. Her initial impression of him was not favorable: while he worked as a clerk in the local police station, he had a slight hunchback despite being in his twenties, so she hesitated for nearly a year before accepting his pursuit. The final push came from her mother, who attempted to arrange a match between her and an accountant from a department store. Disliking this prospective match, she decided to proceed with the introduction from her workplace superior in order to offset her mother's suggestion, and in 1965 married the local police station clerk.

In 1966, when the Cultural Revolution erupted, it was government policy to dispatch medical professionals to the countryside to help develop village clinics. Grandma Mu wanted to change her profession to avoid being sent away, but her husband, sensing an opportunity to help his family, insisted that she be sent to his home village in order to care for his widowed father and younger siblings. As a result, between 1968 and 1978 Grandma Mu and her three children endured a decade of rural hardship and family conflict, while her husband remained in the city and gradually climbed the ranks to become head of a local police station. Returning to her urban hospital in 1978, Grandma Mu worked tirelessly and eventually became head of her medical unit. How-ever, her responsibilities as a caregiver for her grandchildren prompted her to apply for early retirement at the age of fifty in 1992. After her husband was formally diagnosed with cerebral congestion (excessive blood in the vessels of his brain) in 1999, she became his primary carer for fourteen years (in addition to her grandmothering duties), until his death in 2013. When asked whether she would choose the same husband again, she remarked, "I think being single is the best option. All the hardships stem from marriage and family. If neither existed, there would be no suffering. All dealings with relatives originate from marriage. Friendships are different; if you have a strong connection, you re-main friends; if not, you just drift apart. But in marriage and family, there are countless situations that are difficult to understand and sort out [*shuobuqing de li, libuqing de shi*]."[14]

Born in 1967, Son Mu's schooling was disrupted by the Cultural Revolution, so in 1985 he started work in a state-owned factory. His future wife was distantly related to his family[15] and so they had known each other since adolescence, and well before Grandma Mu indicated to him that she could be a potential marriage prospect. Initially, Son Mu harbored reservations, but gradually his resistance waned, and they were married in 1990 and then given temporary accommodation by his work unit (something eventually upgraded into the two-bedroom apartment they still lived in). Their familial landscape expanded with the birth of a son in 1991 and during this period, Son Mu also assisted his wife in caring for his ailing in-laws who both ultimately passed away in the late 1990s. In 2003 the respective state-run work units of Son Mu and his wife closed in response to urban economic restructuring, but their financial instability was alleviated by support from his parents and brothers.[16] Of his wife, Son Mu commented: "How can I put it . . . She has a strong personality, but she sees things clearly, unlike some wives who harbor resentment and grievances. I don't like hypotheses, but I'm very satisfied with her in my life. Having this life with her is quite good enough for me."

Grandson Mu (born in 1991) was the graduate of a local university. He had had a university girlfriend, but they broke up upon graduation. It was in his first workplace, a research unit, where he thought that he met the love of his life. He was initially attracted by her beauty and gradually they developed strong feelings for one another. However, there was a sturdy opposition from the girlfriend's divorced mother, on the grounds that he was five years younger than her daughter. Her mother worried that he would always have an advantage over her in the relationship and might abandon her when her youthful good looks faded. Despite this opposition, they secretly dated for three years until the girlfriend turned thirty and her mother set her up to marry a man she deemed suitable. Grandson Mu confronted the girlfriend's mother, arguing she should not draw upon her own marital experience to judge them, but with little success as the girlfriend had been brought up by her mother singlehandedly, meaning they were very emotionally close, and she was not prepared to continue their relationship without her mother's consent. Broken-hearted, Grandson Mu left this workplace and when I first met him in 2017 (a year after the breakup), he was still in the process recovering emotionally. In 2018 through a work opportunity, Grandson Mu met his current wife, a goodlooking university educated woman who was as ambitious as he was for career development and worked in the media industry. Although one year older than he was, her parents accepted him (not least because there was the same age pattern in their relationship) and they were married in 2020.

Marriage Decisions

In the Confucian family system, parents played a prominent role in making marriage decisions for their children. From early imperial China, elite families were expected to arrange marriages among status equals,[17] a principle that grew into the popular Chinese idiom "matching households," which continues to be used today. Ordinary parents in premodern China had more flexibility in choosing marriage partners for their children and sometimes took the child's welfare into consideration as well as the family's long-term benefits.[18] However, daughters were located at the bottom of the kinship hierarchy and conceptions of women as male property persisted in Chinese history. While the dowry was practiced among some upper-class families and in some regions, Confucian ideologies and state institutions prevented the development of a full dowry system[19] and instead families followed a property regime that favored transmission through males.[20] As a result of such institutionalized gender asymmetry, Chinese society was prone toward hypergamy (women marrying up).[21] While urban elites of the early twentieth century promoted the ideal of "freedom in courtship and freedom in marriage," its impact upon the wider society was very limited. After 1949 the party legislated and campaigned to transform Chinese marriage from a quasi-commercial exchange of women, arranged by senior kin, to a personal relationship between individuals. Thus, a key question for scholars has been whether the traditional arranged marriage has given way to free choice of mate selection.[22]

Negotiated Marriage

A pervasive motif of much existing scholarship on Chinese families is the (supposed) contrast between the greater individualism of one generation with the stronger family orientation of another. For example, Yan[23] argued that individual agency and autonomy had been increasing since the 1970s. Similarly, Lui[24] suggests that urbanities born 1976–1990 were heavily influenced by individualism and so did not "reflect the strong moral sense of obedience that is common among the older generation." This linear transition is not borne out by my data, which suggests there is no clear evidence of a move from familism to individualism (or vice versa) from the older to the younger generation. Across the three generations, there were varying ways in which an individual got to know their spouse (ranging from arranged, introduction-based to self-initiated approaches). While becoming acquainted is no more than a first step toward a marriage decision, securing the consent of parents and senior family members remains crucial. Except for the early cohort of rural G1s (e.g., Grandma Zhao), the majority of interviewees from each generation sat on a continuum and the choice of spouse involved varying degrees of negotiation, compliance, or agreement among family members. Rather than being trapped in a dichotomy between free-choice marriage and arranged marriage, negotiated marriage[25] is a dominant feature of all three generations.

In the Mu family, although Grandma Mu opposed her mother's chosen candidate, there was no fundamental conflict between them. After marriage, the couple provided her mother with financial support and maintained an amicable relationship with her. Son Mu was initially unhappy with his semi-arranged, or encouraged, mate selection because such interference had been considered "backward" by state discourse since the 1950s, so he thought he would prefer to find a mate using his own networks. However, after several encounters with his future wife, he willingly accepted her because she was "good-looking" and had "a good personality" (that is, got on well with both sets of relatives). Grandson Mu appeared a free agent, as his mother explained: "He normally selected highly educated and lovely girls from his own circles. So we let him decide." However, rather than being an innate natural right, Grandson Mu's autonomy was earned (an example of "obedient autonomy," for which see chapter 1). In his interview, Grandson Mu described how his mother had been very controlling of his academic study as a child, but had suddenly adopted a much more relaxed approach when he came top in the local district exam competition during his final year of primary school. Ever since, his mother had trusted his judgement. The girlfriends Grandson Mu courted were all university educated, white-collar professionals, from local urban families, who got on with his parents. In short, the "free choice" that Grandson Mu exerted reflected the use of criteria endorsed by his parents. His choice was also nonetheless constrained by the fact that his first choice of bride had been vetoed by the woman's mother.

Despite the diverse ways in which they chose their spouse, the three generations of the Mu family share and reflect a common theme with the wider sample, that is, the self-pursuit of desire does not necessarily conflict with filial obligation toward senior generations. On the contrary, filiality is an important personal trait that weighs heavily in the process of choosing a spouse. The traditional patrilineal and patrilocal ideology led men to give greater weight than women to filial considerations, as reflected in Son Mu's and Grandson Mu's assessments of potential spouses' ability to get on with their family members. In the G3 generation, filial considerations also affected women since both urban and rural daughters had come to assume responsibility for caring for their aging parents, as seen in Mr. Gao's filial declaration toward his in-laws (at the start of the chapter). Thus, loving one's spouse can go hand in hand with loving one's parents. Contrary to the individualized self in new modernity writers' work,[26] Chinese sense of self is relational, entailing a balance between individual interests and those of other important protagonists.

In the process of intergenerational negotiation, both individual autonomy and parental authority are not static but elastic (see the Introduction). Individuals' socioeconomic resources, as well as the familial demographic profile, are two noticeable forces that affect intergenerational power dynamics and so parents who hold higher status and resources relative to their children are more likely to exert influence over their children's marriage choice. At the same time, such parental power is relative and embedded in webs of multilayered relationships. Thus, by way of illustration, Grandma Mu orchestrated the relationship between middle Son Mu (who had a "good" temperament and was a factory worker) and his wife, but did not intervene in the mate selection of her eldest son (who was the "most rebellious child among three sons" and a civil servant).

This "elastic individuality" was also evident in rural families' marital choice negotiation. While introduction-based marriage, allowing adult children the right to veto, was the dominant village norm among rural G2s and G3s, there were varied process of intergenerational configuration. The experience of the six children of Grandma Zhao (from eldest to youngest: one girl, one boy, three girls, and one boy) illustrate this. The two sons entered university (at the expense of their sisters' education)[27] and built a life in the city so they were "exceptions" and exempt from the village norm: both met their spouse through their own circle of friends. The four sisters all had introduction-based marriages in the village, albeit with varying levels of intergenerational negotiation. Elder Sister Zhao and Second Sister Zhao in particular highlighted parental pressure as an influence shaping the acceptance of their marriage proposal, considering themselves sacrificed by their natal family in their personal interviews. However, Grandma Zhao's two youngest daughters had considerable autonomy in selecting a husband. For example, although facilitated by a village matchmaker, the third daughter chose a man from another village whose family was poor but whom she viewed as having considerable entrepreneurial potential.

These dynamics become even more visible in the mate selection of the urban one-child generation. Parents focused disproportionately on the child's marital decision since his or her choice of partner was likely to influence future relations with their only child, only grandchildren, and impact on their plans for old age. There were cases in which the negotiations became very intense. On the one hand, skyrocketing house prices accentuated adult children's dependence upon their parents in obtaining marital accommodation; on the other, as sole heirs, the one-child generation possessed crucial bargaining capital. The solution to this conflict was generally a temporal one. When G3s were still in their early twenties, parents could and did exercise considerable power in vetoing their children's choice, leading to some interviewees adopting a delaying tactic by not revealing they had a girlfriend or boyfriend until they were in their mid-twenties. But by the time children reached their late twenties, parental preoccupation was directed to whether, rather than with whom, their child would marry. This new preoccupation led to the emergence of matchmaking corners in urban public parks where anxious parents gathered with pictures and resumes of their late-twenties and early-thirties sons and daughters, trying to scout out marital prospects.[28]

Sense and Sensibility

Like the characters in Jane Austen's novel *Sense and Sensibility*, interviewees were affected by two intertwined frames—rational choice and emotional sensibility—in their mate selection. A pervasive theme of much existing literature is a perceived attitudinal shift from less emotionally involved early generations to more emotionally committed younger generations. In their study of young urban residents from the 1970s, Whyte and Parish[29] speculated that the absence of a dating culture as well as a tendency to place status criteria ahead of personal feelings might have resulted in marriage between couples who were incompatible and not in love. Commenting on post-Mao urban China, Jankowiak and Moore[30] argue that growing affluence, exposure to Western ideas and values, and the establishment of a dating culture led the one-child generation to place an increasing emphasis on the importance of emotional connection and affection.

The three-generational portrait presented here highlights how complex it is to make sense of generational transformation over time. While it is difficult to quantify whether interviewees' emotional attachment increased or decreased over generations, it might be more effective to assess how an individual's emotion is shaped by the sociocultural frames of their time.[31] Grandma Mu felt emotionally attached to the army officer she courted while disliking the candidate set up by her mother, because the latter dressed "inappropriately" (*buzhengpai*) for their introduction meeting and she felt this unbefitting of the political rightness of the time. In other words, her like or dislike of a potential partner was conditioned not merely by emotional or sexual feelings, but also by Maoist ideological values in which an individual's political credentials and comportment weighed heavily.

As for the youngest generation, Granddaughter Zhao conveyed the emotional bond with her husband in the following words: "We've been married for quite a few years now, but we still have strong feelings for each other, unlike some couples whose feelings fade or disappear after marriage. My husband buys clothes for me—he did the same when we were courting and still does it now; last month he spent over 2,000 yuan on clothes for me." Making this connection between consumer behavior and emotional intimacy is by no means atypical, since post-Mao society is increasingly typified by materialism and consumption and money has become an important mediator in intimate life. An urban G3 woman commented: "We had a strong connection with each other; in particular, I was really touched when he bought a flat and put it solely in my name prior to our marriage." Although this case was unusual, as her husband had been head of a company and so was very wealthy,[32] it is clear that following the commercialization of housing from the late 1990s onward, housing had become an overwhelming marriage consideration among the G3 generation. Refashioning patrilocal tradition, men with property were therefore more desirable in the marriage market. These narratives of the grand-child generation echo findings from the United States, where researchers have found the monetization of economic life to produce similarly profound trans-formations in intimate relationships.[33] Contrary to the one-dimensional in-terpretation of the woman in these relationships as a gold-digger, an image despised by official state media, the feelings (*ganqing*) these young women conveyed were genuine, transcending the dichotomy between sense and sen-sibility and combining both sentiment and rationality.

In general, ability (*nengli*), personality (*xingge*), and appearance (*zhangx-iang*) were the common reasons one person fell for another. The important aspects of "ability" were influenced by the institutional context of the time. In the Mao era, good political credentials could be converted to resources and other benefits, but from the 1980s economic and financial capability became more important. In terms of personality, a frequently highlighted trait was a capacity to get on with people and other family members (*weiren chushi*). This was shaped within the cultural sphere, reflecting the relationship-based nature of Chinese society.

While parents and adult children generally shared views on desirable characteristics through a process of intergenerational molding,[34] the precise definition of these factors and the various ways people weigh these factors may vary, and so become potential sources of intergenerational disagreement. For example, the "matching households" idiom was frequently cited as a legitimiz-ing resource in mate selection at the turn of the new millennium.[35] A small proportion of urban G3s (20 percent) emphasized couples' compatibility grounded in personal abilities or characters (kindness or being filial, being university educated, having a good urban job) and ignored the incompatibili-ties of families (urban versus rural), which angered some parents and inter-generational negotiations ensued. Nevertheless, more than 50 percent of G3s shared their parents' interpretations of the idiom (an emphasis upon family's capability as well as individual abilities).

There was, however, a gender twist. For men, women's appearance is often considered the most important with personality and ability behind, while for women, men's ability is considered the most important with appearance and personality following. This gender asymmetry can be traced to a premodern Chinese ideal, epitomized in the commonly used vernacular phrase "talented man and beautiful woman" (*lang cai nu mao*), which was initially used in a popular Yuan Dynasty (1271–1368) play to indicate a perfect match.[36] Given the dominance of the civic exam system in shaping social mobility in premod-ern China, a talented man was expected to convert his knowledge to status and resources. A man's value was therefore marked by his ability, while a woman's value was marked by her appearance. This cultural ideal of a perfect match complemented the patrilineal custom that prioritized property transmission through male heirs, leading to the persistence of hypergamy.[37] Since 1949, while the Communist Party has mobilized women into paid work, varied forms of gender inequalities in public spheres across the Mao and post-Mao divide[38] compel women to resort to marriage as a means of social mobility.[39] The pervasiveness of inherited cultural norms and expectations was highlighted in the fact that most women in my sample still married a man of the same or higher social status.

A combination of hypergamy and the institutionalized urban-rural divide resulted in persistent urban-rural segregation in the choice of spouse across the three generations.[40] Only a minority of cases (15 percent of all marriages) involved an urban man or woman marrying someone from a rural family. While there are cases among the G1 of urban men marrying women from a rural background and no formal urban employment, where an urban woman married a man of rural origin, the man was always someone who had settled in the city after receiving a university education and / or attaining a professional job (for example, Grandma Mu and her husband). Within the urban or rural subcategory, assortative mating—a contemporary adaptation of the traditional principle of matching households—persists. For example, growing up in a rural background, Grandson Gao (real estate manager) married a woman of rural origin but she also had a white-collar occupation (nurse). Granddaughter Zhao's sister who was a low-paid factory worker married another low-paid factory worker. These narratives reveal that social stratification has been inscribed in the Chinese mate selection process, reproducing existing social hierarchies.

Additional factors contribute to the Chinese contours of contemporary dating and courtship. Influenced by a socialist legacy that regarded romance and sexual relations as depleting energy that should be devoted to study and work, adult children were discouraged by parents and schools from experiencing romance too early.[41] Unlike their American counterparts, who began dating in high school and often even in junior high school, the first dating experience of Chinese G3s occurred at university and for many took place in their early twenties after graduation. Social pressure to marry by their mid- or late twenties meant there was a relatively short period for Chinese youths to enjoy romance in its own right and, due to persistent gendered cultural scripts around sex, women needed to take extra care in managing the courtship and dating processes (for example, refraining from sex; see chapter 3)[42] to prevent a dating history from tarnishing their reputation.

The continuing weight of parental influence and the universality and compulsoriness of marriage that pressurize individuals to marry by a certain age,[43] the lack of a "dating" culture, the overwhelming consumer culture in shaping emotional sensibility, continuing social inequalities, the gendered moral implication of sexual behaviors—all work against the youngest generation in making a "free" and thoroughly "informed" choice of marriage partner. Here, there appears to be a convergence between the grandchild generation and early generations. For example, due to her father's political history, Grandma Mu felt she could not pursue the relationship of her own choice and settled for the second best for marriage. Similarly, Grandson Mu, due to parental resistance, could not marry the person he most desired. He commented: "In my heart I like the former girlfriend best. My wife, she is the most suitable person for me at the time. Of course, I have feelings for my wife. But we are also living a life together [*guo rizi*]. So there is love as well as responsibility. Chinese marriages are after all the unions of two families. My in-laws also treat me very well so I cannot let them down."

Grandson Mu's answer indicated an ambivalence toward his wife that was not atypical and reflected nearly 50 percent of G3s: they had feelings for their spouse but they were not particularly intense (sometimes with reservations or ambivalence). Only 30 percent of G3s felt an intense emotion when getting married (such as Granddaughter Zhao), while 20 percent of G3s felt under great pressure and agreed to "make do" (*couhuo*) marriages. Whether entering marriage with reservations, or deeply in love, these initial feelings were not a sufficient determinant of marital bliss as the latter is largely dependent upon how the couple conduct the day-to-day family practicalities. As one G3 put it, "Easy to fall in love, hard to get along" (*xiangai rongyi xiangchu nan*).

"Men Dominate the Outside, Women Dominate the Inside"

This traditional idiom was frequently invoked by interviewees to justify the division of labor in the family. However, while its meaning is understood in common parlance, it was originally used to indicate the control and subordination of women in premodern China, that is, women should be confined to the "inside" or domestic sphere, excluded from public life, and denied access to education or eligibility for examinations, while men should be given free rein to explore and dominate the "outside"/wider world. Throughout the twentieth century, various nationalist projects attempted to assist women in crossing the inner-outer boundary. The early Communist Party in particular believed that women's emancipation would be realized through their full-time participation in paid work outside the home and, after taking power in 1949, there was a mass mobilization of women into full-time employment during the 1950s.[44]

Nevertheless, research has consistently found that despite their involvement in "outside" paid work, women have taken on a disproportionate share of the housework.[45]

Across all three generations, women remained symbolically responsible for domestic work. For example, during the short time I lived with Elder Daughter Zhao's family,[46] both the husband and the wife worked during the day, but in the evenings Elder Daughter Zhao did the cooking and washing-up, as well as tidying the house. Her husband either visited his neighbors or his (male) village friends came to visit him, drinking spirits and chatting with each other until late into the night. I asked the wives of various ages why housework continued to be women's responsibility and the answer was commonly that "southern Fujian men are chauvinistic" (da nanzi zhuyi). The gendered pattern of housework was largely replicated in cities. Grandma Mu, despite being in a professional occupation in urban China, gave a remarkably similar account about the noninvolvement of her husband in housework: "As soon as he finished dinner, he went out to play cards with colleagues in the work unit compound. Eating, work and play were his three major activities."[47]

There was a greater level of concession by the husbands in the domestic division of labor in migrant households than in those where the couple remained in the countryside. When Younger Daughter Zhao's second child started primary school her time during the day was freed up and she opened a street vending stall. Her reduced availability, as well as the material necessity of a second income to cover the educational expenses for both children, compelled her husband to compromise by taking on more housework, such as cooking for their children and sending them to school. However, this "masculine compromise"[48] did not extend beyond the low-paid migrant households. In successful migrant family enterprises, such as that of Granddaughter Zhao, gender segregation was reinforced through the mobilization of her mother-in-law to act as a cook for the employees. Meanwhile, both daughters-in-law chose to engage in *online* retail business, giving them the flexibility to look after the children while male members concentrated on running the family business.

Comparatively speaking, one-child generation urban women did the least housework as they relied heavily on the older generation of women and / or engaged paid domestic help. As they grew up, both male and female members of the urban one-child generation had very limited experience of doing housework (see chapter 1). In addition, as a consequence of the late 1990s and early 2000s economic restructuring, many of the older generation of urban women were made redundant, freeing their time to help their adult children with housework and childcare (see chapter 4).[49] This experience was very different from earlier generations, for whom parental and in-law support was divided among three or four siblings and intergenerational support in housework tended to heavily lean toward a co-residing or nearby adult child (with sons prioritized). Some affluent one-child generation couples reserved their parents or in-laws to oversee childcare but were primarily dependent upon an hourly domestic worker (*zhongdian gong*), normally a rural woman or older working-class urban woman, to cook and clean. Grandson Mu's nuclear family, for example, hired an older woman for three hours a day to undertake these tasks.

While wives have retained the symbolic role of housekeeper despite engaging in full-time paid work outside the home, husbands have retained the symbolic role of breadwinner despite many marriages consisting of dual-earner couples (and in my study this extended across all three generations). The role of breadwinner entitles a man to put his career above that of his wife and frees him from family work but at the same time entraps masculinity with economic power. Men are therefore expected to "succeed" and a husband's occupational achievement becomes a chief criterion in evaluating his contribution to the family.[50] The failure of a man to fulfill his gender prescribed role can lead to resentment and antagonism within his marriage. Mother Jing, a work unit accountant, born in 1945 and married in 1969, said of her husband, "From the age of 40, I started to look down upon him. All my male peers have been promoted to become a section chief [*kezhang*], but he was still where he started. I become more and more disdainful of him." Her daughter, a grassroots government unit head, born in 1974 and married in 2000, said of her own husband: "He has no proper job nowadays. The so-called career he is engaged in has generated no income. I wish I could have a husband who had the ability to earn more money. . . . I hoped for a man with a stronger career than mine so I could have a sense of security psychologically. A husband's career is not only his achievement but also his wife's achievement as well as a family's support."[51]

Both in this mother-daughter pair would not choose the same spouse again and one of the reasons given was their husband's failure to fulfill the gender expectation of a successful career man. There are, however, a couple of observations worth highlighting. First, both husbands undertook a considerable amount of housework—indeed, Daughter Jing's husband did the majority; but this was insufficient to earn a currency of gratitude in the marriage as he had failed in his primary responsibility as the main financial provider. Only if a husband has fulfilled his responsibility as a breadwinner, as well as helping with the housework, does he enhance his position in the "economy of gratitude."[52] Second, despite Daughter Jing achieving educational and occupational mobility, especially compared to her mother's generation, she expected her husband to strive and push forward in his career. This gendered yearning reflected the hypergamy tradition shaping conjugal expectations, something that persists among the educated women of the one-child generation. The men from the one-child generation acknowledged this gendered expectation, like one G3 born in 1994, who said: "Chinese women are not really feminists, even those highly educated ones. They still want to find someone who they can rely upon financially. So for us men, the pressure is particularly high."

These entrenched gender roles in the family domain are interconnected with the persistent gender inequalities in the labor market, creating a "cycle of vulnerability."[53] For example, the wage gap between husband and wife seemed to widen over time. Grandma Mu's pension was 1,000 yuan (20 percent) less than that of her husband. By contrast, although they both had a university education, Grandson Mu's salary was three times that of his wife. Even more extreme, in the case of an urban G3 couple who had married in 2009 and worked in the same company, the wage ratio between husband and wife during fourteen years had increased from 3:1 to 20:1.

Increasing gender inequality in wages and employment[54] has also impacted the way in which wages of the husband and wife are managed and distributed in the family. In urban families, in the early two generations, dual wages were pooled to pay living expenses, often managed by the wives (for example, both Grandma Mu and Daughter-in-Law Mu were responsible for family finance). Conversely, in the urban one-child generation, while some couples pooled their income, one third of the husbands (often the affluent ones) resisted doing so[55] and a new model in managing family finances developed in which the husbands' wage was largely used to cover housing costs, educational expenses, and everyday living expenses, while the wives' wage was "pocket money" for herself. Rural families presented a mixed set of family finance practices, including both men-dominated and women-dominated[56] management across all three generations. Rural families did, of course, have more limited resources than their urban counterparts, with struggling to make ends meet, borrowing money and repaying debts a recurring theme in rural households.

Interwoven Lives

Fei's seminal study of rural China in the Republican era suggested that in order to obtain efficiency for the family enterprise, discipline and prescribed family relationship rules, rather than personal feelings, were required and conjugal ties were secondary to intergenerational ties.[57] Drawing upon ethnographic data in the 1990s, Yan focused on the individual and examined dating and premarital sexual experiences of youth in a village, revealing a demand for intimacy, love, and privacy and concluding that conjugal ties took precedence over vertical ties.[58] Below I introduce a life course perspective and argue that the dynamics between conjugal ties and vertical ties *fluctuate* over the life course of a marriage. Going beyond a dichotomy, conjugal intimacy continues to be firmly anchored within the interdependent web of family and kin relations.

Son Mu and his wife were one of the few deeply loving couples when they were courting as well as at the time of my fieldwork. Son Mu described their courtship: "During daytime we were both working so our main activities were in the evenings. We went to the movies a lot and sometimes went out drinking and playing. I remember vividly at the time pop songs from Taiwan and Hong Kong had just started being imported so we two spent a lot of time listening together to Deng Lijun [a famous singer in Taiwan in the 1980s]." However, this "two-person lifestyle" (*erren shijie*) soon ended when their son was born a year after marriage and they needed to coordinate his childcare. Daughter-in-Law Mu's mother was not available as she was the sole carer for her sick husband. Grandma Mu was also initially unavailable, as she was still working while taking on some share of the childcare for her elder son's child. As soon as Grandma Mu took early retirement, the couple solicited her help to provide day care for their son and then assist with the pickups and drop-offs at a kindergarten until he reached the age of seven and started primary school. (Grandma Mu then went on to provide childcare support for her youngest son's family.) Afterward, Son Mu and Daughter-in-Law Mu became primarily responsible for the childcare and education of their son again.

While their son was in primary school, Daughter-in-Law Mu's father's dementia worsened. Having witnessed the difficulty her mother had with her father's care, the couple invited them both into their conjugal apartment in order to help out. This was a very challenging period for all concerned, as there were episodes in which the dementia-suffering father disappeared in the early morning, when everybody was sleeping, and a search party needed to be organized to find him. After two years the father-in-law passed away and the mother-in-law moved back to live on her own, though she herself died of an acute illness one year later. Soon after, Son Mu's own father became ill; although Grandma Mu served as the sole carer, her three sons' families offered emotional support during the weekends (Daughter-in-Law Mu had been an only child so the options for support were narrower). When Grandfather Mu passed away in 2013, Grandson Mu had finished university and he still lived with his parents, but this marked the point at which Son Mu and his wife's "two-person lifestyle" resumed. Daughter-in-Law Mu said: "I like singing and dancing. I wanted to go to the movies and dance halls. But he didn't like going out anymore. So we compromise and do evening walks together around the neighborhood. We both like poems and history, so we talk a lot together. If my son is at home, he joins our discussion too." Since Grandma Mu was healthy and Grandson Mu did not have any children yet, the conjugal intimacy for Son Mu and his wife peaked during this phase of their marriage.

The near thirty-year marriage of Son Mu reveals three layers of analysis. First, the exact timing of when conjugal intimacy triumphs over intergenerational intimacy varies, dependent upon specific family circumstances and temporalities—however, generally speaking the marriage phases exempt from care responsibilities (whether to the young or to the old) are marked by the potential peak of conjugal intimacy.[59] Second, tackling bilateral family responsibilities together and managing them well can strengthen conjugal intimacy. Daughter-in-Law Mu commented on various occasions: "He is a very kind person [haoren]. He treated me very well and treated my parents very well." Son Mu explained that during the period of care for his father-in-law, his mother occasionally remarked upon his heavy involvement in her family and that these remarks antagonized his wife at the time. Since he continued to provide support, his wife appreciated this and in turn, he appreciated her understanding in not harboring any grievances toward his mother. The interactions between Son Mu and his wife were therefore indicative of mutual appreciation, mutual support, and mutual accommodation, which were considered the most important elements in a Chinese marriage by an overwhelming majority of interviewees (see "Transformation of Intimacy?" below). Finally, the nature of the Chinese familialist welfare regime plays an important role in perpetrating the interdependence between conjugal ties and vertical ties. Although the state pension and medical care was introduced during the period covered by the book—albeit to varying degrees across the three generations and between urban (since the 1950s) and rural China (since the 2000s)— personal care (both childcare and old age care) was predominantly carried out by family and kin members across the three generations. For example, both the father-in-law and father of Son Mu had their medical expenses covered by their work unit. However, everyday care was shouldered exclusively by their family members with no support from state institutions.

According to patrilineal and patrilocal tradition, women are viewed as outsiders to their husband's family. As they age and bear male heirs, women's authority increases and they ultimately serve as the supervisor overseeing younger women in household management, meaning the mother-in-law / daughter-in-law dyad was often viewed a source of intergenerational dispute. Since 1949, the patrilocal custom has been modified to varying degrees in urban and rural China—for example, the work unit housing allocation enabled two thirds of the urban G1s in my sample to obtain conjugal accommodation from their workplace.[60] In rural villages, in a multiple-siblings structure, after household division, neolocal residence (living apart from the families of either spouse but provided by the husband's family) was the norm for a considerable number of rural households since G1.[61] Despite an evolution of patrilocal residence, a gendered tradition in the material basis of marriage has re-emerged in different eras. In the Mao era and early reform era, married male workers were more likely to obtain work unit housing, making marriage a material necessity for women (e.g., both Grandma Mu and Daughter-in-Law Mu moved to the flat allocated to their husband). As part of the transition from a planned to a market economy, housing allocation by the work unit officially ended in 1998 and a commercial market for urban housing grew rapidly. Since 2000, urban families have converged with rural families in mari-tal housing provision, that is, the husband's family is expected to provide marital housing, reinforcing gendered intergenerational wealth transfer.[62] In Grandson Mu's case, his parents funded his marital flat in its entirety (by selling the flat owned by Son Mu's parents-in-law after they had passed away). In families who could not afford the full price of an urban flat, the husband's family is expected to cover the deposit for the flat. While it is increasingly popular in single-daughter urban families to purchase a car for the daughter when she marries, the cost of a car is far less than the deposit for a flat. Because of this persistent gendered difference in intergenerational wealth transfer, men are more materially indebted toward their parents and so they must delicately balance the intertwining of conjugal and vertical ties. Just as women were responsible for a disproportionate share of domestic work, men—especially those in earlier generations—were often obliged to expend con-siderable emotional labor in helping preserve a smooth relationship between their wife and parents.

Balancing Act

Grandma Zhao held a deep grudge regarding her husband's unbalanced deal-ing with the relations between conjugal and vertical ties. She felt her husband had "colluded with" his family to abuse and bully her in the early years of marriage. Conversely, despite sharing the same domineering and abusive mother-in-law, Grandma Zhao's sister-in-law spoke very highly of her hus-band's balancing act: "He was afraid of his mother too and he did nothing when she scolded me. But in the evenings, we ran outside and hid under a tree. He would hug me as we cried together." In other words, his vacillation between a "frontstage" performance for his extended kin and "backstage"[63] behavior in the privacy of their conjugal life was a deliberate strategy to disentangle the complex web of conjugal and vertical ties. Frontstage, he behaved in accor-dance with norms associated with the cultural expectations of intergenera-tional hierarchy. Backstage, he was a caring husband toward his wife.[64] This front- and backstage oscillation takes various forms as men balance the parties involved. Son Mu termed his own strategy—"deceiving both sides" (*liangbian hong*). In his private interactions with both his mother and his wife, Son Mu "casually agreed" (*suikou fuhe*) when one party expressed grievances against the other in order to avoid confrontation with either of them.

If a husband failed to handle the balancing act well, the consequences could be detrimental to both his conjugal intimacy and intergenerational intimacy. In Chen's family in Tianjin (see chapter 5), Son Chen (G2) first became acquainted with his wife at their workplace. For both of them it was their first time they had fallen in love and their feelings for one another were extremely close when they got married. However, Son Chen had always been his mother's favorite child and he had formed a strong bond with her. Upon their marriage, the young couple moved in with his parents and occupied one room of their two-bedroom flat. After his wife had given birth to a child, their relationship soured, and increasing acrimony between his wife and mother left him feeling isolated and hard pressed by them both. He signed, "At that time, I was very young and didn't know how to deal with these conflicts. I felt backed into a corner. To be honest, there were moments when I even felt suicidal. I hated going home. On my way back home, I rode my bicycle extremely slowly, feeling that my head would explode as soon as I got there."

When mortgages became available in late 1990s, the couple moved into their own flat, however the relationship between his wife and mother did not improve. The juggle between conjugal ties and vertical ties also distanced Son Chen from his mother: "My mother cared so much about me when I was young. However, since my marriage, with all the things we went through, she perhaps felt that I was no longer hers and had taken the side of my wife. . . . For example, nowadays she behaves very formally [*keqi*] toward me. The other day when I took her to see a doctor, part of the medical bill required self-payment. I just tried to pay the bill on the spot, but she kept refusing to accept it. I felt really upset."

Sadly, none of the people involved in this disastrous triad relationship emerged as a winner. Daughter-in-law Chen compared the relationship with her husband at the start of their marriage and now: "I used to feel that I was the most important person in his life. He always paid great attention to me. Nowadays I feel that his feelings for me blow hot and cold [*you yida mei yida*]. For example, when I talk to him these days, he always seems to be thinking of something else."

When asked if she would choose to marry him again, she replied firmly: "No. It's a definite no." When asked the same question, Son Chen also replied firmly: "No, definitely no. As a woman, she has her merits: for example, she does a very good job at keeping the house tidy. But human beings are also emotional creatures. . . . I remember that when we were courting and I asked her if she thought there might be a conflict with my mother in the future, she replied 'Impossible.'" His reference to human beings as "emotional creatures" highlights the critical role of conjugal intimacy in accommodating existing intergenerational ties of intimacy.

In the two early generations, there was a default perception that the mother-in-law and daughter-in-law would conflict with one another. This perception subsided among the youngest generation. Multiple factors contribute to this emerging "peaceful coexistence" of both conjugal and vertical intimacy. The shrinking demographic profile of urban and rural families has reshaped the emotional landscape of intergenerational ties. In the earlier two generations, parents commonly had one or two favorites among their many children, causing bitterness between generations and among siblings. In contrast, the urban one-child generation and the rural only-son generation did not have competition from siblings (brothers in rural families) and experienced a high level of emotional devotion from their parents in comparison with the children of earlier generations. When asked whom they considered the most intimate persons in their life, the majority of G3s, both single and married, chose their parents. This dynamic had implications for the spouse, a Guangzhou G3 woman interviewee commenting: "I can tell my husband feels closer towards his mother than towards me." While she was not as intimate with her mother-in-law as she was toward her own mother, she behaved "respectfully," explaining, "I accept that both I and his mother are equally important to him." (It is noteworthy that this particular mother-in-law had been a senior civil servant and her professional gravitas might have played a role in reproducing respectful behavior.)[65]

With the benefit of their own experience, G2 mothers were reflective and hoped to create an easier environment for their child to manage the intertwining relations between conjugal and vertical ties. Daughter-in-Law Chen commented "I will care about my son-in-law as much as I care about my daughter. This is because my love toward my son-in-law will make my daughter happy." This reveals how intimacy is relationally constructed: a mother's intimacy toward their child may be transposed into intimacy toward their child's spouse. In turn, they increase the gratitude felt by their children, thereby strengthening intergenerational intimacy.

Finally, maintaining close bilateral family ties has become a widespread trend, necessitating a balance of conjugal ties with bilateral vertical ties. The bilateral intergenerational exchange practice is already seen at work in the urban G1 generation,[66] and in recent years, as rural daughters' old age support has increased (see chapter 5), rural households are slowly catching up with their urban counterparts, albeit with stubborn remnants of the legacy of the patrilineal tradition continuing to persist.[67] In Elder Daughter Zhao's two-floor house, while allocating a floor for their only son's marital accommodation, she also reserved two rooms for her married daughters to use when they visited with their families. Her younger daughter, Granddaughter Zhao, was the mostly economically capable child and she sent around 10,000 yuan per year to her parents and also bought various appliances (such as an air conditioner and fridge) for them. Although the financial transfers to her natal family were derived from her own earnings, Granddaughter Zhao appreciated her husband's support in maintaining a close tie with her natal family. One way in which she showed her gratitude toward him was to stay on friendly terms with her mother-in-law by often praising her on her WeChat profile and taking particular care to thank her whenever she came to cook for them. A new equilibrium has been built for the intertwining of conjugal and vertical ties; as one G3 male interviewee put it, "If I treat your parents well, how could you not treat my parents well?"

Women's Power and Resistance

Commenting upon the rural women she encountered in Taiwan in the 1970s, Wolf[68] suggested that, because of their structurally disadvantageous position in the Chinese kinship system, married women were keen to cultivate a uterine family consisting of their own children. This uterine family strategy was most noticeable in rural G1 women with unsatisfactory marriages. When asked why she had kept having children despite being mistreated by her husband, Grandma Zhao commented: "I thought that, after my children grew up, they would help to protect me. At the time when my children had grown up, my husband would be old, and my son will be in charge and have the power. That's why I gave the name 'power' [quan] to my son."

Her pursuit of a uterine strategy to transform her miserable life was shaped by the micro institutional context in which she was trapped. She had no control over her income as, at the time, payments for collective farm work were handed over to the family head (first her father-in-law and then her husband when they lived separately from the in-laws).[69] She had no wider support network as, like the majority of rural G1 women at the time, she had been married into a different village to her own natal village, and lack of infrastructure (such as roads) meant frequent visits to her natal family were impossible. In contrast, urban G1 women had personal access to their work unit wage and, with a natal family located in the same city, a uterine family strategy was a less necessary form of resistance. Nevertheless, women in unhappy marriages do continue to develop strategies in order to show their discontent. Against the background of persistent and worsening gender inequality in public spheres, marriage and family became important sites for women to maneuver and exercise power.[70]

Crafting Disharmony

Crafting an inharmonious atmosphere through deliberate emotional outbursts and / or instigating quarrels has often been the resort of Chinese wives seeking to "tame" their husbands. Such disharmony can be staged inside the family and / or in the public domain. Younger Daughter Zhao, who faced the challenges of living as a rural-to-urban migrant alongside her husband, explained: "I found it very annoying that he didn't pull his weight, and so I kept nagging him. Look, he was obsessed with playing mah-jong rather than working hard to make money, won't it make me angry? Once at dinner time, I called him to come home to eat. But he ignored me and carried on playing mah-jong downstairs. I was so angry that I went downstairs and threw the mah-jong onto the floor. If he had dared to hit me, I'd have hit him without any thought of saving his face."

Most of the time, Younger Daughter Zhao nagged and scolded her husband at home, when, as far as her daughter could remember, he normally remained silent. But, on this occasion, the wife took the stage in the public domain, hoping that this would bring her husband to heel. Underpinning her tactic, various forces were at work. First, thanks to a strongly gendered notion of emotionality, a woman is entitled to openly display strong emotions, whereas the same action by a man would invite censure. In short, for women in particular the deployment of emotions acts as a form of resistance. Second, in a relational society, such as that of China, the social focus during a woman's emotional outburst is not only directed to the person who displays the emotions, but also to the perceived "wrongdoer" who has triggered the display. By extension, those witnessing the outburst can be expected to question the behavior and morality of the person who is the object of the woman's anger. In the Chinese context, an extreme example is a woman's resort to suicide as a form of ultimate revenge and its use as a shaming strategy vis-à-vis the person(s) who have done her wrong. Third, given the sociocultural emphasis upon harmony,[71] the complementary and relational dynamics between masculinities and femininities, embodied in the notion of yin and yang, imply that in response to a woman's emotional outburst, a man should restore calm and help reestablish a harmonious equilibrium.[72] By further implication, a wife's emotional outburst poses a potential threat to her husband's masculinity, which may cause him to lose face.

The multifaceted strategy can produce an emotional response among men. When confronted by Younger Daughter Zhao's emotional outburst described above, her husband went gray and silently followed her home and for a while curtailed his mah-jong playing. Other examples of the successful use of the quarrelling technique included wives compelling their husbands to undertake more housework, forcing their husbands to share a greater proportion of his income, and (among urban G3s) pushing their husband to add their name to the title of deeds of the martial flat purchased by his parents. However, if overused, this mechanism can lead to a loss of conjugal intimacy, as exhibited in Son Chen's case.

The strategy of crafting disharmony was not practiced by all women with grievances in their marriage. As the husband's masculinity and face are undermined by the humiliation of this process, he may respond with physical violence. Indeed, Younger Daughter Zhao had already considered this risk and, as noted in her narrative, had also decided upon her response. In the Shandong and Fujian villages, where domestic violence persisted as a social norm, Younger Daughter Zhao may well have felt less emboldened. For example, Grandma Zhao hated her husband for most of their marriage, but according to the memories of her children, her emotional outbursts (such as scolding and hitting) were directed toward her children but not her husband.

Speaking Bitterness

Speaking bitterness (*suku*) was a popular oral genre of Chinese rural society. Adopted and reinforced by the Chinese Communist Party in a series of Maoist ideological education movements, it was used as an essential tool to mobilize class struggle and strengthen identity among peasants, workers, and women.[73] By providing a framework in which a political narrative could unfold, it encouraged and enabled protagonists to denounce past pain and sufferings inflicted on them by the pre-1949 social norms and values, while simultaneously celebrating the joyful benefits conferred on them by the Communist Party.[74] Among my interviewees, I found that wives who had experienced unhappy marriages resorted to this narrative technique in telling their life stories, but with a focus upon recounting past marital woes. In the two extended family case studies, except for the three women—Granddaughter Zhao, Elder Daughter Zhao, Daughter-in-Law Mu—who had had happy marriages, the narratives of the remaining wives placed great emphasis on the sufferings they had endured in their marriage. One dominant theme that emerged from them concerned the anguish and distress relating to childbirth and / or child-rearing. Grandma Mu reported, "After I'd given birth, nobody looked after me. I looked after myself. My husband had work trips and sometimes disappeared for several weeks. At the time, there were so many political movements. In the mornings I had to take part in communal physical exercising and in the evenings

I needed to attend meetings. It was extremely difficult to look after the babies. All I could do was to lock them indoors and came back during breaks to breast-feed them." Younger Daughter Zhao likewise recounted, "Other wives' husbands were always close at hand when their wives gave birth but I was alone, just like a beggar, to look after my new-born baby. Nowadays I have headaches and pains all over my body—all caused by not being looked after at that time." And Grandma Zhao described how she had suffered:

> After I gave birth to my children, nobody looked after me. Nobody cared whether or not I died. I remember vividly that when I gave birth to my third daughter—at around 11 in the morning—my husband asked my sec-ond daughter: "Boy or girl?" She replied, "Girl," but he didn't even bother to come upstairs to have a look at the baby. He left home in the afternoon to enjoy himself and didn't return until the next day. I had no rest after childbirth. I had hardly anything to eat but had had to get up to do the washing-up, feed the children and feed the pigs. So that's why my health was ruined and I've now ended up with a lot of illnesses.

Interviews with the younger generations confirmed the children of these women were well versed in the suffering their mothers had endured, as these grievances had been repeated frequently during intergenerational discussion. For example, the daughter of Younger Daughter Zhao told me, "The seeds of many of my mother's illnesses, such as rheumatism, migraine and tinnitus, were sown in the lack of proper care when she gave birth to me. I really feel sorry for her." Son Mu commented, "Except for work, my father neglected everything in the family. All our needs—cooking, washing and going to school—were seen to by my mother. My mother suffered a huge amount of stress at that time." These mothers had successfully transformed a political disciplinary technique into a personal tool of resistance in the family setting. Their narrative performances were a reminder to their children of the contri-bution and sacrifices they had made through their reproductive and child-rearing efforts, thereby strengthening their children's gratitude and in-debtedness to them.

Transformation of Intimacy?

Goode's second subsidiary hypothesis predicts a shift away from marriage as an alliance of families and domestic economies toward the rise of companion-ate relationships between spouses. This narrative has been implicitly incorpo-rated into the discourse on Chinese marriages by Jankowiak and Li.[75] Drawing on interviewing data of couples in the 1980s in Hohhot and in the 2000s in other Chinese cities, Jankowiak and Li identified a cultural shift in family be-havior in two urban cohorts. The "dutiful spouse" model, characteristic of those born from the 1960s to 1977, is "grounded in the ordinary life of family practicalities and explicit duties, stresses the diligent and responsible fulfill-ment of family duties by both spouses and, when necessary, an accepted sexual division of labor." By contrast, the cohort born since 1978 conform to the "emotionally involved" model, in which "the husband and wife prefer to define themselves as socially interconnected and, ideally, intensely emotionally intertwined."[76] This generational shift is assumed to be closely linked to the shift from the "language of duty" to the "language of love" apparent in the institution of dating and the new value placed on the formation of a conjugal love union.[77]

Meanings of Love

MOTHER QIAN: Love, [pause for a short while], love is where two people get on and are considerate towards one another. I feel that if I am considerate towards you and you are considerate towards me, that's what love is. In my generation, love isn't something that is complicated.

Q: Could you describe the moment of falling in love?

MOTHER QIAN: No, at the time, we didn't feel that sort of love—loving someone so much that you weren't able to sleep. At that time, it was really very simple—he treated me very well and as a result I felt good. Something like that.

Q: What is it that connects you and your husband in your marriage?

MOTHER QIAN: Our hearts are aligned [xin dou neng xiang yikuai qu]. He has accommodated me in various ways. When I sometimes lost my temper, he accommodated me. During the time when I was ill, he was even more considerate toward me. I feel that he is kind-hearted. When I devoted a lot of my time to my natal family, he had no complaints at all. All this has sustained our marriage down to the present day. (Mother Qian, born 1957, married 1983, Tianjin)

SON QIAN: The meaning of love is too broad to be able define it. Look, nowadays do we love each other? There is still love in our marriage, but it's perhaps more in the way of familial love [qin qing].

Q: Could you please describe the feeling of falling in love?

SON QIAN: That was at the beginning of our relationship, when we were attracted to each other, very nervous, our hearts throbbing, selflessly and unconditionally giving ourselves to each other.

Q: What is it that connects you and your wife in your marriage?

SON QIAN: In the beginning it was more to do with our feelings for one another. But after having children, nowadays it's more to do with family responsibilities. After all, I'm now a father, I have to work hard to earn money to support my son and my family, and there's the fact that my parents are also getting old. (Son Qian, born 1984, married 2014, Tianjin)

As illustrated by this mother and her son, "love" is a word that is used to indicate many things (passionate love, companionate love, enduring love, familial love, etc.) and so it is exceedingly challenging to define. In the absence of a clear and unambiguous definition, it is difficult to test the popular hypothesis suggesting that the younger generation in China experiences love more readily than their older counterparts. However, one observable finding is that members of older generations, such as Mother Qian, were less likely to have experienced the sensation of "falling in love." In the two case studies, apart from Son Mu and his wife, G1 and G2 members did not experience the "passionate love" phase. For the one-child generation, those who admitted to having "fallen in love" did so in their early twenties and / or as university students, influenced by institutional changes, including privatization of marriage and intimacy and greater exposure to Western and media products relating to romantic love. Even so, eventual marriage partners were not necessarily those about whom they had felt most passionately. Like Grandson Mu, Son Qian's feelings toward his wife were ambivalent: "I got married to my wife because I met her at the right time. I was already thirty and all my peers had wives, and I felt really anxious to get married. If it had been ten years earlier, I wouldn't have chosen her."

Whirlwind romances, as so often portrayed in media,[78] were not the kind of relationship experienced by most interviewees in their marital life. Son Qian vacillated between two notions of love: on the one hand, he outlined a transition from "passionate love" to "familial love"; on the other hand, when he narrowed down the meaning of love to "passionate love," he posed a duality between "love" and "responsibility."[79] Overall, however, he was talking in terms of more or less rather than offering an either / or dichotomy. By contrast, Mother Qian's perception of love as something grounded in "mutual consideration" was the analogue of her depictions of marital practices centered around mutual understanding, mutual accommodation, and mutual support. In short, the notion of "love" highlighted by Mother Qian inherently embraced a notion of responsibility evidenced by each couple's mutual care and support behavior.[80] Finally, one feature that the mother-son pair shared was their understanding of family responsibilities grounded in an interwoven web of both conjugal and vertical ties.

Jankowiak and Li's study described the one-child generation's marriage aspirations as "shared empathy and mutual respect, alongside other reciprocal processes such as consideration, cooperation, and compromise" and these ideals were taken to be specific to the one-child generation.[81] However, my data reveals that a marriage model grounded in mutuality was already—whether rhetorically or functionally—part of the mindset of previous generations. When asked what they regarded as the most important elements in their marriage, almost all my interviewees responded by citing "mutualities" such as mutual understanding, mutual support, and mutual accommodation. Son Mu commented: "Judging from my own experiences, the most important things are mutual support, mutual assistance and mutual consideration." It is worth emphasizing that the three mutualities Son Mu referred to are not merely reciprocal with each other but also extend to each spouse's families (see "Interwoven Lives" above). Grandma Zhao shared this view, though from the perspective of an unhappy marriage: "Mutual consideration and mutual accommodation is the most important thing in a marriage. My husband never cared about me or accommodated me." Several factors contribute to the circulation of this marriage ideal. Since 1949, the party-state has promoted love and mutual companionship as key criteria in mate selection.[82] This mutuality discourse circulates in popular culture (for example, in the wedding ceremony described at the start of this chapter) and has been also handed down from generation to generation. The daughter of Younger Daughter Zhao recalled a conversation about love and marriage involving several of her female relatives: "My maternal aunt said, 'Let me tell you that once the love phase is over, what matters is familial love. You need to find a way of getting on [guo rizi] with whoever you are married to. The two of you must learn to support [bangzhu] and accommodate [baorong] each other.' The other aunt [the wife of her uncle] echoed this, saying: 'Yes, absolutely.'"

Studies of Chinese families often highlight the lives of the one-child generation as being quite different from those of previous generations. However, my findings indicate strongly that viewing the entirety of their life course is critical to understanding the experiences of this generation. The one-child generation described in Jankowiak and Li's study mainly comprises young men and women in their early twenties (the oldest being thirty-four). The findings from my previous investigations[83] of the one-child generation in their twenties echoed those of Jankowiak and Li in acknowledging the importance for this generation of the emotional connection with a partner[84] and the ideal of conjugal intimacy. However, when I conducted the fieldwork for this book, many of the interviewees born in the 1980s were edging toward their forties. For these now *middle-aged* singletons, as demonstrated in the comments made by Son Qian and many other interviewees, the "duty narrative" was strongly in evidence. In short, attitudinal and behavioral differences among married couples in China highlighted in previous scholarship may have reflected the impact of changing life courses rather than inherent generational differences.

Practices of Intimacy

Chinese interviewees described a range of conjugal practices, varying from practical to emotional, that were considered intimate. The most frequently highlighted and valued aspect of conjugal intimacy (whether having experienced it or not) across all three generations was the act of care and support. For example, when both Mother Qian and Mother Gao (mother of Mr. Gao, the groom at the start of this chapter) were diagnosed with breast cancer, their husband took on the main carer role such as accompanying them to hospital and cooking for them while they were bedbound, acts that were highly praised by their wives. It is noteworthy that wives often illustrated how their husbands *cared for* them, reflecting the underlying assumption that women are presumed to hold this default role in a marriage.

Gift-giving was considered a practice of intimacy, although the persistent vertical segregation by gender and wage inequality meant gifts are or were prone to flow from the husband to the wife. In early generations, the gifts could be clothes, food or anything used in daily life. For example, Daughter-in-Law Mu recalled an episode in which her husband went on a work trip to southern China and carried a batch of sugarcane for her on the long train journey home. She told the story for humorous effect, but it revealed her appreciation in little acts of conjugal intimacy. Among the younger generation, the rise of consumerism has meant that gift-giving has increasingly become a quasi-ritualized symbol of love and intimacy. On Valentine's Day and Chinese Lover's Day (Qixi—seventh day of the seventh lunar month) retail companies frequently promote and publicize romantic dinners and gifts.[85] Grandson Mu, and other well-off husbands explained that they were expected to bring home luxury goods such as bags and skin care products from international brands whenever they were on foreign business trips (obviously a considerable step up from sugar cane just one generation prior), and there were two extreme cases in which the husband bought a separate flat to be put solely in his wife's name as an ultimate declaration of love and intimacy.

Chatting and communication (*liaotian* and *jiaoliu*) were highlighted as forms of intimacy, especially among urban and younger interviewees, although they do not necessarily capture the "mutual" "self-disclosure"—constantly revealing one's inner feelings to each other—described in Giddens' conceptualization.[86] Here are two contrasting narratives of urban G3 wives, both of whom said they would choose the same husband again, yet had different takes on communicative intimacy. First, Ms. Fang reported: "Chatting together is a form of intimacy for a couple to show that they care about each other." When asked who usually initiates such chats, she responded, "Most of the time it's me. For example, when things happen at work, I don't know what to do. So I go and chat to him. Once I've let off steam, he gives me suggestions about how to deal with the difficult issues at work. . . . So basically it's whenever I have any issues that I chat to him. For most of the time, he's the listener." Ms. Jiang on the other hand reported that

> When we were dating [*tanlianai*], we chatted a lot. No matter whether it was something big or small, we always called and told each other about it. At the time I felt closer to him than to my best female friend [*guimi*, female confidant). These days we still talk a lot, but about things like what restaurants we should go to, what extra-curriculum courses our daughter should choose, what kinds of gifts to buy for both sets of parents, etc. As we've grown older, I've found it harder to confide in him. For example, I sense that my husband isn't happy with his current job. When we were in our twenties, I'd have simply told him to quit his job and try and find a job that he'd enjoy. But now, we have a teenage daughter with expensive private school fees to pay. How could I afford to encourage him to try out another job? These external forces make it harder for us to communicate heart-to-heart. He also avoids talking to me about these issues.

Ms. Fang's narrative reveals a wife longing for communicative intimacy while her husband remains emotionally reserved.[87] This difference is closely related to the gendered notion that "emotionality is antithetical to traditional understandings of masculinity."[88] Moreover, the communicative pattern described by Ms. Fang is a gendered model with the husband as advisor to his wife, reflecting the hypergamy principle (women marry up). Interviews with middle-aged G3 husbands indicated that some suffered anxiety and issues at work, like Ms. Jiang's husband, but were unwilling to talk to their wives about these problems in order to maintain their masculine image as a "capable" husband. Mr. Ren (urban, middle-level manager) is one such husband: "I still serve like a dog at work. But I don't tell my work troubles to my wife. First, she can't help. Second, it looks as if I am useless."

The genesis of why both Ms. Jiang and Mr. Ren's narratives dispute Giddens' disclosing intimacy model lies in the contrasting underlying assumptions of the self. Giddens' model relies upon an agentic self, a "self-made" self. Chinese interviewees, on the other hand, confirm Mead's conception of the self: a self that is inherently social, possessing agency but at the same time very much embedded in everyday sociality.[89] A social self is relational, as it "exists and adapts through the ability to locate oneself within the social world of others."[90] This explains why Ms. Jiang could open up to her husband in the early years of their relationship, but found it much harder later: both she and her husband had evolved and adapted to the marriage and family institution and were no longer carefree selves in a two-person dating context.

Intimacy is a social field where social relations are reproduced and reinforced. I echo Illouz's observation (drawing upon US data) that class inequality is intertwined with the experiences of romance and intimacy. Illouz argues that the culture of capitalism "articulates a powerful utopia of love promising transgression though the consumption of leisure and nature."[91] The ritualized symbols of romance and intimacy, widely circulated in media and popular culture, have privileged certain practices of intimacy, often experienced by the affluent and highly educated urban middle class, as an ideal and reshaped the vision of other social groups in the society. However, life conditions, limitations in income, leisure time, and education can hinder the realization of intimacy, leading to anxieties, negotiations, and contestations.

Younger Daughter Zhao had spent nearly thirty years of marriage in the city. On the one hand, she lectured her daughter about the unrealistic portrayal of conjugality in the media: "Marriage is not as described in those romantic TV dramas; marriage is about daily necessities—eating, drinking, pissing and shitting." On the other hand, she lamented that her husband never bought her any gifts or knew how to say words that were pleasing to her: "I said to my husband, 'Look, it's Valentine's Day today, other husbands have bought something for their wives. What have you got for me?' He replied that roses were too expensive on Valentine's Day and that even if he'd bought them for me, I'd also complain that they'd cost too much."

The modest economic means and lack of emotional articulateness of poorly educated migrant men were at odds with the intimate ideal adopted by their wives, a source of conjugal disharmony among low-paid migrant households. Interestingly, despite her husband being similarly "unromantic" and lacking in communicative affection, such discord did not feature in the narrative of Elder Daughter Zhao, who still lived in the countryside—perhaps because she was more shielded than her sister from the urban ideal of intimacy that privileged affluent middle-class households over other social groups.

Conclusion

Alongside the profound social and economic transformations since 1949, there have been many changes in the way people marry, including in the criteria for an ideal spouse, an increase in the average age of marriage, and customary financial transfers associated with children's marriages. However, there were also continuities underlying the three generations of Chinese marriages: parents remain important players; women tend to marry up; and urban-rural segregation persists, as do gendered division of labor and gendered practices of intimacy. Marriage remains effectively obligatory and there is huge social and parental pressure on young people to marry. As members of the G3 reach middle age, there is a convergence with older generations in their attitude and practices of conjugality.

Have Chinese marriages evolved into the "companionate marriage" ideal described in Goode's model? The answer to this question is complex. On the one hand, Chinese respondents' emphasis upon mutualities (whether rhetorically or functionally) captures elements of companionate love. On the other hand, the companionate marriage model is based on the idea of an exclusive emotionally and sexually intimate relationship between a man and a woman that is satisfying to both partners. Chinese marriages differ in various respects. First, there is an *embeddedness* of conjugal intimacy within extended family ties. Chinese parents continue to matter greatly in children's lives, from choosing a spouse and getting married, to managing conjugal life. As the life course evolves, the configuration of conjugal intimacy and intergenerational intimacy fluctuates. While there is greater attention to romantic love in both public and private domains over time, the meaning of conjugal love has evolved into a model that emphasizes support and care for each other as well as an obligation toward bilateral ties. Conjugal intimacy does not therefore stand on its own but exists interwoven with intergenerational intimacy. Whether or not vertical ties are managed well can greatly impact the quality of conjugal intimacy. Second, contrary to an emphasis on emotionality in the companionate love, Chinese marriage entails significant financial investment and negotiation. As in the case of parent-child relations (see chapter 1 on "The Value of Children"), material considerations now go hand in hand with the emotional elements of an intimate relationship. As Chinese society has modernized, alongside the commercialization of housing, property ownership became a prerequisite for marriage among the one-child generation. In short, the Chinese marital relationship is a composite, a mixture of emotion, materiality, duty, and commitment.

Further, contrary to the democratization narrative embedded in the new phase of modernity writings, intimate relationships are not automatically emancipatory;[92] instead, intimacy is reinscribed in existing social structures. Echoing Jackson and Ho,[93] this chapter finds that modernization has involved, redefining gender roles that de-traditionalize as much as they re-traditionalize them. While the Maoist commitment to gender equality ensured Chinese women were mobilized into paid work outside the home, domestic work remained predominantly a woman's responsibility across all three generations.

Alongside widening gender inequalities in the labor market, hegemonic gender role models (e.g., housekeeper versus breadwinner) have become more entrenched over time. In addition, the urban-rural segregation in marriage choices is a continuing feature across three generations. Influenced by growing consumerism and materialism, certain practices of intimacy are privileged and inequalities are reproduced in the intimate domain.

3

Having Sex

I: What are your thoughts on premarital sex?

A [born in 1992, male, recently married]: It has become quite common nowadays.

B [born in 1995, female, in a stable relationship]: It is considered normal in China now. For those who wait until they have their wedding, I think there must be something wrong with them.

A: Many couples also end up getting married because of pregnancy. Chinese people are generally open to it [sex], but we don't like to talk about it like the Japanese do. Japanese are more comfortable discussing it openly. [Pause] Ideally, men prefer having multiple sexual partners, but they also expect their wife to be a virgin.

B: The virginity complex still exists, but finding a virgin is quite rare these days.

A: Having this ideal is one thing, realizing it is quite another.

C [born in 1993, female, engaged and about to get married]: I don't agree. Personally, I feel it's better not to rush into "that thing" [sex] too early.

A [pointing at C, jokingly]: She's already entering the stage of no "couple life" [meaning sex, *fuqi shenghuo*].

C: I believe it's not good to engage in it [sexual activity] too early. I don't think we necessarily have to wait until marriage, but at the very least, both parents should have agreed on the marriage proposal. My mother always advised me not to engage in such activities before marriage. She would never accept the idea of getting married solely because of pregnancy [*fengzi chenghun*]. She strongly disapproves of such behavior.

A [pointing at B]: The concept you mentioned [the virginity complex] still remains the mainstream ideal. However, some people can achieve it while others cannot. These traditional ideas still subtly and unconsciously influence people [*qianyi mohua*].

B: Yes, we—the 90s generation—are neither traditional nor avant-garde. We may want to embrace an avant-garde lifestyle, such as being single and carefree, but reality often prevents us from achieving that.

C: I agree. Those of us of the 90s generation are both traditional [*chuantong*] and open-minded [*kaifang*].

On a blisteringly hot summer day in Xi'an in 2018 I had originally planned a follow-up meeting with one of my interviewees at his office. However, at the last minute the interviewee pulled out due to a work commitment and so I found myself loitering in the company's air-conditioned office, wondering what to do next and whether to brave the midday sun. Three curious white-collar office workers—all of them university- and college-educated and working as sales professionals—showed an interest in my research and background. Seeing their enthusiasm, I initiated an impromptu group discussion, delving into various topics covered by my project. The extract above is taken from this unplanned, but enlightening, focus group.

Several themes emerge from this discussion on premarital sex. The first and most obvious is the recognition of the prevalence of premarital sex, albeit located within a spectrum of attitudes and practices. Second is the persistence of gendered sexual mores (for example, the virginity complex), even if these are open to challenge because of ambiguities surrounding their realization. Third is the persevering influence of tradition and of parents (compare this with, for example, C's mother) in shaping young people's views, leading to a confused understanding of the debts they owe to "modern" and "traditional" values. Fourthly, because the topic remains a cultural taboo,[1] the language available to discuss "sex" is limited. In the focus group and other one-on-one interviews, "that thing" was a frequently deployed euphemism to refer to sex. The responses to my question that open this chapter offer a thumbnail sketch of the sexual transformations experienced by the youngest generation of professional adults in contemporary China.

Given the cultural sensitivity in talking about sex, existing studies on Chinese sexual attitudes and experiences are predominantly grounded in survey methods[2]—many of which have been led by Chinese sexologist Pan Suiming, focusing upon the occurrence of, regularity of, and satisfaction with various sexual activities. While these surveys map out general trends, they infer interactions between sexual partners instead of examining the process directly. This chapter[3] enlivens the statistical data by highlighting the dynamics, contradictions, and complexities embodied in people's narratives of sex. Further, the proliferation of publications and media products with a sexual content, and the increase of nonmarital sexual activities in post-Mao China, have led Pan Suiming and others to claim that China is undergoing a sexual revolution.[4] Critics argue that this narrative may obscure the empirical realities of the Mao era and reiterate the dichotomy between tradition and modernity.[5] Grounded in a three-generational comparison, this chapter throws new light upon the debate by revealing paradoxical change and continuities over time: sex in China is changing in ways that are linked closely to past views and offers women less liberation than men.

My analysis of sexual attitudes and practices is informed by a social interactionist approach—"sexual scripting." Sexual scripting includes *cultural codes* (the understanding of sexuality that circulates within any given society), *interpersonal scripting* (shaping cultural codes into scripts relevant for a specific context—e.g., sexual interaction and everyday gossip of a sexual nature), and *intrapsychic scripting* (through which individuals make sense of culturally available knowledge and personal experiences—e.g., individual thoughts, desires, and fantasies).[6] Each of these levels of sexual scripting are captured in the above group discussion: cultural codes (the virginity complex highlighted by participant A), interpersonal scripting (in the mother-daughter conversation recalled by participant C and the group discussion itself), and intrapsychic scripting (the sense-making concluding comments made by participants B and C). I begin with a brief overview of sex in Chinese history to contextualize the evolution of cultural codes; this serves as a cumulative repertoire of discourses that people deploy to make sense of their sexual life. I then move onto discussions on premarital sex, conjugal sex, and extramarital sex and examine how institutional transitions from the Mao to post-Mao eras contribute to shifts in sexual experiences and perceptions and how people negotiate multiple levels of sexual scripting. The analysis highlights how, as a result of gendered cultural codes being refashioned in various eras—as well as being reproduced through gendered intergenerational transmission—men and women are positioned unequally in China's ongoing sexual transformation.

Sex in History

China's history spans a broad spectrum of attitudes toward sex.[7] Unlike the Christian association of sex with sin, classical Chinese philosophy viewed sexual desire as an innate physical need.[8] Early Daoist texts advocated a healthy harmony of yin (female) and yang (male) through intercourse[9] with sex closely linked to health and the extremes of abstinence and overindulgence discouraged. Women's sexual pleasure was emphasized, though it was often regarded as a means to fulfill men's healthy needs.[10] Confucians largely shared Daoist principles, but their focus was on procreation, and concubinage was legitimized to ensure continuity of the family lineage.[11]

During the Song Dynasty (860–1276), influenced by neo-Confucianism, significant efforts were made by the state and elites to shape sexual behavior according to moral standards, restricting reproductive sex to married couples. This moralistic attitude toward sex was deeply gendered, allowing men to have multiple sexual partners (such as concubines and courtesans) while fidelity was considered the highest virtue for women—leading to the widow chastity cult in the Ming and Qing dynasties (1368–1911).[12] Consequently, while men's status was often tied to their occupation, women's status was defined by both the occupations of their male relatives *and* their sexual conduct.[13] The highly gendered moral codes instilled in young women a pervasive awareness of sex as a source of danger and risk.[14]

In the early twentieth century, Western natural science became an integral part of intellectual discussion and "sex" was essentialized as a biological drive for heterosexual intercourse.[15] Socially, the modernizing rhetoric of the New Culture Movement (an intellectual movement in the 1910s and 1920s that criticized Confucian ideas and promoted a new Chinese culture based on modern notions of science and democracy) introduced new sexual practices, such as premarital sex and cohabitation, but these experiments were primarily limited to urban elite and intellectual circles. After 1949, the Communist Party undertook drastic measures to enforce a normative model of conjugal heterosexuality across the whole of China. Concubinage and prostitution were eradicated during the 1950s, and premarital virginity again became emphasized as a virtue for both males and females.[16] During the Cultural Revolution, the expression of sexual feelings in public spheres was suppressed and the open expression of physical intimacy forbidden.[17] Literary and artistic works related to love and sex were banned, and any sexual behavior outside legitimate conjugality was considered immoral and subject to political criticism and attack.

In the post-Mao era, with the depoliticization of everyday life, the decline of the work unit system, and China's opening up to the rest of the world, there has been a gradual relaxation of socialist sexual morality.[18] Public discourse on marital sex for pleasure has expanded. There is a growing deployment of a sexualized femininity in the market domain, leading to the commodification of women for commercial activities[19] and a reemergence of the sex industry.[20] Tensions have also intensified between a neoliberal governance approach based on self-regulation[21] and recent moves toward a more authoritarian regime under Xi's leadership.[22]

Rather than viewing cultural codes relating to sex as a straightforward replacement of ideas from the past to the present, or mere hybrids of Chinese and Western ideas, I consider them characterized by a "mosaic temporality"[23] in which Daoist influences, Confucian doctrines, socialist legacy, Western liberal attitudes, and capitalist modernity all figure. Situated in this mosaic temporality, Chinese men and women grapple with anxieties and contradictions, as well as opportunities, as they navigate their sexual lives.

Premarital Sex

All urban G1s stated that they refrained from premarital sex, although men and women tended to provide different explanations for their choices. Women often cited the influence of a gendered cultural code that linked a woman's status to her sexuality. One G1 women explained, "Engaging in it [premarital sex] is deemed inappropriate and, borrowing from common parlance, shameless. 'Shameless' is a particularly harsh label for a woman." The gendered notion of shame was reinforced during Maoist political campaigns, with several female interviewees recalling the distressing experience of witnessing women who had engaged in nonmarital sex being labeled "broken shoes" or "whores" during political attacks.[24]

Male G1s placed greater emphasis on adherence to official regulations and the socialist moral code of the time. One G1 male explained: "Engaging in that [premarital sex] was strictly prohibited. The work unit had the authority to impose punishment or even expel individuals for such behavior. It was crucial to maintain a sense of purity and cleanliness [qingqing baibai]." This comment captures the regulation and policing of sexual conduct exercised within the work unit system at the time.[25] Those who engaged in premarital sex were branded "impure" and "hooligans" subject to disciplinary measures by the work unit.[26] While rural G1 respondents were less explicit in their explanations, they indirectly affirmed their abstinence from premarital sex by noting they had hardly any opportunities to interact with their spouse prior to their wedding day.

During the early reform period, while the legal definition of premarital sex as "hooliganism" persisted,[27] the focus of work units gradually shifted away from a form of political surveillance to one with much greater focus on their economic viability in the market economy. Although official representation of premarital sex retained the cautionary tone of the Mao era, public discourse centered on love and intimacy, featuring cultural products and references from the West that displayed more explicit expressions of sexuality.[28] Amidst the depoliticization of everyday life, a subtle trend of relaxation began to emerge, particularly among G2 male respondents. A small proportion (20 percent) of rural G2 men from Fujian, who migrated to urban areas for work before getting married, hinted that some young men resorted to commercial sex while living alone in the cities.[29] Likewise, urban G2 men began to adopt a more ambivalent attitude, moving away from strict moralism. Below is an extract of a conversation with Mr. Dong (Xi'an):

> MR. DONG: Back then, it [premarital sex] was acceptable. If you found the right person, it was okay to engage in it [sexual activity].
> I: Did premarital sex always lead to marriage?
> MR. DONG: Not necessarily. But men of my generation still thought it important that their wives should be virgins.

His sentiment underlined that female virginity remained a significant criterion for men when selecting a spouse and yet they were open to premarital sex with their girlfriends, showcasing an assemblage of liberal attitudes toward sex and traditional notions of female chastity. This assemblage of ideas was gender-specific, catering to men's diverse desires while creating conflicting expectations for women. Women were pressured by their boyfriends to maintain the relationship through sexual involvement, but were also expected to preserve their chastity for their future husband. In contrast with her husband, in her private interview, Mrs. Dong was shy and fidgeted when asked about premarital sex. She hinted at having engaged in sexual activity with Mr. Dong prior to marriage, that it was her first sexual encounter, and marriage brought her a sense of relief. Nevertheless, she remained hesitant and ambivalent, citing the case of a female friend who failed to marry the individual she had her first sexual experience with, leading to gossip and judgment within her social circle.

Unlike Mrs. Dong, the majority of G2 women distanced themselves from premarital sex. One urban G2 woman commented: "My generation adhered to a moral guideline. We must absolutely maintain a physical distance during courtship, and there's one distinct boundary [premarital sex] that we should not cross. Beyond this, we were free to do whatever we wanted together." Similarly, a rural G2 woman underscored the potential repercussions for women: "In my generation, a woman's virginity held a significant value. If a husband discovered his wife was not a virgin on the wedding night, her status within the marriage would be diminished, and the husband could make life difficult for her." Approximately 10 percent of G2 respondents (all from urban areas)[30] acknowledged having engaged in premarital sex, but always within the context of their impending marriages.

During the late 1990s and 2000s, revisions to state legislation eliminated legal barriers associated with premarital sex. The charge of hooliganism was abolished, and the term for unmarried cohabitation changed from "illegal cohabitation" (*feifa tongju*) to "nonmarital cohabitation" (*feihun tongju*).[31] Si-multaneously, the relaxation of university regulations and expansion of leisure venues removed practical obstacles for young couples to engage in premarital sex.[32] The rapid expansion of the internet over the last two decades has also facilitated a widespread dissemination of information about sexual behavior.[33] Finally, the age of first marriage has also been rising steadily in recent decades. Using results from the 2010 China Census, Yu and Xie[34] found an overall in-crease in median first marriage age from 21.2 (men) and 20.8 (women) born before 1950 to 25.3 (men) and 23.4 (women) born 1980-1984. Clearly, later mar-riage gave young people more time to engage in premarital sex.

These social transformations have contributed to a broader acceptance and increasing occurrence of premarital sex.[35] As noted in the focus group discus-sion at the start of the chapter, the prevalence of premarital sex in G3s was significantly higher compared to earlier generations, with reported rates of 60 percent among women and 80 percent among men. However, the number of sexual partners the G3 generation has before their eventual spouse did not increase substantially: women averaged between 0 and 1 and men between 0 and 2. Thus, Chinese premarital sex largely serves as a "transitional stage"[36] leading to marriage.[37] While the G3 generation has become more accustomed to premarital sex, the interplay of various codes embedded in "mosaic temporality" has introduced significant new tensions, particularly for young women, as they navigate and manage their own desires and the expectations of peers, family, and society.

The Virginity Battle

The decision over whether to lose their virginity during dating was a pivotal struggle among women of the one-child generation born during the 1980s, often becoming fiercely contested between women's defensiveness and men's persuasiveness. Ms. Zhuang was an only child within a Guangzhou working-class family. Viewed as a promising candidate for marriage by her peers, she met her first boyfriend during the final year of university. Prior to this she had been pursued by several suitors, casually accepting their designation as "ordi-nary friends" without making any genuine commitment. When her boyfriend emerged on the scene, she swiftly terminated these associations.

Standing tall at 1.8 meters and possessing relatively good looks, Ms. Zhuang's boyfriend exerted an allure. He hailed from a privileged family, with his father holding a prominent role in the hotel industry and his mother serving as a civil servant. Following an initial period of dating, their relationship entered a stable phase of courtship, during which Ms. Zhuang's boyfriend began to pres-sure her into sex. While she deflected her boyfriend's requests with "wait until we're married," he invoked the newly emerging sexual mores then coming into vogue, insisting that "if you loved me, you would sleep with me." He also said, "Your reluctance to have sex stems from your desire to be with someone else!"—an observation that carried some validity, as Ms. Zhuang was not entirely convinced about the prospect of marrying him given he was less industrious and capable than herself, with his advantages primarily stemming from his parents' social and economic standing. While he never resorted to physical violence, the boyfriend's attempts at persuasion ranged from sulking and pestering to verbal outbursts.[38]

Caught in an ambivalent stance over the potential for marriage, and compounded by her boyfriend's persistence for sex, Ms. Zhuang performed nonpenetrative activities (using her hands and mouth) to delay vaginal-penile intercourse. The virginity battle persisted for two years until Ms. Zhuang met someone new at work (from a reputable family and with ambitious career aspirations). She deemed her new prospect more suitable and, in their subsequent relationship, she more readily acquiesced to his sexual advances, culminating in their marriage one year later.

Ms. Ma (Xi'an) succumbed to her now husband's persuasion and they had sex prior to marriage. Reflecting on her thoughts during their disagreements at the time, she said she had pondered whether a breakup would lead to judgment over her non-virginal status by a future partner. She concluded: "I went along with it [premarital sex] because I planned to marry him. But it was also true that, after we did it, I felt I ought to marry him." In contrast with Ms. Ma, who was obliged to marry her boyfriend, by preserving her "virginity" Ms. Zhuang empowered herself to terminate the relationship with her first boyfriend and transition to an alternative partnership with her eventual husband. The outcome of the virginity battle therefore played an influential role in determining who held the upper hand in exercising agency in the desire market. To an extent, the conflict between men's insistence on sexual activity and women's efforts to postpone intercourse was perceptible in the earlier generation, for example, Mr. Dong and Mrs. Dong. However, this battle intensified among the one-child generation as the advancing market economy and heightened competition fostered a more pronounced calculation in dating choices and mate selection.

Mr. Dai (Xi'an) was one of the 1980s male interviewees who expressed difficulty with the notion of a nonvirgin wife, feeling such a woman was "used." While acknowledging that rape placed its victims in a special category, he was less accommodating toward women who had lost their virginity in other circumstances. Although he was pleased that his wife had been a virgin when they met, he lamented that one of his life's regrets was not having sex with his first girlfriend, believing that it could have solidified their relationship. He confessed that they had spent a night in the same hotel room but did not progress due to his inexperience and hesitancy. When questioned about the possibility of a woman choosing not to marry him despite losing her virginity, Mr. Dai casually responded: "I wouldn't lose anything. After all, I would have been with a virgin." When I asked, "But you'd have lost your virginity too?," he responded, "That's trivial for men. It doesn't matter." Some other men were more preemptive, one remarking, "If you want to marry someone, have sex with her; take the first step to gain an advantage [*xian xiashou wei qiang*]."

Women and men are unequally positioned in the desire market. The concerns of both Ms. Ma and Ms. Zhuang stemmed from contradictory expectations of male peers regarding a bride's virginity, on the one hand, and a woman engaging in sex to demonstrate love and commitment, on the other. This exposes the enduring influence of the "male in the head" complex in which women evaluate their own sexual behavior based on male expectations.[39] In the absence of men relinquishing the virginity complex, a new sexual script that frames sex as an expression of love and commitment introduces tension and obstacles for young women as they navigate the realms of sex, intimacy, and marriage. Conversely, the combination of the virginity complex and the new sexual script becomes a strategic maneuver for men to "capture" their desired partner (male interviewees' original term, *zhuaizhu*).

When I initially asked male interviewees about consent in the context of first sexual encounters, all asserted a respect for their girlfriends' wishes. However, as subsequent discussions unfolded, a noteworthy shift occurred among a significant minority (30 percent). Several admitted that the first time they had sex with their girlfriend it resembled an act of forceful imposition,[40] epitomized in the everyday vernacular *baiwang ying shanggong* ("a general forcefully pulls the bow"). One respondent was explicit: "Although my girlfriend said no, her body said yes so I entered her." The notion of consent could therefore be manufactured by men and, as a female counterstrategy, being a virgin could be manufactured too (as illustrated in Ms. Zhuang's case).

"Torture" or "Fun"

A discernible shift toward premarital sex emerged between the 1980 and 1990 cohorts of G3s, underscored by the focus group discussion opening this chapter—in other words, "the virginity complex still exists, but finding a virgin is quite rare these days." An urban woman from Guangzhou elaborated, shedding light on its underlying causes: "As women, we usually take part [in sexual relations] with the intention of marrying the man. However, not all relationships last since men frequently choose unilaterally to end them."

Acknowledging this reality, 1990-cohort urban men displayed greater ambivalence, one professional stating, "Personally, I don't have a strong preference, but I can't speak for all my friends." However, an intriguing observation is that, despite their seemingly liberal attitude, more than half of the men claimed their wives or their girlfriends were virgins when they first met. Whether or not the virginity complex remains part of young men's mindsets, the code that sex is an integral aspect of a loving relationship has become normalized among the 1990 cohort. To consider the impact on women of this way of thinking, I juxtapose below two contrasting examples of how women navigated the normalization of premarital sex within distinct micro-institutional environments.

Born in 1992 into a Xi'an professional urban family, Ms. Kong successfully avoided sex in her first two relationships. However, with her third boyfriend, someone she cared for and aspired to marry, she acquiesced to his request for sex at the age of twenty-four, but the experience proved to be a source of inner turmoil.

> MS. KONG: When I was with him, I felt utterly disoriented. He assumed the role of guiding me through various acts, and I found the entire experience torturous. I felt like a complete novice, mechanically following his instructions to take various positions. My mind was constantly plagued by the question of whether such a behavior was right or wrong.
>
> I: What were your thoughts?
>
> MS. KONG: They perhaps had a lot to do with my obedient nature toward my parents. I was raised to be truthful and avoid deceit, yet I found myself attempting to conceal and shield them from this aspect [premarital sex] of my life, dreading their discovery. So, every time I had sex with my boyfriend, I was gripped by fear. Firstly, I was anxious about my parents finding out. Secondly, I worried about the possibility of an unintended pregnancy.
>
> I: Did you use protection?
>
> MS. KONG: Yes, but there's always a chance of pregnancy, even with a condom. There's the risk of it tearing, for instance. I also fretted about the prospect of him not being the right person to marry, which could compel me to find someone else. What if the parents of that future "someone else" took issue with the fact that I wasn't a virgin?[41] Consequently, love-making didn't provide any sense of pleasure. Instead, it felt like a form of torture, particularly for my mind.

The relationship with Ms. Kong's third boyfriend ultimately came to an end as he did not want to marry her and, while Ms. Kong's now husband did not comment on her nonvirgin status when they consummated their relationship, the unspoken past continued to cast a shadow over her thoughts.

Miss Lu (born 1992), growing up in a rural family in Shandong, encountered her first boyfriend at a university and their relationship lasted two years. She lost her virginity at the age of twenty-two after a slightly inebriated Christmas celebration, recalling: "It was a pleasant sensation, leaving me desiring more. Both my boyfriend and I were experiencing this for the first time so our curiosity and passion were palpable. We even procured a range of inexpensive sex toys to enhance our exploration."

At the time, Miss Lu considered her first boyfriend marriage material, but his family and village were even more impoverished than her own and this engendered strong opposition from Miss Lu's mother. When Miss Lu received an offer to pursue a postgraduate degree in Guangzhou her boyfriend joined her, but the relationship failed to flourish. Miss Lu became associated with a close-knit group of friends who interacted with foreigners and feminist activists, broadened her horizons, and drove her to consider ending the relationship. But her boyfriend vehemently resisted and a middle ground was reached in which Miss Lu was free to have sex with other men on the condition that she avoid pregnancy, thereby preserving the prospect of their potential marriage. Through dating apps, Miss Lu met a series of foreign lovers, leading to a number of brief, intimate liaisons albeit marred by instances of fear, encompassing concerns of potential sexual violence and the risk of infection.

Miss Lu's relationship narrative underwent a pivotal transformation when her boyfriend found a new partner and she became more seriously involved with a much older European man whom she deemed the ideal partner for her. She recalled, "Thanks to the significant experience he brought to our relationship, our intimacy was seamless. However, his Catholic upbringing made him shy when it came to taking certain sexual positions. For reasons unbeknownst to me, but which were perhaps rooted in trust issues or other factors, he was hesitant or even refused to take part in certain kinds of sexual activity. During the final year of our relationship, our sexual interactions dwindled significantly and we eventually split up."

One major factor contributing to their break-up was disagreement about future plans—in particular, Miss Lu's wish to settle in Europe clashing with his preference to stay in China. As a result, Miss Lu moved on to another relationship with a different foreign man, about which she commented: "As things are at the moment, we rarely bother to engage in elaborate foreplay. This perhaps stems from our deep mutual trust, allowing us to transcend the romantic pretense often portrayed in cinematic depictions of love-making. Our encounters are characterized by untainted sensuality, a quality that I genuinely appreciate—uncomplicated and enjoyable." While Miss Lu was satisfied sexually, an underlying tension with her mother persisted, her mother commenting: "My daughter had a big ambition [to marry a foreign man] but none of them seems keen to get married."

The sexual histories of Ms. Kong and Miss Lu defy the binary narrative of modern (urban) versus traditional or backward (rural) perspectives. Ms. Kong grapples with the ethical quandary between her boyfriend's pressure for sexual intimacy and her parents' admonitions against premarital sex, while Miss Lu emerges as a sexual adventurer. The juxtaposition of their experiences elucidates how their respective micro-institutional environments yield contrasting interpersonal and intrapsychic scripts.

Ms. Kong, raised as an only child, remained under her parents' watchful gaze, dwelling alongside them until her marriage. The underlying assumption is that, for sexually reputable women, a proper place to sleep at night is either their parents' or husband's home.[42] Her parents refrained from providing comprehensive information about sex, with her mother's counsel limited to "not allowing anyone to take advantage of you." School also offered no guidance and dating was prohibited.[43] Pursuing higher education in her hometown[44] further perpetuated her parents' influence over her conduct. This sheltered environment imbued Ms. Kong with a perception of sex as fraught with danger and risk, paralleling observations made about young women in eighteenth-century China.[45]

Conversely, Miss Lu's upbringing unfolded in a Shandong farming village. Confronted with the demands of raising two children and securing their livelihood, her parents directed less attention and energy toward their daughter than their son. Before going to study at a university in Ji'nan (the capital of Shandong province), Miss Lu's mother offered her no warning or counsel. Relocating to coastal Guangzhou, where attitudes toward premarital sex were more liberal than in northern cities,[46] significantly expanded her horizons. The turning point came when she took up with a close-knit group of friends who interacted with foreigners and feminist activists. She was then introduced to local Guangzhou initiatives such as *The Vagina Monologues*, which exposed her to the interpersonal scripting that featured women's agency and pleasure in sexual encounters. A connection with a university roommate, who was also actively engaged in premarital sex, forged a deep friendship, enabling an exchange of insights. Despite Miss Lu's rich sexual experiences, her microenvironment remained constrained by the broader societal context and this was one of the reasons she wanted to move abroad. Chinese men (including the young and educated) continue to label young women who have embraced their sexual agency with derogatory terms like "slut" (*sao*) or "broken" (*lan*) to highlight their disapproval and disdain, and Miss Lu strategically pursued partners drawn exclusively from a circle of foreign men.

Within my sample, Ms. Zhuang and Ms. Kong represented the G3 norm and Miss Lu the exception.[47] Numerous urban G3 women pursued their university education within their hometowns, living with their parents until marriage. Although some of these women engaged in premarital sex, the majority eventually married the individuals with whom they shared those experiences or devised strategies to preserve their virginity.

A Hierarchy of Premarital Sex

Mr. Gang was in his final year of undergraduate studies in Guangzhou when we first met. He enthusiastically described to me four categories of premarital sexual practices among his male peers at university. The first category involved casual sexual encounters or "hookups" (yuepao) with the ethos "I enter your body, not your life." These encounters were facilitated through online dating apps—the same avenue through which Miss Lu connected with her foreign acquaintances—and relied heavily on the physical appearance of potential partners, showcased through profile photos and videos. The success rate for securing such hookups was relatively low, Mr. Gang noting that "Seven of us tried, but only one succeeded."

The second category encompassed premarital sex within a relationship. Mr. Gang engaged in non-penetrative sexual activity, similar to that of Ms. Zhuang during her "virginity battle," with his first girlfriend, but did not progress to full intercourse before the relationship ended. His second girlfriend was "perfect" in his eyes so he ensured that they engaged in full intercourse. However, uncertainty loomed due to her plans to undertake postgraduate study abroad.

The third category entailed high-end commercial sex. One of Mr. Gang's close friends, the son from a wealthy family with a beautiful girlfriend from a compatible background, felt unsatisfied with his girlfriend's physique ("too thin"). He therefore paid 4,000 yuan per service for high-end commercial sex workers, without his girlfriend's knowledge. Mr. Gang commented, "I find this behavior not very commendable. However, if I had the money, I might try it too."

The final category was low-end commercial sex, often pursued at leisure facilities such as saunas and costing 300–400 yuan per service. Young men such as Mr. Gang considered this "sordid" (wocuo) and associated it with low-income middle-aged men. Nevertheless, some male classmates resorted to this option in order to lose their virginity.

Mr. Gang's portrayal of the sexual landscape broadly aligns with trends across China. Findings from the Sexuality of China Surveys indicate an increase in the proportion of Chinese men aged eighteen to forty engaging in commercial sex, rising from 11.0 percent in 2000 to 22.3 percent in 2015;

similarly, the proportion of Chinese men aged eighteen to thirty-five seeking sex online rose from 6.6 percent in 2010 to 8.3 percent in 2015.[48] Given the lengths many of Mr. Gang's female urban peers went to, and the mental anguish they endured, in order to preserve their virginity, my findings reaffirm the assertion of Parish et al.[49] that there is a reemerging double standard in premarital sex behavior, where men enjoy greater social latitude for sexual experimentation.

Mr. Gang's narratives also underscore the intricate interplay of masculinity, class, and intimacy. While a notion of masculinity is constructed through the control and "consumption" of female sexual bodies, to be "autonomous" consumers[50] in the realm of intimacy, men need economic capital. This unveils a global hierarchy of men. At the top are white Western men, representative of global capital flows but also highlighting a colonial legacy that is reinforced in media stereotypes that cast non-white men as less attractive or less "masculine" and whose allure threatens established relationships—illustrated, for instance, in the possibility of Mr. Gang's girlfriend finding someone else when studying abroad. Closely behind are affluent urban men, such as Mr. Gang's friend, who legitimize their sexual practices by equating financial power with masculinity. At the bottom of this hierarchy are poor rural men. Miss Lu's rural boyfriend was willing to accommodate her sexual escapades to maintain their relationship because he was aware of his inferior standing within the realm of intimacy compared to both urban Chinese and foreign men in Guangzhou.

Gendered Intergenerational Transmission

Amidst a broader societal discourse that accentuates women's responsibility for their sexual reputation,[51] the senior generation of women, including mothers and grandmothers (G1 and G2), wield a pivotal role in transmitting gendered sexual scripts to their female descendants. As with Ms. Kong's mother in Xi'an, many urban mothers caution their daughters against engaging in premarital sex. Grandmothers also contribute to this moral guidance, as shown by a G1 from Tianjin who said, "I always urged my granddaughter not to engage in it [sex]. I told her, 'Don't follow others. If you get pregnant before marriage, you'll carry that stigma for life. It won't just be future in-laws who look down upon you, but your future husband too. If you two have future disagreements, he might hurl the word 'shameless' at you. You must be mindful of this [sexual] aspect and safeguard your reputation."

Conversely, when asked about advice given to one-child generation men, many mothers were taken aback by my question, one (G2, Guangzhou) commenting: "I haven't really considered that. When my son and his girlfriend traveled together and shared a hotel room, I didn't give much thought to it." This attitude underlines the view that women are more adversely affected by premarital sex, stemming from the disproportionate impact of unplanned pregnancy on women (including physical and reputational harm).

Rural mothers were less explicit than their urban counterparts, but this did not signify a lack of concern about their daughters' virginity. G3 migrant women reported their mothers inquiring about interactions with male co-workers in their migration destination and details of female-only factory dormitories. They also discouraged dating in the city and set up their daughters with young men from families in local or neighboring villages. However, differing conditions in Shandong[52] and Fujian villages generated contrasting behavior. The former, a low-income locale, offered only low-paid migration opportunities mainly in factory work and on construction sites. While sharing a similar skewed sex ratio,[53] the relatively small income disparity among families reduces the significance of the virginity complex in marriage negotiations. A G2 Shandong mother encapsulated this sentiment: "It was already challenging to find a wife for my son so we didn't ask about that." Conversely, the Fujian village boasts affluence, with a widening wealth gap between villagers. With wealthier rural families willing to pay a substantial bride price for the proposed bride's clean sexual history, women's virginity acquires a monetary value in marriage negotiations.[54] Ms. Zhao (G3, Fujian village, see chapter 2), a university graduate, was in a stable three-year relationship with her university boyfriend. Although marriage plans were in motion, uncertainties remained. An exchange between her and her mother illustrates the delicate dance of navigating virginity within the Fujian marriage market:

I posted a picture of myself and him together on my WeChat. My mother chided me, "You're naive, not knowing how to protect yourself." She urged me to remove the photo from my WeChat. She advised me that in future relationships, be it dating or marriage, I must never divulge my past, as men often mind women having multiple relationships. . . . She recounted to me an instance where one of my cousins' sexual history became known, leading to a significant reduction in her option for potential partners. As a result, she ended up marrying an older and less affluent man.

Two years later, after disclosing this exchange, Ms. Zhao's relationship ended. Her mother wanted her to pursue hymen repair surgery[55] but Ms. Zhao remained ambivalent: "I understand my mother's intention is to shield me. Yet, I struggle with the idea of deception." Ironically, while Mother Zhao advised her daughter on strategies to conform to the male expectations of marrying a virgin, she simultaneously expressed annoyance with her son for not engaging in premarital sex: "Your brother has no balls. He lacks courage to do it [sex]. I bet that he won't dare to sleep with a woman until he gets married."

Marital Sex

MS. SHEN: I don't know how to put it.

I: For example, did you feel happy when you did it or did you feel that you had to do it?

MS. SHEN: Feelings towards each other are most important. When two people have a good relationship, the experience [sex] is bound to be a happy one. But if you had to do it, that wouldn't be good; it would be as if you were forced.

I: Did you initiate sex in your marriage?

MS. SHEN: Well, shall I put this way: it's something both husband and wife can ask for.

(Ms. Shen, G1, illiterate, farmer, three sons, Shandong)

MS. MU: When we were very young, it wasn't particularly pleasurable. I feel as we've grown older, our feelings deepen and that [sex] changed too.

I: When did it change?

MS. MU: Until my son was five or six years old. Before that I didn't have a strong desire myself but I could go along with him [my husband] when he asked for it. My desire grew stronger after that period.

I: Did you say no when you didn't have the desire?

MS. MU: No, I didn't turn him down nor did I treat it as a chore [yingfu] either as I do like him. As we've grown older our feelings have deepened. The longer we are together, the better we know each other. The more inseparable we become, the greater love we have for each other. It is like us becoming one. That's a great pleasure, ecstasy. Nowadays it's [sex is] just wonderful. Whichever one of us asks for it, the other always readily responds, unless I or he is too tired or busy.

I: Did you initiate sex?

MS. MU: Yes, of course. He actually felt very happy when I do.

(Ms. Mu, G2, middle school education, worker, one son, Xi'an; see chapter 2)

MS. JIANG: When we were young, it [sex] was not very harmonious. He could only satisfy his own needs but not necessarily mine. Nowadays, he is more mature and calm—quite different from when he was young. It [sex] is becoming more and more enjoyable. Between 25 and his early 30s, he changed jobs and the pressure for him to succeed was high. I had given birth to our daughter. There were all kinds of demands and it [sex] didn't feel very pleasurable. Nowadays, he is much calmer, considerate and he seldom loses his temper. He knows my likes and I know his. After so many years of adjustment [*mohe*⁵⁶], we know each other very well. It [sex] feels mutually fulfilling.

I: Did you initiate sex?

MS. JIANG: Throughout my life, I haven't been very active in taking the lead nor do I have strong physical desire. Perhaps this is linked to our Chinese culture. Over time, my mind has taught my body to be passive. My husband has a much stronger sexual drive. I don't have many such needs, but I don't resist it [sex] either.

(Ms. Jiang, G3, master degree, manager, one daughter, Guangzhou)

Sex, Intimacy, and Marriage

Pan Suiming argues that the one-child policy (1979–2015) and other factors like the availability of abortion and contraception have played a significant role in creating a new space for marital sex in China by decoupling it from procreation. In my study, while younger generations were more eloquent in articulating their sex life, there is not a clear generational shift from sex for procreation to sex for pleasure. As exemplified in the above narratives, feelings between husband and wife play a critical role in constructing women's sense of sexual pleasure. As conjugal intimacy is deeply embedded in wider family ties and life (see chapter 2),⁵⁷ through the link between sex and conjugal intimacy, Chinese marital sex is responsive to the dynamics and rhythms of family life and therefore becomes "familial sex."

The three women's narratives are indicative of satisfactory "familial sex" from the wives' perspectives. Despite different eras and socioeconomic status, their family life shared certain characteristics. For example, husbands fulfilled their financial responsibility for the family (albeit without doing much housework) and husband-wife interactions were healthy with limited conflict. Both Ms. Mu and Ms. Shen admitted to having short tempers and praised their husbands' tolerance, with Ms. Jiang noting that her husband had the ability to calm her down when she was hotheaded. Despite specific periods of difficulty, the relationship with extended families⁵⁸ was largely positive. Ms. Shen and Ms. Mu's in-laws had three sons who agreed to an equal distribution of old age care among them. Ms. Jiang and her husband did not have any siblings (due to the one-child policy) so extended family relationship management was much easier, albeit with a greater burden of care for older generations falling upon their shoulders. Deep intimate knowledge and interdependence deriving from years of mutual support and adjustment (*mohe*) produced a feeling of intimacy between these women and their husbands, which in turn is reflected in the sensuality of sex.

Male participants echoed the link between conjugal intimacy and sex: "Two people manage everyday affairs. Only when the relationship between them is good, 'couple life' [i.e., sex, *fuqi shenghuo*] is good. If there are lots of conflicts between them every day, the conjugal relationship is bad and 'couple life' becomes bad too" (urban G1, male). Because of the gender and age differ-ence between myself and interviewees in this study, older men were generally less forthcoming about their own sexual experiences and feelings. Men from the one-child generation were more willing to reveal their own stories; for example the middle-level manager Mr. Lin (urban G3) explained how his sex life had evolved:

> MR. LIN: I feel that with experience I have developed from a novice to an expert. Contrary to feeling unfamiliar and awkward when we first started, nowadays you know when the other person wanted it [sex] with merely a small gesture.
>
> I: Did you feel sex is pleasurable or an obligation?
>
> MR. LIN: It [sex] is a normal biological need. The only time I felt it was an obligation was when we were trying to have a child. We got married in 2009. For the initial few years, the money was tight so we opted to delay having children. In 2012, when we wanted to have children, all of a sudden we found it so difficult to get pregnant. My wife was calculating the days when she was ovulating—that was the only phase I felt it [sex] was an obligation. After childbirth, when her bleeding ended, we restarted it [sex]. Perhaps I have a stronger sexual drive than my wife so I wouldn't regard having it [sex] as an obligation. I often wake my wife up in the middle of night. She will say "wait until tomorrow." But I am insistent. She will then say, "okay, okay," go to the toilet to wake herself up, and then cooperate.
>
> I: Does your wife ever take the lead?
>
> MR. LIN: I think this comes with experience. At the beginning, she knew nothing. Nowadays she will sometimes take the lead, for example, lying on top of me when we are doing it [sex].

Mr. Lin's account acknowledges women's view (e.g., that of Ms. Mu and Ms. Jiang) concerning the impact of intimate knowledge on familial sex life. However, women's sense of pleasure is "relational," resting on the notion of "mutuality" and encompassing their feeling of love (in Mu's case) or attentiveness (in Jiang's case) from their husband. Mr. Lin does not derive sensuality from his wife's response but it is grounded in a narrative of *self*, constructing his pleasure as an innate biological need. This difference cannot simply be attributed to the gender stereotype that men are sexually driven and women are emotionally oriented. Mr. Lin explained that "if two people can achieve a deep emotional bond [*shenjiao*], the process of love-making would be more beautiful," implying that his feeling for his wife has not yet reached the highest possible level and therefore the quality of sex could also still improve. This gender difference might be more attributable to the social construction of men's and women's positions in a marriage. As Evans[59] reveals, despite changing modes of female representation in different eras (reformist discourse, Maoist discourse, and post-Mao discourse), a key theme that reproduces and resurfaces is a notion of wifehood that centers upon a wife's service and responsiveness to her husband. Men's pleasure is therefore grounded in a male-centered conjugality while women's pleasure is a means to reaffirm and strengthen conjugal intimacy.[60]

There are degrees of gender fluidity in familial sex practices. Where there is conjugal intimacy, the cultural script of sex whereby men are active and women are passive can loosen up and be disrupted. As in the words of Ms. Shen (rural G1) and Ms. Mu (urban G2), women could equally initiate sex when they had the desire. However, fluidity in initiating and performing sex did not mean that the gender script was undone. Ms. Jiang explained that "my mind has taught my body to be passive," reflecting how deeply gendered cultural codes are entrenched in Chinese society. When both Ms. Jiang (urban G3) and Ms. Mu did not enjoy sex, they tried to "accommodate" (*peihe*) the needs of their husbands for the sake of the relationships. Ms. Jiang's husband preferred to have sex first thing in the morning and persuaded her to adapt to this. For Mrs. Lin (urban G3), forcing herself to wake up and cooperate was her form of "accommodation." In these accommodating acts, conventional gendered sexual labor was completed as part of the tacitly agreed heterosexual contract.[61]

Sexual harmony / pleasure emerged as a dominant discursive theme through which younger, urban women interpreted and explained their marital experiences, whether positive or negative. This phenomenon is closely linked to the transition in public discourse on marital sexuality from being silent in the Mao era to treating sex as a key facet of married life in post-Mao China.[62] Although marital sexuality has received increasing attention in public discourse, whether the significance of sex in marriage has risen or declined over time is difficult to ascertain. Older interviewees, who experienced the constraints of socialist production schedules and more limited marital privacy, tended to believe the younger generation placed a greater emphasis on sex in marriage due to their increased resources and leisure opportunities. Younger interviewees felt the pressures of China's market economy, including extended working hours and heightened competitiveness, compelled them to prioritize familial responsibilities, such as providing for their families, educating their children, and caring for aging parents. However, one thing all generations agreed upon: while sex is important in marriage, it is not the singular driving force and instead it ebbs and flows in conjunction with the rhythms of family life.

Life Cycle

The intimacy of familial sex intersects with a family life cycle but in differing ways for men and women. Like many women, Ms. Jiang and Ms. Mu highlighted the period when their child was young as the time when they felt sex was least pleasurable. Both were in full-time employment[63] and returned to work after their maternity leave. However, childcare and full-time work caused considerable stress as these women tried to fulfill their family and workplace obligations. In Ms. Mu's case, due to her three-shift rotation factory work pattern, she needed to coordinate and accommodate her mother-in-law in arranging childcare (see chapter 4 grandparenting). In Ms. Jiang's case, her professional job involved overnight business trips that conflicted with her new childcare responsibilities. While Ms. Jiang's parents helped during her daughter's infant years, responsibility for her daughter's educational development (identifying and taking her to after-school activities) fell on Ms. Jiang's shoulders and this burden caused her own career to stagnate (see chapter 1 on gendered intensive parenting). Ms. Jiang's husband was unaware (or willfully ignorant) of her frustrations and this led her to experience feelings of depression and to contemplate divorce.

Ms. Kong (see "'Torture' or 'Fun'" above) became a mother in 2021. While she appreciated the way in which conjugality provided a legitimate space for her to relax her mind during sex, she commented: "Right now sex is something I can do or do without, but it's not a must as there are so many roles [mother, wife, daughter, and full-time professional] I need to take on; all these family demands make me so tired."

Parenthood affected men's sex lives too. As Mr. Lin's wife co-slept with their child, he needed to identify the right moment and be careful not to make a sound in the same bed when their child was asleep. Needless to say, the impact upon men was more related to the practicality of accessing sex rather than negotiating conflicting demands between work and family, as the women did.

Old age was another phase in which familial sex required adaptation. Ms. Zhu (G1, Guangzhou) enjoyed a good sex life up to her sixties when it became "not very harmonious." She explained how she managed the transition:

> After 70, men's sex desire and function decline rapidly. For women, I feel the decline is less. You [pointing to me] haven't reached that age, so you wouldn't know. From my own experience, as long as being alive, women still have sexual desire. But for men, their sexual performance deteriorates as they get older. So there is a dissonance. Certainly there is hugging and kissing and so on, depending on how we feel [qingdiao]. We also like traveling together and holding hands. All this feels very nice, so we just go with the flow [shunqi ziran].[64]

Her narrative suggests a few things. First, in contrast with pathologized and marginalized assumptions[65] that sexual deterioration is an inevitable accompaniment of aging, Ms. Zhu and her husband worked together to find supportive solutions to overcome late-onset barriers to sex. Second, Chinese couples' understanding of sex is often confined in the domain of vaginal-penile intercourse: while Ms. Zhu considered her sex life "not very harmonious," she recognized the pleasantness in other non-intercourse intimate activities. Third, the dynamics between gender and sex shift across the life course. Men's sex drive peaks at puberty but declines gradually from their mid-thirties, while women's desire and pleasure in sex, discouraged in their younger years by childbearing and rearing, is more likely to peak in later life.[66] Ms. Zhu still had the desire, but her similarly aged husband was unable to perform. The reversal in sexual prowess as men and women age was also reported by Ms. Mu who felt she "now" (i.e., her early fifties) enjoyed the most satisfying sexual experience with her similarly aged husband, although there were occasions "when he wanted [to have sex, but] his body wouldn't let him." Nevertheless, she considered this "part of the life processes" they shared.[67]

Control and Resistance

When a relationship is less intimate and satisfying,[68] familial sex can shift from being an expression of feelings and intimacy to a means of control and resistance. Ms. Ho (urban G2, Xi'an) was unhappy with her marriage and vowed that she would not choose the same husband if she had the chance to relive her life.[69] She commented:

> Our conjugal life was not that harmonious, sometimes we did it [sex] a bit reluctantly, at others it was more like a routine. Once it [sex] was done, it was over. I didn't have any strong sensuality. We have been sleeping

separately for several years. I sleep in another room with my grandson. Sometimes if he came to the room [for sex], I just said that I needed to brush my teeth or to be with my grandson. He then left angrily. I think I have managed to suppress his desire to the point that he has almost none now. We haven't done it for two years but it doesn't worry me at all.

The same word "suppress" (*ya*) was used to describe her husband's dominance over her in everyday affairs. It became clear that Ms. Ho's deliberate suppression of her husband's sexual urge was a means of dealing with the dissatisfaction she felt about her marriage and combating the power exerted by her husband in their everyday interactions. Ms. Ho was triumphant in the way she reported her reverse sexual coercion, implying that this was not merely about sex but a conjugal power struggle and one she felt she was winning. In contrast with Ms. Mu and Ms. Zhu, Ms. Ho did not feel that she had a sex drive herself, which she attributed to the fact that she looked after her four-year-old grandson full-time and found this exhausting. Ms. Ho's lack of sex drive reflects a second major child-rearing phase in the familial sex cycle for women and so Ms. Mu's enjoyment of the best sex experience being later in life might prove to be short-lived once her son becomes a father.

In some relationships where the husband did not acquiesce in his wife's rejection of his advances, familial sex turned to violence. Ms. Tian (rural G2, casual laborer and farmer, Shandong; see also "Extramarital Affairs" below) was a victim of such domestic abuse.[70] In addition to being beaten by her husband (sometimes at the order of her father-in-law), she endured a traumatic sexual relationship. Mr. Tian wanted to have sex every day, and while she constructed excuses to refuse his advances,[71] he forced himself upon her even during menstruation and pregnancy leading to vaginal infection and a premature childbirth. While the domestic violence subsided over the years, the sexual coercion continued up to the point of my fieldwork, although lessened because her husband had become a long-term migrant worker in the city and only returned to the village sporadically. In contrast with Ms. Mu (also G2), Ms. Tian's experience of sex was "torturous" (*jian'ao*): "I felt sore every time, tears in my eyes and my brain hurting. Sometimes I couldn't control myself, when he did it [ejaculated], but had not yet got off me, I would slap his face. He said that he was most afraid of this act of mine."

While their conjugal relationship was clearly a broken one, and they found each other "annoying" (a word they both used to describe the other), the husband continued to pressure his wife to have sex with him. Given his status as a low-paid, unskilled migrant worker, sex appeared to be one of the few ways by which he could exercise his masculine control and power. With her restricted capacity to circumvent familial sex,[72] Ms. Tian's slapping of her husband after sex was a form of conscious resistance.

Sex Education

Across the three generations, the trajectory of sex education has evolved from self-exploration to pornographic consumption. While daughters were warned against premarital sex, across all generations, no guidance was provided for men and women upon entering marriage. Interviewees noted that the only time parents might give advice on familial sex was when the young couple had difficulty conceiving a child. Older generations primarily relied on self-discovery. For most, information on "sexual harmony" and other sexual matters was scarce to nonexistent in their work unit or village committees.[73] With no information from other sources, older generations resort to a naturalized approach; when I asked how she learned about sex, Ms. Shen (rural G1) replied: "Dry tinder is bound to catch fire, one will naturally know." Unfortunately, some rural women suffered as a result of their husbands' ignorance—for example, getting urinary infections—and Ms. Mu reported that her husband did not successfully penetrate her until several weeks into their marriage.

For the one-child generation, the lack of a comprehensive sex education[74] has led to an increased reliance on pornography as an instructional tool. Many young men, such as Lin and Dai (see "The Virginity Battle" above) used erotic novels and videos during their high school years for both pleasure and to increase their understanding, while some couples watched soft porn together. Pan argues that, since the high rates of pornographic consumption (79.4 percent among males aged eighteen to twenty-nine in 2015) have not resulted in a corresponding rise in sex crimes in China, pornography does not necessarily violate the interests of women and should be tolerated.[75] However, I would caution against viewing pornography as a legitimate source of education. While it can provide information on sexual positions, it does not address underlying gender inequalities and can reinforce gendered sexual scripts. For example, some women reported feeling pressured to emulate certain behaviors witnessed in pornographic content, leading to uncomfortable dynamics in the bedroom. Ms. Ma (see "The Virginity Battle" above) complained: "After watching those movies, my husband also expected me to perform in this way, for example oral sex, which I really hate." Another G3 woman commented: "I am normally quiet during the process [sex] but my husband somehow got the idea that women must moan and make 'appropriate' sounds in order to show their enjoyment; nowadays I have to make this noise too."

Like the feminized construction of childcare (see chapter 1), there is an expectation that men are "naturally" better in knowing about sex and so women should comply with their ideas. Ms. Jiang (G3) explained, "I have no knowledge [of sex], it all comes from my husband. It seems that men know all sorts of aspects about it [sex], as if they are born to know about it." Such a biologically determinist notion of gender and sexuality, which has persisted across various eras in China, before and after 1949, perpetuates the hierarchy of men and women in sexual relations.[76] A better form of sex education in China, in particular one that is more balanced between men and women, seems to be a pressing requirement.

Extramarital Affairs

There has been a consistent increase in extramarital sex in China over the past two decades; rising from 16.5 percent among men and 4.5 percent among women in 2006[77] to 33.4 percent for men and 11.4 percent for women in 2015[78] and then 35 percent of married men and 23 percent of married women in the most recent 2020 China Private Life Survey.[79] The Chinese infidelity rate is now similar to some developed countries, and above that of the United States.[80] Institutional transitions such as improving living standards, increased mobility (rural to urban migration causing marital separation), reduced surveillance from the work unit system, increased opportunity (e.g., through business trips), and a flourishing media focusing on topics like intimacy and love in the post-Mao era have collectively contributed to the environment and opportunities for extramarital affairs.[81] Nevertheless, extramarital sex remains socially stigmatized, with survey findings consistently indicating a high level of disapproval—81 percent in the 2020 China Private Life Survey.[82]

In my sample, the older generation (G1) overwhelmingly disapproved of extramarital affairs, viewing them as "immoral" and potentially "harmful to children and families." While no one admitted to having an extramarital affair themselves, some rural G1 participants shared anecdotes about women during the Mao era who exchanged their bodies for food and resources in times of extreme poverty. Among the middle generation (G2), a portion of interviewees (30 percent, mostly male) expressed sympathy and understanding when recounting stories of extramarital affairs involving others. In contrast, a majority of G3 male respondents (70 percent) were quite open to the idea of marital affairs. One G3 (married, Xi'an) said, "Love and marriage don't always go together. Many marriages are loveless. Many love stories don't end in marriage, so we should be more tolerant towards extramarital affairs. You can't guarantee that you'll only love one person in your life. As long as the affair doesn't disrupt family life, it should be acceptable."

Young female respondents held diverse views, with some strongly disapproving due to concerns about potential harm to children, while others followed the male logic that affairs could be kept separate from "normal" family life. Between these views was a belief that women could have an "emotional lover" (*lanyan zhiji*) without crossing the physical boundaries of engaging in sexual intercourse—a refashioned cultural code of female chastity. Interviewees who held more tolerant views of extramarital affairs tended to differentiate between emotion-driven affairs and those focused on monetary exchange, generally favoring the former and disapproving of the latter. Nonetheless, due to the moral implications associated with extramarital affairs, interviewees often distanced themselves from personal involvement. Only twelve (all G2 and G3) out of 260 interviewees admitted to or hinted at an extramarital affair of their own. The following two case studies have been selected to represent voices from different socioeconomic positions, providing insights into the complex and multifaceted human narratives underlying this trend.

Marital Retribution—"For Whatever I Can't Get from My Husband, I Can Get from Him"

Ms. Tian spent her formative years in a subsistence farming family in Shandong. At the age of twenty-two, she was introduced to her husband through a village matchmaker, and they married the following year. Despite having three potential suitors at the time, her mother vetoed the alternatives[83] and favored her now husband due to his perceived honesty and good looks. While Ms. Tian had reservations,[84] she found him physically attractive, and their meeting marked her first intimate connection with a man outside her family, which she described as her "first awakening of love" (*qingdouchukai*). Pressured by her family, particularly given her younger brother's earlier marriage, Ms. Tian agreed to a quick marriage. However, the union soon became fraught with difficulty. Poverty and financial instability[85] strained their intimacy, and domestic violence shattered any emotional connection Tian had felt toward her husband.

In 2016, Ms. Tian met a married middle-aged party officer from another village at a social event. Their connection deepened through WeChat communication, eventually leading to a secret extramarital affair.

> MS. TIAN: We regret meeting each other so late in our life. When we are together, it feels so comfortable. He is tall [1.78 m], educated [to senior middle school] and extremely caring towards me.
>
> I: In what ways?
>
> MS. TIAN: If he had visited a restaurant with his colleagues, he'd find a way to take me there. As long as he can afford it, he buys me the

clothes I like. We never visit those luxury shops because he said we
need to wait until he can afford it. Sex with him is fabulous—just
wonderful—as if he'd been born for me.

I: Is this because of his technique?

MS. TIAN: No, not technique. It's because of the feelings we have for one
another. Whatever I can't get from my husband, I can get from him.

The affair was well hidden and they made a pact to "live together as a
couple" when they are eighty years old.

Ms. Tian framed her affair as a form of retribution against her husband,
motivated by her resentment toward him, citing the Chinese idiom, "It's never
too late for a gentleman to take his revenge" (*junzi baochou, shinian buwan*),[86]
to emotionally bolster her actions. She could not divorce her husband out of
concern for her children and natal family; her husband was a low-paid migrant
worker, and she worried that divorce might drive him to drastic action such as
physically hurting her natal family and / or children.[87] She also emphasized,
"I need that 20,000 yuan" (her husband's annual income) to support her two
children, adding: "If I had plenty of money and if I were an orphan, I could
give him some money and then take my children far away from here." She
admitted having wanted to run away on many occasions in her life but had
never been able to.

Ms. Tian's situation reflected the common finding in both Chinese and
Western literature[88] that the quality of a couple's relationship is a critical factor
contributing to extramarital affairs. However, there is a risk of treating extramarital affairs as merely a form of individual transgression as this explanation
overlooks the workings of broad structures in shaping individual choices in
life. The institutional context includes stagnant rural development that perpetuates urban-rural inequalities, a market economy that reproduces gender
discriminations in pay and the reluctance of the state to directly confront
familial patriarchy.[89] The village committee and the local police did not intervene as wife-beating is viewed a normal and a domestic issue. There is a
cultural tendency to blame the victim for failing to meet her conjugal obligations, so Ms. Tian did not ask her natal family for support, but on some occasions, hid from her husband at the home of female friends.

While it may seem that her affair brought Ms. Tian some welcome (and
perhaps deserved) relief from years of marital misery, her full narrative added
nuance to this as she vacillated between idealizing her lover as a perfect partner and using the language of "play" to distance herself from this ideal. On the
one hand, Ms. Tian perceived the relationship with her lover as deepening,
likening it to that of a husband and wife, and welcomed the mutual support,
such as accompanying each other to hospital visits and helping with household

repairs. However, on the other hand, Ms. Tian acknowledged that her lover had other liaisons and she turned a blind eye to these.

MS. TIAN: We spend time together just for relaxation, play and fun! As long as he buys me food and clothing, I just let him do as he wants.

I: Do you want to get married to him?

MS. TIAN: Children, parents . . . They all need a stable and complete family. And if we do get married, perhaps we wouldn't be as happy as we are now.

I: Why?

MS. TIAN: Chinese men all have their shortcomings as they inevitably have several women in their life.

Ms. Tian's narrative reflects a complex interplay of cultural codes, captured in her use of words such as "feelings," "play," and "exchange." These codes were utilized to make sense of the multifaceted extramarital relationship.[90] However, inconsistencies among the codes generated anxiety for Ms. Tian, who struggled to reconcile her actions with societal moral norms; the resurgence of neo-Confucian family ideologies in public discourse adds tensions to her intrapsychic scripting. Several months after disclosing her affair to me, Ms. Tian shared an article with me that had been circulated on WeChat entitled "Never Sleep with Anyone Other Than Your Husband," which emphasized female fidelity to one's spouse. While I initially dismissed the article as controlling and baseless propaganda, Ms. Tian's ambivalence persisted, leading her to question whether challenges, such as her lover's health issues and her children's unmarried status, were karmic consequences of her infidelity. Thanks to this moral dilemma, Ms. Tian felt trapped in a state of uncertainty about whether or not to continue the affair.

Desiring Subject—"I Wish I Were a Man so that I Could Have 'Three Wives and Four Concubines [sanqi siqie]'"

Ms. Shi (G2), grew up in the working-class milieu of Guangzhou. Following her graduation from senior middle school in 1990, she responded to a local government recruitment initiative that sought service workers for state-owned entertainment establishments (hotels and massage saunas) in Shenzhen. Her workplace was frequented by businessmen and government personnel and from these clients she met her first boyfriend, the son of a government official. They got engaged, but before they could be married her fiancé was killed in a violent border conflict between Shenzhen and Hong Kong and so Shi returned to her hometown of Guangzhou heartbroken.

After a period of mourning, Ms. Shi was able to draw upon her early connections within local government and secure sponsorship to attend business courses at a prestigious university and this in turn enabled her to become a company manager by the age of twenty-six. While working, she fell in love with a fellow company manager, but family pressures led him to choose to marry the daughter of his parents' friends, ending their relationship. Shi then agreed to marry her third boyfriend, a medical doctor. He treated her very well—however, she became gradually disappointed in him as she felt that he lacked career ambition. After being married for two years (with no children), Ms. Shi divorced him in 2000 and married her current husband (another company manager). Although she never openly admitted to having had an extramarital affair, the short time that elapsed between her divorce and second marriage, as well as the financial generosity she displayed to her former husband, whom she paid 700,000 yuan as a divorce settlement, certainly hinted at an affair having occurred.

When asked in what way her gender had influenced her life choices, Ms. Shi commented:

> I wish I were a man so that I could have "three wives and four concubines." [Laughter] To be honest, even after getting married, I did develop crushes on good-looking men. When I was young, I found I couldn't control my feelings towards other men . . . It's OK for a man to have a wife and lovers too. He can provide material and emotional support to all of them. Others won't accuse him of philandering—they just say that he's lucky. But for a woman, the same thing isn't possible. It is embedded in our tradition.

Conscious of how the gender system structured sexuality, Ms. Shi took precautionary measures to anticipate and manage any potential extramarital affairs that her husband might have:

> MS. SHI: Although I know my husband hasn't had extramarital affairs in the past, I cannot guarantee how he might behave in the future. If he happens to meet someone he falls in love with, he can easily abandon me. However, if he has a strong sense of responsibility, he'll care about his family. Since his child is his own bloodline, he won't abandon his child. That's one of the reasons why I decided, once I'd given birth to our daughter, to have myself sterilized.
>
> I: Why?
>
> MS. SHI: My husband would never be able to take my child away if he divorced me. The judge would not allow this to happen knowing that I couldn't have any more children. I have seen it too much in my circles. I feel that all men are unreliable. When I was young I could easily find

someone else to love me. But when you get into your 40s and 50s, men still can find younger women but women can't. That's why you often see that once women reach a certain age, they use every means not to let a husband go when he has an affair. If she's a very proud person, the humiliation and anger can even make her ill. So it's better to be prepared. Think of all the things that you can get hold of and control—like children and money, for example. If you want to trap your man or make it emotionally painful for him, a child is a powerful bargaining chip. In my case, my child will always belong to me, even if he leaves me.

Ms. Shi's narrative offers important insights into how extramarital affairs are viewed in China. Firstly, it underscores the gendered nature of such relationships, shaped as much by cultural and institutional factors as by mere biological desires. The gendered cultural script of sexuality serves as a legitimizing resource for men, epitomized in everyday vernacular: "three wives and four concubines." This cultural legitimization is facilitated by the vertical segregation of the labor market producing far more rich men than rich women. Second, Ms. Shi's account reveals how the dynamics between "living for oneself" and "living for others" shift for women across their life cycle—an example of the "elastic individual" (see the Introduction). When she was young, Ms. Shi embodied the desiring subject in Rofel's theorization of post-Mao neoliberal governance[91] and envisioned being free from all kinds of constraints: "From the age of 18, I haven't spent a single penny of my parents' money. I spent whatever I earned. I was very self-centred. Nobody could control me." At the time, her "elastic individuality" was stretched to full. However, following the birth of her child, her life became oriented toward her daughter, for whose sake she gave up her managerial job and instead focused on investing her savings in order to spend more time with her daughter. The child, symbolically serving as a cushion or backup, provided her with a sense of security that her husband did not ("all men are unreliable") and in this way, despite being a modern successful woman, Ms. Shi had resorted to the same strategy of building a uterine family as that used by rural women in Taiwan in the 1970s.[92] Ms. Shi's evolution from a desiring subject to an insecure wife, reveals the intertwining impact of ageism and sexism in the political economy of desire—contributing to the weakening of the "elasticity" of her individuality. For Ms. Shi, the concern was not that her husband might have an affair, but his potential abandonment of the family. Older men, viewed as mature and successful, can continue to attract younger women but older women, viewed as out-of-date and asexual, become deserted in the desire market. In short, the desiring subject in post-Mao China is profoundly gendered, classed, and aged.

The accounts of Ms. Shi and Ms. Tian illuminate the nuanced landscape of divorce in China.[93] Ms. Tian felt unable to petition for a divorce, while Ms. Shi initiated the divorce from her first husband, but then feared divorce from her second husband. With limited resources and weak support from her natal family (which was also materially disadvantaged), Ms. Tian found it impossible to escape from her marriage. At the age of twenty-eight, Ms. Shi—rich and without children, felt that divorce was no impediment to the fulfilment of her personal desires and happiness. However, by her mid-thirties[94]—only a few years after she had married her second husband—despite still having access to considerable resources, Ms. Shi felt that she had become devalued in the desire market and so needed to take drastic defensive action to prevent a divorce. These dynamics resurface in the one-child generation; a female Guangzhou G3 summed it up: "In Guangzhou, quite a few of my female classmates divorced and then remarried. For divorced women after 30, it would be challenging to find a suitable partner. But unless they already have a child, divorced women between 20 and 30 are still popular and eligible."

While the common view holds that men have a much longer shelf life in the desire market, average married men remained cautious toward divorce, even if they had an outside lover. A married male (G3, professional) in Xi'an explained:

> In China, the cost of a divorce is far than a man can afford, especially when his child has already reached primary school age. He stands to lose all his savings, having to start again from scratch [baishou qijia]. This is because the Marriage Law takes the view that the spouse who is involved in the extramarital affair is the faulty party and must therefore carry the full financial penalty. . . . When all is said and done, it seems to me that those who turn the Coloured Flag [lover] into the Red Flag [wife] are still rare.

Nevertheless, while Chinese law is designed to preserve and protect the institution of marriage, affluent men—for example, Ms. Shi's husband, who was the head of a company and had accumulated a considerable fortune—are still able to afford the financial penalty. It was for this reason that Ms. Shi took the precautionary action of having a child before undergoing sterilization.

Arising from a combination of institutional factors—including limited dating prior to marriage, depoliticization of everyday life, exposure to Western media, the social and material barriers to divorce, and continuing significance of the family institution—discreet extramarital affairs have become an effective mechanism for Chinese men and women in post-Mao China to satisfy their desire to experiment with sexual and emotional intimacy while continuing to fulfill routine family obligations. These extramarital affairs offer a glimpse of a "pure relationship" (where individuals stay together only insofar as their self-development and erotic needs are being met) and "plastic sexuality" (a decentered sexuality freed from both reproduction and subservience to a fixed object) described by Giddens[95] and provide an escape from conventional familial roles, allowing participants to experience a more liberated and fulfilling form of intimacy. For example, while Ms. Tian was effectively a victim in her familial sex life, she took a proactive role in her extramarital sexual activity, explaining, "I can behave playfully. I like making noises when I feel high. I like trying all kinds of positions."

Despite periods of freedom, gender norms continue to influence extramarital relationships. Ms. Tian expected her lover to cover all the expenses involved, a normative condition for their "pure relationship." Ms. Shi, despite her wealth and status, reported taking the initiative to chat up a handsome young man in a bookshop when she was in her early thirties, but then cut him off as soon as she found out that he lacked "substance" (i.e., ability and ambition). These narratives illuminate a complex tapestry of gender, class, and desire. While offering a temporary escape from conventional norms, extramarital affairs remain rooted in an allegiance to social relations that both transgress and perpetuate established social divisions.

China's Sexual Revolution Revisited

Pan Suiming has been a prominent advocate of the notion of a sex revolution in China. His argument posits that the sex revolution, with its fivefold characterization (see below), commenced in the late 1980s and culminated in the early twenty-first century, when China entered what he terms a "sexualized era." However, the findings presented in this chapter challenge the revolutionary narrative, revealing a paradoxical process of change and continuities across three generations.

First, my investigation does not conclusively establish the one-child policy as the pivotal factor in this transition from procreative to pleasurable motives[96] (i.e., a revolution in sex philosophy). As noted by previous scholarship,[97] China's fertility rate had begun declining prior to the one-child policy's implementation, owing to the "later marriage, longer birth spacing, fewer children" initiative in the early 1970s. This had already extended the nonreproductive sexually active period for a substantial number of individuals, evidenced by the limited two (urban) to three / four (rural) children per couple among the G1 generation born in the 1940s. A very important observation that emerges from my analysis is that far from marital sexual behavior displaying a clear generational shift over time, a common theme across all three generations is that not only the quality of the conjugal relationship but also the rhythms of family life have shaped the way in which familial sex ebbs and flows across the life course of a married couple.

Second, the proliferation of publications and products with a sexual content as well as the spread of pornography has constituted a veritable revolution in the public representation of sex in China—one that stands in stark contrast to the suppression of any public reference to sex during the Cultural Revolution. However, this chapter also highlights what has remained an enduring challenge across all three generations: namely, the reluctance to discuss sex openly, as shown by my interviewees' frequent use of euphemisms when referring to sexual activity. In short, sex is still a cultural taboo in China.

Third, my findings confirm a progressive increase in sexual experimentation over time but suggest this as a gradual evolution rather than a revolution in sexual behavior. Earlier generations approached familial sex with a self-exploratory attitude and some interviewees (for example, Ms. Mu) acknowledged the invention of new positions and initiatives to invigorate their sexual relationships, though they were unable to label these positions. The pivotal distinction between members of early generations and the youngest cohort was in the embedding of such practices in post-Mao Chinese public culture, transforming them into elements of a system of sexual knowledge much of which derived from the consumption of pornography.

Fourth, there has been an escalating prevalence of premarital and extramarital affairs spanning three generations, but this does not unequivocally support the notion of a disassociation between sex and marriage. Instead, these behaviors are frequently contextualized within the framework of Chinese marriage and family, imbuing them with legitimacy and justification. For instance, while premarital sex becomes increasingly normalized, many instances of such behavior serve as a "transitional stage" leading eventually to marriage. Even within the sphere of extramarital affairs, the simultaneous pursuit of individual desires and fulfilment of familial responsibilities remains the preferred option of many men and women.

Fifth, my findings dispute a revolutionary narrative in women's sexuality. With the exception of a minority of women who openly embrace feminist principles to assert their sexual agency and pleasure, the majority of women remain considerably constrained both in their mindset and behaviors. Although some fluidity has emerged in gender roles within spheres of sexual intimacy, gendered scripts often tend to adapt themselves to new eras.

The scope of China's sexual revolution[98] has been notably limited. While the public portrayal of sex has witnessed a significant expansion, other aspects of change have been marked by gradual adaptations as well as continuities with the past, culminating in an assemblage of traditional and modern elements rather than a linear model of social change. The impact of social change has also been uneven as individuals are positioned in varying social structures and so have negotiated the change differently. Either way, the pervasive sexualization of everyday life in China in the twenty-first century (Pan's "sexualized era") has distinctly favored men and a privileged elite, perpetuating entrenched social divisions rooted in gender and socioeconomic disparities.

The institutional changes during the transition from the Mao to post-Mao era have been overseen by the party-state; therefore, the various changes in Chinese sex life have effectively been facilitated by the state. However, the state has simultaneously played a key role in limiting the potential that China's sexual revolution has for women, in particular remaining silent on gender inequality in sexuality while enforcing a normative model of conjugal heterosexuality and reinforcing a biological determinist understanding of wifehood and motherhood across the Mao and post-Mao divide. Miss Lu, the exceptional case in my study, poses some hope for an alternative sexual imaginary for Chinese women; yet the recent authoritarian moves, curtailing a space for an independent feminist movement and promoting the reemergence of neo-Confucian ideologies, suggests the tide may have already turned in another direction. For the majority of women, their capacity to mix new and old values in sexual toolkits is limited, obliging them constantly to fall back upon gendered cultural scripts to make sense of their experiences as well as perpetuating them through generational transmission.

4

The Old Caring for the Young

I: How does the childcare experience of your elder son differ from that of your younger son?

DAUGHTER HUANG: My mother took on most of the responsibility for my elder son's childcare since he was born. She looked after him until he was well into his primary school years. I recognize that her help was critical and I am grateful to her for it. But living with her so closely on a daily basis also gave me headaches. For example, she constantly nagged me for being no good at doing housework, and sometimes she bragged about how the children of other older people in the neighborhood were so filial, implying that I was unfilial! When I had my second child, she was unwilling to offer the same level of childcare so we paid a market premium for a nanny to live with us. Raising the second child was far more expensive.

I: Which mode of childcare do you prefer?

DAUGHTER HUANG: [Pause] Probably I would prefer to engage a nanny rather than have help from my mother. At least once I had paid the nanny, I could order her around. But there is no way to tell my mother what to do.

Daughter Huang (urban G3, born in 1983) and I first met in a Cantonese restaurant in downtown Guangzhou in 2017. At the time she was the mother of a four-year old son and, intrigued to know who was looking after her son that evening, I asked how the childcare arrangements for her son had evolved since his birth. *Phase one*, Daughter Huang's postnatal confinement, was spent in the city where her husband grew up (a second-tier city in central China). As her parents-in-law were part of a care coordination plan for her husband's frail grandparents, they could not travel to Guangzhou to welcome their first grandchild. It was for this reason that Daughter Huang went to her husband's home city to give birth. Since her own grandparents had already passed away in the 2000s, she was accompanied by her retired parents, who were originally from Guangzhou. Her husband's family also engaged a rural female relative to serve as a live-in postnatal carer (*yue sao*) to look after Daughter Huang and the baby for two months.[1] Daughter Huang's bilateral extended family provided supplementary support. For example, her mother-in-law took charge of going to the market to buy fresh and nutritious food and other supplies, while her own parents washed the clothes of the mother and child. Because of his limited paternity leave, Daughter Huang's husband, a middle-level company manager, came back for one week but then returned to Guangzhou to continue work.

At the beginning of *phase two*, when Daughter Huang had two months' maternity leave left,[2] she and her parents returned to Guangzhou with the baby. To support her daughter, Mother Huang moved in with the couple and occupied the second bedroom of their two-bed flat, while Father Huang stayed in their flat, around fifteen minutes' walk from where the young couple lived. Daughter Huang and her mother were the main carers for the baby day and night. During *phase three*, when Daughter Huang resumed her full-time job as an administrator in a government service unit (*shiye danwei*), her mother became the main carer for the baby during weekday working hours (9:00 a.m.–5:00 p.m.) and her father helped with shopping and preparing meals. In the evenings Daughter Huang took over care of the baby and then shared a bed with him at night. Her husband normally came home quite late (around 9:00 p.m.) and so his main interactions with his son took place at the weekend. During *phase four*, when Daughter Huang's son reached his third birthday and was eligible for kindergarten, Mother Huang moved back to her own flat to live with her husband, but took charge of pickups and drop-offs to and from kindergarten. She also cooked the evening meal for her daughter's family. On evenings when Daughter Huang had to work late or be away for other social events (including meeting me), her mother would stay over and sleep with her grandson. The fourth phase of the childcare pattern continued into the son's primary school years. Mother Huang continued to play a critical role in providing after-school support, cooking dinner for the grandson and keeping an eye on his general welfare. But as the boy grew older, Daughter Huang's role as his educational mentor also increased. Daughter Huang organized various extracurricular activities for him and she and her mother shared the responsibility of taking him to different classes. Mother Huang spent her free time at neighborhood events such as plaza dancing,[3] something she had taken up during phase three.

In 2021 Daughter Huang became unintentionally pregnant. When told of the news, Mother Huang tried to persuade her to have an abortion: first, she felt that with her daughter soon to reach forty, it would be too tiring for her to raise another child; second, she was herself reluctant to take on more childcare responsibilities, stating, "I want to have own life back." Daughter Huang's in-laws were far more keen, but as they were still carers for their own parents were unable to offer practical assistance to the couple and instead paid the deposit on a larger three-bedroom flat to demonstrate their support and hope for the arrival of their second grandchild. Daughter Huang, meanwhile, was some-what ambivalent about having a second child: on the one hand, she found the idea of having to bring up and educate two children daunting, but on the other hand, she was concerned about both the physical and mental implications of an abortion. In the end, she had the second child (a boy).

A lack of practical support from Daughter Huang's parents and in-laws meant the experience of raising the second son was completely different from that of the first.[4] In Daughter Huang's words, the second son's child-rearing was "socialized" (*shehuihua*, meaning marketized).[5] She and her husband paid for a postnatal nanny to live with them for the first two months, then they hired another live-in nanny (*yuyin shi*),[6] who took sole charge of looking after the second son as well as cooking meals for the whole family. Daughter Huang explained, "She's completely in charge of my second child for the entire 24 hours. She feeds him, sleeps with him, takes him out to play . . . basically does everything. I have no spare time or energy as I need to focus on our older son whose studies in the primary school are getting intensive."

I caught up with Daughter Huang in 2023 and she explained to me that she planned to employ the same nanny until her second son was three years old and could enter kindergarten, but had not yet decided whether to pay some-one to do the kindergarten pickups and drop-offs or find some means of doing them herself. When asked why childcare responsibilities in her family had remained so gendered, Daughter Huang was accepting of her circumstances: her own career had stagnated, while her husband had been promoted to the senior management at his firm, meaning he earned considerably more than she did and this covered all family expenditure including the mortgage repay-ments on their two flats (i.e., her own income was for her discretionary spend-ing). Since Daughter Huang's husband successfully fulfilled the breadwinner role expected of men, she did not challenge his lack of involvement in bringing up their two sons.

While Daughter Huang's growing family affluence resolved what might otherwise have become a childcare crisis when she had a second child, her narrative highlights the tensions and challenges faced by many child-rearing families in China. Since the 1950s, Maoist political campaigns mobilized Chi-nese women to participate in work outside their homes and conferred upon G1 and subsequent generations the identity of a full-time worker. As a result, returning to work after giving birth becomes a familiar and expected rite of passage for young mothers. Unfortunately, the disparity between state maternity leave (which varied by generation from two to four months) and shortage or absence of childcare facilities for infants and children forced women to seek help from their own mothers and / or mothers-in-law. In this chapter, I first outline the ubiquitous phenomenon of grandparenting in contemporary China. Through an analysis of two case studies—those of Family Huang (an urban family living in Guangzhou) and Family Xu (a rural family in Hunan village)—I examine how grandparenting has morphed into a familial obligation across three generations, albeit with contrasting institutional configurations among urban and rural families. Finally, I explore the intergenerational and gender dynamics involved in grandparenting, revealing a nonlinear portrait of generational change, continuity, and diversity.

Ubiquitous Grandparenting

In many countries grandparenting is a common response to childcare pressures.[7] However, there are several features that make Chinese grandparent-grandchild ties distinctive, compared to those of US and Western European societies. First, in contrast to the bilateral but matrifocal kinship structure found in the West, patrilineal and patrilocal Confucian kinship rules prioritize ties with paternal grandparents over those with maternal grandparents.[8] This prescriptive hierarchy is exhibited and enforced in Chinese linguistic terminology, which contrasts "grandchildren" (the children of one's son) with "outside grandchildren" (children of one's daughter).[9] A second distinction is the sheer scale of childcare provision by Chinese grandparents. By the mid-2010s, according to the 2015 Chinese families development report, grandparents were the main carers for 60–70 percent of children aged six and under,[10] more than double that of the United States, where around 30 percent of grandparents provide childcare support.[11] Further, unlike many Western grandparents who have custodial care of their grandchildren because of parental drug abuse, divorce, or imprisonment,[12] Chinese grandparents provide childcare on a full-time basis even when their adult children's families remain intact.

The prevalence and intensity of grandparenting in China has led some scholars to argue that grandparenting is "an expression of cultural continuity"[13] rooted in Chinese culture, that "emphasizes blood ties and intergenerational support."[14] Ubiquitous grandparenting is viewed as a normative cultural practice and is a taken-for-granted care arrangement in contemporary Chinese families.[15] A contrary line of argument is that the grandparenting phenomenon represents a clear break with the traditional Chinese cultural pattern of intergenerational exchange embodied in the concept of filial piety.

Grandparenting could therefore be seen as an example of Chinese "neo-familism" / "descending familism" whereby the dominance of the senior generation has given way to a situation in which the focus of both grandparents' and parents' love and care is channeled into the grandchildren.[16] A third interpretation of Chinese grandparenting argues that as family members adaptively respond to changing external constraints and opportunities for the benefit of the household, grandparenting has become a strategy to maximize the well-being of the entire family.[17]

This chapter throws new light upon these claims through generational and urban-rural comparison. First, because existing scholarship is predominantly grounded in cross-sectional data, there is a lack of understanding of grandparenting practices in the past. Did grandparenting exist in previous generations? If so, what form did it take? Under what circumstances was it activated? The answers to such questions help delineate institutional configurations whereby grandparenting in China has morphed into a social norm over time. In particular, I show below how state institutional arrangements affecting grandparenting differed between urban and rural families. Urban socialist institutional arrangements—the combination of more or less mandatory full-time employment of women below the age of fifty and the adoption of unusually early and gender-differentiated retirement ages (fifty for blue collar women workers, fifty-five for white collar women workers and sixty for men)—has encouraged and facilitated a much more active role for grandmothers in helping bring up children since the 1950s. During the reform era this trend has been intensified by changes in the state's childcare policies for children under the age of three. Contrastingly, for rural families, it is mainly the state institution of the *hukou* system that has worked to make grandparenting ubiquitous, particularly during the reform era. The loosening of migration restrictions and the huge surge of migratory labor, combined with the daunting obstacles to raising and educating rural *hukou* children in cities, have given rise to the large number of left-behind children under the sole care of grandparents in rural areas.

Second, disputing a linear interpretation of generational change that charts a power shift from the old to the young, I reveal the existence of a variety of intergenerational cooperation patterns affecting the care of grandchildren and illustrate how these patterns have been shaped by configurations of multiple forces. These forces include state childcare policies, demographic profile, living arrangements, other family care commitments, and kinship rules, all of which have exerted varying degrees of pressure at different points in time. Finally, beyond the umbrella of the collective family welfare, I posit a delicate micro-level intergenerational negotiation in which individual family members seek to achieve a balance between prioritizing family interests and protecting individual self-interest. As with other family practices—for example, when children are growing up and choosing spouses (chapter 1 and chapter 2)—grandparenting is also embedded in a constant process of adaptation and realignment between and within generations.

Case Studies

The Huang Family in Guangzhou

I have already outlined above the childcare arrangements for Daughter Huang's two sons. Here, I trace the previous two generations' memories of grandparents and their role in providing childcare. Mother Huang (urban G2, born in 1951, the second out of four siblings) was born into a working-class family in Guangzhou. Her parents were first-generation settlers who had migrated from the suburban villages of Guangzhou before 1949 and since the 1950s had worked in a state work unit. Both her grandmothers died before she was born, while she only met her grandfathers once, on the single occasion they both visited the family in the city prior to their deaths in the 1960s. With no support network in the city, her parents adjusted their shift pattern (her mother taking the day shift while her father worked at night) so that they could provide coordinated care for their four children. As the elder sister, Mother Huang also helped her parents look after her younger siblings. During her middle school years, in 1968 she was sent to work on a farm in rural Guangdong as part of the Cultural Revolution. In 1977 she returned to the city and was initially allocated work in a textile factory before being transferred to another factory making food, where she remained until she retired at the age of fifty.

Father Huang (urban G2, born in 1948, the youngest of three sons) also grew up in a working-class family in Guangzhou. In the 1940s his parents moved to Guangzhou from one of its suburban villages to undertake manual work. He never met his paternal or maternal grandparents, all of whom passed away prior to his birth. After graduating from senior middle school at the age of eighteen, he worked in a state department store until retirement at the age of sixty. Through a work colleague introduction, Father Huang met and married Mother Huang in 1980 and their daughter was born in 1983. Since Father Huang was the youngest son and his elder brothers had already moved out of the family home,[18] the couple lived with Father Huang's parents for many years in a one-room shack of around twenty square meters. Despite this shared living arrangement, Father Huang's mother took no part in the childcare of Daughter Huang.

Daughter Huang (urban G3, born 1983, an only child) was initially sent to the nursery school affiliated with the textile factory where her mother returned to work after her maternity leave of fifty-six days. At three, Daughter Huang was sent to the kindergarten affiliated with Father Huang's work unit as it was thought to be of superior quality. Until the age of ten, Daughter Huang lived in the one-room house, but because of the tension and petty squabbles that arose from the close living arrangement, particularly between her mother and her paternal grandmother, Daughter Huang valued her relationship with her maternal grandparents—and the escape it offered—more highly than that with her paternal grandparents. After 1993, Father Huang secured accommodation through his own work unit and the nuclear family moved out, but Daughter Huang's preference for her maternal grandparents continued. During the summer holidays, her mother often sent Daughter Huang to spend the day with her maternal grandfather who lived near Mother Huang's work unit. (The maternal grandfather was the primary carer of his wife, Daughter Huang's grandmother, who suffered from dementia.) As the only grandchild who stayed with them at the time, Daughter Huang was the sole focus of her maternal grandfather's love and attention: "I vividly remember my grandfather holding my little hand and taking me to eat dim sum [zaochai]. He never scolded me and always gave me whatever I wanted. I felt extremely close to him."

Son-in-law Huang (urban G3, born 1982, an only child) grew up in a provincial city in central China. Like Daughter Huang, he felt closer to his maternal grandparents than his paternal grandparents during his childhood. His paternal grandparents lived with his father's younger brother and seemed to prefer him. As a result, Son-in-Law Huang had limited interaction with his paternal grandparents, paying occasional visits at weekends or during Chinese festivals and he described the relationship as "so-so" (yiban). By contrast, his maternal grandmother came to live with them when he was born and looked after him until he entered kindergarten at three years old. During his primary school years (age seven to twelve), he was also sent to live with his maternal grandparents on summer vacations. This extensive provision of childcare was made possible because Son-in-Law Huang's mother was the eldest of four siblings (with one younger sister and two younger brothers), which meant for an extended period he had been the only grandchild on the maternal side of his family. He excelled at school and entered a university in Guangzhou. After graduation, he worked in a trade company and met his wife through a mutual friend.

The Xu Family in Hunan Village

Grandpa Xu (rural G1, born 1931, the third of five siblings) never met his grandparents, all of whom died young. His own parents also died when he was around twelve years old and so, along with his younger siblings, he was brought up by his elder sister who was five years older. In 1946, at the age of just fifteen, he married a cousin in accordance with a family proposal arranged prior to his father's death and the couple went on to have seven children, of whom only three survived (a daughter and two sons). His wife, and mother to his children, died in the late 1950s and so in 1961 he married Grandma Xu (rural G1, born 1934, the fourth of five siblings), whose previous marriage had failed because of her infertility.[19] Grandma Xu did meet her paternal grandfather during her childhood as he lived with her father; however, her grandfather took no part in her upbringing as he considered it her own mother's responsibility. Grandpa Xu and Grandma Xu spent their entire life in the village, working in the fields and raising animals for sale. When they reached their mid-seventies, they ceased their agricultural work and the two sons started to provide them each month with fifty kilograms of grain and cash of 600 yuan per year.

As he grew up, Elder Son Xu (rural G2, born 1956, the second of three siblings) did not meet his paternal grandparents as they died before he was born. He also had very limited memories of his maternal step-grandparents, who lived in another village and died in the late 1960s. In contrast, Daughter-in-Law Xu (rural G2, born 1957, the eldest of four siblings) lived close to her paternal grandparents, although they provided no childcare assistance. Instead, as the eldest of the four children, Daughter-in-Law Xu helped her mother look after her three younger brothers.[20] When she was eighteen, her parents died suddenly in a work accident, leaving her to bring up her three siblings, the youngest of whom was only ten. She explained:

> My paternal grandparents were still alive but didn't care about [bu guan] us. Indeed, we four grandchildren provided for them for six years. My father had provided for them financially [yang; see chapter 5] and after my parents died, we four did the same [yang]. As my parents had died at work, the production brigade compensated us with 3,000 work points—1,000 points for each brother. My paternal grandparents thought that with so many work points we were quite well-off; my paternal uncle [her father's younger brother] was also a bit calculating. He made us give 30 or 40 yuan to my paternal grandparents every year. We did this for six years until they passed away.

Elder Son Xu and Daughter-in-Law Xu had two sons. In his thirties, Elder Son Xu migrated to a coastal city for better paid construction work, but he returned to the village within a few years due to poor health. Thereafter he worked on the family fields to which he added the land of fellow villagers who had left the village in search of migrant work.[21] Daughter-in-Law Xu undertook housework and helped her husband with farm work, although in more recent times her primary responsibility had shifted to looking after the two daughters of their elder son.

Elder Grandson Xu (rural G3, born 1980, with one younger brother) never met his maternal grandparents because they died before he was born, but he often saw his paternal grandparents in his childhood as they lived only ten minutes' walk from his home. As his mother had remained in the village (rather than temporarily migrate to the city for work), his paternal grandparents only had an occasional role in helping to bring him up—for example, during the harvest. Despite this, Elder Grandson Xu still felt close to his paternal grandparents and recalled vividly how Grandpa Xu had often lectured him about studying hard. Unfortunately, these lectures and the will of his extended family, fell on deaf ears because Elder Grandson Xu did not progress beyond junior middle school and he became a migrant worker at the age of sixteen, working in various industries, including manufacturing, construction, and, most recently, on a food stall in a supermarket in the city of Dongguan. Grandson Xu earned more than his parents, and his financial status, as well as the close relationship he enjoyed with his paternal grandfather, was reflected in his shared contribution with his brother—on behalf of his father—to a banquet for his grandfather's eightieth birthday.

Granddaughter-in-Law Xu (rural G3, born 1982, the fourth out of five siblings), wife of Elder Grandson Xu, grew up in a neighboring village. Both her paternal grandparents died before she was born, and she was brought up by her mother and elder sisters. Because her family was poor, she dropped out early from junior middle school at the age of thirteen and became a migrant worker in order to help fund her younger brother's education. She met her husband through an introduction arranged in her home village, and they were married in 2002. They had two girls (born in 2002 and 2007). Under Xu family pressure, she underwent two abortions before eventually having a son in 2011. She left her first two children with her mother-in-law when they were only a few months old and planned to do the same with her third child. Speaking of such arrangements, she sighed: "People like us have no options so we have to leave the children with my mother-in-law. We asked my mother-in-law to keep an eye on their studies. If the grandparents don't bother to do so, there's nothing else we can do. We have to work outside to make money and we can't bring the children with us."

The Emergence of Grandparenting

As in other industrializing societies, women's increased participation in the labor force and significant increases in life expectancy have played a key role in activating grandparenting. In China, however, since 1949 various microinstitutional configurations have encouraged urban and rural families to turn to grandparents as a major source of childcare support.

Pre-1949 Conditions

Due to widespread severe poverty, many grandparents passed away before their grandchildren were born. For G1 whose grandparents lived long enough to meet them, interactions with paternal grandparents were closer and more frequent than those with their maternal grandparents because of the strength of patrilineal and patrilocal norms. These themes were commonplace in the narratives of many urban and rural families prior to 1949. In more affluent families, paternal grandparent(s) were likely to feature in children's lives as they grew up, although the senior generation generally eschewed any responsibility in looking after their grandchildren. As a male G1—one of six siblings—who grew up in a three-generational courtyard home in Xi'an explained: "Although my paternal grandparents [who owned a grain store] lived in the same courtyard as us, they didn't look after us. Occasionally, when they visited relatives, we grandchildren would join our grandparents. But that was all—quite different from nowadays when one grandchild is the focus of attention and cared for by four grandparents."

The general perception of cases in which grandparents did display more involvement in caring for the children was that such behavior was driven by sentiment and affection. One woman from Tianjin who had grown up with four younger sisters in a three-generational household where her grandfather was the owner of a chain of bookstores recalled: "We all lived together. I was my paternal grandmother's favorite as I was the most obedient child. I remember vividly how she patiently combed my long hair into plaits after washing it. It was my paternal grandmother to whom I felt closest when I was little." Nevertheless, her mother remained her everyday carer and her paternal grandparents would not allow her mother to go to work as they felt it was her responsibility to raise her five children. Indeed, for most G1s, their mothers and / or elder siblings were the main carers and they were predominantly brought up at home. Concealed in this reality was a desperate shortage of childcare facilities before 1949; for example, in the 1940s in Tianjin—a city with a population of 1.71 million—there were just twenty-eight nursery schools, caring for a mere 1,388 children in total.[22]

In the patchy memories of another era, grandparents tended to emerge as largely symbolic and remote figures of respect within the extended family. Some G1s brought up in multigenerational households recalled that as children they had to bring water to their grandparents' room in the morning for them to wash their faces and again in the evening to wash their feet. Grandparents merely followed their own wishes in their interactions with grandchildren without a familial or social expectation to care for them. Caring for grandchildren was voluntary, occasional, and reflected the degree of intimacy they felt

toward them. The portrayal of close grandparent-grandchildren relations in
G1 interviews is reminiscent of the vivid depiction of a happy grandparenthood captured in the well-known Han dynasty phrase, "enjoying sweets and
playing with the grandchildren" (*Hanyi nongsun*).

Post-1949 Conditions—Urban Families

In the 1950s the Chinese Communist Party effected a mass mobilization of
women into paid work in the belief that women's liberation could only be
achieved through employment outside the home. Since childcare responsibilities were constrained by work commitments, the state encouraged work units
to set up their own childcare facilities.[23] Additionally, childcare facilities were
put in place by street neighborhood committees and individual childminders.[24] However, there was a persistent shortage of childcare facilities for most
age groups and availability varied considerably between different work units
and different urban neighborhoods. Given the demanding work schedules of
urban young mothers and fathers and against the background of an earlier
retirement age for older women, even in the 1950s grandmothering had become a necessity.

Another institutional factor that increasingly encouraged urban grandmothering was grounded in the state's changing policies toward childcare
facilities for children under the age of three. In early post-1949 years, public
care facilities for children (up to the age of three) were prioritized, and between 1949 and 1956 the number of nursery schools[25] increased from 119 to
5,775.[26] The Great Leap Forward (1958–1961) witnessed a further explosion of
nursery school provisions, but many of these closed in the 1960s and it was
not until 1975 that the admission rate returned to the mid-1950s level.[27] After
the Cultural Revolution, to alleviate the burden on women workers, the state
prioritized the reestablishment of childcare facilities—for example, in 1980,
28.3 percent of children aged three and below were in nursery schools
nationwide,[28] and a survey of nine cities subsequently revealed that, by 1987,
42.3 percent of children up to the age of three were in nursery schools.[29]

Economic restructuring of state enterprises in the late 1980s and early
1990s, as part of an effort to improve efficiency, prompted a shift in state discourse on provision of childcare. A 1989 policy recommendation on children's
education issued by the Ministry of Education decreed that care of children
aged three and under would no longer be part of the state's welfare remit[30] and
official publications subsequently called for the marketization of former work
unit childcare facilities. As a result, childcare facilities catering for children
aged three and under began to disappear—between 2000 and 2005 the number of nursery schools throughout China declined by 70 percent.[31] By 2017 a

mere 2.2 percent of Chinese children up to the age of three were enrolled in a nursery school with grandparents assuming the dominant role in caring for their grandchildren, especially in the early years.

STATE BENEFICIARIES (1949–1990S)

About one-third of the urban families I interviewed, who had their children prior to the 1990s, were affiliated with a work unit that had sufficient financial resources to provide childcare facilities or were willing to bear the cost of childcare. These circumstances left grandparents as the second choice in the provision of childcare. In the Huang family, Father Huang and Mother Huang both emphasized that childcare provision was a welfare entitlement (*fuli*) and had no expectation of grandparenting involvement when their daughter was born in 1983. Drawing on the findings of the existing literature on ubiquitous grandparenting, I asked Mother Huang why she had not sought help from her parents and in-laws:

> MOTHER HUANG: My mother-in-law was not keen to help, and in any case we didn't need her help since my work unit had its own nursery school. I could travel on a work bus, and as soon as I'd completed my maternity leave I took my daughter with me to the factory's nursery school. At the time, this was an employee benefit enjoyed by many women workers.
>
> I: Why didn't you ask your own parents to help?
>
> MOTHER HUANG: I lived quite a long way from them. In any case, my own parents were also getting old and I didn't want to bother them. After all, I had access to a work unit nursery school so that there was no need to ask them.

Grandparenting is not an established cultural tradition in China, and its adoption was closely linked to the availability of childcare facilities in the mother's work unit. The case of Ms. Jing (G1, Tianjin) vividly illustrates the relationship between changes in intergenerational care patterns and the vagaries of state childcare benefits. Ms. Jing had two daughters, born in 1970 and 1974, and worked in a government administrative bureau that contributed to the private childcare costs incurred by its employees. For the first eighteen months of her life, her elder daughter was sent to live with a childminder,[32] after which her mother-in-law, who lived with the family, took over care responsibilities. Her second daughter was sent to live with the childminder until she was seven years old and ready to join a primary school. Each child stayed full-time at the childminder's home and was taken home once a week. This outsourced childcare arrangement was undertaken despite the fact that

Ms. Jing lived with her mother-in-law, with whom she had a relatively good relationship and who had no job to constrain her availability to help. Ms. Jing explained that her younger daughter had been in the care of the childminder for considerably longer than her first child because of her work unit's childcare reimbursement policy: "When my elder daughter was born, my work unit's policy was to reimburse the fee from the end of the maternity leave until she was one-and-a-half-years-old. But then the policy changed and in the case of my younger daughter the work unit was willing to reimburse the childcare costs until she was seven years old." Unlike childcare provided by a family member, the cost of which was not recoverable, Ms. Jing regarded the work unit childcare policy as a form of welfare benefit she should make use of. As such, it was an economically rational decision to choose a private childminder rather than a grandmother to look after her child.

Daughter Huang and other G3 child-rearing women often asked me about the nature of care provision for children under the age of three in the United Kingdom. When told parents could send their children to nursery school from three months old, the overwhelming response was one of shock: "How could anyone send a baby of such a young age to a nursery school?" and "Wow, what a difference in culture! We Chinese would never do that." However, these responses conceal the reality that not so long ago—one generation in the case of the Huang family and two in the case of the Jings—Chinese babies were sent to a work unit nursery school or a childminder's home when they were only two months old.

COMPETING FOR GRANDPARENTS (1949–1990S)

Parents whose workplaces did not have childcare facilities relied on their own bilateral families for help. The traditional patrilineal kinship norm generated an expectation that children would be closer to paternal grandparents than maternal grandparents and this positioned the paternal grandmother at the top in the hierarchy of carers, albeit with terms and conditions attached. In particular, the grandmother's work status, the absence of other care commitments, and the nature of her living arrangements determined the willingness and ability of a paternal grandmother to assume care responsibilities for a child. Only very rarely, for example, did a paternal grandmother simultaneously look after more than one child under the age of three (although where there was a significant age gap between the children, the number might increase).

As G1s had on average four surviving siblings, negotiations among siblings' families took place to determine which child would enjoy the benefit of being cared for by the paternal grandparents. The consensus among G1s was that their parents should prioritize the care of sons' children. In families with more than one son, priority should be given to the children of the son with whom the grandparents lived. If the grandparents lived independently, a careful assessment of each individual sub-family's circumstances (including availability of public care facilities, each child's age and needs, and the distance between each sons' family residence and that of their parents) was undertaken to ensure all the male siblings were treated fairly. Since most G1s had between two and four children of their own, and, on average, four siblings, each extended family generally contained at least eight grandchildren, making it practically impossible to rely solely on paternal grandmothers. As a result, among G1 and subsequent generations, maternal grandmothering had emerged (although this was only possible if the grandmother was not already involved in looking after her own son's child). If a G1 had one brother and several sisters, mothers were usually able to secure some maternal grandmothering support; but if there were several brothers, access to maternal grandmothering was, at best, sporadic.

Competition for grandparenting support forced young parents into a delicate juggling act, involving outsourcing some care to a private childminder, synchronizing the couple's work schedules, and coordinating with bilateral grandparents. In the Guan family, Mr. Guan (a G1 living in Xi'an) had two younger brothers and two younger sisters. He and his brothers all had their first child within two years of each other in the mid-1960s. While his youngest brother's family used a childminder near where they lived, Mr. Guan's parents looked after his son and his middle brother's son separately for three days and three nights each week. Of the remaining four days, Mr. Guan's son stayed with his wife's parents for one day and Mr. Guan and his wife took turns to balance the rest (something more difficult at this time since there was still a six-day working week). From the outset, Mr. Guan's parents made it clear that they were prepared to look after their grandchildren only up to the age of three and, when second grandchildren began to arrive, they would prioritize the youngest son's family.

The competition persisted into the 1980s among the first cohort of the one-child generation: sibling formation and living arrangements continued to shape a family's ability to take advantage of grandparenting. For example, as a child, Son-in-Law Huang spent little time with his paternal grandparents because they lived with his uncle and cared for his cousin. By contrast, he was his maternal grandparents only grandchild for some time as his mother was much older than her three siblings. Moreover, while son preference had long existed, the One-Child Policy heightened the significance of having a male child to the extent that care of a grandson was prioritized over the care of a granddaughter.[33] Despite being the "outside grandson" (*waisun*), Son-in-Law Huang retained a prominent position in the minds of his maternal grandparents as the only boy among all their grandchildren. This privileged status weakened only when his youngest uncle, who had had difficulty conceiving a child with his wife, eventually had a son who replaced Son-in-Law Huang to become the maternal grandparents' favorite grandchild.

Among the 1990s cohort of the One-Child generation, one or both of whose parents often had a single sibling under the 1970s "later marriage, longer birth spacing, fewer children" (*wan, xi, shao*) state initiative, the degree of competition for grandparenting witnessed in the early cohorts had weakened. As a result, it became much easier to reach agreement with the parents' sibling and both sets of grandparents. Alongside a dramatic contraction of state childcare facilities for children under three during the 1990s, grandparenting gradually emerged as the dominant social norm of childcare in urban China.

COMPETING FOR THE GRANDCHILD (2000S)

By the time the 1980s one-child generation married and had a child, grandparenting was taken for granted as a familial arrangement. In the one-third of G3 families in which each parent was an only child, the grandchild was so outnumbered by its four grandparents that, within the space of a generation, competition for the care services of a grandmother had given way to competition between the two grandmothers for the care of their only grandchild. In the 2000s, this competition intensified because of a sudden increase in grandmother availability following the forced redundancy of a large number of female workers as a result of state enterprise restructuring.[34]

Ms. Sun was laid off from a Tianjin factory in early 2000s (although her husband retained his job as head of a government organization and so her family was better off than many others). She recalled the care arrangements for her only grandchild: "From the birth of my granddaughter until she was 27 months old, I looked after her in our flat. Then she went to live with her maternal grandmother [also been made redundant], who lived close to a bilingual kindergarten. Nowadays my husband and I go to see her twice every week."

Although her son's family could have covered the cost of the kindergarten, Ms. Sun still opted to pay the fees in full (more than 200,000 yuan over three years) because, as she put it, "I feel this is the paternal grandmother's obligation since we have only one grandchild." This gesture conveyed two important messages to the other set of grandparents. First, it reaffirmed the traditional hierarchy of paternal grandparents in the kinship system. Second, it served, indirectly but intentionally, to demonstrate Ms. Sun's family wealth to her daughter-in-law and natal family: "My daughter-in-law's father was an engineer: their situation was okay, but they certainly weren't as well off as us." This gesture boosted Ms. Sun's decision-making power within the bilateral extended family in making plans for her granddaughter's future—in other words, "money talks" (*caida qicu*).

In the case of any competition between two grandmothers, a child's mother (G3) often favored the maternal grandmother since it was thought that the "natural" intimacy generated by blood-related ties would make it easier for the wife to get on with her own mother than with her mother-in-law. Although this perception also existed among earlier generations, only thanks to the demographic profile that emerged in the wake of the one-child policy could maternal grandmothering be realistically secured. This new form of behavior was captured in an idiomatic expression that became common in Tianjin: "As soon as the child is born, the maternal grandmother starts bringing it up" (*shengle haizi laolao dai*).

NEGOTIATION AND AMBIVALENCE (2010S)

The intensity of competition for grandparenting during the 2000s has given way to a "new normalcy" of negotiation, based on the availability of grandmothers and shaped by their work status and other family care commitments. In some respects, these considerations are similar to those of previous generations. However, a major difference is that whereas grandmotherly availability in earlier generations tended to reflect siblings' family formation (including the birth of their children), in today's China increasing life expectancy and the single-child family structure have introduced a new complicating factor in the form of a tension between fulfilling grandparenting responsibilities and caring for grandparents' own parents. In the Huang family, old age care responsibilities prevented Daughter Huang's parents-in-law from visiting Guangzhou to care for their two grandsons, but they helped the young couple buy a second flat and gave their grandchildren significant sums of money during the Spring Festival. Mother Huang hinted at her feeling of powerlessness: "Every day I looked after the baby [her first grandson]. I was the main carer. The paternal grandparents did not take on the grandson's care responsibility because they still had two 90-year old parents to look after, which made it impossible to come to look after the grandson. What could I do?"

Research has found that, following the introduction of the two-child policy in January 2016, in big cities only 5–6 percent of couples opted to have a second child,[35] while a national survey revealed that 86.5 percent of the families cited the unavailability of a carer as the main impediment to having a second child.[36] In other words, grandparents' willingness to provide care played an important role in many couples' decision whether or not to have a second child. In the Huang family, Daughter Huang had initially hoped to secure Mother Huang's support, and when this was not forthcoming she and her husband resorted to hiring a live-in nanny. Other less affluent couples abandoned any thought of having a second child. For example, when, like Daughter Huang, another G3 interviewee accidentally became pregnant with a second child, she underwent an abortion because her husband's parents were in poor health and her own mother, who had helped bring up the first child, was unwilling to offer further support.

Although nearing their seventies, most urban parents of the one-child generation were generally in good health, but remained ambivalent and were often reluctant to look after a second child.[37] First, many felt that having already looked after the first child, they had fulfilled the familial obligation expected of them. Second, sightseeing had become a popular pastime among urban pensioners, and many spoke of wanting to enjoy their old age while they were still mobile. Finally, many grandmothers confided that although they enjoyed the companionship of looking after a grandchild, the intensity of the labor left them exhausted. Mother Huang explained, "Looking after a grandchild is far more tiring than outside work or doing housework." In short, the fact that fewer than 10 percent of urban interviewees in the 1980s cohort went on to have a second child is in no small part attributable to grandparents' refusal to provide help in bringing up the child.

Post-1949 Conditions: Rural Families

In the 1950s, like their urban counterparts, rural grassroots officials were urged to respond to central government calls to set up childcare organizations to facilitate mothers' participation in agricultural work. However, because of inequalities in welfare provision between cities and the countryside, rural childcare facilities differed markedly from their urban counterparts in a number of respects. First, in contrast with urban facilities, funded by the work units or directly by the state, those in the countryside were largely financed by the production brigade and the mothers[38] themselves.[39] Second, unlike the permanent (year-long) support provided in urban facilities, rural childcare services were often organized on a seasonal basis (e.g., to coincide with the agricultural harvest), and / or arranged in the form of mutual aid assistance.[40] Third, rural facilities were most likely to be set up in suburban villages close to cities and / or in town or county seats. These characteristics meant that the provision of childcare facilities[41] was patchy and very uneven across rural China.

Across all three generations access to state childcare facilities among rural families has been severely limited and, for many, nonexistent. Only among the children of G3 rural families has the concept of year-long kindergarten care entered child-rearing narratives. In contrast to urban families, for whom grandparenting was facilitated by socialist institutional factors and eventually became virtually universal thanks to shifts in government childcare provision policy, quite different institutional factors have shaped the practice of grandparenting as a social norm among rural families.

MAO AND THE EARLY REFORM ERA—RARE EXCEPTIONS

There were cases of *paternal* grandmothering from the Mao era onward arising as a result of the state's mobilization of women into agricultural production. However, this practice was contingent, its most likely sole beneficiary being families with single sons that co-resided with the grandmother. In rural Shandong, Grandma Chang (see chapter 5) and her husband lived with her parents-in-law until they passed away. She had been married in 1951 and did not initially work in the fields, except during the harvest season. But after the village was integrated into a commune in 1958, she participated in collective farm work from morning until evening, leaving her mother-in-law to cook for the entire family and care for her four young children. However, as she explained, the childcare support provided by her mother-in-law was an exception to the norm: "In those days the senior generation behaved differently from old people of today. If they wanted to help with grandchildren's care, they would do so. If they didn't want to, there was no obligation. I was lucky to be married to a husband who was the only surviving son. The prevailing view was that parents themselves should bear the responsibility for raising their children."

Grandma Chang's statement was echoed by other villagers. For example, in Grandpa Gao's extended family (see chapter 5), although his parents (Go) lived in a large courtyard with their four married sons, Grandpa Gao's mother played no part in looking after any of the grandchildren. Grandpa Gao's wife recalled: "I had two children [one subsequently died], my second sister-in-law had five, my third sister-in-law had four, and my fourth sister-in-law had another four. The age gap between the children was small, so how could my mother-in-law have looked after so many of them? And anyway, at that time it wasn't the norm for grandmothers to look after grandchildren [*buxing kan*]—not like nowadays when you see the grandmothers everywhere carrying their grandchild around all day."

Except for a small number of families, most mothers juggled childcare responsibilities with participation in collective agricultural work. It was common for mothers to carry their babies to the fields to breastfeed them during their work breaks and, when the child was slightly older, leave it all day in the care of older siblings.

Agricultural de-collectivization in the early 1980s made the rural household responsible for the costs of production, as well as allowing them, after they had fulfilled the state's fixed grain quota, to dispose of any remaining output as they wished. While the state remade the household as a basic unit of production, there was no increased public provision to support the social reproduction activities of the household. As a result, competing demands were placed on family labor to fulfill both nonproductive childcare responsibilities and the needs of productive farm work. In the Xu family, since Grandma Xu was actively engaged in household farm work, she was unable to help care for her grandchildren, leaving her daughter-in-law with no option but to look after her children herself. Daughter-in-Law Xu (G2) did so in time-honored fashion: when she worked in the fields, she carried her youngest child on her back; when she was engaged in housework, she tied her young children around the waist to a house fitting, such as a window, so that they could not walk away from the house. Although her two sons interacted more with their paternal grandparents as they grew up, the latter offered no ongoing childcare support.

THE ERA OF MIGRATION: THE NORM

From the late 1980s and early 1990s, an increasing demand for cheap labor in the expanding urban economy led to a relaxation of restrictions on movement between the countryside and cities. In search of better living standards, migration became popular among members of Daughter-in-Law Xu's (G2) generation and, in some families from the same Hunan village, wives followed their husbands into the cities. In her own family her husband was the only one to move to a city in search of work, although ill health forced him to return after a few years. Despite earning more than they would have working in agriculture, migrants faced institutional discrimination in cities, where they were treated as second-class citizens and deprived of various employment benefits to which registered urban citizens were entitled.[42] Although the plight of migrants' children has received increasing media attention and the concept of "left-behind children" has entered common parlance in the last two decades, it has remained very difficult for migrants' children to gain admission to urban schools.[43]

In the face of institutional discrimination in the urban labor market, and hostility toward incoming migrant families, rural migrants relied on left-behind family members to look after their children when they were working away. In short, as soon as mothers absented themselves from their household, paternal grandmothering needed to step into the void and it has gradually become an intergenerational norm in village life throughout China. Daughter-in-Law Xu assumed a custodial role for all her elder son's children.[44] The first grand-daughter was born in the village in 2002, her mother having returned to give birth but subsequently returning to the city when the baby was eight months old. The birth of the second granddaughter in 2007 took place not in the village, but in the city where the migrant parents were living. On the latter occasion, Daughter-in-Law Xu went to the city prior to the birth and returned to her village with the baby girl as soon as Granddaughter-in-Law Xu's postnatal confinement period was completed. The third grandchild—but first grandson—was born in the city in 2011, but since his birth clashed with the harvest, Daughter-in-Law Xu was unable to leave her two granddaughters behind to travel to the city. As a result, Granddaughter-in-Law Xu's own mother came to help during the birth and postnatal confinement period. However, when their son was about two months old, the young couple took him back to their home village to be cared for by his paternal grandmother.

Granddaughter-in-law Xu commented: "No young people stay at home in their villages any more. They all leave to make money. Nowadays everybody leaves their children behind in the villages to be looked after by their paternal grandmothers [*nainai*]. If we stayed in our home village, how could we afford the cost of child-rearing? At least nowadays we're in a position to meet the material needs of our children and all the other costs of bringing them up." Working in an urban supermarket provided Granddaughter-in-Law Xu and her husband with a combined annual income of around 50,000 yuan. They sent one third of this home to cover their children's living and educational expenses, used another third to cover their own living costs in the city, and put the rest into savings with the intention of eventually using it to set-up a small business that the husband would manage. Elder Grandson Xu explained, "If in a few years we do manage to set up our own business and make big money, we hope to bring my children and my parents to the city. But for the time being we just don't have enough money to do this."

Although confessing that looking after two children full-time for a protracted period was exhausting, Daughter-in-Law Xu was generally positive about the intergenerational care arrangement. Without remittances from the city, she and her husband would have been wholly reliant on subsistence farming to cover all expenditures, including kinship management within the village,[45] and also the medicine expenses for her husband's chronic illnesses. The amicable nature of relations within the extended family was underlined by the reciprocity of ex-change gestures between the generations. For example, Elder Grandson Xu, who was aware of his parents' financial constraints, volunteered to cover his father's share of the cost for Grandpa Xu's eightieth birthday banquet.

While maternal grandmothering has become a popular feature of childcare arrangements among urban G3 parents, paternal grandmothering has remained dominant in rural areas. At the time of my interviews, for example, Granddaughter-in-Law Xu had three married elder sisters and one unmarried younger brother. Her sisters' children were all looked after by their respective paternal grandmothers, despite their maternal grandmother being free of any existing care commitments. The birth of the third child of Granddaughter-in-Law Xu was the only occasion on which the maternal grandmother's help was solicited, and this was regarded as an unavoidable, temporary arrangement rather than an obligation. Such cases apart, there were also rare exceptional circumstances in which rural G3 women moved to cities through university education (for example, Ms. Wang in chapter 1). Some of these were able to secure help from their own mothers in looking after their children. However, the quid pro quo was that in due course they would be expected to provide financial support to their brother—for example, by contributing to the bride price—and natal family.

Intergenerational Power Dynamics

Normativity and Variance

Before grandparenting became an accepted social norm, the older generations in both urban and rural society held the upper hand in deciding whether or not to offer childcare support. In the Guan family (see above) the grandmother refused to look after any grandchild who was still being breastfed. In the Chen family (see chapter 5), Grandma Chen's mother-in-law refused to care for her granddaughter because she felt the proposed "fee" (*huoshi fei*) was insufficient to cover the child's living expenses and so the granddaughter became a latchkey child who arranged her own meals throughout her school years. Among rural families, Grandpa Gao's mother took no part in caring for any of the fifteen grandchildren who lived in the same courtyard. Following the death of Daughter-in-Law Xu's own parents, her paternal grandparents refused to help care for her three younger brothers, leaving her to assume sole care responsibility at the age of eighteen.

As grandparenting gradually transforms into a social norm, it acquires the capacity to enforce the normativity needed to justify and legitimize social values and behavior.[46] The normalization of grandparenting has incorporated expansive childcare into the list of intergenerational obligations of parents and legitimized a familial and social expectation that the older generation will provide care support for their grandchildren in exchange for reciprocal support in their old age. The outcome has been to shift the intergenerational power balance, effectively forcing the elderly to conform to the new childcare obligation. It is also noteworthy that the emergence of grandparenting does not neatly fit with Yan's "inverted family" narrative, which is characterized by "the constant decline of parental authority and power and the parallel increase in youth autonomy and freedom in both urban and rural Chinese families."[47] While on the surface, parental power seems to have waned because parents need to contribute more in the intergenerational reciprocal arrangement, this power shift is not motivated or paralleled by an increase in children's autonomy but rather as a result of the legitimization of grandparenting as a social norm. Furthermore, the trajectory of this generational power shift has been uneven and nonlinear, causing a variety of intergenerational configurations.

By way of illustrating this, I compare four sets of grandparents to reveal how they are varyingly positioned in the negotiations between generations and within a given generation on whether / how to offer childcare services. Located on the top of this decision-making hierarchy is Daughter Huang's parents-in-law who were former civil servants. Old age care responsibilities exempted them from the major grandchild care provision. However, to obviate any hard feelings between the generations, and in recognition of the familial expectation of grandparenting, they used financial support to compensate for their lack of involvement. This gesture was possible because of their generous Civil Service pensions (around 12,000 yuan per month each). In addition to putting down the deposit for their son's second flat in Guangzhou, each Spring Festival Daughter Huang's parents-in-law gave each of their grandchildren 20,000 yuan in red envelopes—a sum forty times larger than that given by Mother Huang and her husband (both of whom were former factory workers). This financial support ensured a smooth and respectful relationship existed between Daughter Huang and her parents-in-law, contrasting with the frequent quarrels that characterized her negotiations with her own mother when raising her first child.

Second in the hierarchy is Daughter Huang's own parents. Although their financial resources were far more limited when compared with Daughter Huang's parents-in-law, they enjoyed a privileged position of being "urban" in terms of material well-being and were able to bluff their way out of looking after their second grandchild. With a monthly state pension (around 3,000 yuan), more than twenty times greater than that of her rural counterpart, as well as being the owner of a two-bed flat in central Guangzhou valued at more than one million yuan, Mother Huang refused to help care for the second grandchild, commenting, "I can't help you now. When we get old, we won't need you to look after us either. When the time comes, we'll move into an old age home." In her interview, Daughter Huang interpreted this comment as a ruse used by her mother to avoid any grandmothering responsibility: "Of course I won't let them go into an old age home. As their only daughter, I will definitely look after them in old age. She knows that perfectly well!"

Third in the hierarchy is a rural grandmother who remained economically active in the city. From the late 1990s, Daughter-in-Law Xu's fellow villager Ms. Zhou (a rural G2 migrant worker) joined her husband in a city of Guangdong, where they worked as street shoe repairers, earning a daily income of between 40 and 200 yuan. Because their only son and his wife (rural G3) earned low wages in a factory (45 yuan per day each), the young couple joined the family business instead. Ms. Zhou refused to care for the granddaughter when their son's wife gave birth to a baby girl in the city: "My daughter-in-law wasn't working in a factory [instead doing piecework at home, e.g. making necklaces] so she was responsible for sending her daughter to the kindergarten. If I had to do pickups and drop-offs, I wouldn't be able to help my son with his business." Ms. Zhou was an integral part of a small-scale family business in the city, set up with her husband, which provided a livelihood for the extended family. This economic relationship between generations empowered Ms. Zhou while the daughter-in-law disguised her own economic productivity with homework and in so doing further subjugated herself.[48] Ms. Zhou refused to embrace her grandmothering obligation while she was in the city and prioritized the family business, although she acknowledged that when she returned to the village and no longer had access to the family business, she would follow the norm of looking after her grandchildren in order to enable her son and his wife to earn money in the city.

At the bottom of this hierarchy is Daughter-in-Law Xu (rural G2) and her husband who stayed in the village as farmers. Due to ill health, her husband's life as a migrant worker had been cut short and they were wholly reliant on subsistence farming to cover their expenditures. As a result, they were financially dependent upon the younger generation for income and not in a position to decline the grandparenting expectation. Daughter-in-Law Xu was fortunate in two respects: first, she had only three grandchildren to look after, with the care responsibilities for her second son's child being assumed by their urban maternal grandmother; and second, her family relations were marked by amicable reciprocal exchange between generations (partly enabled by Elder Grandson Xu's ability to send sufficient remittances back to the village).

In some rural families with two sons, rural grandmothering could be a huge burden, both physically and financially. It frequently involved raising five or six grandchildren for a lengthy period—typically until they had reached junior middle school age. If the younger generation were not faring well economically in the city, and could not send enough money home (in some cases only to cover school fees, but not living expenses of children), the grandparents who stayed behind endured financial hardship. This financial strain could dampen intergenerational ties and throw doubt upon the intergenerational contract, as a rural grandmother in this situation commented: "Nowadays they ask me to do the childcare, I do it for them. But I have no idea in future how they will look after me."

The distinctive positions of these four sets of grandparents highlight several layers of analysis. First, they reveal how individuals' capacities to act are shaped by their social positions and the level of resources they command, generating uneven intergenerational configurations. As a result, there is variation and contestation of grandparenting practices both within a generation and between generations, making any linear prediction of a generational power shift untenable. Second, they indicate that socioeconomic status has regained its prominence as a key factor in structuring family practices in post-Mao China. With rising income inequalities and persistent differences in access to state welfare, the urban-rural divide has been further consolidated. Occupational differences (professional versus working-class; agricultural versus nonagricultural) have also caused stratifying effects within both urban and rural sectors with stay-behind subsistence farmers being the most vulnerable. These trends run counter to the democratizing narrative of family relationships in the new phase of modernity writings that predict the dissolution of social structures. Third, they illustrate how Chinese society's increasing preoccupation with wealth accumulation has given money an important role in mediating family relations. While money cannot forge intimacy, wealthier grandparents, such as Daughter Huang's parents-in-law, can be more selective in defining the nature of the childcare they offer while continuing to enjoy a moral reputation for fulfilling their familial obligation. By contrast, grandparents with limited financial resources, such as Daughter-in-Law Xu and other stay-behind farming grandparents, have no option but to undertake practical care work.

MONEY

Money is empowering as well as disempowering among family members. While money can lubricate family relations, it was one of the most frequently cited sources of conflict across both urban and rural families. In rural families, the conversations and conflicts concerning money in large part originated from material necessity. In urban families, although the survival need was not as pressing, money negotiations were an important way for individuals to achieve a balance between prioritizing family interests and protecting individual self-interest. In the Huang family, when they started co-living, the plan was for the young couple to give Mother Huang 1,000 yuan per month to cover food costs for the whole family. However, after a few weeks, both sides were unhappy. Mother Huang complained that 1,000 yuan was not enough to cover food price inflation while Daughter Huang complained that the ingredients acquired were of poor quality and might not equal the money given. After a few months' bickering, the family agreed to an alternative model in which Daughter Huang purchased the ingredients and Mother Huang cooked whatever was bought. This worked fine but then Mother Huang started to raise further financial grievances in the presence of the young couple—for example, after she took her grandson to play: "Every time we went out, so much money was spent [on toys, food, etc.]!" Following the hint, Daughter Huang and her husband agreed to give 500 yuan[49] per month to Mother Huang to cover ad hoc expenses and ensure that she would not spend any of her own money on the child. In addition, Son-in-Law Huang, on behalf of the young couple, gave each parent-in-law 2,000 yuan at the Spring Festival for sightseeing and annual health check costs.

Unlike the paternal grandparents who were retired civil servants and could lavish money upon their grandchildren, Mother Huang was presented as "calculating" in the younger generation's narratives. However, her actions were grounded in her material reality as the recipient of a pension of around 3,000 yuan per month (less than 25 percent of the pension of Daughter Huang's in-laws). Speaking of her old age plan, Mother Huang revealed an ambivalence common among many G2s (see chapter 5): "If she is able to, of course I would like to be looked after by her [the daughter] in old age. But nowadays she can't even cook for herself, how could I rely upon her in future?" In an era of considerable change, carefully guarding her material interests was rational and necessary, especially in the context of high old age care costs. Moreover, it is noteworthy that all parties overlooked a highly valuable but hidden contribution Mother Huang had made, that is, her care labor that was not valorized. If calculated at the market rate of the live-in nanny, Mother Huang helped to save the young couple 300,000 yuan in care costs, far more than the rich paternal grandparents gave to the grandchildren. Like other care work conducted within the family setting, grandmothering is viewed as "natural" and not even considered for commercialization. This perception—the naturalization of family care—is being built upon and reinforced in Chinese legislation and public propaganda, against the backdrop of a welfare regime that emphasizes family responsibilities and the state's residual function. Aligned with this public discourse, negotiation between generations concerning childcare costs centered around the expenses (*huoshi fei*) of the child rather than on grandmothering. Here, what Mother Huang managed to achieve was not to spend any of her own pension on the day-to-day expenses of the grandchild.

While an inverted population pyramid is emerging in China, intergenerational relations, especially micro-level intergenerational dynamics, are not necessarily "upside down" as Yan's new edited volume title indicates.[50] Following Mother Huang's grievances, and the perceived need to display filiality (see chapter 5), the young couple more or less complied with her requests. In the residential compound where Mother Huang interacted with other grandmothers, there was an implicit ranking within her peer group in relation to how their respective adult children treated them. Adult children could confer "face" on their parents in the eyes of the latter's peers through their filial demonstrations (giving money to parents, taking parents on holiday, etc.). By citing examples of other filial children in the neighborhood, Mother Huang exerted peer pressure to perform filiality on Daughter Huang. While this was a source of considerable resentment, Daughter Huang and her husband did make behavioral changes[51] in the direction Mother Huang desired. Existing literature often states that submission to parental authority is no longer an essential component in the redefinition of filial piety in contemporary Chinese families.[52] However, the mother-daughter exchanges of the Huang family show that parents have no intention to relinquish their authority; instead, they continue and, indeed, strategize in order to exert power over their adult children, drawing upon their generational position and access to filial discourse, albeit in an indirect and subtle manner.

Although grandparenting has been hailed by existing literature as a strategy to maximize the well-being of the entire family, the microenvironment in which multiple generations closely interact is not necessarily smooth and amicable. As shown in the quote at the start of this chapter, Daughter Huang preferred the "nanny model" since the relationship with the nanny was transactional and avoided the emotional complexities of having to deal with her mother. In turn, there were fewer interactions between Mother Huang and Daughter Huang, generating less friction and a more harmonious mother-daughter relationship.

Gender

Grandmothers versus Grandfathers

While the Maoist commitment to gender equality ensured Chinese women were mobilized into paid work, childcare continued to be a woman's responsibility across all three generations. Women—mother, grandmother, or child-minder / nanny—remained emblematically and unambiguously responsible for providing childcare with male responsibility largely absent. While grandfathers did start to appear in the care of G3s, they remained in a subsidiary role. For example, a G3 college student in Xi'an recalled that as he was growing up, his grandmother provided everyday care, such as cooking and cleaning, while his grandfather often took him to play outside and showered him with toys. In the Huang family, Mother Huang was the primary caregiver and closely involved in everyday tasks, such as feeding, co-sleeping, and bathing, while Father Huang served as a helper in these tasks. As the grandson grew older, Father Huang assumed the role of playmate for the grandson.

While urban grandfathers such as these were generally retired and available, rural grandfathers needed to keep working in the fields and were largely absent during the day when their wives were in charge of childcare. When the grandchildren reached school years, rural grandfathers, such as Grandpa Xu and Elder Son Xu, lectured their grandchildren about the importance of studying hard in order to escape the countryside and be socially mobile.

Gender Intersecting with Generation

There was a correlation between grandparents' participation and a husband's involvement in urban childcare. In the Mao era, when grandparenting could not be always secured due to multiple-sibling competition, a husband was compelled to get involved where necessary to alleviate a care crisis. For example, as explained above, when Mr. Guan's (G1) son was not cared for by the child's bilateral grandmothers, Mr. Guan and his wife were responsible for the care of their son during their nonwork hours. However, in recent decades as normative grandparenting has coincided with an emphasis upon a child's academic achievement, a new division of intergenerational labor has formed in which grandmothers focus upon practical care tasks (cooking, cleaning, etc.),[53] with the mother as education manager,[54] leaving no obvious role for the father (meaning the husband's involvement in child-rearing has reduced or even been waived). This gendered effect of grandparenting was summarized by one G3 woman when she described how her husband's behavior changed dependent upon the presence of the grandmother: "When the grandmother is present, the husband is a lazy pig [*lanzhu*]; when the grandmother is away, the husband becomes a teammate [*duiyou*]."

It is worth highlighting that a re-traditionalization of gender roles within the family (as also shown in chapter 2) is facilitated by persistent gender inequalities in the public sphere. Like many urban G3 couples who started out with similar university qualifications, a few years after childbirth Daughter Huang's career stagnated while Son-in-Law Huang's career and income followed an upward trajectory. This gender bias operated in both public and private spheres to create a "cycle of vulnerability"[55] by further consolidating women's inferior position in the household and the labor market.

Gendered Intergenerational Storytelling— "Structured Remembering"

Since women are disproportionately entangled in the grandparenting arrangement, they strategize to bend the kinship rules that traditionally favor a husband's parents in the hierarchy of extended family relations. While this patrilineal kinship custom persists in rural areas, maternal grandparents gradually gain recognition as the most intimate people in an urban G3's childhood memories. The mothers of urban G3s played an important role in driving this shift, partly as a response and retaliation against the unfriendly treatment by paternal grandmothers.

Daughter Huang recalled her early childhood:

> My abiding memory of my paternal grandmother is that she didn't like us. . . . Five of us lived in a cramped space of less than twenty square meters. My paternal grandparents slept on the mezzanine level, while the three of us were downstairs. We ate separately; they had one set of cooking utensils and my parents had another. She didn't like my mother and my mother didn't like her. My paternal grandmother drank a lot and would then constantly shout loudly in the street. We all felt awful, so my parents tried hard to move out.

When asked about her relationship with her maternal grandparents, Daughter Huang said, "I think perhaps because I was not close to my paternal grandparents, I felt close to my maternal grandparents. I guess that my mother complained to them about the unpleasant experience of living with her in-laws, and so they treated me very well whenever I was with them."

Rejection by her paternal grandparents pushed Daughter Huang closer to her maternal grandparents. However, the distant relationship with her paternal grandparents also reflected a reconstructed narrative of the past based on recollections of her mother. A key mechanism mothers used was to inject their own strong subjective feelings into a narrative when speaking of the past to their child, something I refer to as "structured remembering" in intergenerational storytelling.[56] Daughter Huang recalled, "When I was very little, I fell from a chair onto the floor. My paternal grandmother didn't even bother to pick me up. My mother told this story to me so many times that I felt my paternal grandmother really didn't like me."

Mothers' frequent use of such discursive devices successfully made their own perception of the past part of the child's own memory, reinforcing the discourse of rejection by paternal grandparents. The objective was to weave a child into a closer relationship with their natal family than with that of their in-laws. Among the one-child generation of women, structured remembering in intergenerational storytelling was largely absent, partly because maternal grandmothers are already closely involved in the grandchild's life. Further, frictions arising from close encounters in mother-daughter relationships, as seen in the Huang family, have made some one-child generation women return to a more balanced mode—that is, engage both sets of grandparents equally in the raising of a grandchild. For example, some families follow a pattern of "grandparenting rotation," whereby each set of grandparents lived with the young family for a month.

Conclusion

While grandparenting is ubiquitous in contemporary Chinese families, the three generation analysis reveals that its prevalence is only visible in the rearing of G3s' children. Grandparenting has evolved through several phases: although initially the practice was quite rare, demand for childcare generated fierce competition for grandparents' services, and ultimately it became a de facto obligation. While grandparenthood is traditionally honored in Chinese families, far from being rooted in Chinese culture, grandparenting is quite recent in origin. It is a reinvented and reimagined "tradition" in response to the challenges presented by socioeconomic change and demographic transformation that have taken place in China in recent years.

Theoretically, this chapter throws new light upon the existing claims surrounding the practice of grandparenting. Rather than attributing grandparenting to an essentialist cultural value, this chapter highlights how micro-institutional configurations have become a critical driver in morphing grandparenting into a familial responsibility and social norm, and how these institutional arrangements affecting grandparenting differed between urban and rural families. In the Mao era, the mandatory full-time maternal employment and the adoption of early gender-differentiated retirement ages initiated grandmothering practices. In the reform era, accelerated by the state's changing childcare policies for children (up to the age of three) and facilitated by the shrinking family demographic profile, the involvement of urban grandparents in bringing up children especially in early years has expanded rapidly and become ubiquitous. In rural China, due to a lack of state provision, child-rearing was de facto the mother's responsibility through the Mao era to the early reform era and grandparenting remained contingent and voluntary. The post-Mao mass rural-urban migration and the hostility of cities in receiving rural families has normalized rural grandparenting as a standard part of everyday village life. In short, it is the state institution of the *hukou* system that has made rural grandparenting ubiquitous, above all during the reform era.

This chapter also adds more nuance to the existing literature on grandparenting as a sign of intergenerational solidarity and strategy to optimize overall family well-being. It reveals a variety of circumstances in which the older generation take on grandparenting willingly or unwillingly and identifies a delicate intergenerational configuration whereby family members balance their own self-interest and the collective welfare. The capacity of an individual to steer their own self-interest is shaped by their positions in the relevant social hierarchy, the most vulnerable constituency being rural grandparents engaged in farming.

This chapter challenges the modernization narrative on nuclearization of family life. Rather than a universal triumph of conjugal intimacy, the interactions between grandparent and grandchild generations increase, and intergenerational interdependence tightens, as modernization proceeds. For example, while early generation grandparents (especially in urban settings) mostly looked after grandchildren up to the age of three, younger generation grandparents were involved in everyday care until the child entered primary school or junior middle school. One interpretation of these shifts is that they reflect a weakening of the older generation's authority at the expense of a rise in that of the younger generation, exemplified in Yan's "inverted family" model.[57] However, this chapter suggest that the intergenerational power shift has not been linear. While the force of normativity binds older generations with this newly established familial obligation, the young generation's autonomy and freedom does not necessarily increase and there continue to be complex and sometimes agonizing processes of gendered and intergenerational contest and compromise in the household.

Paradoxical changes and continuities occur over time. Grandmothers continue to shoulder a disproportionate burden in raising grandchildren. However, those grandmothers and grandparents with greater socioeconomic resources are more likely to determine the form of childcare provision. Although classic modernization theory predicts a shift from patrilineal to bilateral kinship structure as societies modernize,[58] the Chinese case study reveals that such a transition is uneven. While urban maternal grandmothering grows in popularity, in particular in the rearing of the children of the urban one-child generation (like Daughter Huang's family), rural grandparents continue to comply with the patrilineal norm so as to prioritize the raising of a son's children over a daughter's children.[59] Even in an urban setting, looking ahead, the dominance of maternal grandparenting may not persist as evidence relating to care arrangements for the second child of the one-child generation suggests. Thus, the changes and adjustments in family practices are nonlinear but gradual and partial or even cyclic.

5

The Young Caring for the Old

I: What is the current care arrangement?

GRANDMA CHANG: Each child spends five days with me on a rota, one after another. Relying solely on my sons won't work, and relying solely on my daughter won't work either.

I: What do they do when they come here?

GRANDMA CHANG: They bring meals, take me to the toilet and my daughter washes all my clothes.

I: Do the sons wash clothes for you?

GRANDMA CHANG: No. They don't know how to do it. I have a daughter so don't need them anyway.

I: Who do you want mostly to care for you?

GRANDMA CHANG: The Second Son. He visits most frequently. My elder son lives slightly further away [a twenty-minute walk] so drops in every two hours. But the younger son comes at least twenty times a day—he lives very close by [a five-minute walk].

I: How do you feel about the current arrangement?

GRANDMA CHANG: The care they provide is quite good so I can't feel dissatisfied. But not being able to move about is really hard. Who would have thought growing old would be so difficult?

When I first met her in 2011, Grandma Chang (G1, rural Shandong) had been bedbound for four years. Her house (see Appendix C) was located in a small courtyard, about five minutes' walk from her younger son's courtyard accommodation. It contained three rooms in a row, with her small bedroom positioned at the far end. Because she had problems with her legs, she spent most of her time confined to her kang bed.[1] Next to her bed was a table on which was a small black-and-white television, a water cup, and some medicine. Two wooden chairs were the rest of the furniture in the bedroom. The floor was uneven and made of earth. Grandma Chang was evidently cheered to have some visitors.[2] After her younger son introduced me and left, I sat down on a chair next to her bed and started chatting to her.

Grandma Chang was born in 1932. She had only one (older) surviving brother who had been sent to school and later became a teacher. In keeping with the gender norms of the time, she herself had not received any education. Instead, she was kept at home and taught how to spin cotton and weave cloth. In 1951, as a result of an arranged marriage, she moved to her husband's village located about three miles from her natal village. A few years after her marriage, agricultural collectivization got under way and she began to work in the fields alongside her husband to earn work points. She had three sons and one daughter. She wanted her sons to succeed educationally, but all dropped out of school as they did not want to study as well as help with farm work. Her daughter was sent to school for only one year. Her youngest son died of a serious illness at the age of twenty-one, while the other two sons were married within the village and each had three children and a grandson. Her daughter was married into a nearby village and had two children.

In 2007, Grandma Chang suffered a cerebral thrombosis and was subsequently diagnosed as hemiplegia. As a result, she became bed-ridden and her husband became her everyday carer. The further consequence was that the old couple handed over their field to their two sons' families to tend. In return, the two sons provided them with grain and other necessities such as coal. Grandma Chang and her husband contributed their entire life savings of 2,000 yuan toward the cost of her medical treatment, the remaining bill being divided equally among the two sons' families.

In 2009 Grandma Chang's husband suddenly died of stomach cancer, and for the next five months her daughter moved back home to care for her. Thereafter, her daughter and two sons' families established a rotation care arrangement whereby each adult child looked after Grandma Chang on a rolling five-day basis. The daily care tasks involved sending her meals, dressing her, helping her to the toilet, and sleeping in her house at night. The chores of washing dirty clothes and bed sheets were undertaken by the daughter when she was looking after her mother. Grandma Chang lived on the food and cash provided by her two sons' families, in addition to which during important Chinese festivals her daughter and grandchildren often gave her gifts, including food and money.

Although she voiced no complaints about the old age support provided by her children, Grandma Chang's total dependency upon them made her extremely upset and emotional:

> I get angry easily, not about others but with myself. It angers me that I can't move around. My children can't stay with me all the time. When they're

busy, I can't tell them to stay with me, otherwise how can they work and make a living? . . . To be frank, I don't want them to leave me on my own. When they leave, I cry. I don't cry in front of the children because I'm well fed and looked after. So what is it that makes me cry? . . . I feel very upset and sometimes cry for several hours. But crying is no use. The best thing for everyone would be if I were dead. I am ready to die. Tell me, what do I live for?

When she began sobbing in front of me, I felt intensely inadequate in my role as a researcher. Grandma Chang was trapped in a situation from which she could not escape because of conflicting constraints in which she and her children were caught up. She was bedridden, illiterate (like many other rural G1s) and unable to use a phone or read. The outdated television set in the room could still receive a few channels, but she did not feel like watching anything. The physical company of other people was critical to her emotional well-being. However, her children had to juggle working for a living while fulfilling their obligation to take turns looking after her, and they sought to fulfill these competing claims on their time by popping in and out to see her when it was their turn to look after her. Her younger son, who was emotionally closest to her, visited her twenty times a day when it was his turn, but his employment as a piece worker in a village enterprise prevented him from staying with her all the time. Her elder son had to migrate to find work as his family was still in debt; during his absence, he sent his wife to see to all the essential tasks, although she too was unable to stay with Grandma Chang because she had work to do in the field as well as helping look after her own grandson (G4). To end the misery that they all felt, Grandma Chang had considered suicide, demonstrating the lengths to which she was prepared to go to reduce the care burden carried by her adult children. Nevertheless, this merely posed a new dilemma, for as she explained, she could not afford to die by suicide: "This life of mine is pointless. But if I were to die like that [suicide], it would cast a shadow on my children's reputation by giving the impression that they were unfilial. But in fact, they aren't unfilial."

After this emotionally charged encounter with Grandma Chang, I felt I ought to do something to alleviate Grandma Chang's misery. I spoke to other members of the family and villagers about the possibility of buying an electric mobility scooter designed for older people suffering from mobility issues. However, this conversation was fruitless: first, because they had never heard of such a machine and anyway wondered if they would be able to afford it; second, because they felt that the uneven village lanes would make it impractical for old people to maneuver a scooter or wheelchair on their own. All that the other villagers could suggest was that the family should carry on taking turns looking after Grandma Chang.

The interviews with Grandma Chang's other family members accurately reflected the complex realities of each family member's care obligations. However, my separate conversation with her elder daughter-in-law highlighted further tensions embedded in the intergenerational support arrangements. Frictions in the Chang family were closely related to parental emotional favoritism as well as the perceived unequal distribution of family property among male heirs. During the initial intergenerational household division made roughly sometime in the 1990s, Grandma Chang's three sons drew lots to determine the allocation of the houses that were available—Grandma Chang and her husband being allowed to reside until death in the house received by the elder son. Sadly, her third son died in his twenties, which left the house allocated to him vacant. At that time, the second son (G2) stated that since his own son (G3) was doing well at school and would eventually be able to find work and settle in the city, so his family had no need of the additional house. Since the old couple (G1) lived in the house allocated to the elder son, the elder son and his wife (G2) moved into the house originally destined for the third son. However, when the grandson (the second son's son, a G3) did not manage to settle in the city, the second son needed land for a new house in anticipation of his son's marriage. Since the second son was Grandma Chang's favorite, he persuaded his mother to reallocate the house Grandma Chang lived in to him. This angered the elder son's family as when the initial household division took place the other house had been allocated to them, in addition to which their own son (G3) also needed land for a marital house. Although unhappy, the elder son felt he had no option but to accede to his mother's decision. However, thereafter the elder son's wife held a deep grudge against Grandma Chang. She performed all the care tasks for the bedbound Grandma Chang during her husband's absence in order to avoid village gossip that might accuse her of being unfilial. However, despite the tiring care work she had to perform, she admitted that she hoped Grandma Chang would not get better because she "wanted to continue seeing her suffer."

When I revisited the region in 2018, I learnt that Grandma Chang had died in 2012 and that the younger son's family had taken over the house where Grandma Chang had lived until her death. Superficially at least, the relationship between the two brothers' families was harmonious. Although the elder daughter-in-law felt that her family had been exploited, she would not risk undermining the relationship with her brother-in-law's family since, as she put it, "You never know when these ties may be useful in the future." In any case, after Grandma Chang's death there was a shared sense of relief in both brothers' families that they had now moved beyond the life phase in which "above has the old generation, below has the young generation" (*shang you lao, xia you xiao*).

Given the rapidly aging population in China, absence of comprehensive state welfare provision (similar to issues of childcare resources, for which see chapter 4) and limited development of retirement communities and nursing homes, whether the young can fulfill normative obligations and care for their parents in old age is a central question in existing literature. Empirical findings to date are mixed and patchy because many studies focus on cross-sectional data and are grounded in one location. Without data from previous generations, there is a tendency, especially among the work produced on the post-Mao era, to compare findings with "tradition," which carries an epistemological risk (see the Introduction). Further, there is an overwhelming emphasis on filial piety as the main factor shaping familial support. This preoccupation reflects a common assumption underpinning classic modernization theory that familial support is mainly driven by obligatory norms.[3] However, what emerges from the case of Grandma Chang is that the filiality or otherwise of her children was irrelevant to her unhappiness and suffering. Yet, because of the public preoccupation with filial piety, she was unable to disclose the true cause of her misery as being grounded in the structural inequality with which so many aging rural residents and their extended families must contend.

In this chapter, using comparable data from three successive generations, I aim to map out how familial support practices[4] have shifted from the Mao era to today's China. Through an analysis of two case studies—those of Family Chen (an urban family) and Family Gao (a rural family). I outline paradoxical changes and continuities in familial support processes that are shaped by institutional, intergenerational, and temporal forces. First, I examine how institutional transitions from the Mao to post-Mao eras have transformed family members' "capacity to care" (that is, "physical and mental ability, opportunity and resources required to engage in caregiving")[5] and reshaped the pattern of old age support from one driven by egalitarianism to one tending to subcontract filial piety. Notwithstanding the changes, interdependence underlies the ties between parents and children across the three generations and familial support for aging parents has remained strong over time. Second, I highlight how intergenerational configurations—for example, intergenerational property transmission and the emotional quality of relationships—are enmeshed with the traditional moral imperative of filial obligation in shaping adult children's "motivation to care," albeit with urban and rural families following divergent destinies. Finally, I explore the role of temporal dimensions in shaping old age support processes (an un- or under-studied aspect in existing scholarship). In the Chang family, for example, this is highlighted through a comparison of the experiences of the elder and younger sons, whose differing sub-families' life cycles affected their ability to provide old age care at different times. Through a multidimensional treatment of time, my analysis reveals how the dynamics and tensions among various temporal rhythms impact a person's or a family's care capacities and practices.

Case Studies

The Chen Family (Tianjin)

THE PROVISION OF OLD AGE CARE FOR G0 BY G1

Grandma Chen's mother (a G0, 1916–2001) was never formally employed. Throughout her life she did occasional odd jobs for a local neighborhood committee in Tianjin. Grandma Chen's father (1912–1987) had followed an army career in his early life and subsequently worked as a clerk in a government unit. However, in the 1970s alcoholism led to him losing this well-paid job. Although he was denied a civil servant pension, in his old age he received a basic livelihood allowance from the local neighborhood committee in recognition of his service in the army, as well as for having been a long-term Communist Party member. The entire family—parents and four children—initially lived in a one-bedroom house (nine square meters), but when their son (the eldest child, 1934–2012) was married in the mid-1950s they were rehoused by the local housing bureau into a two-bedroom house, in which the son's family occupied one room and the rest of the family lived in the other. When the son's four children grew older, their nuclear family moved into a slightly more spacious accommodation. After all three daughters were married and had moved out, the old couple continued to live in this two-bedroom house until they passed away.

When they started working, all the adult children (G1) gave most of their wages to their mother. This pattern continued until they married, when some of this money was returned to them in the form of bride price (for the son) and dowry (for daughters). After they were married the adult children continued to give their mother a share of their wages. Grandma Chen (G1) recalled, "After marriage, at first we gave her 10 yuan per month, which we increased to 20, then 30 and eventually, in the 1980s and 1990s, 50 yuan. My mother was very thrifty and saved this money. We also bought her clothes and various daily necessities. After she died, she left us 8,000 yuan, which she had saved over all these years."

Proximity was the dominant factor in determining which children assumed the main responsibility of visiting and providing practical support. Grandma Chen's youngest sister, whom her mother and older siblings persuaded to marry a neighbor's son, recalled: "I took most of the responsibility because I lived closest to my parents. I was only a five-minute walk away. I went to visit them every day, helping with washing clothes, cooking and carrying coal for the stove. If I missed a day, my mother would scold me, and if I didn't help with the chores, she would also criticize me." All the other children visited the couple frequently, usually about once a week or every two weeks, depending on how far away they lived. During their visits, they offered practical support to help with chores around the house.

Grandma Chen's father drank heavily and died of bronchitis in 1987. In his final months, his wife assumed the main responsibility of caring for him. Grandma Chen recalled: "The doctors suspected that my father had a tumor, but decided against operating on him because of his age. He was in bed at home for several months before he died. It was mainly my mother who looked after him, although we also visited and sometimes changed his bedsheets."

After her husband died, Grandma Chen's mother remained in reasonable health until the late 1990s, when she developed heart problems and became bedbound until her death three years later. During this period her four children looked after her, each child providing twenty-four hours of care on a rotating basis. Since the mother had not worked for a work unit, her children also shared her medical costs.

THE PROVISION OF OLD AGE CARE FOR G1 BY G2

Grandma Chen (G1, born in 1943) initially worked in a factory affiliated with the middle school that she had attended, but in 1962 was formally allocated to a job in a manufacturing factory. It was here that she met her husband whom she married in 1967. Because of the housing shortage at that time, their first week as a wedded couple was spent in her in-laws' one-room house, which they (the in-laws) temporarily vacated, staying with their neighbors. Thereafter, Grandma Chen returned to live with her natal family, while her husband stayed in his factory dormitory. After a year's wait, their work unit allocated them a single room, where they had two children (a daughter and a son); by the mid-1980s this had been upgraded by their work unit to a two-bedroom apartment. Daughter Chen (G2) left home after her marriage and moved to live with her in-laws in 1990. After he married in 1992, Son Chen (G2) and his conjugal family occupied one of the bedrooms in his parents' two-bedroom apartment. Grandma Chen's everyday relationship with her daughter-in-law was tense, and in 1999, by which time an urban commercial housing market had emerged, the young couple took out a mortgage and moved into a flat of their own, leaving the older Chen couple (G1) to live on their own.

With state allocation in jobs still in place in the 1980s, Son Chen and Daughter Chen handed over their monthly pay to their parents as soon as they started working. But after getting married, they ceased doing so and instead they gave their parents money at important festivals and birthday celebrations. This change reflected economic restructuring that took place shortly after they started working and affected both enterprises in which they were employed, resulting in their incomes becoming irregular. By the 1990s the financial strain this caused had become the source of tension between the two families living together (i.e., Son Chen's family and the elderly couple).[6] In early 2000s both children lost their state jobs and were forced to rely on self-employment and short-term contracts.

Grandma Chen's husband had a stroke in 1995, but remained mobile until 2002 when he fell and suffered brain damage. Thereafter he was mentally disabled and bedbound for two years until his death in 2004. Sixty percent of Grandpa Chen's medical costs were reimbursed by the Urban Medical Insurance scheme, leaving the balance to be paid out of their savings. Everyday care became Grandma Chen's responsibility. She recalled, "I often cried in the toilet. It was both physically and mentally tough looking after him and sometimes I felt I wanted to die. I needed to move him five times a day in order to prevent bedsores. But whenever I did so, because of his mental disability, he hit out at me and scolded me."

Son Chen lived nearby at that time and visited every day for ten to twenty minutes to see if there was anything he could do to help, such as cutting his father's hair or shaving his beard. Daughter Chen, who lived much further away, visited once a week and assisted with washing dirty clothes. Son Chen had been close to his mother since childhood and spoke feelingly of these years: "I was really grateful to my mother. She carried too much on her shoulders, but she insisted to me, 'I can't help you with your daughter's school pickups. But leave your father with me, I'll care for him.' She lightened the younger generation's burden. I am really touched by what she did." What makes this intense experience of looking after her husband even more impressive is the fact that it followed on the heels of Grandma Chen having been part of a three-year rotational care arrangement for her own mother.

When Grandma Chen became widowed in 2004, her son and daughter each agreed to give her 100 yuan per month. After one year, Grandma Chen refused to accept further payments because she felt that "their circumstances weren't very good: both had been laid off from work and were doing odd jobs." When asked about her own plans for old age care, she said that her preference would be to receive "care from children on a rota basis. But I really hope that day never comes." Daughter Chen, who by now lived only ten minutes away by car, called her every day, but visited her only every three or four months. Son Chen did not live nearby, but because of his much stronger emotional attachment, he visited her every two or three weeks. In her seventies she felt quite lonely living on her own and worried what would happen if she died without anyone knowing. In recent years Grandma Chen had occasionally felt heart pain in the evenings and made sure that medication was close to hand in case of emergency. When she mentioned this to her children, Son Chen suggested that he and his sister should take turns to stay with her at night. But Grandma Chen rejected this, feeling that such an arrangement was premature and preferring to delay it until it became essential.

THE PROVISION OF CARE FOR G2 BY G3

Daughter Chen (G2, born in 1968) was initially allocated a job in a textile factory in 1988. She met her husband, who was also a factory worker, at a local dance hall. After marrying, they lived with her husband's parents for ten years until they were able to obtain a mortgage to buy a one-bedroom flat for their conjugal family. As a result of urban economic restructuring, in the early 2000s Daughter Chen and her husband both lost their jobs and found employment via a series of short-term contracts—many of which were mediated by bilateral extended family members—and as self-employed workers. In 2006 when housing prices were still relatively low, they bought a slightly bigger flat that was more suitable as their son was growing up, and rented out their original one-bedroom flat. This turned out to be the best financial decision they had ever made, for in 2012 Daughter Chen's husband—then working as an unlicensed taxi driver—was involved in a car accident. They sold their one-bedroom flat to pay compensation to the victim in the accident and used the remaining money as a deposit for the purchase of a one-bedroom flat that became their son's marital home when he married in 2016. Their current source of income was from renting a stall in a shopping mall where they sold small toys and appliances.

After completing his college education, Grandson Chen (G3, born in 1991) was introduced by a relative to a state-owned company that he joined in 2010. Since his pay was quite low (an initial monthly wage 600 yuan rising to 2,000 yuan in 2016), he wanted to leave and find work in a non-state enterprise. But his extended family opposed this idea partly because they felt that the state company offered stability, but also due to the belief that in the absence of an elite university education Grandson Chen would find it difficult to compete for jobs in the market economy. He met his wife [an urban only child] through an introduction by his schoolmate, and they were married in 2016 and had a son the following year.

At the point in their life trajectory when the interviews took place, Grandson Chen was the recipient rather than provider of support. Because of his low income, after he was married his mother continued to contribute 1,000 yuan per month toward his mortgage, leaving him to pay the balance of 700 yuan. As his marital accommodation was close to his mother's flat, the young couple from time to time visited his parents' home for dinner. After the birth of their child, his mother-in-law—a former laid off worker who did occasional odd jobs—took on the responsibility of looking after his son (G4).

When asked about plans for their parents' old age, Grandson Chen unhesitatingly expressed his wish to reciprocate and fulfill his filial responsibilities: "It'll definitely be down to us. I'm an only child and my parents only have me to depend on. It's the same with my wife and her parents. . . . When they become immobile, I will definitely look after them. What else could I do? If necessary, we will move and live with them or they may move in with us."

However, speaking of her old age plan, his mother revealed ambivalence: "I haven't thought about that stage. Take one step at a time. . . . If he is able to, of course it would suit me best to live with him. No one voluntarily wants to live in a care home for the elderly, do they? But if there's no alternative solution, I shall have no choice but to move into a home."

The Gao Family (Shandong Village)

THE PROVISION OF OLD AGE CARE FOR G0 BY G1

Grandpa Gao's father (G0, 1908–1986) was born in a village in western Shandong. The Gao family lineage was relatively affluent until Grandpa Gao's grandfather's generation, when a considerable area of farmland was sold off to provide dowries for four sisters in the family. When Grandpa Gao grew up, before 1949 the family owned limited farmland (around 20 mu, or 1.34 hectares). As a result, before joining the village production team in the 1950s Grandpa Gao's father had engaged in street vending by making and selling buns, as well as helping with agricultural work in the fields. These bun-making skills had been passed on to Grandpa Gao and his brothers. Grandpa Gao's mother (G0, 1905–1996) did little work in the fields as she had bound feet, but throughout her life had woven cloth to earn some money. They had four sons and three daughters, but none of the daughters survived beyond childhood. Grandpa Gao's parents lived on their own until the mother was widowed, when each of her sons' families took it in turns to provide her with food and accommodation.

The support given by Grandpa Gao and his siblings to their parents occurred in three stages. At the heart of *stage one* was the provision of regular financial support (*yang*). In contrast to their urban counterparts who received regular cash transfers from their children as soon as the latter started work, rural adult sons began to offer financial support only when their parents no longer had a stable source of income (for example, because they had ceased working in the fields). Grandpa Gao recalled, "When they were in their sixties, they stopped working in the fields. So at that point we started to provide financial support [*yang*]. Our four families were responsible for providing grain and firewood."

Stage two was characterized by the provision of regular practical support—specifically, serving daily meals to parents—in addition to financial support.[7] It was initiated when aging parents became ill and / or lost a partner in old age. Where families had several sons, meals were provided by each son's family in turn. Grandpa Gao's Fourth Brother explained the process in detail:

> After my father died in 1986, we formulated a rotation plan to look after my mother who was by now not far off her 90s. Until her death in 1996 each family took turns in looking after her for a five-day stint. . . . She was still quite mobile so didn't need us to wait on her: she wasn't bedbound and in need of constant care. The daughters-in-law did the cooking and washed her clothes, but all the other tasks were done by the sons since unlike her daughters-in-law who were from outside the family, my mother found it easier to order us sons around.

The distinctive feature of *stage three* was the additional provision of regular personal care (*cihou*).[8] Grandpa Gao's Fourth Brother defined the initiation of this stage as the point at which a parent "became bedbound and required constant care"—a phrase that exactly corresponds to the circumstances in which Grandma Chen (from Tianjin) and her siblings provided support for their mother in the final three years of her life. Many of the rural families I interviewed did not in fact experience this stage, not least because the limited nature and poor quality of healthcare available to rural households made it difficult to sustain life for a protracted period in old age. Grandpa Gao explained: "Neither of my parents required extended care [*cihou*]. My father died quickly, within two months of falling ill. Only during the final twenty days of his life, when he became bedbound, did we four sons take turns being at his bedside to assist with feeding, etc. My mother died even more quickly—a mere three days after becoming unwell."

THE PROVISION OF OLD AGE CARE FOR G1 BY G2

Grandpa Gao (G1) was born in 1929. His marriage in 1951 was an arranged cousin marriage[9] (Grandpa Gao's mother and his wife's father were siblings). Grandpa Gao and his wife found it difficult to conceive and their daughter was not born until 1966. They married her into a family in the same village in the hope that she would provide old age support. They had also adopted another girl, who sadly died of a stomach tumor when she was twenty-one, despite most of their savings having been used to cover the cost of an operation to remove the tumor in the county hospital. Grandpa Gao was full of remorse for her death, realizing that all the financial and care responsibilities for their old age would now fall exclusively on his daughter. His wife injured her leg in 2007 and thereafter could only walk with the help of a crutch. She became reliant on her husband to deal with all the domestic work, and it was at this point that they handed over their field to their daughter to tend. In return, the daughter provided them with grain and covered various other costs, such as medical expenses. In 2010 Grandpa Gao also developed mobility problems after injuring his back; at this point his daughter began to visit her parents two or three times a day, preparing their meals, washing their clothes and dealing with all the household chores. She also sent her own daughter (a rural G3) to stay with the old couple during the night to look after them. This pattern continued until Grandpa Gao passed away in 2012, after which his wife moved in with her daughter, with whom she thereafter continued to live. In addition to looking after her own parents, Daughter Gao's conjugal family shared the financial responsibilities of caring for her widowed mother-in-law with her brother-in-law's family.

Grandpa Gao's Second Brother was born in 1935 and married the first potential marriage partner to whom he was introduced in 1956. They had three daughters and two sons together. Sadly, his wife died of an illness in the early 1990s. After he became a widower, the two sons took over his field and—on an equal basis—provided him with grain. However, despite having relinquished his land, Grandpa Gao's Second Brother continued to work. In 2011 when I first visited the village, he was involved in various odd jobs, such as cleaning pigsties, preparing food for pig farmers, and washing dishes in a village restaurant. In 2018, he was less active, but still earned some cash by making ropes at home and trading candles in the street market. When asked why he kept working despite being in his eighties, he replied, "I feel that as long as I can handle the job in hand, I want to continue working. If I can do one more year, I'll do one more year so as to make some money. In this way, if in future I get ill, I'll be able to ease the financial burden on my children, right? If I find I can't do it, that's when I'll stop working."

Through his hard work over the years, he had managed to accumulate 30,000 yuan in savings, which he kept in two equal savings accounts. He asked his two sons to look after the savings account books, worrying that if one day he became seriously ill and unable to communicate, nobody would know the whereabouts of the money. When asked about his old age care if and when he became unable to move about, he replied, "Eating by rotation [*lunzhe chi*]— sons taking it in turn to provide food is the custom here. Some take it in turn every month, others do so every five days. That's the norm. As long as I have food to eat and something to drink, that's all I need."

In 2011 his younger son was working as a migrant on an urban construction site. Whenever he set out for the city, the younger son went to see his elder brother and asked him to visit their father frequently in order to watch over him. In return, he promised to carry a bigger share of financial responsibility, should their father need it. In fact, at the time of my interviews their father had not sought financial help from either son. During his younger brother's absence, the elder son visited his father once a week to see how his father was getting on and to check if any work, such as house repairs, needed doing. The three daughters, who had married into families in various neighboring villages, visited their father once a month, bringing him some gifts (such as food and other daily provisions). All of them had invited their father to move into their homes to live with their families, but their father declined: "When all is said and done, living on my own gives me the most freedom. If I lived with them, I'd have to fit into their routines in terms of when to get up, what time to eat and so on. And all of them have such busy schedules and I might get in their way."

In 2011 the two sons agreed that the time might be approaching when their two families should start living with their father on a rota basis in anticipation of modernizing his house and turning it into a suitable marital home for Grandson Gao (the second son's son). But in 2018, it turned out that after graduating from university Grandson Gao (see chapter 2) had settled in the nearby city. Rather than modernizing his grandfather's old house, with financial support from his parents Grandson Gao had bought a city flat. As a result, his grandfather continued to live on his own in his old house.

THE PROVISION OF OLD AGE CARE FOR G2 BY G3

Depending on the educational and work trajectories of G3, it is possible to discern a variety of likely old age scenarios. The family of Son Gao (the elder son of Grandpa Gao's Second Brother) is an exemplar of the first scenario, characterized by all G3s working in low-paid manual occupations. Son Gao had two daughters and a younger son, none of whom were educated beyond junior middle school level. The two daughters followed their cousin to work in a manufacturing factory in Hebei province, where eventually they were joined by their brother. According to Son Gao's wife, all three children were obedient (*tinghua*) and always handed over their wages, which the parents subsequently returned to them as a dowry or bride price.[10] All three children agreed to "introduced marriages" and each of them married someone born in a neighboring village. After each gave birth to their first child, the two married daughters and the daughter-in-law stayed behind in their villages, while their husbands continued to work in cities as migrant laborers.

Following the patrilineal custom, Son Gao's wife was mainly engaged in providing support to her daughter-in-law in bringing up the grandson (G4). When the grandson was an infant, it was the daughter-in-law who assumed the main care responsibilities, while Son Gao's wife helped to make some clothes for him as well as working in the fields. When he became older, Son Gao's wife took him to and from school and provided after-school care while her daughter-in-law worked in a nearby township enterprise. Thinking ahead to future care arrangements for him and his wife, Son Gao (G2) commented, "It's a son's obligation. My son ought to look after us." When asked, "What if he doesn't?," Son Gao replied, "We treat him well, how could he not look after us?" By contrast, while his wife acknowledged that a son should carry the main responsibility, she hoped that her daughters would be more involved: "Psychologically, it feels easier to order my own daughters around. But as for my daughter-in-law, I don't know whether by then she'll listen to me or not [*ting bu ting hua*]."

The second scenario, characterized by widening class differentials between siblings, is exemplified by the family of Daughter Gao (the only daughter of Grandpa Gao). The elder of Daughter Gao's two children was a daughter (G3), born in 1991. She graduated from junior middle school and wished to take her education further, but failed to pass the senior middle school entrance exam. She did not join other young village migrants as her mother wanted to ensure that she would be on hand to lend help, should her grandparents need her care and support. Instead, from the age of eighteen she became a street vendor in the village market. In 2014 she married a young man in a neighboring village to whom she had been introduced. Her husband had worked as a migrant in a coastal factory and continued to do so after his marriage. The younger child, a son (G3) was born in 1994. He graduated from a non-elite university in Shandong province and found an office job in the city close to his home village. Looking ahead to the care arrangements for his parents in their old age, he commented: "It's most likely that I'll bring my parents to live in the city. As a son, that's my responsibility. If she's willing and happy to do so, my sister may also look after them for some of the time." When I pressed him further on potential generational conflicts between his parents and his future wife who might just turn out to have been born into an urban family,[11] he replied: "I will try to minimize the chance of their having to live together. As long as my parents are still mobile, I'll let them continue to live in the countryside. I'll cover all their costs so that they won't have to work on the farm, and if my sister is available, I'll ask her to keep an eye on them for me."

Three-Generational Comparison

Although details may vary, the preceding narrative reveals that at the everyday level support for elderly parents from their children has diminished across the three generations among both urban and rural families. Urban families have witnessed a shift from regular financial transfers and practical support to gifting at festival times and focused care provision dictated by parents' physical needs. Among their rural counterparts a trend toward delayed delivery of financial support and a more compressed package of care has emerged against the background of large-scale rural-urban migration by younger generations. Are these shifts in old age support practices a result of eroding filial piety, as predicted by theorists of modernization and aging? In answer to this question, the findings paint a complex picture.

Filial piety as a moral imperative has remained strong in both Mao and post-Mao China. Several factors have accounted for this. First, since 1949 there has been consistent official endorsement of the notion of filiality, which has persisted across the divide between the Mao and post-Mao eras. During the former, although political campaigns condemned submission to parental authority, far from attacking the idea that old age support was the responsibility of their sons, the party endorsed the notion of filial responsibility and even extended it to daughters.[12] In the post-Mao era the state has also consistently endorsed the ideology of filial support through further legislation.[13] Second, at the everyday level, families have consciously sought to transmit filial beliefs and behavior across generations. Thus, Daughter Gao (G2) spoke of having tried to teach her son to be filial during his childhood: "When I helped to wash his feet in the evenings, I said to him, 'I wash your feet now. When I'm old, when will you wash my feet?' He replied: 'When you can no longer move about, I'll definitely wait upon [cihou] you and wash your feet.'" The filial values Daughter Gao wished to inculcate in her son center around a lifetime obligation to reciprocate, an essential principle that underlies Chinese intergenerational ties. The successful reinforcement of filial values, endorsed by the state and embodied in family behavior, was captured in the responses of my interviewees across all three generations, almost all of whom, when asked about family tradition, cited filial piety as one of its major elements. While this avowal may have reflected the interview setting, filial piety as an ideology is deeply ingrained in the everyday Chinese psyche.[14] How do we reconcile the persistently strong filial attitude with the changes in old age support practices across three generations? Moving beyond the filial piety framework, I examine below the impact of the institutional configurations on the old age support practices of Chinese families during the Mao and post-Mao eras.

Egalitarianism with a Gender Twist[15]

Egalitarianism among siblings was a dominant feature characterizing G1 provision of old age support for their aging parents. It was reflected in the flat fee (urban) or the equal amount of grain and coal (rural) that each adult child was expected to provide to their parents. Although proximity dictated the frequency with which children could offer everyday practical support, in the enactment of personal care, an egalitarian division of labor among children was the norm regardless of their living patterns. Such practices accorded with the broader institutional context of the time. In the Mao era the planned economy guaranteed job security for life, enabling urban G1s to respond more readily to the needs of their extended families. One of the helpful work practices referred to by some G1s was the right to apply for temporary leave for up to six months without threatening their job security. Similarly, in rural China the ban on migration meant that adult male children lived close to their parents, facilitating the provision of regular old age support. There was a high degree of material egalitarianism among rural siblings and their families, albeit against the background of a much lower living standard than in cities. Notwithstanding urban-rural differences, in the countryside and in cities the quality of old age lives differed little across occupational divides.

However, the principle of egalitarian division played out differently in urban and rural families regarding whether or not to include daughters in the share. In urban families, daughters' close involvement in their parents' care is observable from as early as women of the G1 generation. Although married sons were far more likely than married daughters to live with their parents, women took an active part in the care of their own parents as well as that of their in-laws. Brothers and sisters both made the same regular payments[16] to their parents, not least because women of this generation had a stable income from their state-allocated employment. In addition to providing financial support, daughters were active in lending practical and emotional support, as well as taking an equal part in their parents' care rotation plans. Although many G1 women had a tense relationship with their mothers-in-law, daughters-in-law generally complied with the filial obligation to help them in old age. Contrastingly, rural women G1 devoted a considerable amount of time to fulfilling their obligations toward their in-laws, while their contribution to their own parents' old age support was minimal, being mainly confined to visiting them when they became ill. In a small number (five) of rural cases, daughters were the main sources of financial support and practical assistance, but such daughters were viewed as "substitutes" for brothers who had died or were absent.

Coordination among Children

Since the market reform of the 1980s a new institutional landscape has unfolded in China. As a result of the economic restructuring of state enterprises, many urban G2s were laid off within a few years of starting work, and from 1995 the "iron rice bowl" (de facto permanent employment) was abolished. The resultant precariousness of employment has made it difficult for adult children to allocate significant amounts of time to their extended families without suffering financial consequences. In rural China, following the agricultural de-collectivization, with increasing demands for cheap labor in the expanding urban economy leading to the lifting of the migration ban, younger members of rural households started to migrate to the cities for work in order to maximize their cash income. As China transitioned from the central planning to a reform-led "socialist market economy," these institutional changes were accompanied by a reduction in practical support provided on a daily basis by the younger generations as well as an accelerated widening of wealth and income gaps between siblings, families, and regions.

As post-G1 individuals and families pursued their varying livelihood trajectories, their "capacity to care" followed diversified paths, generating contrasting models of old age care provision.[17] Where all G2 siblings were working class or low-paid income earners, egalitarianism continued to operate in Chinese families, as shown in the case of Grandma Chen's family. However, in families characterized by widening income gaps between siblings, a new dominant model centering on coordination among siblings emerged, in which adult children organized support arrangements in accordance with their economic capacity and availability. In the Ho family in Xi'an (see chapter 3), Mr. Ho's widowed mother, who had four sons, initially lived with her second son. Later, when she became bedbound, it so happened that her eldest son had recently retired and was therefore available to care for her. As a result, his mother moved in to live with him and his family. Although the eldest son—a former company manager—was also the most financially affluent of all four children, the three other sons all made monthly cash contributions—varying according to their economic conditions—toward their mother's expenses, as well as visiting her at weekends. A further notable finding is that when no child is free to look after their parents, the choice of one of them to step down from work in order to care for aging parents is sometimes determined by adult siblings' earning power. Mr. Ho's widowed mother-in-law spent her final years with Mr. Ho's second sister-in-law who had worked as an assistant in a small shop, the other siblings (an elder brother and two younger sisters) having persuaded their sister to sacrifice her job on the ground that it was less remunerative than their own jobs. In return, they contributed 400–600 yuan each month toward their mother's living expenses and as compensation for their sister's job sacrifice.

In the countryside, families caught up in varying migration trajectories resorted to contrasting models of old age support. Grandpa Gao's Second Brother's family circumstances were representative of most families in the Shandong village. Because of the more limited migration history of this village and the more sporadic involvement of male G2s in migration, not all sons had left the village in search of work as migrant laborers. In such circumstances there was an expectation that sons would adopt a coordinated approach toward parental care—the migrant son assuming a larger financial responsibility, while the stayed-behind son who remained in the village provided more practical support. Nevertheless, the patrilineal model of old age support continued to emphasize the role of sons as the main financial providers. One notable change was the increased involvement by daughters in providing care for their own parents when their brothers left home to become migrant workers. When parents needed regular personal care, daughters were included into formal care rotation plans. This was confirmed in the Chang family (see the opening paragraphs of this chapter), where her two sons' families provided food and cash for Grandma Chang, while her married daughter also became part of the care rotation plan formulated together with her brothers.

A different model was observable in the Fujian and Hunan villages, where because of arable land shortages and greater exposure to economic opportunities in coastal regions there was a longer history of outward migration. As a result, many G2 men and women had been involved in migration for more than thirty years. Moreover, unlike male G2 migrants in Shandong who mainly worked on construction sites, Fujian and Hunan villagers formulated more versatile migration strategies involving self-employed work. In families where the entire middle generation was absent, G1s were largely self-reliant in managing their everyday lives. If regular financial transfers from migrating children (the *yang* stage) had not yet been established, elderly parents continued to work in the fields. Even after their children began to send regular remittances, as long as they remained mobile many of them continued to engage in some income-generating activities, such as tending the family vegetable garden or raising farm animals.

For those parents who became terminally ill before the date on which their children had planned to return to the village, the original old age care plan was necessarily superseded by terminal care arrangements. In chapter 2 we encountered Younger Daughter Zhao, who had married into the Wu family in a village in Fujian. Grandpa Wu and his wife, who had three sons and two daughters, lived on their own in the village.[18] But in 2019 Grandpa Wu was diagnosed with late-stage stomach cancer and was given only six months to live. When he was told this, he decided to abandon his medical treatment in order to avoid burdening his children with major financial expenses. His second son—his only prosperous child—took him on a sightseeing tour of the province. In the final month before Grandpa Wu died, all five of his children returned to the village from the cities to which they had migrated and took it in turns to be at his deathbed. His funeral expenses were shared by the three sons.

A distinctive feature of the Hunan and Fujian villages is that since G2 women as well as G2 men migrated to cities, married daughters were increasingly expected to make a financial contribution toward support for their own parents.[19] In a small number of families in which the earning capacity of married daughters far exceeded that of their brothers, a capacity-orientated approach overrode the gender principle, making daughters the main sources of financial support for their aging parents. In the Hunan village, the Zheng family comprised a widowed mother (G1) and her five G2 children (three sons and two daughters). The middle son suffered from coronary artery disease, as a result of which he was forced to return to the village after working as a migrant in a city for only five years. The responsibility of providing financial support for the widowed mother was carried entirely by his elder brother (an engineer in the city) and two younger sisters (successful business entrepreneurs in Vietnam). He and his younger brother's family (his younger brother was a low-paid migrant in a city whose wife had returned to the village to raise their grandchild) merely provided firewood and grain for their mother.

A characteristic of both models illustrated here—that of Shandong in northern China and of Hunan and Fujian in the south—is that the heaviest care responsibilities fell on the shoulders of different cohorts of women. In the Shandong model, it was the women of the middle generation whose care burden grew heavier as a result of their brother or husband leaving the village in search of migrant work. As shown in the case of Daughter Gao (G2), many daughters who remained in the village assumed care responsibilities for *two* families—their husbands' and their own. By contrast, in southern villages, from where both men and married women tended to migrate, the gendered division of labor and generational inequalities produced a differentiated impact of migration characterized by a disproportionately heavy burden being carried by older women (G1). Given women's longer life expectancy and the fact that husbands were usually older than their wives (this was the norm in the two southern villages), wives were likely to incur the heaviest responsibility of looking after their husbands.

Subcontracting Filial Piety

For more than a decade urban China has witnessed the expansion of commercial old age-care insurance schemes, as well as a boom in fee-based institutional care. Some scholars have interpreted such developments as a re-alignment of the shared interests of state, family, and market in the provision of old age security and care for the elderly.[20] However, this implicit commodi-fication of filial piety, endorsed by the state, has generated varying effects among Chinese families.

There has been a persistent aversion toward institutional care in Chinese society. Under Mao, state-run care homes for the elderly were first established in the 1950s to provide food and accommodation for those who were childless and unable to work. In rural families, a strong antipathy toward old age care homes has persisted because of their original function as homes for the child-less and the social stigma attached to childlessness. When asked if he would consider living in a care home for the elderly, Son Gao's (rural G2) response was a robust one: "Absolutely not! I have children. How could I go into a home?" By contrast, in urban families the aversion toward care homes felt among urban G1s[21] gave way to greater ambivalence among G2s, reflecting a perception that the one-child policy had rendered the "coordination model" obsolete among urban G3s. A shared concern expressed by many G2s is cap-tured in this comment by a mother living in Tianjin: "Whenever I think about this matter [old age care], I worry. Nowadays each family has only one child. How can you expect them to look after you when they still have to make a living and provide for their own family?" Within the last decade all three urban field sites have seen the construction of new commercial retirement communi-ties boasting facilities equivalent to those of a five-star hotel in their provision of meals, daily support, medical care, and leisure activities. However, all of these are targeted at high-income families.

Urban parents in China have had recourse to a variety of strategies designed to reconcile the increasing scarcity of children to look after them and Chinese families' aversion to institutional care. One of these is the practice of "coopera-tive aging,"[22] as illustrated in this explanation of collective living alongside other relatives given by a father in Xi'an: "Some of us who get on well could find a flat or house together—for example, my brother, my sister and my wife's sister. We four families would then live together. Ideally, the children of all four families would take turns to visit us—each adult child's family spending a day with us."

Another strategy involves the use of paid helpers at home, although here it deserves stating that regional variations have overlapped with generational shifts. Thanks to the city's more advanced level of development and the more rapid commercialization of care,[23] in Guangzhou the employment of paid carers dates from several decades ago, when some G1s adopted the practice in order to help provide care for their G0 parents.[24] The commodification of filial care has not yet spread to rural society. Rural G3s are more firmly anchored in personal familial care, albeit on the basis of a coordinated approach involving sons and daughters. Anticipating his inability to return to his home village or relocate his parents to the city, Grandson Gao had contemplated soliciting the help of his left-behind sister to undertake more practical and personal care, leaving him to assume the financial responsibilities. Implicit in this plan is an assumption that adult children with sufficient financial capital can choose which aspects of filial support they are willing to offer, leaving asset-weak siblings with limited capacity to resist or propose alternative plans. The consequence is that because of their economic vulnerability and "visible" presence in the village, left-behind married daughters (rural G3) are likely to carry a disproportionately heavy care burden vis-à-vis both their own and their husbands' families.

Filial Piety, Love, or Money

An "intimate turn" has occurred in family life. . . . With the redefinition of the traditional virtue of filial piety, the development of intergenerational intimacy is especially noteworthy.[25]

In the classic patriarchal system, and what survived of this system in the Maoist period, filial connection was an absolute moral imperative, to be fulfilled even in the absence of any affection, or even in the presence of concealed intergenerational hostility, particularly between fathers and sons and between mothers-in-law and daughters-in-law. . . . At the present time, however, elders have little institutional or economic control over the lives and careers of their adult offspring, and as grateful as the latter might be for their birth and upbringing, elders have lost the power to compel obedience or even emotional connection. So filial piety has evolved into a relationship in which elders must earn, as it were, the support of their children by building emotional connections.[26]

These two comments are taken from the introductions of the two most recent and influential edited volumes on Chinese families. Underlying them is an implicit model embodying a linear transition from a past driven by filial obligation to a present emphasizing emotional intimacy. However, the data from my three-generational family analysis do not fit neatly into this transitional model. Rather, in trying to interpret my project findings in order to analyze people's motivations in providing old age support, I find British sociologist Janet Finch's early work on family obligations particularly helpful. Finch developed a nonlinear analytical framework that sought to examine the balance between feelings of affection, moral imperatives of obligation, and material calculations in order to explore "how the particular sets of economic circumstances in which women and men are placed shape the character of that balance at any point in time."[27] By highlighting the various forces that may simultaneously motivate family support at a particular juncture, Finch's work makes available a dynamism that is absent from a linear transition model.

Filial Piety

It has long been argued that filial piety has played a key role in shaping people's filial obligations in China. However, there are several inherent ambiguities in the filial discourse that have escaped attention in the scholarly literature, but an awareness of which is crucial in analyzing the motivations for old age support. First, filial piety, as expounded in Chinese classical literary and philosophical texts, emphasized the general principle and function of old age support in Chinese families. In measuring the quality of old age support, individuals were evaluated against benchmarks of everyday rituals (for example, how to dress, talk, sit, and walk in front of parents and in-laws), as specified in the Confucian classical text the *Book of Rites* (*Liji*).[28] While subscribing to the principles of submission and support, actual care practices were individualized to accommodate different elite lineage groups in different historical eras, and this was reflected in these groups' own family teachings (*jiaxun*).[29] In short, filial piety has embodied an adaptability to suit the material conditions of different historical eras, albeit at the expense of generating varying degrees of ambiguity. While all forms of care behavior can be embraced as integral to old age support, what constitutes "good-quality" filial practice is a more subjective and flexible concept.

Second, in analyzing premodern Chinese society, Hamilton[30] noted that since filial piety is symbolized in the duty of submission, the prescribed emotion that best defines the relationship between children and parents in a family is that of respect (*jing*). This contrasts with Western practice, where the correlative emotion is that of love. Hamilton added that although respect does not preclude a closer attachment, it does not *require* any personal involvement. What, however, is left unsaid is whether within the protocols of classic filial piety a closer personal attachment will generate qualitatively different support practices.

Third, there is an inherent contradiction concealed in the role of material interest in old age support provision. Classic filial piety emphasizes the "unconditional" nature of altruistic support provided by adult children[31] and carries the implication that material gain should never serve as a justification for filial piety. At the same time, however, in the Chinese context sons' unfilial behavior *may* lead to the imposition of economic sanctions and exclusion from inheriting parental property.[32] Such ambiguity in relation to motives points to the need for methodological caution: material considerations may underlie filial support even if individuals are unwilling to admit that this is the case. Fourth, filial piety serves as a form of public morality. People tend to present themselves and their families to the outside world according to their "understanding of the dominant and acceptable public norms of family life."[33] Given the importance of "face" (*mianzi*; see chapter 1) in China, there is a strong performative element involved in filial piety.

Intergenerational Intimacy

In the two early generations, most families had several children—at least three or four siblings in the case of the G1 generation, and at least one or two among G2s. Such demographics often led parents to display an emotional bias toward one or two favorite children, and this was reflected in varying degrees of intimacy between parents and their *adult* children. For example, in the urban Chen family, as her mother's favorite daughter Grandma Chen felt most closely attached to her mother. In her interview, she gave several examples of her mother's particular fondness toward her: "After I was married, whenever I visited her, she always gave me 50 cents for my bus fare home. I told her that I had plenty of cash and there was no need, but she always insisted. Whenever I left her house, she would be standing outside watching until I disappeared at the end of the lane." But Grandma Chen's only brother was the child their mother loved most, and in early years he responded to the favoritism she showed toward him by supporting his parents and his younger siblings. However, he and his wife later came to hold a more grudging attitude toward his mother because they felt that she had failed to observe what was then the norm of prioritizing bringing up a son's children over that of a daughter (see chapter 4 on grandparenting).

By contrast, when Grandma Chen and her siblings recalled their father, there was no sense of intimacy at all. They did not like him, and complained that he "was selfish and didn't care at all about the children." Grandma Chen's mother also hated her husband because earlier in their marriage he had often beaten her. Nevertheless, in his old age, when Grandma Chen's father became critically ill, Grandma Chen and her siblings visited their mother and helped her change his bedsheets and dirty clothes, as well as undertaking other kinds of terminal care. As Grandma Chen put it, "We were never close to him. . . .

but after all, he is our father"—these words poignantly capturing the inescapable and binding nature of parent-children relations encapsulated in the notion of filial obligation. To some extent, the old age support extended to the father could be interpreted as an act of intimacy toward the *mother*. Overall, adult children's old age support helped their extended family in retaining a "filial" image in the neighborhood.

Prior emotional attachment—or its absence—did not determine whether or not adult children provided filial support to their parents, but stronger emotional attachments certainly enhanced the *quality* of old age care. When Grandma Chen's mother became bedbound, all the Chen siblings took it in turns to look after their mother—each looking after her for twenty-four hours. This rotational care arrangement continued for three years. When it was the turn of Grandma Chen's family, she covered the day shift, while her two children (G2) took turns to provide night care. Grandma Chen also changed and washed her mother's dirty clothes and bedsheets. But when it was her brother's family's turn, he or his wife only sent meals, but took no part in washing or changing sheets. Nor did anyone from his family stay overnight.

These varying degrees of intergenerational intimacy also characterized Grandpa Gao's family. For example, Grandpa Gao's Fourth Brother was their mother's favorite child. By way of reciprocating his mother's feelings for him, as part of the care rotation program for her, he devised a format that offered her psychological comfort during the rotation changeover between families: "My brothers agreed with me that when a changeover between families took place, we should avoid taking her to the next family. In other words, after she had been staying in my eldest brother's home for five days, my second brother would come and collect her rather than my elder brother sending her away so that this would make her feel more at ease, as sending her off seemed a bit like abandoning her, whereas coming to collect her hopefully made her feel that she was still wanted."

In the G1 and G2 generations, the multiple-sibling structure and parental favoritism could cause bitterness between generations and between siblings. By contrast, the one-child generation had no competition from siblings and received the exclusive emotional attention of their parents. When asked who were the people to whom they were closest in their lives, many G3s chose their parents. This high-level emotional attachment to parents embodied a firm commitment of filial support for parents in old age, as Grandson Chen explained: "My parents are definitely number one in my ranking of those to whom I feel closest. Supporting them in their old age is without question my responsibility." The attitude was similar among rural G3s where, despite the one-child policy having been modified to enable rural families to have a second child if their first child was a girl, the number of sons in each rural family

has fallen to one. For Grandson Gao, the feeling of affection and filial obligation had merged in his psyche: "I have deep feelings for them [his parents].
Of course I will look after them in old age."

Western scholarship on care has drawn attention to two different but interrelated dimensions of care, captured in the English expressions "caring for"
and "caring about." "Caring for" reflects positive activity, often associated
with meeting needs, performing specific tasks, and fulfilling obligations; by
contrast, "caring about" someone is a state of feeling, related to affection, af-
finity, and emotion.[34] The Chinese language does not contain the equivalent
of an encompassing word like "care," although various terms are used to
describe caring relationships. The terms *zhaogu* and *zhaoliao*[35] are the closest
equivalents to "caring for," while *guanxin* approximates most closely to "caring about." While "caring about" often generated "caring for" activities (cf. the
experiences of Grandma Chen with regard to her mother, Grandpa Gao's
Fourth Brother and Grandma Chang's younger son), care activities alone did
not automatically embody genuine "caring about" feelings (see the case of
Grandma Chang's elder son's wife). In short, transcending generational and
urban-rural divides, a feature common across three generations of families is
the existence of a qualitative difference in old age support between intergenerational relationships built on intimate ties and those bound merely by duty
and obligations.

Property Transmission

Parental property transmission has been viewed by scholars as an important
means of structuring relations between generations and among adult siblings.[36] Household division[37] was central to the enactment of property transmission in pre-1949 China and traditionally followed the principle of "equal
division among sons" (*zhuzi jufen zhi*). It customarily took place when parents
passed away, although it could legitimately proceed if parents agreed to a request made by adult sons.[38] Under the impact of socioeconomic and political
change, since 1949 a variety of "micro-institutional" settings[39] have emerged
to which household division has had to adapt. Thus, the ways in which property transmission has structured intergenerational relations and old age support have varied across generations and sectors (urban and rural).

URBAN FAMILIES

In urban China the impact of parental property transmission was not a powerful influence on the relationship between G0 and G1. From the 1950s urban
families experienced the nationalization of housing, which transferred the

private rental housing stock to local government, while housing built for their employees by state institutions and enterprises became a significant form of social welfare. Against this backdrop, traditional household division practices were abandoned,[40] leaving many parents with little of material value[41] to pass on to succeeding generations. Even for those few who did retain private housing, its monetary value was low thanks to the undeveloped state of the real estate market.

There was, however, a revival of material interest in the wake of the commercialization of housing in the late 1990s and the subsequent rapid increase in property prices.[42] For the very few G0s who survived into the 2000s, the property boom gave parental housing a role to play in formulating their old age care arrangements. For example, Grandma Chen's mother-in-law was mostly fond of her youngest son, and after selling her city flat, she bought a suburban two-bedroom flat for his family, with whom she lived until she died. The other adult children visited Grandma Chen's mother-in-law only during important festivals. It is noteworthy that G1 women were largely excluded from the benefits of parental property transmission despite playing an important role in the care of their own parents. In the Chen family, for example, all three sisters shared equally with their brother the responsibilities of caring for their elderly mother. However, on her deathbed Grandma Chen's mother said to all the daughters: "If you want anything from this room for yourselves, please take it. After all, you daughters bought me the TV, the electric fans and everything else. But as for my house—that will pass to your brother. Don't you dare argue about that."

In G1:G2 pairings, as the value of urban G1s' residential housing has steadily risen, parental property transmission has become an important point of leverage in negotiations between generations, as well as among siblings. One of the most fundamental shifts has been the changing logic guiding daughters' participation in their parents' old age support. Although none of the G2 women I interviewed admitted that parental property had been an incentive in their involvement in the provision of old age support, most expected to be a beneficiary of their parents' estate when the latter died. The shift in attitude shaping these women's involvement in caring for their parents derives from two interrelated factors. First, many G2s lacked a university education and had been badly hit by the economic restructuring of urban state enterprises in the 1990s that removed the lifetime employment guarantee. The material constraints imposed by this structural societal change accentuated economic considerations in intergenerational ties. Second, booming Chinese real estate values introduced a very high material premium into children's planning for the future since the equity tied up in urban parental property had acquired the potential to significantly transform their adult children's wealth profiles.[43]

In G2:G3 pairings, although conflicts and competition among siblings over parental property transmission have not been in evidence, parents have consciously guarded its timing as a useful tool to prevent children from straying from the filial path. Although Mother Zou (G2) paid the deposit for her son's (G3) marital housing, she objected strongly when, having floated the idea of buying another flat near a good school, he suggested that the best way of doing so would be to sell the flat his parents owned rather than his own marital housing on the grounds that the former was worth more. Mother Zou recalled the conversation with her son:

> MOTHER ZOU: If you sell our flat and buy a new one, the new flat will be in your name and we'll no longer have a flat in our names.
> SON ZOU: How could we not look after you in old age?
> MOTHER ZOU: It's impossible to predict the future. I watch TV every day and there are plenty of news stories describing how adult children's behavior can quickly change. If we become old and lose our mobility, how will we be able to protect ourselves?
> SON ZOU: I could never allow such a thing to happen. All the relatives are there watching me. How could I not look after you?
> MOTHER ZOU: If you really think it's necessary to sell our flat, you must find a way to put both your and your father's names on the title of deeds, and you must also sign a letter to confirm that this flat actually belongs to us.

In the end, Son Zou (G3) secured financial help from his wife's parents—his wife was also an only child—to fund the purchase of the second flat. From Mother Zou's perspective, she was being asked to give up ownership rights to their accommodation without any guarantee for the future, forcing her and her husband to rely on a filial commitment which her son might or might not fulfil. As a result, she maintained a firm stance in intergenerational negotiations and deployed housing as an additional weapon to ensure that her son's filial ideology would eventually be embodied in practical action.

Like G1 and G2, not a single urban G3 I interviewed cited the prospect of inheriting parental housing as a factor encouraging their filial commitment. Nevertheless, in cases where family property inheritance was disputed, children's intensified material self-interest sometimes overrode emotional intimacy. In one—admittedly exceptionally bitter—case, a widowed mother (Go, born 1916, died 2019) left a property in the center of Xi'an valued at about 5.6 million yuan. As no clear rota care arrangements had been in place, her four G1 children had conflicting views about how to share the property's value, some of them insisting on a larger share on the grounds that they had contributed more to their mother's care. G2 and G3 extended family members also became involved in the dispute in the hope of being rewarded with a larger share of the inheritance for their own nuclear families. Although family members had previously enjoyed close relationships, the dispute generated numerous bitter family quarrels across all three generations. The family tried to avoid litigation, which would have reduced its social standing among their friends and relations, but none of them was prepared to make significant concessions. At the time of writing, the issue remained unresolved, and since the property had been frozen by the Municipal Bureau of Housing, it remained unsold.

RURAL FAMILIES

Among urban families, a clear trend was observable across the three generations, highlighting the increasing importance of parental property transmission as a bargaining chip in intergenerational negotiations on old age care. By contrast, the opposite trend has emerged among many rural families, reflecting the *diminishing* significance of parental property transmission because of accelerated rural-urban migration and the much lower market value of rural residential accommodation. Among G0:G1 pairings, in the absence of housing allocation by a work unit, the impact of parental property transmission on family relations and old age support made itself very strongly felt. Low incomes, the absence of savings, and narrow intergenerational wealth gaps in the rural sector during the Mao era meant that considerable value attached to any parental property. If the residential property of parents was destined to be left to one son, that son's family would be expected to take primary responsibility for their old age care. Even in families in which an equal distribution of property was expected to take place, the various ways in which parents' estates were actually divided still impacted on family relationships.

Grandpa Gao's parents lived in rooms around a large courtyard, and a few years after each son was married their family was given some rooms. The principle of egalitarianism was mainly respected, but was also undermined by parental favoritism. Grandpa Gao and his third brother were each given two rooms, but his second brother was given three—albeit on the understanding that in order to conform to the egalitarian principle he should give some money to his parents in return. As the parents' favorite son, the fourth brother was given three rooms that were mostly newly built and better constructed. In order to pacify other sons, Grandpa Gao's parents defended their decision by arguing that the fourth son, having spent so many years at school, had been the last to enter employment and was therefore less well-off.[44] All the other brothers appeared to have accepted this argument and made no complaint. When it became necessary to put in place rotational support for their elderly widowed mother, the four sons' families equally shared their care obligations.

However, when I interviewed Grandpa Gao and his wife, both referred to the nepotism shown by Grandpa Gao's parents and hinted that the fourth brother should have borne a greater share of such responsibilities. A further source of tension was their feeling that having shared equally the old age responsibilities despite the unequal nature of the parental property transmission, the fourth brother should also have acknowledged a greater indebtedness toward his other siblings—a dimension that was absent from their limited interactions at the time of my fieldwork.[45]

Differences in the importance attached to parental property transmission emerge in the rural G1:G2 pairings. Thanks to the much shorter history and limited scope of migration, many Shandong household divisions took place after G2s married. Aware of the sensitivities associated with property transmission experienced by G1s when they were young, a new method of "drawing lots" (*zhua jiu*) was introduced in order to prevent unequal distribution among sons. However, the extent to which property transmission affected family dynamics was dependent upon the life trajectories of the G3s. In the Chang family (introduced at the beginning of this chapter), all the grandsons were married in the village. As a result, the shortage of local rural residential land for new marital houses heightened the value of the land on which G1 families' houses were built.

By contrast, there was no competition for G1 land in Grandpa Gao's extended family, several G3 members of which had graduated from university or college (albeit non-elite institutions) and found mundane office jobs in a nearby tier-four city. After graduating, for example, Grandson Gao (see chapter 2) started work as an estate agent. In preparation for his marriage, rather than modernize the house currently occupied by his grandfather, his parents paid a deposit of 130,000 yuan to facilitate the purchase of a flat in the city. Grandson Gao made clear that he had no intention of settling in the village, but said that he would return there if in the future it became necessary to look after his aging parents. We may infer that this expression of filiality was much more a reflection of his emotional attachment toward his parents than one of material considerations since his parents' residential accommodation in the village, which would one day be inherited by him, would be unlikely to have played a significant role in encouraging him to provide care for his elderly parents.

With a much longer history of larger-scale migration under way since the G2 generation, the declining significance of parental property transmission accelerated more dramatically in the two southern villages. Here, for the more elderly cohort of G2s, who were born in the late 1950s or early 1960s and migrated to cities a few years after getting married, the pattern of household division was similar to that of the Chang family in Shandong. Using savings accumulated through migration, they modernized old houses (acquired through household

division) and extended them upward to make them two- or three-story dwell-
ings in anticipation of one day returning to the village (see Appendix C). Adding
extra floors was a conscious strategy designed to provide accommodation for
their own son's (G3) family in the future, should the latter repeat the previous
generation's life trajectory and become low-paid migrants. Nevertheless, using
their own money to undertake the task of rebuilding the house had in effect
disguised and diluted the significance of G1 parental property transmission.

Many of the younger cohort of G2s, born in the late 1960s or early 1970s,
had no experience of the household division practice,[46] having migrated before their marriage. Instead, when they returned to their village to marry, they
were merely allocated some rooms in their parents' accommodation—a practice that also reflected the shortage of land for residential use by the younger
cohort of G2s. Another option open to would-be G2 returnees was that of
buying a flat in a nearby county or tier-four city.[47] As one Hunan migrant put
it, "In our village it costs around 200,000 yuan to rebuild a house. This is almost the same as the price of a small two-bed flat in the nearby county where
town life is much easier. That's why I plan to buy a flat there." His comment
reveals the ambiguities of valuing village accommodation. The cost of modernizing or rebuilding a rural house was about 200,000 yuan, but this did not take
into account the value of rural residential land. As China still lacked a genuine
free market for the purchase and sale of rural family houses, he felt it sensible
to buy a flat commanding a "proper" market value.

Among G2:G3 pairings, further variations have emerged. G2s who had
bought a city flat followed the example of their urban counterparts in using
parental property as an additional material incentive to facilitate the provision
of old age support by their only sons. For G2s who had remained living in their
villages, the likelihood of their property being a significant bargaining chip in
future old age care negotiations was dependent on their ability to secure an
appropriate market valuation of their house and land. Some villagers joked that
the value of village accommodation was bound to rise significantly if urban
developers bought it with a view to turning it into a holiday resort or residential
compound. Such developments have in fact taken place in suburban villages
(jinjiao cun) next to big cities and have profoundly transformed the wealth
profile of village beneficiaries. But the same is most unlikely to happen in villages more distant from nearby cities (yuanjiao cun).

"Surface Work"

Being filial is critical to one's public perception in Chinese society, and displaying filial piety is as important as the practice itself. The performative element
allows the caregiver to move along a spectrum between the private practice of

intimate care and a public act at least partially designed for an audience, thereby potentially reshaping the caregiver's motivation and the quality of his or her care. I have reformulated Hochschild's[48] concept of "surface acting" (describing how people manage their emotions socially) as "surface work"[49] in an effort to capture the ways in which people behave in order to fulfill normative perceptions of filial support, even in circumstances in which they would choose to behave otherwise. Surface work thereby becomes a mechanism enabling people to negotiate circumstances where no emotional or material bond exists between the caregiver and care recipient.

In Grandma Chen's family, in 1999 Son Chen used his own savings plus mortgage finance to buy a flat, but in 2005, after being forced to sell it in order to pay off debts accruing from a separate unsuccessful investment, he and his conjugal family had to move in with his widowed mother. In 2012, when an urban policy initiative designed to support low-income families offered an opportunity to purchase a flat at a heavily discounted price, he persuaded his mother to sell her flat and use part of the proceeds to buy one for his own family from the government. Since the location of the new flat was decided by the government and his wife did not like his mother, Son Chen used the remaining proceeds as a deposit to buy a second flat for his mother near to where his sister lived in the hope that she (Daughter Chen) would provide more hands-on support.

Daughter Chen acceded to the gendered bias with which her mother's property had been divided. But her sarcastic comment to her brother—"I won't fight with you over our mother's flat"—conveyed her sense of unfairness,[50] and she reduced the amount of money she gave her mother at festivals and birthdays, although she displayed her filial piety by continuing to phone her every day. Daughter Chen's practice reflected the gendered assumption that women are "naturally" good at communicating and should therefore provide more emotional support.[51] Nevertheless, communicative intimacy was not necessarily part of such emotional support: because of the favored position since childhood of her brother, she had never been as close to her mother as her brother—something recognized by both mother and daughter in their private interviews. Thus, when Grandma Chen became ill, Daughter Chen did not visit or take her to see a doctor. Although, when interviewed, Daughter Chen affirmed her commitment to sharing in the provision of care for Grandma Chen, she did so without much enthusiasm. By contrast, in addition to telephoning his mother twice a week, Son Chen visited her at least once a month, took her to see a doctor whenever she was ill, and insisted on paying her medical bills. His emotional closeness to his mother was very clear, and he wept when he spoke of her in a private interview. In Son Chen's case, the emotional closeness he felt and the material benefit he had gained from selling his mother's flat strengthened his filial ideology and practice. For Daughter Chen, deprived of material benefit and starved of emotional intimacy, filial piety was stripped to "surface work"—the public display of filiality.

Why did Daughter Chen feel the need to display filiality? The answer is not only because being filial is "to be properly Chinese"[52] but also because she was embedded in webs of interdependence in which personal relationships (*guanxi*)[53] operated as a key mechanism in Chinese society. At the heart of the web of *guanxi* networks are family kinship relations. Practical welfare needs and the uncertain and sometimes unstable nature of the China's social environment—reflecting political upheavals and impoverishment in the Mao era and the vagaries of market reform in the post-Mao era—have compelled family members to come together for support and protection. At the same time, the cultural tradition of reciprocity[54] still dictates that in order to secure support from the extended family, an individual must fulfill his or her familial obligations to sustain the interdependent family network. Accordingly, Daughter Chen should have displayed filiality to her mother and brother in order to retain membership in her natal family, whose support she might at some point need, especially in a world whose future had become uncertain. However, thanks to emotional reserve and the de facto financial loss resulting from her mother's nepotism, her filial piety was translated into mere "surface work," such as phoning her mother every day but doing little else of substance to help her. Grandma Chen and her son recognized the superficiality of her behavior, but chose to ignore it. They did so for two reasons: first, because they too were embedded in a network of interdependency that might yet require Daughter Chen's involvement in future care rotation arrangements; and second, because filiality affects not only the public standing of an adult child, but also the "face" of the extended family in the wider kinship and social circles.

Intersecting Consequences

While making sacrifices for the collective welfare of Chinese families, mothers of all three generations are more likely than their male counterparts to form closer bonds with other family members because of both the gendered division of labor in the domestic sphere and gendered notion of emotionality. However, men's greater advantage as economic laborers declines as they age, and having invested insufficiently in the "emotional bank," older men are less likely to receive high-quality support and care than older women. This gender effect is further mediated by urban-rural and generational differences. In contrast to city flats owned by urban G1s, the houses of most rural G1s had a low market value. Moreover, unlike the strong emotional attachment seen in relationships between a G2 couple and their only G3 son, rural G1s commonly had many sons, engendering inter-sibling conflict and bitter competition for resources. Therefore, rural male G1s are most susceptible to the risks of elderly abuse and neglect. In the absence of material incentives and emotional closeness, the most they could expect to receive from their adult children was therefore "surface work," designed to fulfill public perceptions that filial piety had been discharged. In concrete terms, this often meant no more than the provision of short-term terminal care and payment of funeral costs. It does, however, deserve emphasizing that the impact of these micro-level intrafamilial dynamics is shaped by the financial circumstances that determine adult children's capacity to provide care. In other words, even if adult children are both emotionally close to their parents and also materially incentivized to support them, financial constraints are likely significantly to limit the extent to which intrafamilial forces can improve the quality of care.

Temporalities

While there is an abundant literature examining the extent to which filial piety has been eroded or redefined in Chinese families, the temporal dimension of aging and old age support is un- or under-studied. I highlight below several temporal mechanisms that have affected individuals and families' experiences of old age care.

Institutional Time

There are three distinctive phases in Chinese welfare development, all of which intersect with a systemic division between urban and rural areas.[55] During the first phase (1949–78), the urban work unit was able to provide various benefits, such as lifetime employment (the "iron rice bowl"), a state pension, and welfare provision (including heavily subsidized food, housing, and medical care). This ensured an "egalitarian"[56] system of high welfare and low wages. In contrast, while rural able-bodied adults were absorbed into the collectivization of agriculture, the lack of wealth, investment, and development in rural areas meant that none of the other urban benefits were offered to rural residents, although a cooperative medical system of low-cost paramedical personnel—"bare-foot doctors"—emphasizing preventive health care and public hygiene improvements did exist in rural areas. During this period, only those who were disabled, had lost the ability to work, or were childless were provided for by local government.[57]

During the second phase (1978–2000), the primary aim was economic growth with a rapid marketization of the welfare services established in the Mao era. In urban China, the "iron rice bowl" was gradually weakened and eventually abolished in 1995. With millions of former state employees laid off as enterprises restructured, the state introduced social security such as the urban social assistance scheme (*dibao*) and unemployment insurance.[58] By the end of the 1990s, state pension and medical care provided by the work unit system had been replaced by retirement insurance and medical insurance linked to contributions by enterprises as well as individuals.[59] In contrast with a more gradualist removal of work unit welfare protection in urban areas, and commercial replacement, rural China has experienced a vacuum in welfare provision.[60]

The current phase (from the early 2000s onward[61]) involves a renewed state interest in social welfare provision. Urban pension and medical insurance systems have been expanded to cover residents outside the formal workplace. A national guideline on urban old age care promotes "home-based care as the main part, backed up by community-based services and complemented by institutional care."[62] In the last decade, urban communities (*shequ*) have played an increasingly important role in enriching old people's lives by organizing regular leisure activities and classes (music, dancing, chess, cooking, calligraphy, etc.), as well as providing a heavily subsidized dining service for older residents.[63] In rural China, funded by government subsidies and individual contributions, an old age pension scheme for rural residents was introduced in 2009.[64] Rural medical care insurance was piloted in 2003, and gradually expanded to cover all villages by the end of 2015.[65]

The phases of welfare development are conceptualized here using "institutional time" to juxtapose the evolution from the Mao to the post-Mao era with the impact of aging parents' care needs upon Chinese families. During the 1990s, Chinese families were hit hard by shrinking welfare support. While the work unit covered all of the medical care expenses of Grandma Chen's father-in-law prior to his death in the early 1990s, when Grandma Chen's own husband became ill in the late 1990s, his work unit was no longer responsible for any of his medical care expenses and this imposed a considerable burden on the family because his medical insurance only covered 60 percent of the hospital charges. A number of families who required old age medical care at this time complained that hospital doctors deliberately used various methods to charge patients higher fees (for example, by prescribing more expensive medicines or making them take unnecessary tests).

The sudden increase in medical expenses occurred in the 1990s at exactly the same time many G2s were being laid off. Against this backdrop, Grandma Chen's own mother became ill in the late 1990s. As she did not have medical insurance (because she was not formally employed) her children opted to take her to community clinics, rather than city hospitals for full treatment, as this was all they could afford. Ten years later, urban residents like Grandma Chen's mother would have been covered by the medical insurance system for residents. However, the broader inclusion of the population today does not change the fact that insurance is still reliant upon contributions from participating households and government subsidies rather than being citizenship-based. Extensive inequity therefore continues to persist with the health care system privileging those who can afford it. A common saying among urban interviewees is that "a single serious illness can wipe out twenty or thirty years of hard work and reduce you to pre-Liberation [i.e., pre-1949] living standards."

The dual welfare regime also exacerbates existing inequalities between urban and rural families (such as income and infrastructure development) and creates compound inequalities for rural older people. While the pension initiative introduced in 2009 was universally welcomed by rural interviewees, the gap between rural and urban pensions remained strikingly large. In 2019, a retired urban factory worker's monthly pension was around 2,000 yuan while the state monthly pension for a rural resident was a mere 5 percent of this figure at about 100 yuan. On top of this vast disparity in provision, rural residents admitted to city hospitals (where the best medical treatment is available) are required to share a bigger proportion of the hospital charges than urban patients. As a consequence, if an elderly member of a rural family contracted a serious or terminal illness and all the adult children were low-paid, the most common fate was simply to wait for death.

Finally, despite varying institutional time, the nature of the social welfare regime in China is grounded in a residual model shaped by Confucian principles that emphasize the family's responsibilities and the state's residual function.[66] Although the state has expanded pension and medical care insurance provision to rural communities in China, these have mainly taken the form of financial disbursements. In terms of personal care, a comparison of the three generations reveals a strong continuity of exclusive reliance on family members (or their paid substitutes or delegates) across both the Mao and post-Mao eras.[67] In other words, the three-generational comparison offers no clear sign of "re-embedding" in familism in the post-Mao era of the kind anticipated by Yan's individualization thesis. Instead, most interviewees of all three generations were embedded in extended family and kinship ties across the Mao and post-Mao divide.

Biological Time

There is a public perception of older people's "dependency" on younger generations, with old age symbolized by dependency.[68] However, as chapter 4 reveals, Chinese grandparents generally play a crucial role in taking care of their grandchildren and this enables grandparents to accrue moral capital from their families. Old people and their family members are therefore situated on a spectrum of dependency and independency as care providers and recipients over the life course. How old people move across the spectrum depends upon their changing care needs, something that subsequently triggers discrete stages of old age support. This need orientation accounts for the variation in old age support practices within each generation. Despite sharing a similar chronical time, biological time in relation to fragility and mobility fine-tunes aging experiences.

Across all three generations, there was a strong desire actively to resist a stage that rendered them completely dependent. While Grandpa Gao remained mobile and productively active until two years before his death, his experience of old age changed profoundly when he became unable to move around.

> GRANDPA GAO: Living in old age is worse than being dead.
> I: why?
> GRANDPA GAO: Living like me—I can't do any work in the fields, I also rely upon others to bring meals to me. I can't manage anything without my child's help. What is the meaning of a life like this?

His sentiments in this regard were echoed in the remarks of Grandma Chang (at the start of the chapter) who suffered from long-term mobility issues. Two factors underscored why they preferred death to living. First, people like Grandpa Gao and Grandma Chang were well aware of the institutional lacuna in long-term care provision, as it was their family members who exclusively financed as well as undertook the practical tasks involved in care provision. Death would relieve the care burden upon their children and extended family. Second, dependency is popularly interpreted as the antithesis of utility and productivity and so by this basic logic dependency deprived these individuals of a meaning for living. Among other things (such as the value of their considerable life experience), this isolated notion of dependency overlooks the practice of reciprocity over a life course; for example, Grandpa Gao provided support to his daughter at various stages of his life cycle, something I gently reminded him of during our interview together. It is noteworthy that these considerations also featured in the minds of urban aging parents, although with greater financial resources, their strategy was to pay close attention to their health and so to delay the arrival of this "dependent" stage.

The temporal dimension highlights the way in which old people's residence status (whether they lived alone or with one or more of their children) was not a key driver in shaping the pattern of old age support, but is subject to change depending on parents' needs at a temporal rhythm. Both Grandpa Gao and Grandma Chen, like their own parents, lived on their own well into old age until circumstances necessitated that their adult children took them into their homes or cared for them on a rotation basis.

Extended Family Time

Demonstrating Confucian filial piety involves obedience to the senior generation, the production of male descendants to continue the family line, and the support of parents in old age; among these, an inability to continue the family line was considered the most unfilial action of all.[69] Thus, there is an inherent paradox within filial piety: while there is an overwhelming emphasis on the well-being of the senior generation, the future generation is of upmost significance to the lineage and family. As a consequence, there is the unresolved issue of which generation to prioritize if the demands to serve the senior generation and the future generation come into conflict. In practice, a hierarchy of priority toward the younger generation exists[70] and this affects resource allocation in the processes of old age support. In some poorer rural households, G1s confessed that they needed to prioritize the provision of food to their own children over to their parents given scarce resources.[71] An old Shandong man recalled: "I regret deeply that I couldn't be more filial towards my mother. Until her death (in the early 1970s), she never ate a chicken from me. At that time, we didn't have any money, it was impossible to balance three sides—our own children, ourselves, and our parents. Since we could hardly feed our own children, how could we be filial toward our parents?"

The enforced implementation of the one-child policy from 1979 to 2015 made it impossible for urban families to guarantee a male heir, leaving the only child, whether boy or girl, as the sole continuation of the family bloodline. In rural China, where a modified family planning policy offered a greater possibility for a male heir, peer pressure within the community continued to confer a much lower status on rural families without a son. It was widely felt among interviewees that grandparents and parents ought to make sacrifices to ensure the well-being and success of an only grandchild/grandson. The combination of Confucian filial ideology, which emphasizes having children, and China's compressed demographic transition has made the hierarchy of priority among generations more acute and visible.

While the priority in responsibility is tilted toward the younger generation, the older generation is not forgotten and this creates a sandwich generation that bears a care responsibility in both directions for the entire extended family.[72] In line with the analysis in Falkingham et al.[73] of Chinese national survey data, my findings confirmed that the number of families who struggled with the competing demands of older and younger generations at any one time were, in fact, quite low. However, when families did encounter challenges, the households with limited resources faced severe problems. In one Shandong family, a G2 migrant worker became very emotional when recalling the period leading up to his mother's death in 2012: "I couldn't find enough money at the time . . . I was so frustrated. The hospital asked me to hand over cash, but I just couldn't get hold of any money. If only I'd been able to find 30,000 yuan, my mother would have lived for another three or four years. I desperately wanted to secure treatment for her, but there was just no way in which I could help . . . I saw her dying before my eyes—it was the most painful moment of my life." At the time, both his two children and his brother's children were all full-time students and so the two sons had no spare savings between them. (Their only sister worked in a village enterprise, earning even less than they did, while their wives' siblings were also low-paid migrants.) Had his mother become ill four or five years later, when his children had completed their education, he would have been in a much better position to help and fulfill his filial obligations.

Migration Time

A key question in the literature on rural aging is whether migration has a positive or negative impact upon old age support in rural families. I suggest this dichotomous framing of the relationship between migration and old age support has largely overlooked the temporal mechanisms embedded in the migration and care processes. Migration itself has a temporal dimension and so caregiving and care-receiving roles, as well as care arrangements, vary over the life cycle.

Existing literature reveals that the provision of financial support—enhanced by migration—could have positive effects on the financial security and the welfare of parental generations, thereby partly offsetting the disadvantage of living at a distance.[74] However, I found that the cash disbursement made by migrating children was not automatic when they became migrants. The length and history of migration, employment status, and family life cycle of the migrating children all played a role in determining the timing of remittances and capacity to remit. When Elder Son Chang first migrated to the city as a construction worker, he did not make any surplus income during the first two years due to lack of legal protection for migrant workers. Even when he managed to start sending money home, due to the stage of his family cycle (i.e., paying the educational expenses of his second daughter and the wedding expenses of his only son), his nuclear family could hardly make ends meet without borrowing money. And so, despite earning a higher wage than his stayed-behind siblings, his capacity to alleviate his aging parents' sufferings was very limited. As a consequence, when his father was diagnosed with stomach cancer in 2009, the extended family had to send him to a traditional Chinese medicine doctor rather than an urban hospital, as the latter was well beyond the two sons' combined family resources.

The family narratives from the two Southern Villages with a much longer history of migration confirm the temporal dynamics. For example, in the Zhao family of the Fujian village (see chapter 2), it was not until 2014 that Younger Daughter Zhao and her husband's material circumstances began to improve, despite the fact that they first migrated to the city in 1992. Younger Daughter Zhao explained that prior to 2014 they were not in a position to send money to her in-laws or parents since "the biggest item of expenditure was the cost of the two children's education and living in the city." Only after one of their children had finished university did they begin to accumulate sufficient financial resources to be able to contribute to their parents' living and medical expenses.

An overwhelming majority of G2 migrants expressed a strong desire to return to their home village or county later in life. This would normally happen sometime after their son's marriage or after they had paid off the debt incurred for the wedding. Many of those in their early fifties had already taken concrete action to prepare for their return, such as rebuilding and decorating their village house. The absence of migrating G2 children, who were nevertheless determined to return to their home villages, affected the timing and the provision of regular practical support and / or personal care. For parents who became terminally ill prior to their children's return, old age care expectations were necessarily superseded by terminal care needs. For parents who required constant personal care prior to their planned return time, the migrating children delegated care, often to their wife or stayed-behind siblings.

Process Time

Grandma Chang's experience of old age care (noted at the start of this chapter) reveals the tensions between "process time"[75] and clock time. This dimension is critical to understanding care work but has been overlooked in the existing literature on old age support in China. These tensions affected the way care work was being carried out and had implications for the care recipient, particularly in terms of quality of care.

One of the key reasons why Grandma Chang was frustrated with her condition lay in the difference between the "process time" she required (and that was hard to quantify—e.g., chatting, comforting, etc.) and the "clock time" her children were governed by as they still needed to make a living themselves. As she was bedbound and on her own, her emotional needs were upmost. During the days when the Elder Son's wife was responsible, she needed to coordinate the care work for her mother-in-law with her agricultural work in the fields. She therefore emphasized the tasks she needed to complete whenever she visited Grandma Chang, for example, cooking the meal, bringing the food, and helping Grandma Chang to eat, as well as helping Grandma Chang to the toilet. Although the daughter-in-law performed these tasks well, this task-oriented notion of time was not the "process time" Grandma Chang desired.

The younger son of Grandma Chang was similarly constrained by the clock time through which he needed to combine care responsibility with his productive work. However, he had a much closer emotional connection with his mother and he also materially benefited from his mother's nepotism in terms of property division (see above on the impact of intimacy and property division upon old age care process). The younger son was therefore more willing to balance "process time" and clock time during his rotation days. One strategy was to visit Grandma Chang more frequently—once every thirty minutes—so as to be more attentive toward the emotional and practical needs of Grandma Chang, something acknowledged by his mother as a demonstration of his "caring about."

There is a well-known Chinese proverb that goes, "Before the bed of the long-term ill there are no filial children."[76] To an extent, the tension between the "process time" required for long-term care and the clock time adult children are constrained by, especially during their economically productive-years, may be among the contributing factors to the depleting energies or capacities of the adult children in performing long-term care. Given the blurring boundaries involved in "process time,"[77] it is important to acknowledge that long-term care is extremely intensive labor that will stretch beyond the limit of filiality.[78]

Conclusion

In his study of old age support and filial obligations in the 1990s, Whyte[79] cited Polanyi's[80] contention that "market forces foster individualistic tendencies that have a corrosive impact on family and community obligations" and questioned whether "the market reforms, the one-child family policy, global economic and cultural influences, or whatever—will reinforce or undermine filial support for aging Chinese parents." My three-generational analysis of shifts and continuities answers this question by showing that social transformations in post-Mao China embodied forces that simultaneously generated "pull" and "push" effects on the familial old age support system. On the one hand, similar to the institutional configurations impacting grandparenting (chapter 4), external and micro-institutional changes such as the replacement of a planned economy with a precarious labor market, geographic and social mobility of China's market reforms, and the sharp drop in numbers of children have all contributed to declining or delayed everyday support provision. On the other hand, an endorsement of filial values in both public and private spheres, the continuing significance of personal relationships (*guanxi*), and a state welfare framework that emphasizes its residual function have created conditions fostering intergenerational interdependence and solidarity, thereby ensuring that the family has continued to be a critical safety net for ordinary Chinese citizens. Overall, familial support for aging parents (and even grandparents) has remained strong over time and across generations, despite the bewildering array of external changes to which Chinese families have had to adapt.

The findings in this chapter run counter to Yan's model of "descending familism," which describes a downward flow of resources from the older to the youngest generation based upon the experiences of the post-1980s generation. First, a hierarchy of priority among generations existed well before the post-1980s generation and was instead conditioned by the paradox within Confucian filial piety. This marks a continuity with the past that views the future generation as of upmost significance to the lineage and family. It has only become more acute and visible as a result of China's compressed demographic transition since the 1970s. Second, the downward flow of intergenerational resources is not necessarily a sign of the constant decline of parental authority and the rise of youth autonomy (as also with other life phases such as growing up, choosing spouses, and grandparenting) because the impact of a family's life cycle is overlooked. Instead, it is temporarily subject to the care needs of the older generation which may trigger an upward flow of intergenerational resources (for example, covering medical expenses and provision of personal care). The three-generational findings therefore more closely align with an early argument made by Davis-Friedmann[81] drawing upon data collected in the Mao and early reform eras that *lifelong* reciprocity is a dominant characteristic of intergenerational ties in China.

Notwithstanding the continuing functioning of the familial support system, this chapter also reveals the uneven processes individuals and families must respond to in multilayered institutional and intergenerational configurations. For the rural elderly, in particular those who emerged from the Mao era and into the reform era with virtually no "valuable" assets or property, the future has become more uncertain. This is in sharp contrast with urban elderly people who benefited from housing reform that launched them into homeownership in the 1990s as they could use their greater resources to help bind their single child to them through the purchase of a marital home as well as monitoring the timing of the transmission of their own occupied property. Rural residents, and in particular the rural G1s, have also been disadvantaged by a persistent deficit in economic and infrastructure development relative to urban residents.

Theoretically, this chapter redresses two biases in classic modernization and aging theory. First, it challenges the preoccupation with value change and highlights how a variety of factors—structural, intrafamilial, and temporal—have interacted with cultural values to shape the contours of old age support practices. While filial norms serve to lubricate the flow of care for both caregivers and care-receivers, filiality alone is not sufficient to sustain the meaningful enactment of care. The challenges faced by aging parents in China cannot simply be evaluated through consideration of the extent to which their children are, or are not, filial. Rather, essential to such an assessment is an examination of Chinese families' *capacity to care* and exposure to the structural inequalities that those families face but that are often obscured in the public discourse of filial piety.

Second, this chapter has challenged the convergence model underlying modernization and aging theory. Convergence is not only reflected in the Eurocentric assumption that other societies follow a single path toward the "Western model"[82] but is also evident in modernity writers' discussions on relations between urban and rural regions as well as between sexes. In contrast to a pattern of evolutionary progress from the agricultural "rural periphery" to an industrialized "urban core" accompanied by the eventual disappearance of urban-rural differences,[83] the Chinese narrative reveals persistent and even widening differences in the life trajectories of the elderly between urban and rural regions, demonstrating uneven paths of modernization.

The gendered consequence of modernity is also nonlinear. While Chinese families have come to value kinship ties involving both the husband's and the wife's families, the rising status of daughters vis-à-vis sons has generated differing urban and rural contours. Thus, notwithstanding their greater contribution to supporting their own parents in old age, rural daughters continue to suffer the consequences of gendered patrilineal inheritance custom. On the other hand, although today's one-child generation daughters enjoy financial benefits from their natal family, the extent to which such privileges will prove lasting in the wake of the elimination of family planning controls and its unknown impact on the demographic profile of Chinese families remains to be seen.

The findings of this chapter raise two important issues that will need further investigation as the accelerated aging of China's population takes place.[84] The first is the fact that as the income gap among siblings and between families widens, aging experiences and old age support practices will continue to diversify. Against a backdrop of faltering economic growth generating increasing economic uncertainties and the existence of an inverse population pyramid, adult children with sufficient financial resources are more likely to subcontract filial responsibility either to a private care provider (for example, by employing female rural migrant workers or older working-class urban women) or to less affluent siblings or relatives. This could generate the emergence of a "care drain" and / or "care replacement"[85] *within* China. Chinese families located at the bottom of this national care chain—mostly the impoverished rural elderly—are likely to bear the brunt of this old age care transition.

Second, exclusive reliance upon familial old age support is not sustainable. The Chinese state was successful in creating the conditions to consolidate intergenerational solidarity among families during the Mao and early reform eras.[86] During the last two decades, the state has continued to place great weight upon filial piety through legislation, education, and propaganda, building upon and reinforcing the perception that old age support from children to parents is a duty grounded in assumed natural feelings. However, as shown in this chapter, the boundaries between filial morality, intimacy, and economic calculation are more permeable than the government discourse implies. In particular, elderly people with no property to fall back on and / or who have a strained relationship with their children (for example, rural male G1s) are vulnerable to old age neglect and abuse. Such threats make it essential that the state intervenes to offer alternative care beyond the confines of family and market.

Conclusion

IT HAS BEEN the privilege of my professional life to have been given the opportunity to be welcomed into the homes of so many families across various parts of China. Starting as a complete stranger, over time I found myself becoming a family friend—and occasionally a confidant. Those whom I met generously shared with me their life stories and sometimes family secrets, and our conversations were punctuated with numerous intense moments of laughter and tears. These precious occasions provided me with a unique window into the lives of ordinary people in China. The conversations I had with them have been the bedrock on which I have been able to explore the complex change, continuity, and diversity of family practices that have unfolded across three generations of momentous Chinese history.

Three impressions lingered deeply in my mind during my fieldwork encounters. First, I was overwhelmingly struck by the resilience of Chinese families in the face of the tremendous social transformations and upheavals they had endured. Tempestuous events formed the backdrop to the lives of the three generations studied in this book. In the Mao era they include political campaigns of the 1950s, 1960s and 1970s, such as the Great Leap Forward and the ensuing "Great Famine" and the Cultural Revolution. No less life-changing, in the post-Mao years since the end of the 1970s, the lives of Chinese rural and urban citizens have been transformed as a result of economic and social reforms, including the imposition of a one-child policy and widespread redundancies alongside urban economic restructuring and mass migration from the countryside to the cities. Through periods of suffering and sometimes conflicts, family has remained central to people's lives, ideologically as well as functionally. Like a sponge, the Chinese family has absorbed the pain and dislocation caused by efforts to realize successive Chinese administration's visions of modernization, embedded in so many state-engineered projects.

Second, I was shaken by the chasm between living conditions of urban and rural residents in China despite the country having undergone over seventy years of development. Categorized in the terminology of this book as an urban

G3, I grew up in a provincial capital in East China, where I was familiar with an official discourse that viewed rural China as a symbol of poverty and arrested development.[1] However, when I first spent long periods living in rural villages in 2011, I was still shocked by the material deprivation of many villagers. There were no sanitary facilities except for trench privies. In winter when temperatures sometimes fell to minus fifteen degrees Celsius, many rural G1s' houses only had windows covered with paper. Although there was no sign of starvation, most villagers lived close to subsistence level. During the second phase of my fieldwork (2016–19), the infrastructure of all three cities I visited was no different from that of London and other major cities in the developed world. Indeed, the economic circumstances of some urban G3 families I met in China suggested a wealth profile that outdid that of middle-class families I knew in the United Kingdom. By contrast, the pace of change in rural China has been much slower: except for a minority of families who had managed to accumulate sufficient funds from migration to enable them to upgrade their cooking, heating, and bathing facilities, living conditions for other farming households were largely the same as they had been in 2011.

Finally, I was puzzled by the incompatibility between academic models that purported to represent Chinese families—with their emphasis on change and concepts of "individualization of Chinese society," "descending familism," and "the inverted family"—and the complex and intricate family narratives I heard from members of different generations living in various parts in China. At this point I started to reread earlier studies of Chinese families, such as those of Whyte and Parish and Davis-Friedmann in the 1970s and 1980s, where I discovered surprisingly similar findings and conclusions to those I had reached. In particular, I was struck by our shared recognition of the existence of paradoxical changes as well as continuities in Chinese family life over time—this despite our use of differing comparative timelines, in my case a comparison of the Mao (1949–76) and post-Mao eras (1976–2010s), in theirs one of pre- and post-1949 conditions. Out of this and inspired by the critiques of both classic modernization theory and the new phase of modernity theorizing (see the Introduction), in an attempt to accommodate generational changes and continuities I formulated my "embedded generations" framework. I now revisit this framework in summarizing the main findings of this book.

Embedded Generations

As highlighted in the introduction to this book, the concept of "embedded generations" refers to the ongoing, multifaceted, relational, and institutional configuration of family life in which each generation is anchored. First, the family practices of each generation are embedded in the institutional context of their time. Secondly, as family life is linked and shared between generations, a constant process of intergenerational transmission and negotiation is underway at the everyday level. Finally, individuals differ in their capacity to adapt to institutional and intergenerational configurations. As a result, there is variation in and contestation of family practices within a single generation and between different generations.

Institutional Configurations

When invited to comment on family changes taking place over time, one of the mostly frequently used phrases by interviewees was that "as time moves on, there will inevitably be changes." Indeed, as China transitioned from a planned economy to a market economy, the economic livelihood, housing, and welfare conditions of members of the three generations examined in this book were profoundly affected by major policy changes instituted by the government. These institutional transitions were reflected in changes of various family practices, such as the following.

On childhood experiences, across the three generations there is a very clear shift from being "free-roamers" to becoming the subject of "concerted cultivation,"[2] reflecting the institutional transitions embracing improved living standards, smaller family size, and promotion of a knowledge economy, all of which placed a premium on maximizing the educational opportunities of children (see chapter 1). On sex and intimacy, again there emerges a very clear increase in sexual activities in nonmarital settings, deriving from a combination of factors including greater material wealth, increasing mobility (facilitated, for example, by rural-urban migration and professional business travel), depoliticization of everyday life (for example, reduced institutional surveillance in workplaces and universities), and an explosive rise in media focus on topics such as intimacy and love in the post-Mao era (see chapter 3). As for old age support, while giving money to parents on a monthly basis, albeit on a reduced scale after marriage, was the norm among urban G1s, this practice has almost disappeared among the younger cohort of G2s and their G3 successors. This change is closely linked to changes in urban livelihood conditions associated with the shift from lifetime guaranteed employment during the Mao era to the more precarious post-Mao labor market championing competition and efficiency (see chapter 5). Such examples show how institutional changes have, perhaps inevitably, *pushed* families toward changes of their own.

There are, however, also *pulling* effects inherent in institutional changes. What may appear to be a paradoxical pattern of countervailing changes reflects the essential nature of institutions. Thus, since institutions are neither traditional nor modern, institutional transitions generate forces that both re-inforce and undermine a linear pattern of change.[3] As Duncan has put it, in-stitutions are "neither completely new, nor completely traditional, but rather a dynamic mixture of the 'modern' and 'traditional,' and the 'formal' and 'in-formal.'"[4] This is due to the existence of "institutional leakage"[5] whereby "sets of rules are metaphorically connected with one another and allow meaning to leak from one context to another along the formal similarities that they show."[6]

In the case of China, two major institutional transformations have taken place since 1949. The Maoist campaigns of the 1950s sought to dismantle traditional family customs and endorse a new socialist ideology. Subsequently, following Mao's death, the state's imperative shifted to economic develop-ment, involving the removal or reform of practices and institutions inherited from the Mao era. Notwithstanding these two major efforts to break with the past, norms and values of the past have constantly been "re-served" and / or adapted to accommodate the new normal. For example, gendered tradition in terms of the material basis of marriage has been reconfigured in different eras despite changes in the form of marital residence. Throughout the Mao era, while patrilocal custom was affected by public housing allocation, the work unit[7] system favored male married workers, as a result of which marriage was a material necessity for women. Since 2000, following the commercialization of housing, although neolocal residence has become the new trend, the hus-band's family is expected to provide the marital home—a convergence with the practice of rural families throughout the Mao era—effectively adapting the patrilocal custom to the twentieth-first century and reinforcing hypergamy and gendered intergenerational wealth transfer (see chapter 2).

Further, a set of altered institutions and policies could have what appear to be contradictory consequences for different aspects of family patterns. For example, the shift in urban China during the 1950s to nearly universal full-time wage employment of women in work units that also often allocated housing, in combination with the gender differentiated retirement ages, from the 1950s onward helped to undermine the patrilineal bias of urban families and incline urban families to favor their daughters nearly as much as their sons (see chapter 1), long before the one-child birth limits reinforced that tendency, while also helping to undermine parentally arranged marriage and foster freedom of mate choice, at least to some extent (see chapter 2). In these respects, urban Chinese family change tended to appear similar to the trend toward conjugal families that Goode stresses due to modernization (but more rapidly). Paradoxically, as I show in the discussion of grandparenting in chapter 4, those same institutional changes during the 1950s in urban China[8] also made cooperation and mutual assistance between parents and grandparents essential, thus heightening the role of urban grandparents in ways that appear "traditional" and do not fit with the model of conjugal families very well.

Finally, institutional transformations embody a combination of new and old elements inducing change as well as continuity. For example, for the familial support system, China's social transitions from Mao through the post-Mao eras simultaneously exerted pull and push forces. On the one hand, economic and livelihood security, whether achieved through job allocation by the state in the Mao era or the subsequent forces of market competition, conferred a degree of independence from extended family control. On the other hand, the use of personal networks (*guanxi*), often derived from kinship ties, is found to have been common in grassroots economic activities evident, for example, in chain migration displayed by rural G2 villagers and in the reemployment efforts of many laid-off urban G2 workers. While China's opening up exposes the youngest generation (G3) to Western ideologies that champion individualism, cultural values such as filial piety have been officially endorsed and promoted in state legislation and public discourse. Within three generations, state population policies, whether in the form of the 1970s "later, longer, and fewer" initiative or the post-Mao one-child policy (1979–2015), forcefully reduced the average number of children per family from five or six to one (urban) or two (rural). In so doing, they fundamentally reshaped the value placed on children, as well as the power balance and resource allocation control between generations. Yet the welfare regime in China remains strongly family-based, and although important state pension and medical care initiatives were introduced during the period covered by the book—albeit to varying degrees across the three generations and between urban and rural China—it is telling that personal care arrangements for both children and the elderly have remained mainly the responsibility of family and kin regardless of generation (see chapters 1, 4, and 5). These multiple forces and paradoxes have created conditions that simultaneously undermined and reinforced the extended family support system.

Intergenerational Configurations

Intergenerational configurations are another major "pulling" force that has prevented the emergence of a linear pattern of change in family dynamics. One strategy frequently used by parents and more senior members of previous generations to preserve continuity and connectivity between generations has been the intergenerational *molding* of children. This was achieved in children's early lives through corrective physical punishment intended to set clear boundaries between unacceptable and "proper" conduct (chapter 1). As children grew up, parents shifted from this authoritarian approach to

greater reliance on instructional storytelling. Rather than merely being interpreted as a means of democratizing parent-child relationships, the stories that
were told within the family were consciously chosen in order to transmit values
and experiences to younger generations. To this end, senior generations used
storytelling to inculcate filial values into their children and thereby imbue them
with a lifelong obligation of reciprocity. Mothers, in particular, resorted strategically to the device of "speaking bitterness," emphasizing the familial contribution
and sacrifices entailed in their reproductive efforts and thereby strengthening
their children's gratitude and indebtedness toward themselves (chapter 2).[9] Intergenerational storytelling was also frequently deployed when children began
to think about courtship and marriage. Mothers consciously "volunteered" to
offer guidance (see the discussion of Mother Zhong in chapter 1), which sometimes extended to warnings (for example, begging daughters not to indulge in
premarital sex; see chapter 3), in an effort to help their children to have a better
understanding of the world beyond the confines of their homes. In general—
and transcending a simple dichotomy between parental authority and youth
autonomy—the ideal state of governing children was seen as cultivating "obedient autonomy" whereby it was accepted that children should be permitted a
considerable degree of autonomy in living their lives as long as they had been
molded into and conformed with the habitus wished for by their parents.[10]

Apart from "molding," family dynamics are also permeated by a constant
process of negotiation and realignment of family members' interests, which
mediates the impact of linear change in family practices pushed by institutional configurations. Grandparenting is one example illustrative of this
dynamic (chapter 4). Since the 1950s transitions such as the urban socialist
arrangement (mandatory full-time maternal employment and gender-
differentiated retirement ages), the state institution of the *hukou* system, the
inadequacy of public childcare provision, and increasing life expectancy have
all encouraged the activation of grandparenting in urban and rural China.
However, success (or otherwise) in accessing grandparenting depended on
the outcome of intense negotiations between different generations and within
the same generation, and was subject to multiple factors including the demographic profiles of siblings and their children, the nature of living arrangements, the constraints imposed by other family care commitments, and
kinship rules that were in place at particular points in time. Not until the rearing of the children of G3s did the practice of grandparenting become preva-
lent. Going forward, in the unlikely event of future generations responding
positively to the three-child option, competition for grandparenting will re-
emerge. Such considerations lend further weight to the argument that changes
and adjustments in family practices are rarely if ever linear, but tend to follow
a gradualistic, partial or even cyclical pattern.

Another example of intergenerational negotiation and alignment is mate selection (see chapter 2). A common assumption in the existing literature is that as China's opening up has exposed younger generations to Western notions of romance and individualism, the pursuit of personal fulfilment and autonomy inevitably conflict with the enactment of "traditional" values, such as fulfilling filial obligations toward senior generations. Yet as I have shown in chapter 2, such changes *can* be accommodated through an assemblage of the traditional and modern: love for one's spouse (being modern) does not necessarily mean being unfilial toward one's parents (being traditional). Thus, in an effort to square this particular circle, children have increasingly adopted the strategy of incorporating filiality as a key element in choosing a spouse. Among G1s and G2s, patrilineal and patrilocal principles ensured that men were much more strongly swayed by filial sensitivities than were women. However, among the one-child generation, filial considerations also became an issue for women, since an only daughter was now expected to assume responsibility for caring for her own as well as her husband's aging parents. The inference is that for all three generations once a spouse has been chosen, filiality—or at least the display of it—has been an important element in negotiations with the extended family. The origins of such creative, even improvisatory behavioral adjustments are to be found in the relational model of individuality (the "elastic individual") that guides Chinese society, enabling a "modern" emphasis on individual freedom and personal fulfilment to coexist with the enactment of "traditional" values through showing respect and obligations toward important others.

Uneven Process

Individuality is also positional, shaped and constrained by one's position in multiple structures, including family, community/workplace/village, and society at large (see the Introduction). A consequence of this is that the processes whereby an individual responds to institutional and intergenerational configurations is inherently *uneven*. Thus, in chapter 5, I show how intrafamilial issues—for example, intergenerational property transmission and the emotional quality of relationships—are enmeshed with the traditional moral imperative of filial obligation in shaping adult children's "motivation to care." Out of this interwoven web of filial obligation, material interest and emotional intimacy emerge divergent destinies of urban and rural families. For urban families, the commercialization of housing has established a well-defined trajectory characterized by parental property having become an increasingly important bargaining chip in intergenerational negotiation over time. By contrast, many rural families have witnessed a reverse trend in which, thanks to rural-urban migration and the low value of rural housing, parental property transmission has become less significant in intergenerational negotiations. As a result, elderly people with no property to fall back on and / or those (for example, rural male GIs) who have a strained relationship with their children are exposed to neglect and abuse in their old age.

In chapter 3, I showed how women and men have been unequally positioned in the process of China's sexual transformation. For example, while the public emphasis on romance and love in post-Mao China has provided a new sexual narrative that frames sex as an expression of love and commitment, the traditional gendered virginity complex has persisted. For men the coexistence of new and old sexual scripts has created opportunities to use premarital sex with their preferred partner as a strategy to consolidate the relationship. Conversely, women find themselves trapped by the contradictory expectations of male peers who on the one hand value a bride's virginal status, but on the other regard a woman's willingness to engage in sex as a demonstration of love and commitment. Such gendered prejudice, which generates tension and considerable anxiety among women, is reproduced intergenerationally and institutionally. At the intergenerational level, the transmission of gendered sexual scripts targets daughters, not sons. At the institutional level, the state has also played a key role in limiting women's freedom of expression and action, in particular by remaining silent on gender inequality in sexual relations while simultaneously enforcing a normative model of conjugal heterosexuality and reinforcing a biological determinist view of wifehood and motherhood across the divide between the Mao and post-Mao eras. Recent authoritarian initiatives, restricting the space for an independent feminist movement and promoting the reemergence of neo-Confucian ideologies, have merely entrenched gender inequalities even more deeply.

Generated by so many multifaceted and interacting processes, all these pull and push forces—institutional, intergenerational, and uneven—serve to explain and underline the essentially nonlinear nature of changes in family dynamics and behavior. Far from being revolutionary or marking a significant break—let alone a decisive breakthrough—from the past, changes in family life in China have entailed the adaptation and / or "re-serving" of traditional ideas and practices to produce a hybrid of both modern and traditional elements. Changes are also *partial* in the sense of the significant urban-rural variations within China. In short, across the three generations studied in this book the evolution of family life has simultaneously encompassed change, continuity, and diversity.

Convergence or Divergence

My three-generational analysis of Chinese family life does reveal some degree of convergence with family characteristics of Western societies. In the United Kingdom and the United States, documentation of the linkages between socioeconomic bifurcation in family practices and inequality within and across generations highlights an increasing *class* divergence in intimacy and family behavior.[11] In China, it is true that socioeconomic status has become increasingly important in differentiating family practices in post-Mao era, and yet the most fundamental form of social stratification remains the urban-rural divide rooted in *hukou*-based discrimination.[12] Since the introduction of the *hukou* system in the late 1950s, rural *hukou* holders have lagged significantly behind their urban counterparts in the extent to which they have benefited from China's modernization, whether in terms of rising per capita disposable income, access to employment, education and welfare provision (health facilities, pensions, and other benefits), and delivery of economic and social infrastructure. Financial and discursive resources, which differ greatly between those living in cities and the countryside, have a major impact on practices of family life and intimacy. For example, in terms of old age support, although urban and rural residents share similar filial values, rural adult children are constrained in their capacity to care by their limited resources (see the case of the bedbound Grandma Chang in chapter 5). The importance of family background as a determining factor in marriage decisions is the same for both urban and rural households, but across all three generations has manifested itself as a means of maintaining the segregation of urban and rural families (see chapter 2). Finally, as one generation becomes conjoined with another, comparative advantages and disadvantages are not only transmitted, but become starker when viewed across multiple generations. The intergenerational reproduction of urban-rural inequalities is vividly displayed in the comparison of childhood experiences over time (chapter 1). While urban and rural parents' educational aspirations for their children have increasingly converged, the growing urban-rural disparity in parental resources has compounded sectoral inequalities, causing urban-rural stratification to become more firmly entrenched and indeed exacerbated over time.

Much of the research on Western families has found that women are still disproportionately associated with social reproduction and related activities.[13] As for their Western counterparts, unpaid care work in the family has remained a woman's responsibility across all three generations in China. Alongside widening gender inequalities in the labor market, hegemonic gender role models (housekeeper versus breadwinner) have become more entrenched over time. Thanks to an increasing preoccupation with wealth accumulation in post-Mao China, money has also come to play an important role in mediating family dynamics. The intersection between gender and economics has led to the formation of care chains in which the most affluent adult children—because of gender inequality in the labor market these are most likely to be sons—subcontract filial responsibility either to a private care provider (for example, by employing female rural migrant workers or older working-class urban women) or to less well-off siblings or relatives. Those who find themselves at the bottom of such care chains—mostly impoverished elderly rural residents–bear the brunt of old age care transition. In other words, as the difficulties faced by elderly rural residents with long-term mobility issues shows (see chapter 5), a major crisis of care, which Fraser has described as being inherent to capitalism,[14] is looming in rural China. Against the background of faltering economic growth and the exhaustion of China's previous demographic dividend, unless adequate public sector support is forthcoming, this care crisis will undoubtedly worsen.

However, intergenerational and institutional configurations that mediate the relationship between family life and social change are firmly grounded in local history and material circumstances. The outcome is that China's trajectory of evolving family life confounds the predictions of modernization discourse or new modernity grand theorizing, based as these are on the experiences of Western Europe and North America (though Western critics have questioned these theories' empirical base; see the introduction). The most distinctive feature of the Chinese family system is its embeddedness of lifelong intergenerational interdependence and reciprocity—a theme that has persisted across three generations (indeed, longer than that if one were to take an historical perspective), and one sustained and reinforced through institutional transitions and intergenerational transmissions over time.

One consequence of this distinctiveness is that Chinese marriages fail to conform neatly to the paradigm of Western companionate marriages (Goode) or of individualistic marriages (Cherlin), both of which are grounded in exclusive relationships between two individuals.[15] Instead, despite members of the most recent generations showing superficially similar characteristics as those of their Western counterparts (for example, declining fertility, increasing premarital sex, and a predilection for nuclear family living arrangements),[16] conjugal intimacy continues to be firmly *embedded* within the interdependent web of family and kin relations. Chinese parents still matter greatly throughout their children's lives, from choosing a spouse to getting married to managing conjugal life. As the life course evolves, the configuration of conjugal intimacy and intergenerational intimacy fluctuates. While romantic love has attracted increasing attention in both public and private domains, the meaning of conjugal love has evolved into a model that emphasizes not only support and care of each other, but also an obligation toward bilateral ties. Precisely because of these interwoven relationships, Chinese couples tend, especially after they have had a child, to stay together even if their marriages are no longer a source of emotional and / or sexual satisfaction—an outcome vividly captured in the term *jiangjiu* ("making do"). The "pure relationship" visualized by Giddens as late modernity's destination features only briefly in extramarital affairs, the conduct of which in a Chinese context seeks to avoid posing any threat to normative family life through a conscious accommodation of its values and obligations.

The importance of understanding changes in Chinese family dynamics transcends sociological studies of China. It adds to the ongoing and multifaceted critique of Eurocentrism inherent in Western social theories.[17] Through the formulation of a new analytical framework of "embedded generations" embracing the shaping influences of institutional, intergenerational, and many other factors, I hope that this book can be a starting point that stimulates further debate and from which new perspectives will emerge. However, in the end I am most acutely aware that none of this book could have been written without the willing participation of my interviewees. My greatest hope is that it does justice to the life narratives of so many warmhearted but previously unheard ordinary people who have lived through the tumultuous changes of the last seventy-five years of China's political, economic, social, and cultural development.

Appendix

Characteristics of the Interviewees

TABLE 2. Sample Characteristics

	Urban G1	Urban G2	Urban G3
Gender			
Female	24	28	15
Male	15	27	21
Occupational status			
White-collar employment	9	26	33
Blue-collar employment	30	27	2
Unemployed	0	2	1
Marital status			
Single	0	0	9
Married	33	53	26
Divorced	1	1	1
Widowed	5	1	0
	Rural G1	Rural G2	Rural G3
Gender			
Female	26	26	20
Male	20	24	14
Occupational status			
Farmer	35	10	0
Village cadres	4	0	0
Village teachers	1	0	0
Village street vending	6	2	2
Village wage labor	0	7	5
Low-paid migrant workers	0	29	20
Urban white-collar employment	0	2	7
Marital status			
Single	0	0	3
Married	36	49	31
Divorced	0	1	0
Widowed	10	0	0

Family Trees of Case Studies

Note: Interviewees are in bold.

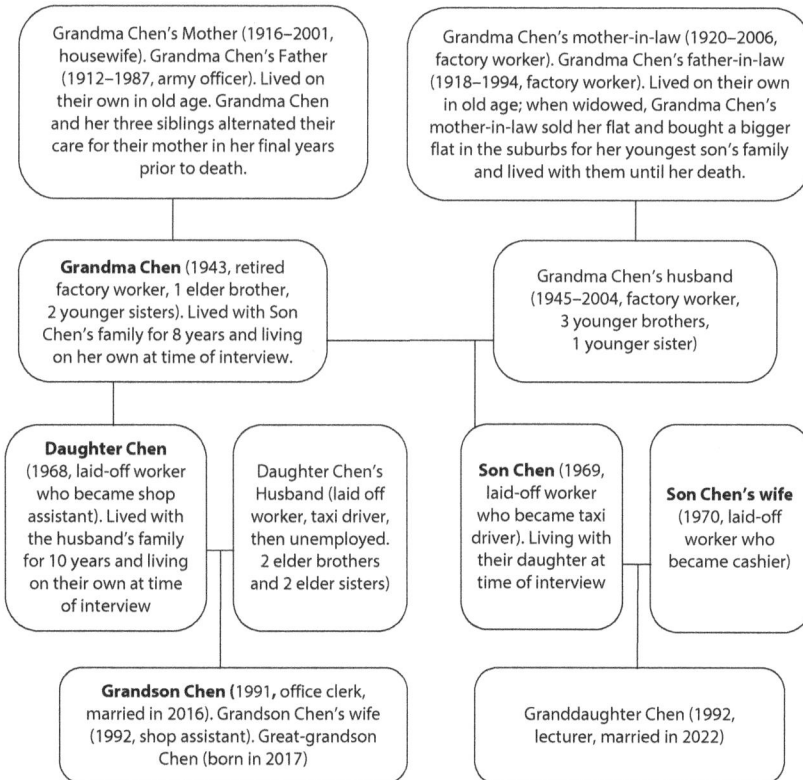

Grandma Chen's Mother (1916–2001, housewife). Grandma Chen's Father (1912–1987, army officer). Lived on their own in old age. Grandma Chen and her three siblings alternated their care for their mother in her final years prior to death.

Grandma Chen's mother-in-law (1920–2006, factory worker). Grandma Chen's father-in-law (1918–1994, factory worker). Lived on their own in old age; when widowed, Grandma Chen's mother-in-law sold her flat and bought a bigger flat in the suburbs for her youngest son's family and lived with them until her death.

Grandma Chen (1943, retired factory worker, 1 elder brother, 2 younger sisters). Lived with Son Chen's family for 8 years and living on her own at time of interview.

Grandma Chen's husband (1945–2004, factory worker, 3 younger brothers, 1 younger sister)

Daughter Chen (1968, laid-off worker who became shop assistant). Lived with the husband's family for 10 years and living on their own at time of interview

Daughter Chen's Husband (laid off worker, taxi driver, then unemployed. 2 elder brothers and 2 elder sisters)

Son Chen (1969, laid-off worker who became taxi driver). Living with their daughter at time of interview

Son Chen's wife (1970, laid-off worker who became cashier)

Grandson Chen (1991, office clerk, married in 2016). Grandson Chen's wife (1992, shop assistant). Great-grandson Chen (born in 2017)

Granddaughter Chen (1992, lecturer, married in 2022)

FIGURE 1. The Chen Family in Tianjin. By the author.

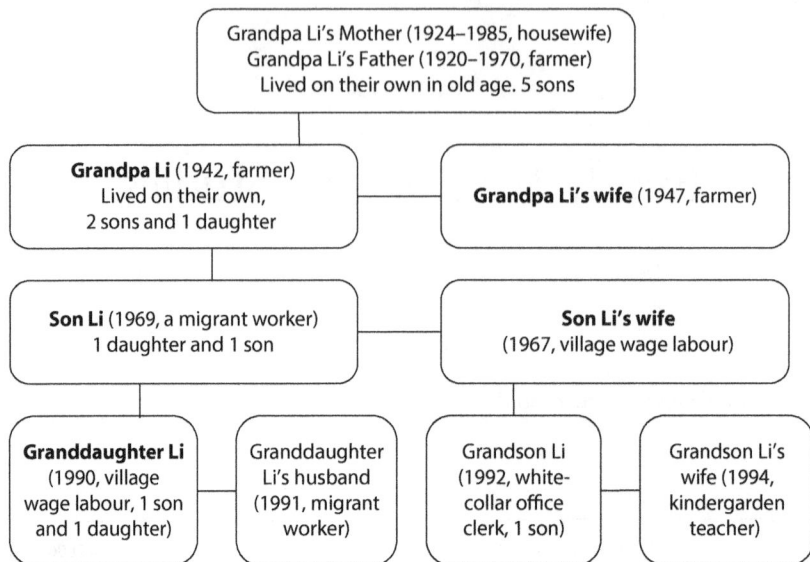

FIGURE 2. The Li Family in Shandong village. By the author.

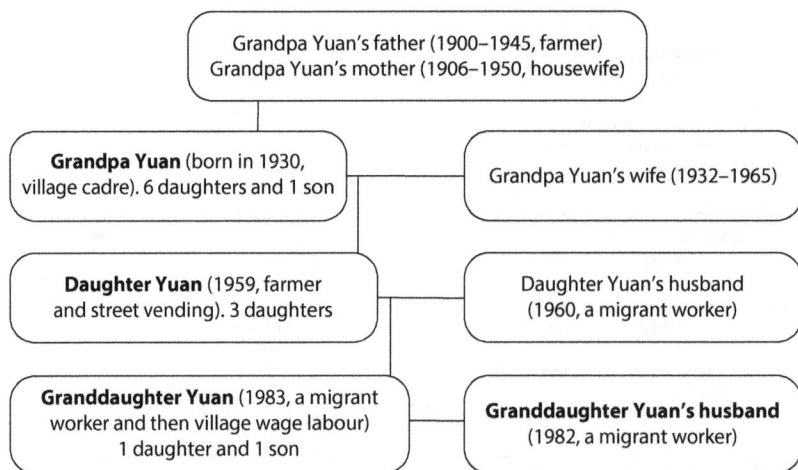

FIGURE 3. The Yuan Family in Shandong village. By the author.

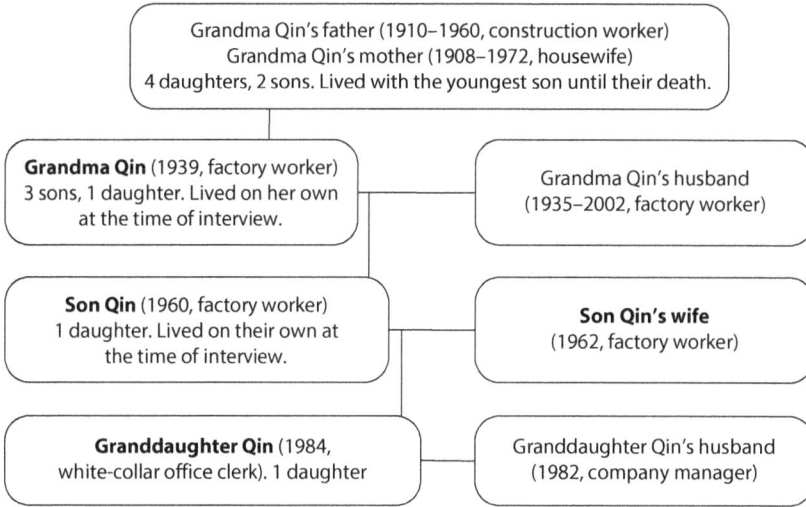

FIGURE 4. The Qin Family in Xi'an. By the author.

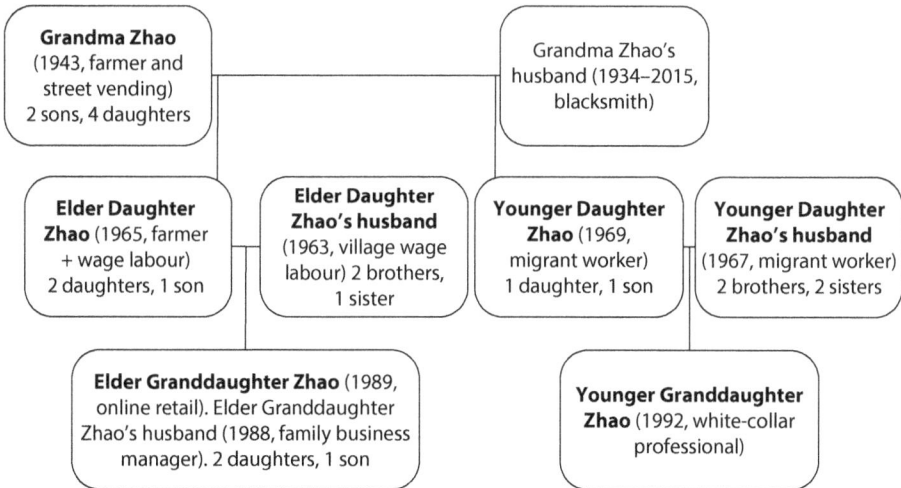

FIGURE 5. The Zhao Family in Fujian village. By the author.

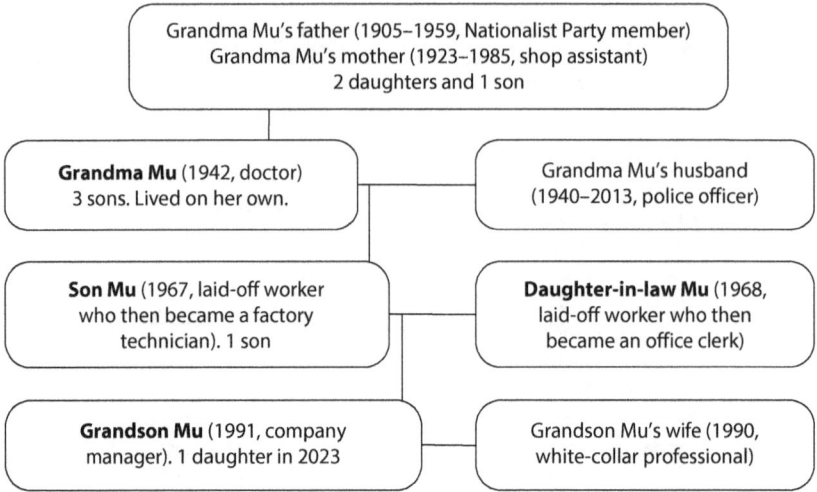

FIGURE 6. The Mu Family in Xi'an. By the author.

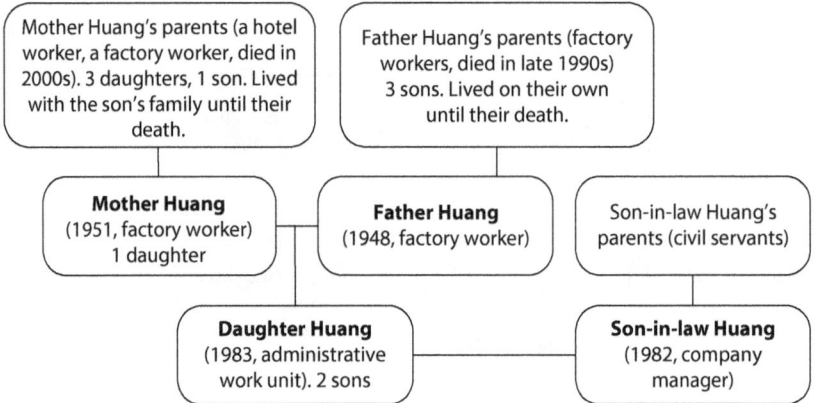

FIGURE 7. The Huang Family in Guangzhou. By the author.

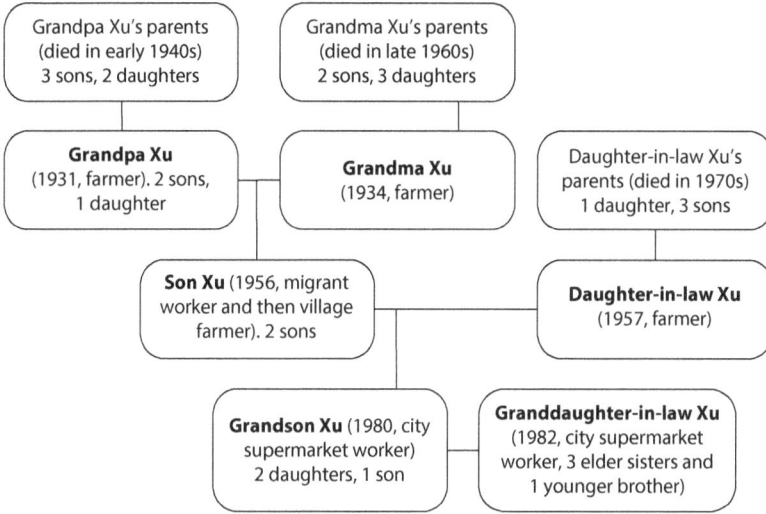

FIGURE 8. The Xu Family in Hunan village. By the author.

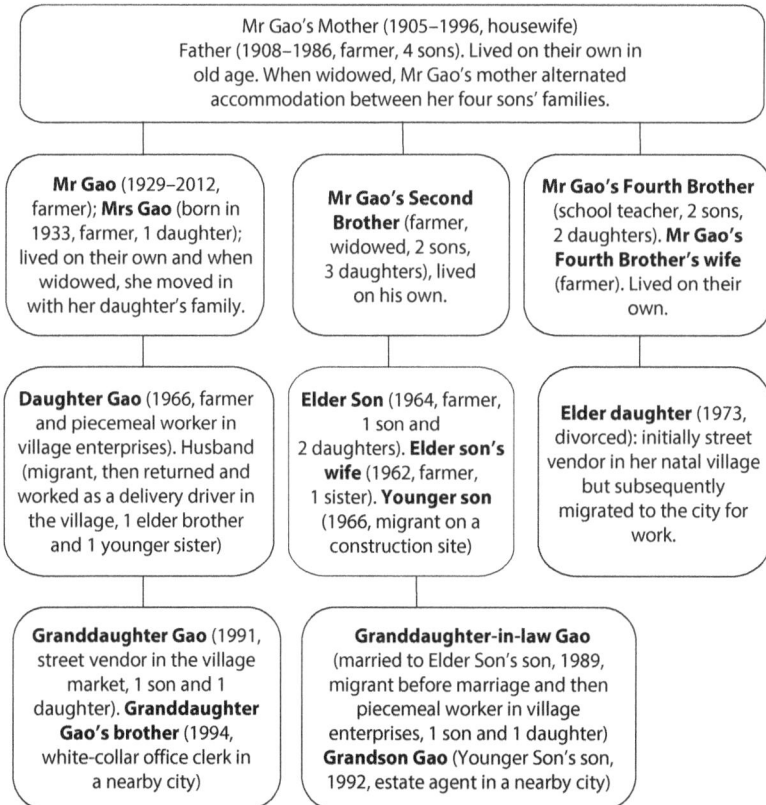

FIGURE 9. The Gao Family in Shandong village. By the author.

Rural Accommodation
in Three Villages

1. G1 Accommodation in Shandong village. By the author.

2. G2 Accommodation in Shandong village. Photo by the author.

3. G3 Accommodation in Shandong village. Photo by the author.

4. G1 Accommodation in Hunan village. Photo by the author.

5. G2 Accommodation in Hunan village. Photo by the author.

6. Accommodation in Fujian village (G1 accommodation in the center; G2 accommodation on either side). Photo by the author.

NOTES

Introduction

1. Chinese do not adopt the spouse's surname when they marry. I choose to label all the interviewees of an extended family under a single surname so that the readers can keep track of the family members of the same unit. In reality, husbands and wives almost always have different surnames in China.

2. This does not mean that at the time his father owned a small business. This derived from the system of class labels assigned after 1949 that were recorded in dossiers; in this case the father was stigmatized by the family's pre-1949 class label. These class labels persisted until the system was abolished at the start of the reform era and were used to advantage or stigmatize Chinese citizens.

3. Yan 2003, Yan 2021.

4. See Jankowiak and Li 2017.

5. Goode 1963.

6. Cherlin 2012.

7. Cherlin 2004.

8. Giddens 1992.

9. Beck and Beck-Gernsheim 1995; 2002.

10. Lesthaeghe 2010, 211.

11. Van de Kaa 2001.

12. See Jamieson 1998; Smart and Shipman 2004; Smart 2007; Heaphy 2007; Carter and Duncan 2018; Jackson and Ho 2020.

13. See McCarthy, Edwards, and Gillies 2003.

14. Jamieson 1998; Duncan and Irwin 2004.

15. Smart 2007.

16. Bengston, Biblarz, and Roberts 2002.

17. Elder 1994.

18. Cherlin 2012.

19. Jackson and Ho 2020.

20. Chai and Chai 1965, 331.

21. Mann 2011.

22. Ocko 1991.

23. Barlow 2004.

24. See Parish and Whyte 1978; Whyte and Parish 1984.

25. Davis and Harrell 1993.

26. Dirlik and Zhang 1997.

27. See Solinger 2006.

28. Palmer 1995.

29. Yan 2021.

30. Ji 2017.

31. The party did switch to encouraging voluntary family planning during the 1950s and Mao was on record in 1957 having forcefully advocated stricter birth control efforts, although initial family planning efforts fell by the wayside in the Great Leap Forward (Freeberne 1964).

32. Whyte, Wang, and Cai 2015.

33. Ikels 2006.

34. See Feng 2020.

35. Whyte 2023.

36. Shang and Wu 2011.

37. Here I do not seek to provide a comprehensive literature review, but merely to outline major trends in recent research on Chinese family dynamics. More narrowly focused studies of specific aspects of family life, often locally based, are referred to in the relevant analytical chapters.

38. See Yang 1959; Davis-Friedmann 1991; Parish and Whyte 1978; Whyte and Parish 1984.

39. Davis-Friedmann 1991, 128–29.

40. E.g., Parish and Whyte 1978; Whyte and Parish 1984.

41. See Davis and Harrell 1993; Huang 1990; Ikels 1996; Ikels 2004; Jankowiak 1993; Judd 1994; Potter and Potter 1990; Siu 1989; Whyte 2003.

42. Whyte 2020.

43. Yan 2003.

44. Yan 2003, 233–36.

45. Yan 2016; 2018.

46. Yan 2018, 182.

47. Yan 2021, 5.

48. Yan 2021, 9.

49. Barbalet (2016, 9) conducted a comprehensive appraisal on the application of the individualization thesis to China. He argues that "factors presented in support of the case for Chinese individualization are shown to be either ambiguous or, on examination, counterindicators." For example, family transformations from the Mao period to the present maintain family obligation. Labor migration, rather than leading to individualization, expresses family commitment.

50. Cf. Xiang (2011, 127): "Ordinary people are acutely aware that individual choices, life trajectory and the possibility of self-determination are conditioned by unequal structures. In other words, ordinary people may be more politically informed and intellectually sophisticated than Yan's theorization suggests."

51. Yan explained in his footnote (2003, 245): "In my case study, I tend to focus on new developments. I also acknowledge the remnants of the traditional family, such as the structural form of the stem family, the male-only inheritance pattern, and the absence of romantic love in many cases of spouse selection. But overall, I pay more attention to what has changed and what is changing."

52. Whyte 2020, 357.

53. Davis and Friedman 2014.

54. Davis and Friedman 2014, 26–27.

55. Santos and Harrell 2017, 27. While recent edited volumes present a diverse range of case studies, the comparability of dissimilar studies may affect the weight of their arguments.

56. Illouz 1997.

57. Sun 2023.

58. Xie, Hu, and Zhang 2014; Xu and Yan 2014.

59. Yu and Xie 2021.

60. Wang et al. 2022; Silverstein and Cong 2013; Silverstein, Cong, and Li 2006.

61. Ji 2017, 2–3.

62. Zhong 2020.

63. Elder 1994.

64. There is an emergent body of literature that demonstrates the influence of intergenerational transmissions on family practices. For example, interviewing migrant workers in Pearl River Delta, Choi and Peng (2016) reveal how parents have continued to exert influence on young male migrants' mate selection and how the latter made compromises to balance aspirations for sexual freedom and their obligations toward parents. Examining homosexual relationships, Choi and Luo (2016) show how parents have also continued to influence their adult children's marriage decisions, effectively forcing their children to strike a similar balance by organizing alternative forms of marriage. Interviewing rural migrant women, Lai and Choi (2021) explore how parental influence has impacted their premarital abortion decisions. Howlett (2021) examines the anxieties and pressures of high school students in their preparation for the national entrance exam in China, revealing how values and aspirations are transmitted to the younger generation. However, all these researchers have addressed only a specific social group at a particular time, and their research does not compare in terms of breadth and depth of analysis to the present book, which examines family life across the life courses of multiple generations in both urban and rural China.

65. Zhang 2017, 249.

66. Yan 2003, 178.

67. Davis-Friedmann 1991, 11, 54.

68. Gabb 2008; Jamieson 2011.

69. See Evans 2007; Liu 2016; Yan 2016.

70. See Yan 2016, 250.

71. Giddens 1992, 61.

72. Giddens 1991, 6. Please note that Giddens' notion of intimacy was originally used in the couple context.

73. Jamieson 1998, 158.

74. See Jamieson 1998; Liu, Bell, and Zhang 2019; Jackson and Ho 2020.

75. Jamieson builds on the concept of "family practices" developed by the British sociologist David Morgan. This concept was formulated to avoid preconceived definitions of family by instead focusing on varied historical and cultural practices that people have used to "do" family. See Jamieson 2011.

76. Zelizer 2005, 288.

77. Giddens 1992.

78. Kurz 2006.

79. Lareau 2003.

80. Thus, Jankowiak and Li (2017): "An emotionally egalitarian marriage is more likely to be built around the 'language of love' as opposed to the 'language of duty.'"

81. Mead 1967.

82. Smart deliberately uses "the personal" in contradistinction to "individual" because of the problems arising out of the individualization thesis. See Smart 2007, 28.

83. Jackson 2010; 2018; both quoted in Jackson and Ho 2020, 118.

84. Fei 1992 [1947].

85. Adam 1996. For Adam, the detraditionalization thesis is "an integral part of the disembededed, disembodied, detemporalised and objective tradition of the Enlightenment" (1996, 146).

86. Yan 2021, 5.

87. Jackson and Ho, 2020, 16.

88. Phillips 2004.

89. Jackson and Ho 2020, 16.

90. Carter and Duncan 2018.

91. The Oxford English Dictionary (2015) defines "bricolage" as "construction or creation from a diverse range of available things." However, since this terminology that may not be familiar to a non-European audience and in order to avoid academic jargon, elsewhere in this book I have opted to use other terms, such as "assemblage" or "construction."

92. Carter and Duncan 2018, 20.

93. Alwin and McCammon 2003.

94. Ginn and Arber 2000.

95. Early feminist scholars identified the absence of consistent state policies and measures to challenge gender ideologies and practices in Chinese households as one of the key weaknesses of the post-1949 women's liberation movement (Judd 1994; Wolf 1985).

96. Evans 1997.

97. Ji 2017, 3.

98. In his study of urbanization in China, Kipnis (2017) proposed a threefold typology of rural villages: (1) villages that had been absorbed into a city; (2) villages that were relatively close to a city (*jinjiao cun*); and (3) villages far away from urban centers.

99. Due to limited land allocated per capita in the 1980s (Fujian: 0.02 hectare; Hunan: 0.03 hectare; Shandong: 0.08 hectare), prior to migration, Fujian villagers were engaged in some form of small business such as working as a blacksmith, grocery shop owner, and street vendor.

100. Skinner 1977.

101. Skinner's nine regions are: Northeast China, North China (including Tianjin and Shandong village), Northwest China (including Xi'an), Upper Yangtze, Middle Yangtze (including the Hunan village), Lower Yangtze, Southeast Coast (including the Fujian village), Lingnan (including Guangzhou), and Yungui.

102. Gladney 2004.

103. Mason 2002.

104. Additional interviews were collected by the project team, comprising thirty pilot interviews conducted during the training of the research assistants and seventy interviews with families living in semi-rural / semi-urban areas. However, because of interpretative difficulties associated with the different degrees of urbanization captured in the semi-rural / semi-urban interviews, I have not used these in the subsequent analysis, although I intend to include them in future publications.

105. I personally conducted 70 percent of the interviews, the remaining 30 percent being undertaken by a team of local Chinese assistants. To ensure consistency and comparability between my interviews and those collected by others, I personally reviewed and annotated interview transcripts and asked the research assistants to conduct follow-up interviews where greater clarity and / or further information were needed.

106. Because of this ethical responsibility, crucial identifiable features of interviewees who appear in the following chapters will be modified in order to protect them from being recognized by the general public as well as by their own family members.

107. For example, through frequent informal catch-up discussions.

108. Carter and Duncan 2018, 22.

109. A further ethical consideration is that individual experiences of sex are inherently very private matters and individuals are likely to want to conceal these from other family members.

Chapter 1

1. China has four national level cities (*zhixia shi*): Beijing, Tianjin, Shanghai, and Chongqing (in terms of administrative levels). In addition, Shanghai, Beijing, Guangzhou (one of my field sites), and Shenzhen are classified as first-tier cities—the most advanced cities in terms of economic and infrastructural development and living standards. My other two urban field sites— Xi'an and Tianjin—have since 2018 been ranked among "new first-tier cities."

2. The government has encouraged private education at all levels since the 1990s. In the late 1990s more than 60,000 high-fee privately owned educational institutions were reported to be offering education to some ten million students (Croll 2006, 193). In 2008, the number had doubled and private institutions constituted 20 percent of all educational and training institutes in the country (Naftali 2016). In my study, no G3s had attended private schools, although some urban G3s' children had done so.

3. China offers nine-year free education to all children. However, each family is required to pay for textbooks, uniforms, and school meals / activities—a considerable financial burden for rural families.

4. The population of migrants' children is steadily increasing in China and over the last two decades growing attention paid to them by journalists and researchers has given rise to the term *liushou ertong* (commonly translated as "left-behind" children).

5. In an ethnographic study exploring how American middle-class families promoted the talents of their children, Lareau (2003) used the term "concerted cultivation" to describe the intense investment by parents to prepare their children for future competition in academic and labor markets. She found that working-class and poor families rely on "the accomplishment of natural growth" in which a child's development unfolds spontaneously as long as basic comfort, food, and shelter are provided.

6. While the first three generations provide the main focus of the discussion, I also touch on the childhood experiences of G3s' children, as described by the early cohort of G3 interviewees.

7. McLanahan (2004, 607) uses this term to describe the two trajectories associated with the second demographic transition in the US and other Western societies: viz., "children who were born to the most-educated women are gaining resources, in terms of parents' time and money" while "those who were born to the least-educated women are losing resources."

8. See Fong 2004; Kipnis 2011; Kuan 2015; Liu 2016; Murphy 2020.

9. Some urban interviewees recalled that they could be away from home for weeks without any intervention from their parents.

10. From the mid-1950s, the party-state mobilized every able-bodied peasant to be part of collective production activities. Through the state's suppression of household sideline production activities and the imposition of a public remuneration system, which forged a direct link between the award of work points and the distribution of grain, collective production became essential to the sustenance of the household. Thus, for rural families, maximizing the number of work points they could earn took precedence over everything else.

11. There is also a Confucian tradition that considers education as a main mechanism for social mobility.

12. Kuan 2015; Naftali 2016; Kipnis 2011.

13. The same emphasis on the variety of food offered to children is noted in Kuan's (2015) study of Kunming families, although her focus is on children from the one-child generation who were much younger than the G3 cohort considered here.

14. Davis 2000.

15. Learning to play an instrument was very much a minority experience among urban G3s, but became the norm among their children.

16. During Chinese Spring Festival (i.e., the Lunar New Year), senior generations customarily give the gift of a red envelope to younger generations. The envelope contains money and represents good wishes for the new year ahead.

17. The empirical evidence of the urban one-child generation's childhood experience given here largely confirms the findings of studies of other Chinese cities (see Fong 2004 [Dalian], Kuan 2015 [Kunming], Goh 2011 [Xiamen]). Other studies that discuss Chinese parental aspirations for and investment in their children's education include Martin (2022) and Howlett (2021).

18. Yuan's family's wish for a son led them to have a third child (a girl) and this breach of the one-child policy resulted in them having to pay a hefty fine.

19. See Postiglione 2011.

20. Hell and Rozelle (2020) found that the urban-rural divide remains pronounced with rural Chinese children continuing to suffer malnutrition, poor health, and substandard education. They argue that the failure to effectively improve health care and educational development among rural children and reduce rural and urban inequality in general could derail China's high economic growth. Friedman (2022) revealed that urban schools favor families with high levels of economic and cultural capital but those deemed not useful are left to enroll their children in precarious resource-starved migrant schools. Ling (2020) examined China's second-generation rural-to-urban migrant youth's experiences of inclusion and exclusion and showed how rural youths are funneled through the school system toward a life of manual labor.

21. In 1990, only 7 percent of rural students went on to complete senior middle school (Yi et al. 2012).

22. According to census and national survey data, in 2015 left-behind children comprised 66.7 percent (68.8 million) of the children of migrants while the remaining 33.3 percent (34.3 million) were "migrant children" who moved away from rural villages (Chan and Ren 2018). G3s' childhood in Shandong village was dominated by a pattern of "absent fathers"; those in Hunan village were featured by a pattern of "left-behind children"; while those in Fujian village were characterized by a pattern of "migrant children in the cities" due to the three villages' divergent migration history. I discuss elsewhere that despite the distinctive growing up patterns, they shared common features reflecting the urban-rural divide and social inequalities embedded in Chinese society (Liu 2022).

23. Zheng and Wu 2014.

24. Over a twenty-year period, a process of school consolidation took place in villages, resulting in a dramatic reduction in the number of schools and the reallocation of educational resources from failing village schools to "central schools" (Xu 2013). This meant that when they embarked on middle school education, village children were forced to become boarders in a county / town school. In turn, higher living standards in counties / towns were reflected in increased educational costs, which put a further strain on family finances. In addition, in the early 1980s the limited cooperative medical support that had been made available in rural areas during the Mao era through the collective system collapsed and was replaced by a payment-based system of medical care (Zhang and Unschuld 2008). The net result was that welfare support costs for both young and old increased dramatically in the reform era.

25. Material living standards in the countryside do seem to have moved on a good deal compared with twenty years ago, as highlighted by village interviewees. However, urban living standards have continued to rise and therefore the urban-rural gap has not narrowed to any significant extent.

26. Rural parents' educational aspirations for their children are also reported from other rural settings (see Kipnis 2011; Hansen 2015; Murphy 2020).

27. Lareau 2003.

28. The luxury to which the family was accustomed is reflected in their frequent choice of the premier Banyan Tree Hotel group for their holiday accommodation.

29. Nunn and Tepe-Belfrage 2019.

30. Another celebrated work that draws on Bourdieu's concepts in the examination of reproduction of inequalities is Lareau's (2003) study, which reveals that parenting strategies are hugely important in transmitting "capitals" to children.

31. Zelizer 1985.

32. Liu 2016.

33. Kagitcibasi 2007.

34. Beehive coal briquettes had to be lighted in order to heat water for laundry and for bathing, and not just for cooking.

35. In 2018, rural interviewees explained that as a result of the government's implementation of a "toilet revolution" village party committees had made available toilet appliances to each household. However, because no corresponding modifications had been made to the villages' sewage system, many rural families continued to use traditional pit latrines.

36. In her study of families in Kunming, Kuan (2015) found that with rising incomes and the growing availability of private insurance and institutional care, some middle-class urban parents had become less committed to valuing children as future providers of old age security. My study has led me to believe that the life course continues to play a role in shaping parental expectations: thus, while urban parents of *young* children envision a future characterized by greater reliance on institutional care, as old age approaches, middle-aged urban parents of the one-child generation display a considerable degree of ambivalence, as shown above.

37. Kagitcibasi 2007.

38. According to Hu (1944, 45), there are two Chinese words—*mianzi* and *lian*—both of which mean "face." *Mianzi* "stands for the kind of prestige . . . [of] a reputation achieved through getting on in life, through success and ostentation. . . . For this kind of recognition ego is dependent at all times on his external environment." *Lian* is defined as "respect of the group for a man with a good moral reputation . . . it represents the confidence of society in the integrity of ego's moral character, the loss of which make it impossible for him to function properly within the community." As I use it here, the meaning of "face" is best captured by the Chinese term *mianzi*.

39. As a result of the "later marriage, longer birth spacing, and fewer children" policy initiative, urban G1s who were married in the 1960s and 1970s were compelled to restrict the number of their children to no more than two.

40. Kagitcibasi 2007.

41. According to Mencius (a Confucian philosopher, 372–289 BCE), the ultimate unfilial act is not to have children.

42. A key reason to want a son in rural China was for old age support due to the absence of pension and continued prevalence of patrilocal postmarital residence transferring the bride's support obligations to her husband's family.

43. Echoing Jackson and Ho (2020), while investing in daughters is a departure from tradition it is also a modification of tradition in the sense that it is part of a wider family strategy.

44. Johnson 2004.

45. Fong (2004) mainly attributes the shift of increasing values in urban daughters to imposition of the one-child policy. It is worth highlighting that the socialist transformation of the mid-1950s produced multiple institutional changes that fundamentally undermined most of the reasons for urban families to favor son over daughters so urban parents could count on married daughters as well as married sons for support in old age (Whyte 2003).

46. Tsui and Rich 2002.

47. Only 23 percent of college students in 1978 were women but now it is over 50 percent (as it generally is in the West).

48. Skolnick 1997.

49. Jamieson 1998.

50. Hays (1996, 8) originally captured this new form of parenting in the term "intensive mothering," which she defined as "child-centred, expert-guided, emotionally absorbing, labour intensive and financially expensive". Subsequently, this concept elicited increasing attention in the literature, either under the original label of "intensive mothering" or that of "intensive parenting" designed to reflect its relevance to fathers as well as mothers (Wall and Arnold 2007). Lareau's (2003) "concerted cultivation" parenting style is an example of "intensive parenting."

51. Whyte 2003.

52. Diamant 2000.

53. Davis and Harrell 1993.

54. Greenhalgh and Winckler 2005.

55. The purpose of the educational reforms was to foster well-rounded children who were intellectually (*zhiyu*), morally (*deyu*), physically (*tiyu*), and aesthetically (*meiyu*) well equipped to compete in a global labor market (Woronov 2008). Thanks to implementative deficiencies, the potential benefits of the reforms failed to accrue to members of the G3 generation. Instead, it has been G3s' children who have carried the burden of these reforms and had to face huge pressure to acquire multiple skills needed to strengthen their competitiveness (not only through orthodox academic study, but also all kinds of extracurricular activities: cf. Ms. Guang quote at the beginning of this chapter).

56. Naftali 2009.

57. Kuan 2015; Fong 2004; Naftali 2014.

58. In addition to Fei, Sun Yat-sen (the first president of Republican China) commented on this differential mode of association in his 1924 public speech on the three principles of nationalism: "Observers say that Chinese are a sheet of loose sand. Why is this? It's because the people as a whole care about the doctrines of the family and clan, but not the state-nation" (Wells 2001).

59. Zheng and Peng 2003. A demarcation between family members and nonfamily members was also noted by Jackson and Ho (2020, 144) among their Hong Kong interviewees. They termed this type of social orientation "protectionist familialism."

60. Although they remembered frequent beatings at the hands of their parents during childhood, G1s and G2s also recalled tender moments when they felt their parents' love for them. However, their consensus was that the expression of love manifested itself more in acts of giving and sharing than through displays of emotion.

61. This is also documented in other studies of the G3 generation (see Kuan 2012; Goh 2011; Xiong 2015). Indeed, judging from G3s' experiences, differences in parental occupation had no clear effect upon child-rearing patterns. Parental beating was also common, regardless of family status (including civil servants and teachers).

62. Evans 2010. Early anthropological literature also suggest that Chinese families were much less likely to openly express affection toward their children, hug them, and praise them (Kipnis 1997).

63. In its original usage, the Chinese character *xiong* conveys a form of verbal communication that was authoritarian, harsh, or stern in the sense of imposing one's position forcefully upon others.

64. An employed nanny was rare among the childhood of urban G3s and only existed in two families in the interview population. One being the Ning family and the other being a Guangzhou family who had benefited from remittances sent by overseas relatives.

65. "Habitus" refers to unconscious and embodied ways of thinking, feeling and acting built through cumulative exposure to repetitive situations (Bourdieu 1977; 1984).

66. In her controversial 2011 book *Battle Hymn of the Tiger Mother*, Amy Chua (Professor of Law at Yale) describes in great detail the incredibly demanding and harsh discipline she used to drive her daughters to excel, patterns that most middle-class Americans found almost fierce.

67. Interviewees subject to physical punishment and / or considerable scolding during childhood, having grown up, sought to justify their parents' actions and so differences in early

parenting methods did not show a major effect in shaping later intergenerational relations. Instead, according to two earlier generations, the different parental treatment of siblings was a source of tension for later intergenerational relationships.

68. These words also suggest the importance of having a daughter-in-law who gets on with other people.

69. Evans 2010.

70. The traditional role of fathers in Chinese families was that of a disciplinarian, as the narratives of G1 interviewees make clear. During the Mao era, as mothers were mobilized into full-time employment, fathers began to help with childcare by cooking for children and doing pickups and drop-offs when the mother was not available. In the post-Mao era, as grandmothers have become more involved in childcare, fathers' involvement has to some extent weakened, although as leisure opportunities expanded, some fathers have devoted more time to playing with their children.

71. Such persistent gender inequalities in parenting work are also documented in Peng's (2024) study of parents in urban China.

72. Lynch 2010.

73. Lynch 2010.

74. Evasdottir 2004, x.

75. The introduction of the one-child policy, with the promotion of state policies designed to foster children as self-governing, individualistic laborers and consumers (Greenhalgh 2011), led some to argue that contemporary Chinese child-rearing and educational paradigms may reflect the construction of an increasingly influential "ethic of autonomy" (Zhang 2008; Yan 2011). However, as I show, Chinese parents have long input their own marks in the normalizing regime of scientific child-rearing, which epitomizes in the cultivation of "obedient autonomy."

Chapter 2

1. This ritual is called "The Worship of The Family Hall" (*baitang*).

2. *Huaqian yuexia* is a Chinese phrase to convey the romantic setting. Regarding the words "pots and pans, firewood, rice, oil and salt," the Chinese phrase is *guowanpiaopeng, chaimiyouyan*, which is used to describe the daily necessities of a conjugal life.

3. I was invited to attend the wedding but due to COVID-19 travel restrictions to China, I was sent the wedding recording afterward.

4. Goode (1959, 39) viewed conjugal love ("the love between settled, domestic couples") as the antithesis of romantic love.

5. Kipnis (2017) also noted an undertone of patrilocality in another contemporary Shandong wedding.

6. For example, an array of expensive cars (hired for the day) was used to bring the bride and her family to the wedding and then parked strategically to project wealth and status throughout the day.

7. While Mr. Gao's parents could have paid a lower bride price, as was custom in Miss Yin's poorer mountainous village, to signify their appreciation and value of Miss Yin, Mr. Gao's family paid a bride price according to their local village standard. As Miss Yin's family had no son (and so no impeding bride price burden), her parents allowed her to retain the money as her dowry.

8. For example, drawing upon interviews with urban and rural Chinese families in the 1970s, Parish and Whyte (1978; Whyte and Parish 1984) found that the importance of the conjugal tie within the family has increased but strong intergenerational ties and obligations continue. Conversely, drawing upon a rural village ethnography in the 1990s, Yan (2003) concluded there had been a triumph of conjugal intimacy over intergenerational intimacy. However, commenting on post-Mao urban China, Davis and Friedman (2014) identify continuing "support for the norm of lifelong reciprocity between generations" alongside new marriage trends.

9. This was not stable employment and contingent on market demand. In September 2017, during the BRICS Summit held in Xiamen (a city about a three-hour drive from the village), all construction work had to be halted to ensure a pristine environment for the meeting. Elder Daughter Zhao's husband spoke with a bitter tone about this government decision, which resulted in him being without income for several weeks.

10. Similar strategies were reported by other rural Shandong families.

11. The boyfriend's family was originally from a neighboring village in Fujian, not far from Granddaughter Zhao's natal village. It was a commonly reported preference among migrants to marry someone whose family was from the same region and so his family approved of Granddaughter Zhao.

12. *Fu erdai* is a Chinese term used to refer to individuals who come from affluent families, often characterized by inherited wealth and privileges.

13. Buying a property is considered a sound investment strategy that also lays the foundation for a future return to their home region when the couple enter old age.

14. *Shuobuqing de li, libuqing de shi* refers to situations that defy rational explanations and are difficult to understand or resolve.

15. His wife was not biologically related to him, but adopted by the cousin of his father.

16. Son Mu's elder brother was a civil servant and his younger brother was a businessman following military service.

17. Ebrey 1978.

18. Watson and Ebrey 1991.

19. Ebrey 1991.

20. Ocko 1991.

21. Freedman 1979 [1961].

22. The empirical picture is patchy. Drawing upon interview data in urban and rural China in the 1970s, Parish and Whyte (1978; Whyte and Parish 1984) identified a clear shift toward a greater voice for the young in marriage decisions, but found parents still played an important role in a number of respects. Yan's ethnographic study of rural youth in Heilongjiang in the 1990s identified a shift toward free-choice matches (from 3 percent in the 1950s to 36 percent in the 1990s), while the matches-by-introduction remained the dominant norm throughout the 1960s to the 1990s (Yan 2003, 47). An ethnographic study of rural youth in Shaanxi in the 1990s found that parents still played a dominant role in local youth's marriage decisions (Liu 2000). For the one-child generation, scholars identified fun-seeking aspects of dating behavior (Farrer 2002; Jankowiak and Moore 2016) but many youths continued to give their parents' opinions a good deal of weight concerning potential spouses (Moore and Wei 2012; Davis 2021). Much recent work on migrant workers has found that rural youth find it necessary to make compromises in order to balance their own desires and the fulfilment of obligations toward their parents (Choi and Peng 2016; Lai and Choi 2021).

23. Yan 2009.

24. Lui 2021.

25. Parish and Whyte (1978, 173) found that in most rural families mate choice involves "double approval and a double veto power; both the young people and their respective parents must agree," although in urban areas they found that there were some interviewees who married in defiance of parental wishes (Whyte and Parish 1984). However, in early 1990s Beijing, Pimentel (2000) found Chinese marriage decisions mostly involved intergenerational negotiation.

26. Giddens 1992; Beck and Beck-Gernsheim 2002.

27. All four daughters received only a few years of primary school education, but were subsequently forced to withdraw from school so that family resources could be used to fund the two sons' educations. Salaff (1981) described a similar pattern in 1970s Hong Kong.

28. Zhang and Sun 2014.

29. Whyte and Parish 1984, 150.

30. Jankowiak and Moore 2016.

31. Here I follow Illouz's conceptualization of emotion which emphasizes that "Cultural frames name and define the emotion, set the limits of its intensity, specify the norms and values attached to it, and provide symbols and cultural scenarios that make it socially communicative" (Illouz 1997, 3–4).

32. Fincher (2014) states that Chinese court rulings tend to favor husband ownership. If a divorce occurs, a wife who has contributed to the costs of the housing is not compensated. However, in the eyes of this urban G3 woman, the extraordinariness of this case seemed to represent the intensity of her husband's affection for her.

33. Zelizer 2005.

34. Parents (often mothers) consciously engaged in conversations with adult children of marriageable age about the type of people they should look for (see chapter 1). These general areas of interest are then reproduced and passed down through generations.

35. Davis 2021. According to a survey of nearly 80,000 people organized by China Youth Daily in 2014, 67.7 percent of the respondents believed that mate selection should embody this principle (Zhou, Shao and Liu 2014).

36. The play is entitled *Wang jiang ting* (The riverside pavilion) and written by Guan Hanqing.

37. The gender difference in mate selection, in which women favor male prowess and status, while men favor female attractiveness, has been found in other societies (e.g., Buss 1995). However, Chinese cultural mechanisms such as hypergamy and patrilineal property transfer have made this gender difference more entrenched in Chinese society.

38. During the Mao era, gender segregation and hierarchy persisted in state-managed work units (Liu 2007). After the 1980s, the restructuring of state enterprises and promotion of a market economy were accompanied by rampant gender discrimination in the labor market (Liu 2017a).

39. Tan and Li (2002) notes marriage is "a form of social capital for Chinese women."

40. In her study of Guangdong interviewees, Lui (2018) also found that the rural-urban inequality erects considerable barriers to intermarriage between urban and rural families.

41. This view was in itself largely influenced by the puritanism in the Soviet Union.

42. Due to a persistence of the virginity complex, young women remain constrained and engage in premarital sex when they intend to marry the person (see chapter 3).

43. The age of first marriage increased among urban and university educated interviewees over time. For example, urban interviewees born in the 1960s and 1970s typically married in the age range of twenty-two to twenty-five, those born in the 1980s typically married in the range twenty-three to twenty-six, and those born in the 1990s typically married in the range twenty-seven to twenty-nine. The youngest rural generation, who were disadvantaged by urban-rural segregation in the education system and so less likely to attend university, typically married in their early twenties (e.g., Granddaughter Zhao, born in 1989 and married in 2010). However, the younger cohort of urban G1s, who were affected by the "later marriage, longer birth spacing, fewer children" state policy in the 1970s, were an exception.

44. Scholars estimate that women's labor market participation rate was 80 percent in urban areas by the late 1980s (Barrett et al. 1991).

45. Salaff and Merkle (1970) disputed the view that women in state socialist regimes had been "liberated" by their active involvement in paid labor.

46. During my fieldwork in the villages, whenever possible, I had tried to immerse myself in interviewees' family life. In Zhao's extended family, I lived in Elder Daughter Zhao's house. In Gao's extended family, I lived in Grandson Gao's parents' house.

47. In his study of conjugality in a rural village in the 1990s, Yan (2003) pointed to the fact that many wives had the final say (*shuo le suan*) as an indicator of women's power in the family. However, as emphasized by Grandma Mu, she had "the final say" in all the domestic affairs because her husband was indifferent to everything at home and she perceived this as a burden rather than an empowerment.

48. Choi and Peng (2016) coined the term to describe similar processes in which migration forced men to renegotiate their roles as husbands.

49. This housework pattern was subject to considerable challenge during the COVID-19 lockdowns, which prevented older generations and domestic workers from visiting. One G3 woman admitted: "The apartment was like a pigsty. Neither my husband nor I bothered to tidy it up."

50. Zuo and Bian 2004.

51. Daughter Jing's husband had been the general manager of a company. Due to workplace politics, he resigned from his company and started a new company but his new endeavor was not very successful.

52. Hochschild (1989, 18) coined the term "marital economy of gratitude" to describe how husbands' and wives' gendered self-images help shape their assessment of an activity in their marriage as either a gift or a burden.

53. Okin 1989.

54. In my early study of the one-child generation, I have outlined the organizational mechanisms that enforce vertical segregation for women professionals (see Liu 2017a).

55. Another group of men were more discreet. Grandson Mu did not tell his wife exactly how much he earned, not least because it was partly commission / bonus dependent. This meant that, if he received 100,000 yuan, he only told his wife he had received 50,000 yuan and gave the rest to his parents to save for him.

56. The cases of female dominance were somewhat facilitated by rural-to-urban migration. For example, in the Shandong village, the husbands migrated while wives stayed behind and so the husband sent back remittances for the wives to manage.

57. Fei 1992, 85.

58. Yan 2003.

59. It is worth highlighting that how much intimacy there actually must depend on the quality of the relationship.

60. Due to a shortage of housing, under the work unit system, there was often a waiting list for accommodation in the husband's work unit so some couples needed to spend the initial years of conjugal life living with the husband's parents.

61. Among rural G1s, the majority of women were married into a different village than their natal village. Among rural G2s, same-village marriages were more common. This meant, for example, that Younger Daughter Zhao's martial house was five minutes' walk to both her in-laws' house and to her own parents' house.

62. Drawing upon interviews with Chinese urban youth currently enrolled in higher education, Eklund (2018) finds that both patrilineality and patrilocality are still important principles for how intergenerational relations play out. She coins the term of "neo-patrilocality" to denote the practice of families channelling resources along the patriline to organize housing for sons in order to enhance their prospect of getting married and having children. The urban G3s' experiences echo Eklund's findings.

63. Here I draw upon Goffman's (1959) concepts of frontstage and backstage personal presentations in analyzing men's strategies.

64. Parish and Whyte (1978, 217) made a similar observation. Rather than the replacement of the parent-son tie with the husband-wife tie, they found a "balancing of two equally important relationships" among their rural interviewees.

65. Studying mother-in-law and daughter-in-law relations in Taiwanese families, Gallin (1994) identified class variations.

66. See also Whyte 2003 on Baoding.

67. For example, rural G2 parents continued to prioritize childcare provision for their son's children over their daughter's children and the patrilineal inheritance tradition remained intact.

68. Wolf 1972.

69. Parish and Whyte (1978, 238) also identified this practice in Guangdong villages where payment is "regarded as earned by members of the corporate family unit rather than as disposable income for each individual member."

70. Here I build upon approaches that consider hidden or covert dynamics of power (Lukes 1974; Komter 1989; Pyke 1994). In contrast with overt measures of power such as decision-making and conflict outcome, which assume power is exercised in a directly observable manner (Blood and Wolfe 1960), the covert power approach instead draws attention to latent and invisible *power processes and dynamics* rather than merely power outcomes.

71. In classical Chinese philosophical thinking, harmony is a central goal of all personal, social, and political relationships (Wang 2005). This traditional notion of harmony has been reemployed in the rhetoric of the contemporary Chinese government, which promotes a "harmonious society" (*hexie shehui*), meaning the word "harmony" (*hexie*) frequently crops up seemingly out of context (e.g., *hexie* is the name of the national high-speed rail network).

72. These relational dynamics have also been found among women's resistance to men's control in Chinese office spaces (see Liu 2017a).

73. Zhou 2015.

74. Zhou 2015.

75. Jankowiak and Li 2017.

76. Jankowiak and Li 2017, 152–53.

77. Jankowiak and Li 2017, 147.

78. A Western movie the one-child generation frequently cited when discussing romantic love was *Titanic*, imported into China in late 1990s.

79. Noting that Son Qian used a more / less term rather than either / or dichotomy.

80. A Chinese understanding of love as "respect," "mutual understanding," and "support" is also found in Pimentel's (2000, 45) survey of Chinese couples in Beijing as well as in the Sexuality of China Surveys. Pan and Huang (2013) highlight that among Chinese couples "love" is highly correlated with being considerate toward the feelings and needs of others, as embodied in the notion of *tiantie*.

81. Jankowiak and Li 2017, 154. However, Jankowiak's (2013) early work acknowledged the similarity of marriage expectations of the one-child generation and their parents.

82. Pimentel 2000.

83. In these two early studies, I interviewed the urban women from the one-child generation in 2002 (most participants were undergraduates; see Liu 2007) and 2008 (most participants were in work but yet not married; see Liu 2017a).

84. In addition to an emotional connection, these young women also emphasized the importance of economic factors when finding a spouse.

85. Facilitated by social media and the internet, gift-giving has become a means of displaying intimacy within the virtual circle of friends and relatives.

86. A key feature of Giddens' "pure relationship" is that it is mainly sustained through mutual self-disclosure, constantly revealing one's inner feelings to each other (Giddens 1991).

87. This echoes the findings of Jankowiak and Li (2017).

88. Gabb 2008, 106.

89. Mead in Jackson 2010.

90. Jackson 2010, 132.

91. Illouz 1997, 10.

92. Studies of the UK families also dispute the democratization narrative (see Jamieson 1998). In this regard, there are similar inequalities in intimate Chinese relationships and Western ones.

93. Jackson and Ho 2020.

Chapter 3

1. Sex was the most challenging area for data collection. Interviewees were less forthcoming and local research assistants more reluctant (and sometimes refused) to ask sex-related questions. I therefore often explored sex-related issues in my follow-up visits, after trust and rapport had been built between myself and the interviewees.

2. The exceptions are the qualitative studies by Jankowiak (1993, on marital sex in Huhhot), Farrer (2002, on premarital sex in Shanghai) and Wang (2017, on premarital sex and dating in Beijing). All of these studies draw upon cross-sectional data.

3. I am grateful to William Jankowiak for his thoughtful and detailed comments on this chapter.

4. Pan 2018; Pan and Huang 2013; Zhang 2011.

5. Jeffreys and Yu 2015; Evans 1997.

6. Gagnon and Simon 1974; 2005; both cited in Jackson and Ho (2020, 135).

7. As this study mainly examines heterosexual family relationships, I have not included cultural codes related to homosexual practices in Chinese history. Hinsch (1992) provides a detailed discussion of how homosexuality was regulated in premodern China.

8. Harper 1987.

9. Wile 1992.

10. Goldin 2002.

11. Van Guilk 1961.

12. Lu 2013.

13. Mann 2011.

14. Theiss 2004.

15. Dikötter 1995, 69.

16. Whyte 1990.

17. Li 1998.

18. Honig and Hershatter 1988.

19. Liu 2017a.

20. Zheng 2009.

21. Rofel 2007.

22. Ho et al., 2018.

23. Ji 2017.

24. Inherent in Stalin's strictly puritanical policies toward sexuality was the belief that an individual's preoccupation with romance and sexuality eroded energy for study, work, and other forms of production. The sexual repression of the Mao era probably owes more to Stalin than to Confucius (personal communication with Martin King Whyte).

25. In the Mao era, college students and factory apprentices were formally forbidden from engaging in romance (*tan lianai*).

26. Tian, Merli, and Qian 2013.

27. Evans 1997.

28. Farrer 2002.

29. Drawing upon the 1999–2000 Chinese Health and Family Life Survey, Parish, Laumann, and Mojola (2007) found that the occurrence of premarital sex is much higher among younger cohorts of men and women. For men, the major increase in premarital sex since 1984 is attributed to commercial sex and short-term relationships. For women, premarital sexual relations since 1984 have remained with a fiancé or possible fiancé. Parish, Laumann, and Mojola (2007) concluded that this represented a reemergence of a double standard in sexual behavior.

30. Due to persistent preference to invest in the education of sons, the majority of rural G2 women only had primary school education. No G2 women had migrated prior to marriage, instead assisting their parents with farm work and other domestic duties, so the opportunities for them to have premarital sex were more limited than their urban counterparts.

31. Yu, Luo, and Xie 2022, 299.

32. Farrer 2002.

33. Liu et al. 2020.

34. Yu and Xie 2021. The increase in first marriage age among those born in the 1950s is sharper, which is influenced by the "later marriage, longer birth spacing, fewer children" initiative of the late 1960s and 1970s.

35. A 2019 survey encompassing nine universities in Zhejiang, Henan, and Yunnan provinces revealed approval rates of 50.4 percent among men and 41.1 percent among women, with 27 percent of men and 13.9 percent of women having engaged in sexual intercourse (Lyu, Shen, and Hesketh 2020).

36. The 2010 Sexuality of China survey revealed that 66.3 percent of men, and 79.6 percent of women, had sex with the person they were certain they would marry and then 74 percent of men, and 87.8 percent of women, eventually married the person with whom they had their first sexual encounter (Pan and Huang 2013, 128).

37. Changes in the gradual acceptance of premarital sex have, of course, been taking place in Western societies. For example, in the United States, there was a general disapproval of premarital sex until the 1960s, that is, in their dating activities, and even with steady boyfriends, although kissing and even "petting" were allowed, girls were expected to resist pressures from their boyfriends to "go all the way" (Whyte 1992). Where premarital sex did occur, as in the case of China more recently, it was generally understood that both parties intended to marry. From the 1960s onward, a different set of norms emerged in the United States, the virginity complex diminished, and women became freer to engage in sexual relationships. The key difference with China is that a dating culture had already developed, and been accepted, in the United States in the first half of the twentieth century.

38. The description of Zhuang's boyfriend's behaviors is not atypical, echoed by other women interviewees' accounts and confirmed in the dating narratives of young professional women in Beijing (see Wang 2017).

39. Holland et al. 1998.

40. Farrer's study found that in the 1990s Shanghai youth acknowledged the notion of mutual consent in premarital sex. However, my study echoed the findings of Wang and Ho (2007) that for one-child generation women in Beijing, many first sex experiences took place coercively.

41. As shown in chapter 2, intergenerational intimacy goes hand in hand with conjugal intimacy, particularly among the G3 generation, many of whom ranked their parents above their spouse on a spectrum of intimacy. Ms. Kong feared that her future husband might tell his parents about her nonvirgin status to create an alliance in the family against her.

42. Some G3s from the 1990s cohort did admit to cohabitation at time during their university life, but kept it hidden from their parents. After university, for those G3s in steady relationships that had been approved by both parties' parents, cohabitation was condoned and could serve as a transitional phase prior to their marriage. Yu and Xie's (2015) statistical analysis reveals that in contrast with early generations (7 percent), cohabitation before first marriage increased among the post-1980s generation (25 percent).

43. Chinese universities expelled students for flagrant sexual intercourse during the mid-1990s (Farrer 2002). While university students have been allowed to get married since 2005, the expectation remains that undergraduate students should prioritize study over dating and sex.

44. As big cities such as Tianjin, Guangzhou, and Xi'an have many higher education institutions, young adults tend to go to university in their home city.

45. Theiss 2004.

46. Hu 2016.

47. Miss Lu's narrative on sex is similar to the liberal views identified by Farrer in his study of youth sex culture in Shanghai (2002). The majority of women in my study did not share Lu's experiences and views; they were more closely aligned with those of the educated women in Wang's (2017) study of Beijing. One possible explanation is the characteristics of researchers—in other words, the sample used by Farrer may have been prone to include a segment of youth who were particularly more open to Western values (like Lu in my study).

48. Pan 2018, 113.

49. Parish, Laumann, and Mojola 2007.

50. Hird 2020.

51. Evans 1997.

52. The economic condition of Hunan villagers was similar to that of Shandong villagers.

53. According to 2010 census data, both Shandong and Fujian provinces have a sex ratio at birth above 120 (Chen and Zhang 2019).

54. Similarly, in Shanghai participants, Farrer (2002, 240) found that women's virginity retained a sexual "exchange value" beyond premarital abstinence; virginity was constructed as a gift of a woman to a man.

55. Steinmüller and Tan (2015, 15) state that it is hard to estimate the number of such surgeries in any city or province in China, but the large number of advertisements for hymen repair surgery, ranging from huge billboards in big cities to posters in the alleyways of minor townships, is a clear indication of its popularity. William Jankowiak also reports mention of hymen surgery in 1982 in Hohhot (personal communications with the author).

56. The Chinese term *mohe* refers to the process whereby frictional forces bring about adjustments to achieve an optimally functioning relationship.

57. Pan et al. (2004, 190) argued that marital sex in China transcends the private act of two individuals and is linked to the family and everyday living circle of the couple—a unique feature of Chinese sex culture. They include the process of cultivating and raising children as part of the couple's living circle. I extend their argument by broadening the boundary of the couple's living circle through including extended family ties and introducing a life course perspective.

58. Patrilineal tradition required the husband to put considerable effort into managing the relationship between his own parents and his wife (see chapter 2).

59. Evans 1997, 142–43.

60. The 2000 Sexuality Study of China Survey found that while love between a Chinese husband and wife is the most important factor in both parties reaching an orgasm, the interaction between love and the orgasm itself manifests differently in men and women (Pan et al. 2004, 209). In men, the orgasm is positively associated with their love *for* their wife. In females, the orgasm is positively associated with feeling love *from* their husband. To women, a major form of feeling love is their "husband being attentive [*tiantie*]" and so this factor is also highly positively correlated with whether a woman regularly orgasms during sex. This gendered finding corresponds with the different construction of sexual pleasure among the men and women in my study.

61. This is very similar to the situation in UK couples (see Gabb 2022).

62. Evans 1997.

63. Following the state's mobilization of women into paid work from the 1950s, full-time and lifetime employment was a standard feature of urban Chinese women's lives from G1 onward. Rural G1 women were expected to resume farm work or earn money when breastfeeding was over.

64. The Chinese term *qingdiao* captures the emotional tone or ambiance that evokes a specific sentiment or mood, be it romantic, melancholic, or a feeling of being at peace.

65. Ménard et al., 2015. Research on older Chinese people's sex lives is rare to nonexistent—for example, the Sexuality of China Survey collects information on men and women aged up to sixty-five.

66. Pan et al. 2004.

67. This corresponds to the finding Gabb et al. (2013) that in the United Kingdom libidinal discrepancies were understood as part and parcel of long-term relationships.

68. According to the 2015 Sexuality of China Survey, 51.2 percent of respondents considered their conjugal feelings very deep, 53.1 percent of respondents considered their marriage very satisfying, and 42.8 percent of respondents considered their sex life very satisfying (Pan 2018, 49).

69. Each interviewee was asked if they would choose the same spouse again if they had the chance to relive their life. Shen, Mu, and Jiang all said "yes" to this question.

70. According to Pan (2018, 129), in the Sexuality of China Survey, wife beating was reported among 19 percent of respondents in the 2000 survey and 10.8 percent of respondents in the 2015 survey. In the rural villages of this study, G1 and G2 women widely reported wife-beating as a village norm. Tian's mother, mother-in-law, and Tian's sister were all beaten by their husband in early stage of their marriage.

71. Excuses, such as being with children or tired, worked effectively when the conjugal relationship was good, even in rural couples. Jankowiak (1993) also noted women's strategies for resisting marital sex in Hohhot families in the 1980s.

72. Ms. Tian explained that if she refused his request for sex during the night, the next day the husband would have a tantrum by throwing things around or refuse to cooperate in other affairs, similar to the first boyfriend's reactions in Ms. Zhuang's story (see "The Virginity Battle"). Ms. Tian therefore felt obliged to comply with the request for sex so as to save further trouble from him.

73. Older generations of women recalled the dominant public advice / order given was related to the reproductive function of marital sexuality, such as contraceptive use, IUD checks, and avoiding sex in specific moments of the female cycle.

74. For the urban one-child generation, sex education at school was largely limited to watching videos about the human body and relevant sex organs.

75. Pan 2018.

76. Evans 1997.

77. Zhang et al. 2012.

78. Zhang, Wang, and Pan 2021.

79. Luo and Yu 2022.

80. Labrecque and Whisman 2017: a 2016 survey found that 16.3 percent of Americans admitted to having had sex outside marriage during their lifetime.

81. I echo Jankowiak's (2021, 205) argument that the transition from the Mao to the post-Mao era did not stimulate an increase in personal introspection; instead, it allowed "for an easier and often more public articulation of personal desires."

82. See Luo and Yu 2022.

83. Of the two potential suitors who were declined, her mother considered one to be "too fat" and, since the other was from the same village and her elder sister was already married to someone from the same village, her mother thought overly homogenous kin ties would reduce the pool of potential girls for her future grandsons.

84. Ms. Tian did not like the fact that her proposed husband was short (less than 1.6 meters) but her mother said that "he would grow taller in future" (which, of course, he never did since he was twenty-three when they met).

85. Upon marriage the couple were allocated three mu of agricultural land (where one mu corresponds to 1/15 of a hectare) but this was mainly used to produce grain. It was necessary to earn an additional cash income to cover family expenses; from the start of their marriage, Ms. Tian's husband temporarily migrated to the city to work in the construction industry; however, his initial period of migration was not economically successful and, even in more recent years, Ms. Tian's husband earned a meagre 20,000 yuan per year. Staying behind, to look after their children (one girl and one boy) and fields, Ms. Tian worked a street vendor, casual laborer at the village school, and more recently as a shop assistant in the village supermarket on 30 yuan per day.

86. This is a Chinese idiom suggesting that a person of integrity and virtue may seek revenge, but needs to be patient and wait for the right time to do so.

87. Drawing up interviews with migrant women, Li (2022) found that divorce litigation often reproduced gender inequality in the family and rural communities. Most of the women in her study walked away from their divorce suits with little or no marital property, child support, or any financial compensation for their husbands' ill conduct or abuse.

88. See Allen et al. 2005; Pan 2018; Farrer and Sun 2003.

89. Li (2022) found a similar institutional context behind migrant women's extramarital affairs.

90. Drawing upon interviews with Shanghai residents, Farrer and Sun (2003, 11) identified various codes such as "feelings," "play," and "exchange" that served in the moral reasoning of the interviewees but operated in different contexts. For example, the code of "play" largely "operates within the contexts of entertainment places with their institutionalized ways of having fun"; long-term associations invoke the code of "feelings," and code switching emerges from a story of romance to a story of exchange when feelings are damaged. I argue that these codes are part of the "mosaic temporality" in which an individual is embedded and there is no fixed rule on context and how these codes may interact and operate.

91. Rofel (2007) contends that neoliberal subjectivities (desiring subjects) are created through the production of various desires (material, sexual, and affective) through engagement with public culture.

92. Wolf (1972) suggested that because of their structurally disadvantageous position in the Chinese kinship system, married rural women were keen to cultivate a uterine family consisting of their own children.

93. There is a gradual evolution in the tolerance and acceptance of divorce in China. The crude divorce rate has risen from 0.98 in 2001 to 3.02 in 2011 (Zhang et al. 2018) and this rise is often viewed as evidence of the "deinstitutionalization" of Chinese marriage (Davis and Friedman 2014). Recent studies recommend a more cautious interpretation of these crude divorce rates. Reviewing the China Family Panel Study 2016, Yu and Xie (2021) introduced a life course

perspective and found that more than 94 percent of marriages formed between 2000 and 2006 in China remained intact after ten years, more than 95 percent of marriages formed between 1990 and 1999 remained intact after twenty years, more than 97 percent of marriages formed between 1980 and 1989 remained intact after thirty years and more than 98 percent of marriages formed before 1980 remain intact after forty years. It seems the shorter a marital period is, the more it is likely to end in a divorce. Nevertheless, Chinese marriages are relatively stable, compared to other East Asian societies in an era of social change (Yu and Xie 2021).

94. Ms. Shi had her only child, a daughter, at the age of thirty-four.

95. These notions are central to Giddens' (1992) transformation of intimacy thesis.

96. Evans (1997) adds that, through explicit association between contraceptive use and marital status, reproduction remains a key organizing principle of the discourse around female sexuality during the implementation of the one-child policy.

97. Whyte, Wang, and Cai 2015.

98. Although the objective of my study was not to provide a comparison between China and Western societies, it is noteworthy that this "revolutionary" narrative has also been questioned in Western societies. Scott (1998, 841) analyzed the survey data on changing attitudes to sexual morality from the 1960s to 1990s in multiple Western societies (the United Kingdom, United States, Ireland, Germany, Sweden, and Poland) and found that, with the exception of attitudes to premarital sex, attitudes had not changed dramatically over the past few decades and the condemnation of extramarital sex remained high. Scott concluded that "change has not been as revolutionary as is often claimed and the demise of traditional values is over-stated."

Chapter 4

1. The postnatal confinement period, *zuo yue zi* (literally translated as "doing the month"), traditionally lasts for a month. However, as urban G3 women increasingly opt for caesarean delivery, postnatal recovery has taken longer and engaging a *yuesao* for two months has become a common practice. The tasks performed by a live-in postnatal nanny include preparing meals for the mother, assisting her in breastfeeding, changing nappies, and looking after the baby during the night. Instead of hiring a live-in nanny, some mothers choose to attend postnatal recovery centers which boast high-level care services for mother and baby. The rate for nannies is around 8,000–10,000 yuan ($1,100–$1,380 USD) per month, while recovery centers in big cities such as Guangzhou charge from 10,000 yuan ($1,380 USD) per month.

2. In 2013, national statutory maternity leave was ninety-eight days, although the Guangzhou Municipal Government added an extra fifteen days of leave for the mother.

3. Plaza dancing (*guangchangwu*), a mixture of dance and gymnastics, has become one of the most popular leisure activities in urban China among middle-aged and older women. It usually takes place in the open air and in public areas (e.g., plazas and parks) in cities. See Sheng (2022) and Huang (2021) on the experiences of older women who had participated in plaza dancing in Nanjing and Chengdu.

4. Following face-to-face meetings in 2017 and 2018, I kept in touch with Daughter Huang via WeChat. We met again in person in 2023 after COVID restrictions had been lifted.

5. Socialization (*shehuihua*) was an official term coined during the 1980s and 1990s to refer to the marketization of welfare services formerly provided by the work unit system.

6. *Yuyin shi* (baby care specialist) is a new term used by many employment agencies to refer to their nanny employees, emphasizing the "scientific child-rearing" skills they possess. In order to find the "right" nanny, Daughter Huang interviewed and employed a few women on a trial basis before finally choosing the one they eventually hired on a long-term basis. Most nannies are from rural areas and towns. Daughter Huang's nanny, who was paid a monthly salary of 9,000 yuan, was from a suburban town and had a college diploma. She worked six days a week, excluding Sunday when she was not required to work.

7. Silverstein and Xu 2022.

8. Ikels 1998.

9. "Outside" (*wai*) refers to the idea that these children belong to their own father's patrilineage and not that of their maternal grandparents (Feng 1967).

10. Lu 2020.

11. Wang and Wang 2017. The Chinese figure is also much higher than that of other Asian countries, such as South Korea and Thailand (Ko and Hank 2014).

12. Goodman and Silverstein 2006.

13. Chen, Liu, and Mair 2011, 4.

14. Hung, Fung, and Lau 2021, 198.

15. Zimmer, Wen, and Kaneda 2010.

16. Yan 2021.

17. Chen, Liu, and Mair 2011.

18. The two elder brothers and their wives had initially also lived with Father Huang's parents, but both families moved out when they were eventually allocated accommodation by their work units.

19. They had been introduced as potential marriage partners on the understanding that Grandpa Xu did not want or need more children.

20. In order to support her younger brothers, her parents also arranged for Daughter-in-Law Xu to marry someone in the natal village.

21. Use of other villagers' farmland was subject to rent, normally in the form of grain.

22. Wang 2015, 77.

23. Yang 2020.

24. Yang 2020.

25. Here I use the term "nursery school" to refer to the childcare organizations for children under three and "kindergarten" for children aged three to six. In the Mao era, nursery schools and kindergartens were provided by work units or run by neighborhood committees. Since the 1990s, nursery schools have largely disappeared and most kindergartens have become privately run.

26. Li, Ma, and Wang 2019, 68.

27. Yue and Fan 2018.

28. Yang 2020, 74.

29. Wu 1990.

30. Yue and Fan 2018, 101.

31. Zhong 2019, 23.

32. Childminders were not formally regulated in the Mao era and tended to be older women living in the same neighborhood who were recommended by word of mouth.

33. Other studies also reveal that, trapped by the competing demands of state patriarchy and familial patriarchy, new mothers with an only daughter were effectively penalized and abused by in-laws who offered limited childcare assistance (see Croll, Davin, and Kane 1985; Liu 2007).

34. Between 1990 and 2015 the female labor participation rate in China declined from 72.7 percent to 63.9 percent (Dasgupta, Matsumoto, and Xiao 2015).

35. Feng 2020.

36. Hong and Tao 2019, 7.

37. Similar sentiments were expressed by grandparents in Zhong and Peng's (2020) sample of families in Guangzhou.

38. It is noteworthy that, in line with the gendered nature of the childcare discourse, mothers' work points rather than those of the fathers were used to pay nursery staff wages.

39. Li, W, 2022; Han 2013. In some nurseries 80 percent of the funding was from the brigade, leaving mothers to contribute the remaining 20 percent, although in other cases, mothers contributed 80 percent of the funding. In extreme cases, mothers contributed 100 percent.

40. Li, W, 2022.

41. In 1958 in rural areas newly established "rural people's communes" sought to establish collective mess halls, nursery schools, and so on, although this experiment was short-lived.

42. See Fan 2007.

43. In 2006, state policy decreed that migrant children could be enrolled in urban public schools without having to pay discriminatory high fees not applicable to urban families. However, in large cities migrant families have continued to face severe difficulties in getting their children enrolled in public schools, because school spaces were reserved on a priority basis for local *hukou* children and many cities began to employ a point system that awarded school places only to families in which the parents were well educated, owned housing, and had worked in jobs with contracts for at least five years—thereby making it impossible for most migrant families to qualify. Friedman (2022) refers to these policies as enforcing an "inverted welfare state" biased toward the already advantaged.

44. After completing his vocational education, Daughter-in-Law Xu's younger son settled in a fourth-tier city as a hotel bartender and gradually worked his way up to being manager of the establishment. In part because of this career progression, he attracted the attention of, and eventually married, a receptionist in the hotel. Since she was the only child of a family living in the city, it was the urban maternal grandparents who looked after the couple's daughter.

45. For example, invitations to relatives' and acquaintances' weddings and birthday banquets carried an expectation that villagers would contribute money in a red envelope as a gift.

46. Cancian 1975.

47. Yan 2021.

48. Feminist scholars have argued that women's homework is one of the most ruthless forms of surplus extraction in capitalist relations. It is a complete interpenetration between production and reproduction enabling a process that hides women's exploitation through excluding them from the wage relation (see Mezzadri et al. 2021).

49. Family living expenses were covered by Son-in-Law Huang's income. Every month he gave 20,000 yuan to Daughter Huang to manage daily expenditure for the whole family.

50. Yan 2021.

51. For example, Mother Huang cited examples of other older people being taken abroad for sightseeing by their children and so, during the next Spring Festival, Daughter Huang organized a trip for Mother Huang to visit Hong Kong.

52. Zhang 2017.

53. When I conducted interviews with urban G3s, if we ate at their home, then the food was entirely prepared and cooked by their parents or in-laws. In contrast, when I held interviews in rural households, G3 women helped their mothers prepare the meal and in the majority of cases did all the cooking themselves.

54. This pattern is also noted in other studies of grandparenting. For example, in her study of families in Beijing, Xiao (2014) identified a division of labor between grandparents who focused upon everyday care activities and mothers whose main involvement was the education of their child.

55. Okin 1989.

56. Other intergenerational storytelling mechanisms include "speaking bitterness" as women accumulate moral capital in their family life (see chapter 2).

57. Yan 2021.

58. Goode 1963.

59. Chen, Liu, and Mair (2011) aggregate the data from nine provinces to reveal that paternal grandparenting was about three times higher than maternal grandparenting. Regional studies show that in villages grandparent-grandchildren ties are particularly strong on the paternal side, while in urban areas maternal grandparenting increases and constitutes 40 percent of grandparenting (Silverstein and Cong 2013 on Anhui; Zhang 2021 on Shaanxi).

Chapter 5

1. This is a style of bed common in rural Northern China. It is built with bricks, and in winter warmed by a fire underneath it.

2. I first checked with the younger son about the possibility of talking to his mother, and my visit took place during one of the periods when he was looking after her.

3. Aboderin 2004.

4. I focus exclusively on familial support for older people in China, mainly because alternative provision is so limited. Over the last decade, fee-paying communities for older people have begun to appear in all three cities; however, they are all targeted at high-income families.

5. Baldassar and Merla 2013, 40.

6. Initially the two nuclear families ate together, each contributing to the common budget (*huoshi fei*) over which Grandma Chen took control. Son Chen's wife complained about the quality of the food provided by Grandma Chen, while Grandma Chen complained that the young couple's financial contribution to the food budget was inadequate. Subsequently Grandma Chen unilaterally decided to dissolve the common budget, after which the two nuclear families ate and managed their budgets separately while still living under the same roof.

7. Miller (2004) documented the adoption of the family contract in old age care in 1990s rural Shandong. However, according to my participants, it is only practiced in the families where intergenerational relations are openly broken down (less than 5 percent of the villagers) so not a common feature of intergenerational relations. As I observed in many families, there are

varying degrees of conflicts between siblings and between generations. Nevertheless, in order to maintain a "filial" image among their relatives and in the wider community, most family members resorted to "surface work" (see below) rather than openly breaking down the relationships (e.g., engaging Head of Village / Court in disputes).

8. Miller (2004) found that in rural Shandong during the 1990s, old age support for parents mainly took the form of providing meals and occasionally also housing. He concluded that "filiality has been distilled to its barest essence"—an observation that only partly corresponds to the findings here. Miller's interpretation does not incorporate the temporal dimension that would have highlighted how discrete stages of old age support reflect changing care needs.

9. Cousin marriage was eventually outlawed during the Mao era, but examples of the practice emerged among both my urban and rural G1 sample households.

10. According to Son Gao's wife, the money handed in by each child prior to marriage was more than enough to serve as a daughter's dowry, but was insufficient to pay for the marital home needed for their son.

11. Marriage between a child of an urban family and one from a rural family is very rare (see chapter 2).

12. Ikels 2006.

13. Zhang 2017.

14. Other quantitative survey-based studies have also found that participants from younger generations demonstrate a strong commitment to the value of filial piety (Zhan 2004; Hu and Scott 2016).

15. These principles are "ideal types" in the Weberian notion, indicative of the norm for the majority of interviewees of each generation. However, the principles are not mutually exclusive and can occur simultaneously in each generation. For example, in the 1990s some Guangzhou G1s reported having utilized paid help (rural relatives or laid-off workers), which is a form of "subcontracting filial piety."

16. This confirms the findings of the 1994 Baoding Survey regarding the provision of monetary assistance to parents by married daughters and married sons: "There is not a statistically significant difference between the assistance provided by daughters versus sons" (Whyte and Xu, 2003, 179).

17. The findings in regard to younger generations' old age support practices confirm Ikels's (2006) prediction that the economic forces unleased by post-Mao reforms would lead to inequalities among the elderly.

18. In 2021, a new development among affluent families in this village was the installation of CCTV cameras in the homes of rural G1s, enabling their migrant children to remotely monitor the movement of their elderly parents in the village and to contact relatives or neighbors should any emergency occur.

19. There is a growing body of work examining care provision for older people in contemporary rural families and this has revealed the increasing role of daughters in the old age care for their own parents (See Cong and Silverstein 2011; Liu 2017b; Shen 2016).

20. Zhang 2017.

21. Not a single urban G1 in the sample had resorted to institutional care, although some interviewees mentioned acquaintances who had done so.

22. Zhang (2017) also noted the adoption of the same strategies in Beijing and Shanghai.

23. Li and Hu 2009.

24. Ikels (2004) also noted the use of paid helpers in Guangzhou families.

25. Yan 2021, 16.

26. Santos and Harrell 2017, 21–22.

27. Finch 1989, 77.

28. Hu and Chen 2007.

29. Tan 2007.

30. Hamilton 1990.

31. Lin 1992.

32. Ikels 2004.

33. Finch 1989, 139.

34. See Thomas 1993.

35. For example, in the authoritative China Health and Retirement Longitudinal Study, undertaken by Beijing University, *zhaoliao* ("caring for") was used in the questionnaire sections relating to care access and provision.

36. Goody 1976, 3.

37. There is an extensive literature on "household division" (*fenjia*) in modern China that provides a detailed examination of its nature (why) and modes of division (who, how, and when). Here I focus on the generational shifts in property transmission and their impact on old age support processes.

38. Yu 2006.

39. Whyte 2020, 355.

40. However, in urban families where parents cohabited with a married adult child's family, the practice of "eating separately" (*fen zhao*) persisted.

41. A parental property or estate may comprise not just land, but also political connection or office (Medick and Sabean 1984). Earlier studies highlight the existence in urban China in the early 1980s of a short-lived practice (*dingti*), whereby an adult child could obtain employment in place of a parent when the latter retired (Davis 1993). However, because of its temporary nature and the timing of the initiative, this practice did not affect all urban families. In those in which one of the G1 siblings (often the youngest) might have benefited from it, the practice had not been incorporated into parents' old age care arrangements because, ironically, the enterprise restructuring of the 1990s resulted in the layoff of many workers from their relevant work units.

42. Ikels (2004).

43. Since the collapse of the Evergrande Group (the second largest property developer in China by sales) in 2021, the Chinese property sector has been in a state of ongoing crisis, which has impacted the price of urban housing and created much anxiety.

44. At the time (c. 1960s), the fourth son, who began work as a village school teacher but had risen to the position of school headmaster by the time he retired, *was* poorer than his other brothers who had been working for some years. However, because of the widening income gap between agricultural and nonagricultural workers in post-1978 China, at the time of my fieldwork (2011) he had become the most prosperous of all four brothers.

45. Speaking of his limited interactions with his brothers, the fourth son claimed that the distance he felt from them reflected the absence of a common language between him and his three brothers, all of whom had spent their entire lives working in the village fields.

46. This is confirmed in other studies of rural China (see, e.g., Jacka 2018; Murphy 2020).

47. The three urban sites of my project were classified as first-tier cities or provincial capitals, in which the prices of residential accommodation far exceeded what could be afforded by even relatively affluent rural families.

48. Hochschild 1983.

49. Finch (2007, 66) argued that families' actions need to be "displayed" as well as "done." Through displaying, "the meaning of one's actions has to be both conveyed to and understood by relevant others if those actions are to be effective as constituting 'family' practices." The term "surface work" embodies elements of Finch's concept of a "displaying family," but seeks to take it a step further in order to capture the irreconcilability between the public perception and rhetoric surrounding what a family "ought to be" and the private intentions and feelings of family members.

50. Booming Chinese real estate values means that the material stakes are high. In 2017, Daughter Chen and Son Chen each received an annual income of around 36,000–48,000 yuan; five years earlier, when their mother's flat had been sold, the sale generated 700,000 yuan.

51. Illouz 1997.

52. Miller 2004, 52.

53. The concept of *guanxi* has generated a scholarly literature that reveals how *guanxi* practices have persisted throughout Chinese history, challenging the modernization narrative and neoliberal discourse that predicted the decline of *guanxi* as China embraced capitalist marketization (see Yang 2002).

54. Yang 1994.

55. Leung and Xu (2016) provide a comprehensive overview of welfare policies in China since 1949.

56. Despite the Maoist rhetoric of egalitarianism, Mao created a deep dichotomy in Chinese society between rural and urban areas (Whyte 2010).

57. Zhang 2016.

58. Solinger 2022.

59. From 1978 to 1999, the central government's share of national health care spending fell from 32 percent to only 2 percent (Hu et al. 2008).

60. The Maoist cooperative medical system collapsed in the 1980s, replaced by a payment-based system of medical care (Zhang and Unschuld 2008, 1866).

61. The time demarcation is approximate. Leung and Xu (2016) selected 2006 as a turning point because it is the year the state formally promoted the building of a harmonious society, pledging to ensure all Chinese people could enjoy equal rights to education, employment, medical care, old age care, and housing.

62. State Council 2006, cited in Shang and Wu 2011, 124. The city of Shanghai, for example, has among the most advanced old age care in China due to its rapidly developing economy and care infrastructure. It has formed a 90–7–3 model, in which 90 percent of old people are supported by home-based care, 7 percent supported by community-based care services (state funded), and 3 percent by market-provided institutional care (Zhang 2016).

63. Two urban interviewees (G3) were the heads of such community organizations and explained in great detail how they organized activities for older people in their communities.

64. This pension scheme covered 10 percent of rural villages in 2009, 24 percent by the end of 2010, and aims to cover 100 percent by 2020 (Zhang 2016). This scheme entitles every rural

resident aged over 16 to contribute 100–500 yuan per year and then, upon reaching sixty, to draw a pension of a minimum of 55 yuan per month.

65. This rural medical care insurance scheme requires individuals, as well as local and central government to make contributions to a fund from which individuals can then draw if they incur hospital fees; with the percentage varying depending upon the region, but ranging from 40 to 80 percent of the total costs. Despite the wide availability of medical insurance, research has found that 31 percent of the rural population cannot afford to pay for their medical care (Li et al. 2014).

66. See Shang and Wu 2011.

67. Recent, state encouraged, private investment in the establishment of social care services targets and privileges those with the ability to pay. A new long-term care scheme is being discussed, and has been piloted in some Chinese cities since 2016, but the effects are too early to be assessed.

68. Gerontology scholars have pointed out the dangers posed by the dichotomy between independence and dependence (Arber and Evandrou 1993), which overlooks the complexities of people's daily lives.

69. See Ikels 2004.

70. The existence of a hierarchy of priority among generations has been termed the "limits of filial obligation" in research on other non-Western societies—for example, Aboderin (2005) on Africa.

71. The desire to prioritize the needs of grandchildren over those of older generations was also highlighted by Davis-Friedmann (1991, 54) in her early study of old age care in China.

72. Drawing upon interviews in Chengdu, Huang (2021) examines retired urban women in collective dance groups to assess how they juggle grandmotherhood (i.e., associated childcare responsibilities), friendship (with fellow dance group members), and self-interest (i.e., participating in dance / leisure activities). Huang's interviewees correspond with women in my G2 generation—the one sandwiched between G1s and G3s. (Although, of course, the experience of being a "sandwich" generation is not specific to G2s, as G1 narratives also reveal they had once been the sandwich generation between G0s and G2s.)

73. Falkingham et al. 2020.

74. Cong and Silverstein 2011.

75. Davies (1994, 278–79) introduced the concept of "process time" to contrast with the dominant temporal consciousness: the linear time of the clock. As a result of industrialization, a linear notion of time emphasizes punctuality, efficiency, and the demand not to waste time. However, care needs are frequently unpredictable and the relation on which the care is premised often requires a form of time that is not predetermined by a quantitative conceptual measure. Therefore, care requires process time.

76. Two thirds of the rural and urban elderly participants agreed with this proverb in a national survey (Zhongguo Laoling Yanjiu Zhongxin 2003).

77. In the notion of "process time," it is impossible to say precisely how much time was spent on an action when relying upon an exclusive quantitative yardstick (Davies 1994).

78. In two long-term care cases where the spouse was the main carer, the wives hated the stressful care process so much that they would not choose the same person again in the next life, despite the fact that they had a relatively happy marriage.

79. Whyte 2003, 310.

80. Polanyi 1944.

81. See Davis-Friedmann 1991.

82. See Kagitcibasi 2007.

83. Friedmann 1966; Goode 1963.

84. At the turn of the century, China became an aging society (Lu and Liu 2019). According to the 2020 census, the number of people aged sixty and above was 260 million and constituted 18.7 percent of the population, compared with 13.3 percent in the 2010 census (National Statistical Bureau 2021).

85. These terms have been used to describe the unidirectional care flows of commodified transnational migrant labor from the global south to the global north (see Lutz and Palenga-Mollenbeck 2012).

86. See Davis-Friedmann 1991; Whyte 2003.

Conclusion

1. I lived in China until 2000 when I came to the UK to pursue a postgraduate degree, thereafter working in several British universities. Before embarking in 2011 on this family project, the focus of my fieldwork and research was urban society. My previous work included an examination of the life histories of urban women workers of the Cultural Revolution generation and, in particular, the factors that had made them so vulnerable to redundancy during urban economic restructuring in the 1990s (see Liu 2007). This was followed by an urban ethnographic project focusing on the experiences of professional women of the one-child generation and their efforts to negotiate the new forms of inequalities in twenty-first-century China (see Liu 2017a). Indeed, my early research on gender inequalities in the workplaces offered me unique insight into the processes in which institutions (socialist work units and then post-Mao state-owned companies) are neither completely "modern" nor completely "traditional."

2. Lareau 2003.

3. This argument also derives from the earlier work of Whyte, Parish, and Davis-Friedmann relating to the Mao era. For example, Parish and Whyte noted that China's transformed rural social structure in the 1950s embodied a combination of new and old elements representative of change as well as continuity, rather than "a gradual disappearance of all old practices or the adoption of new patterns during major campaigns" (Parish and Whyte 1978, 326). Davis-Friedmann (1991, 128) showed that while the state sought to build citizens' loyalty, it also "encouraged and legitimated loyalties rooted in a pre-communist past."

4. Clever 2002, cited in Duncan 2011.

5. Whyte (2020) has used the term "institutional inertia" to describe a similar process in the Chinese context.

6. Douglas 1973, 13, cited in Duncan 2011.

7. In his study of the socialist work unit system—the fundamental unit of social organization for urban citizens in China until the 1990s—the eminent political sociologist Andrew Walder (1986) highlighted numerous characteristics of traditional social roles that have remained firmly embedded in modern enterprises in China.

8. Whyte (2020) emphasizes that while China entered a post-socialist transition after 1978, in some realms the impact of the altered institutions in the 1950s continued on, even up to the

present. This is, for example, illustrated by the fact that urban Chinese maternal employment rates remain higher than in many other societies, while gender-differentiated retirement ages still have not changed.

9. In her work on social memory Blokland (2005) argues that storytelling is not an innocent activity. A storyteller's narrative choice always reflects a particular context and audience, and what is remembered is never purely fortuitous or accidental.

10. It is worth highlighting that educational attainment becomes a more prominent aspect of this molding in the youngest generation, albeit with marked urban-rural differences.

11. Raymo, Park, and Yu 2023; McLanahan 2004; Lareau 2003.

12. As Whyte (2024, 15) has succinctly put it, "Compared with other societies, rural versus urban origin is a much larger source of overall income and other inequalities in China." The major national urbanization plan launched in 2014 was touted as a major step toward eventually phasing out the *hukou* system as a determinant of benefits and opportunities. However, again quoting Martin King Whyte, "It has not produced much progress toward making it easier for migrants to enjoy equal urban citizenship and benefits, and in the largest cities ground has been lost" (2024, 16).

13. Winders and Smith 2019.

14. Fraser (2017) investigates changes in capitalist governance as well as broader transformations in social reproduction institutions (withdrawal of state support in the Global North).

15. Goode 1963; Cherlin 2004.

16. It is worth highlighting that Chinese families remain distinctive in having very few births outside marriage, revealing the continued strength of the norm of marriage before childbirth.

17. There are many perspectives to this critique. They include questions about the grand narrative of development and its implicit assumption of the universality of the Western model of modernity, debate over the comparative claims of socioeconomic development and cultural values in determining family change trajectories (see Whyte 2003; Davis and Harrell 1993; Ikels 2004), and feminist area studies critiques of the gendered consequences of modernization (see Judd 1994; Jackson and Ho 2020).

BIBLIOGRAPHY

Aboderin, I.A.G. 2004. "Modernisation and Ageing Theory Revisited: Current Explanations of Recent Developing World and Historical Western Shifts in Material Family Support for Older People." *Ageing and Society* 24: 29–50.

———. 2005. "'Conditionality' and 'Limits' of Filial Obligation". Working Paper 205, Oxford Institute of Ageing, Oxford.

Adam, B. 1996. "Detraditionalization and the Certainty of Uncertain Futures." In *Detraditionalization*, edited by P. Heelas, S. Lash, and P. Morris, 134–38. Oxford: Blackwell.

Allen, E. S., D. C. Atkins, D. H. Baucom, et al. 2005. "Intrapersonal, Interpersonal, and Contextual Factors in Engaging in and Responding to Extramarital Involvement." *Clinical Psychology: Science and Practice*, 12, no. 2: 101–30.

Alwin, D. F., and R. J. McCammon. 2003. "Generations, Cohorts, and Social Change" In *Handbook of the Life Course*, edited by J. T. Mortimer and M. J. Shanahan, 23–49. New York: Kluwer.

Arber, S., and M. Evandrou, eds. 1993. *Aging, Independence and the Life Course*. London: Jessica Kingsley Publishers in association with the British Society of Gerontology.

Baldassar, L., and L. Merla, eds. 2013. *Transnational Families, Migration and the Circulation of Care: Understanding Mobility and Absence in Family Life*. London: Routledge.

Barbalet, J. 2016. "Chinese Individualisation, Revisited." *Journal of Sociology* 52, no. 1: 9–23.

Barlow, T. E. 2004. *The Question of Women in Chinese Feminism*. Durham, NC: Duke University Press.

Barrett, Richard E., W. P. Bridges, M. Semyonov, X. Gao. 1991. "Female Labor Force Participation in Urban and Rural China." *Rural Sociology* 56, no. 1: 1–21.

Beck, U., and E. Beck-Gernsheim. 1995. *The Normal Chaos of Love*. Cambridge: Polity Press.

———. 2002. *Individualization: Institutionalized Individualism and Its Social and Political Consequences*. London: Sage.

Bengston, V. L., T. J. Biblarz, and R.E.L. Roberts. 2002. *How Families Still Matter: A Longitudinal Study of Youth in Two Generations*. Cambridge: Cambridge University Press.

Blokland, T. 2005. "Memory Magic: How a Working-Class Neighbourhood Became an Imagined Community and Class Started to Matter When It Lost Its Base." In *Rethinking Class*, edited by F. Devine et al. Basingstoke: Palgrave MacMillan.

Blood, R. O., Jr, and D. M. Wolfe. 1960. *Husbands & Wives, The Dynamics of Married Living*. New York: The Free Press.

Bourdieu, P. 1977. *Outline of a Theory of Practice*. New York: Cambridge University Press.

———. 1984. *Distinction: A Social Critique of the Judgment of Taste*. Cambridge, MA: Harvard University Press.

Bowlby, S., L. McKie, S. Gregory, and I. Macpherson. 2010. *Interdependency and Care over the Lifecourse*. London: Routledge.

Buss, D. M. 1995. *The Evolution of Desire: Strategies of Human Mating*. New York: Basic Books.

Cancian, F. M. 1975. *What Are Norms? A Study of Beliefs and Action in a Maya Community*. Cambridge: Cambridge University Press.

Carter, J., and S. Duncan. 2018. *Reinventing Couples: Tradition, Agency and Bricolage*. Basingstoke: Palgrave Macmillan.

Chai, C., and W. Chai. 1965. *The Sacred Books of Confucius, and Other Confucius Classics*. New Hyde Park, NY: University Books.

Chan, K. W., and Y. Ren. 2018. "Children of Migrants in China in the Twenty-First Century: Trends, Living Arrangements, Age-Gender Structure, and Geography." *Eurasian Geography and Economics* 59, no. 2: 133–63.

Chau, A. 2011. *Battle Hymn of the Tiger Mother*. New York: Penguin.

Chen, F., G. Liu, and C. A. Mair. 2011. "Intergenerational Ties in Context: Grandparents Caring for Grandchildren in China." *Social Forces* 90, no. 2: 571–94.

Chen, R., and L. Zhang. 2019. "Imbalance in China's Sex Ratio at Birth: A Review." *Journal of Economic Surveys*, 33, no. 3: 1050–69.

Cherlin, A. J. 2004. "The Deinstitutionalization of American Marriage." *Journal of Marriage and Family* 66, no. 4: 848–61.

———. 2012. "Goode's World Revolution and Family Patterns: A Reconsideration at Fifty Years." *Population and Development Review* 38, no. 4: 577–607.

Choi, Y.-P., and Y. Peng. 2016. *Masculine Compromise: Migration, Family, and Gender in China*. Berkeley: University of California Press.

Choi, Y.-P., and M. Luo. 2016. "Performative Family: Homosexuality, Marriage and Intergenerational Dynamics in China." *British Journal of Sociology*, 67, no. 2: 260–80.

Cong, Z., and M. Silverstein. 2011. "Intergenerational Exchange Between Parents and Migrant and Nonmigrant Sons in Rural China." *Journal of Marriage and Family* 73: 93–104.

Croll, E. 2006. *China's New Consumers: Social Development and Domestic Demand*. London and New York: Routledge.

Croll, E., D. Davin, and P. Kane, eds. 1985. *China's One-Child Family Policy*. London: Palgrave.

Dasgupta, S., M. Matsumoto, and C. Xiao. 2015. *Women in the Labour Market in China*. Bangkok: International Labour Organization Regional Office for Asia and the Pacific.

Davies, K. 1994. "The Tensions between Process Time and Clock Time in Care-Work: The Example of Day Nurseries." *Time and Society* 3: 277.

Davis, D. 1993. "Urban Households: Suppliants to a Socialist State." In *Chinese Families in the Post-Mao Era*, edited by D. Davis and S. Harrell, 50–76. Berkeley: University of California Press.

———. 2000. "Introduction: A Revolution in Consumption." In *The Consumer Revolution in Urban China*, edited by Deborah S. Davis. Berkeley: University of California Press.

———. 2021. "'We Do': Parental Involvement in the Marriages of Urban Sons and Daughters." In *Chinese Families Upside Down*, edited by Y. Yan, 31–54. Leiden: Brill.

Davis, D., and S. Friedman. 2014. *Wives, Husbands, and Lovers: Marriage and Sexuality in Hong Kong, Taiwan, and Urban China*. Stanford, CA: Stanford University Press.

Davis, D., and S. Harrell. 1993. "Introduction: The Impact of Post-Mao Reforms on Family Life." In *Chinese Families in the Post-Mao Era*, edited by D. Davis and S. Harrell, 1–23. Berkeley: University of California Press.

Davis-Friedmann, D. 1991. *Long Lives: Chinese Elderly and the Communist Revolution*. Stanford, CA: Stanford University Press.

Diamant, N. J. 2000. *Revolutionizing the Family: Politics, Love, and Divorce in Urban and Rural China, 1949–1968*. Berkeley: University of California Press.

Dikötter, F. 1995. *Sex, Culture and Modernity in China: Medical Science and the Construction of Sexual Identities in the Early Republican Period*. Honolulu: University of Hawaii Press.

Dirlik, A., and H. Zhang. 1997. *Postmodernism and China*. Durham, NC: Duke University Press.

Duncan, S. 2011. "Personal Life, Pragmatism and Bricolage." *Sociological Research Online* 16, no. 4: 13.

Duncan, S., and S. Irwin. 2004. "The Social Patterning of Values and Rationalities." *Social Policy and Society* 3, no. 4: 391–99.

Ebrey, P. B. 1978. *The Aristocratic Families of Early Imperial China*. Cambridge: Cambridge University Press.

———. 1991. "Introduction." In *Marriage and Inequality in Chinese Society*, edited by R. S. Watson and P. B. Ebrey, 1–24. Berkeley: University of California Press.

Eklund, L. 2018. "Filial Daughter? Filial Son? How China's Young Urban Elite Negotiate Intergenerational Obligations." *Nordic Journal of Feminist and Gender Research* 26, no. 4: 295–312.

Elder, G. H., Jr. 1994. "Time, Human Agency, and Social Change: Perspectives on the Life Course." *Social Psychology Quarterly* 57: 4–15.

Evans, H. 1997. *Women and Sexuality in China: Female Sexuality and Gender Since 1949*. New York: Continuum.

———. 2007. *The Subject of Gender*. Lanham, MD: Rowman & Littlefield Publishers.

———. 2010. "The Gender of Communication: Changing Expectations of Mothers and Daughters in Urban China." *China Quarterly* 204: 980–1000.

Evasdottir, E.E.S. 2004. *Obedient Autonomy. Chinese Intellectuals and the Achievement of Orderly Life*. Canada: UBC Press.

Falkingham, J., M. Evandrou, Q. Min, and A. Vlachantoni. 2020. "Informal Care Provision across Multiple Generations in China." *Ageing and Society* 40: 1978–2005.

Fan, C. 2007. *China on the Move: Migration, the State, and the Household*. London: Routledge.

Farrer, J. 2002. *Opening Up: Youth Sex Culture and Market Reform in Shanghai*. Chicago: University of Chicago Press.

Farrer, J., and Z. Sun. 2003. "Extramarital Love in Shanghai." *China Journal* 50: 1–36.

Fei, X. 1992 [1947]. *From the Soil: The Foundations of Chinese Society*. Translated by Gary Hamilton and Wang Zheng. Berkeley: University of California Press.

Feng, H.-Y. 1967. *The Chinese Kinship System*. Cambridge, MA: Harvard University Press.

Feng, X. 2020. "The Effectiveness of the Two-Child Policy: Assessment and Reflection." *Southeast University Journal* 5. [In Chinese.]

Finch, J. 1989. *Family Obligations and Social Change*. Cambridge: Polity Press.

———. 2007. "Displaying Families." *Sociology* 41: 65–81.

Fincher, L. H. 2014. *Leftover Women: Resurgence of Gender Inequality in China*. London: Bloomsbury.

Fong, V. 2004. *Only Hope: Coming of Age under China's One-Child Policy*. Stanford, CA: Stanford University Press.

Fraser, N. 2017. "Crisis of Care? On the Social-Reproductive Contradictions of Contemporary Capitalism." In *Social Reproduction Theory: Remapping Class, Recentering Oppression*, edited by T. Bhattacharya, 21–36. London: Pluto Press.

Freeberne, M. 1964. "Birth Control in China." *Population Studies* 18: 5–16.

Freedman, M. 1979 [1961]. "The Family in China, Past and Present." In *The Study of Chinese Society: Essays by Maurice Freedman*, edited by G. W. Skinner, 273–95. Stanford, CA: Stanford University Press.

Friedman, E. 2022. *The Urbanization of People: The Politics of Development, Labor Markets, and Schooling in the Chinese City*. New York: Columbia University Press.

Friedmann, J. 1966. *Regional Development Policy: A Case Study of Venezuela*. Cambridge, MA: MIT Press.

Gabb, J. 2008. *Researching Intimacy in Families*. London: Palgrave

———. 2022. "The Relationship Work of Sexual Intimacy in Long-Term Heterosexual and LGBTQ Partnerships." *Current Sociology* 70, no. 1: 24–41.

Gabb, J., M. Klett-Davies, J. Fink, et al. 2013. *Enduring Love? Couple Relationships in the 21st Century*. Survey Findings Report. Milton Keynes, UK: The Open University.

Gagnon, J., and W. Simon. 1974. *Sexual Conduct*. London: Hutchinson.

———. 2005. *Sexual Conduct: The Social Sources of Human Sexuality*. 2nd ed. New Brunswick, NJ: AldineTransaction.

Gallin, R. S. 1994. "The Intersection of Class and Age: Mother-in-Law / Daughter-in-Law Relations in Rural Taiwan." *Journal of Cross Cultural Gerontology* 9, no. 2: 127–40.

Giddens, A. 1991. *Modernity and Self Identity*. Cambridge: Polity Press.

———. 1992. *The Transformation of Intimacy: Sexuality, Love, and Eroticism in Modern Societies*. Stanford, CA: Stanford University Press.

Ginn, J., and S. Arber. 2000. "Gender, the Generational Contract and Pension Privatisation." In *The Myth of Generational Conflict: The Family and the State in Aging Societies*, edited by S. Arber, and C. Attias-Donfut, 133–53. Routledge, London.

Gladney, D. 2004. *Dislocating China: Muslims, Minorities, and Other Subaltern Subjects*. Chicago: University of Chicago Press.

Goffman, E. 1959. *The Presentation of Self in Everyday Life*. Garden City, NY: Doubleday.

Goh, E.C.L. 2011. *China's One-Child Policy and Multiple Caregiving: Raising Little Suns in Xiamen*. New York: Routledge.

Goldin, P. R. 2002. *The Culture of Sex in Ancient China*. Honolulu: University of Hawaii Press.

Goode, W. J. 1959. "The Theoretical Importance of Love." *American Sociological Review* 24: 38–47. https://https://doi.org/10.2307/2089581.

———. 1963. *World Revolution and Family Patterns*. London: Free Press of Glencoe.

Goodman, C. C., and M. Silverstein. 2006. "Grandmothers Raising Grandchildren: Ethnic and Racial Differences in Well-Being among Custodial and Coparenting Families." *Journal of Family Issues* 27, no. 11: 1605–26.

Goody, J. 1976. "Introduction." In *Family and Inheritance*, edited by J. Goody et al. Cambridge: Cambridge University Press.

Greenhalgh, S. 2011. "Governing Chinese Life: From Sovereignty to Biopolitical Governance." In *Governance of Life in Chinese Moral Experience: The Quest for an Adequate Life*, edited by E. Zhang, A. Kleinman, and W. Tu, 146–62. London: Routledge.

Greenhalgh, S., and E. A. Winckler. 2005. *Governing China's Population: From Leninist to Neoliberal Biopolitics*. Stanford, CA: Stanford University Press.

Hamilton, G. 1990. "Patriarchy, Patrimonialism and Filial Piety." *British Journal of Sociology* 41, no. 2: 77–104.

Han, X. 2013. "From Agricultural Nursery to Model Kindergarten: Shan'xi Childcare Facilities for Infants in the 1950s." *Contemporary Chinese History Studies* 3. [In Chinese.]

Hansen, M. H. 2015. *Educating the Chinese Individual: Life in a Rural Boarding School*. Seattle: University of Washington Press.

Harper, D. 1987. "The Sexual Acts of Ancient China as Described in a Manuscript of the Second Century BC." *Harvard Journal of Asiatic Studies* 47, no. 2: 539–93.

Hays, S. 1996. *The Cultural Contradictions of Motherhood*. New Haven, CT: Yale University Press.

Heaphy, B. 2007. *Late Modernity and Social Change: Reconstructing Social and Personal Life*. London: Routledge.

Hell, N., and S. Rozelle. 2020. *Invisible China*. Chicago: University of Chicago Press.

Hinsch, B. 1992. *Passions of the Cut Sleeve: The Male Homosexual Tradition in China*. Berkeley: University of California Press.

Hird, D. 2020. "Knowing Male Subjects: Globally Mobile Chinese Professionals and the Aesthetics of the Confucian Sublime." *China Perspectives* 3: 19–27.

Ho, P.S.Y., S. Jackson, S. Cao, and C. Kwok. 2018. "Sex with Chinese Characteristics: Sexuality Research in/on 21st-Century China." *Journal of Sex Research* 55, nos. 4–5: 486–521.

Hochschild, A. R. 1983. *The Managed Heart*. Berkeley: University of California Press.

———. 1989. *The Second Shift: Working Parents and the Revolution at Home*. New York: Avon Books.

Holland, J., C. Ramazanoglu, S. Sharpe, and R. Thomson. 1998. *The Male in the Head: Young People, Sexuality and Power*. London: the Tufnell Press.

Hong, X., and X. Tao. 2019. "Policies and Practices of Care for Children 0–3, 1980–2020." *Pre-School Education Studies* 2: 3–11. [In Chinese.]

Honig, E., and G. Hershatter. 1988. *Personal Voices: Chinese Women in the 1980s*. Stanford, CA: Stanford University Press.

Howlett, Z. 2021. *Meritocracy and Its Discontents: Anxiety and the National College Entrance Exam in China*. Ithaca, NY: Cornell University Press.

Hu, H.-C. 1944. "The Chinese Concept of Face." *American Anthropologist* 46: 45–64.

Hu, P., and M. Chen. 2007. *Book of Filial Piety and Book of Rites*. Beijing: China Book Bureau. [In Chinese.]

Hu, S., S. Tang, Y. Liu, Y. Zhao, M.-L. Escobar, and D. de Ferranti. 2008. "Reform of How Health Care Is Paid for in China: Challenges and Opportunities." *Lancet* 372: 1846–53.

Hu, Y. 2016. "Sex Ideologies in China: Examining Interprovince Differences." *Journal of Sex Research* 53, no. 9: 1118–30. https://doi.org10.1080/00224499.2015.1137272.

Hu, Y., and J. Scott. 2016. "Family and Gender Values in China." *Journal of Family Issues* 37: 1267–93.

Huang, C. 2021 "Families under (Peer) Pressure: Self-Advocacy and Ambivalence among Women in Collective Dance Groups." In *Chinese Families Upside Down. Intergenerational Dynamics and Neo-Familism in the Early 21st Century*, edited by Yunxiang Yan. Leiden: Koninklijke Brill NV.

Huang, P.C.C. 1990. *The Peasant Family and Rural Development in the Yanzi Delta, 1350–1988.* Stanford, CA: Stanford University Press.

Hung, S. L., K. K. Fung, and A.S.M. Lau. 2021. "Grandparenting in Chinese Skipped-Generation Families: Cultural Specificity of Meanings and Coping." *Journal of Family Studies* 27, no. 2: 196–214.

Ikels, C. 1996. *The Return of the God of Wealth.* Stanford, CA: Stanford University Press.

———. 1998. "Grandparenthood in Cross-Cultural Perspective." In *Handbook on Grandparenthood*, edited by M. E. Szinovacz. Westport, CT: Greenwood Press.

———, ed. 2004. *Filial Piety: Practice and Discourse in Contemporary East Asia.* Stanford, CA: Stanford University Press.

———. 2006. "Economic Reform and Intergenerational Relationships in China." *Oxford Development Studies* 34: 387–400.

Illouz, E. 1997. *Consuming the Romantic Utopia.* Berkeley: University of California Press.

Jacka, T. 2018. "Translocal Family Reproduction and Agrarian Change in China: A New Analytical Framework." *Journal of Peasant Studies* 45, no. 7: 341–59.

Jackson, S. 2010. "Self, Time and Narrative: Re-thinking the Contribution of G. H. Mead." *Life Writing* 7, no. 2: 123–36.

———. 2018. "Why Heteronormativity Is Not Enough: A Feminist Sociological Approach to Heterosexuality." In *Gender Reckonings: New Social Theory and Research*, edited by J. W. Messerschmidt, P. Y. Martin, M. A. Messner, and R. Connell. New York: New York University Press.

Jackson, S., and S.-Y. Ho. 2020. *Women Doing Intimacy: Gender, Family and Modernity in Britain and Hong Kong.* London: Palgrave Macmillan.

Jamieson, L. 1998. *Intimacy: Personal Relationships in Modern Societies.* Cambridge: Polity Press.

———. 2011. "Intimacy as a Concept." *Sociological Research Online* 16, no. 4.

Jankowiak, W. 1993. *Sex, Death, and Hierarchy in a Chinese City.* New York: Columbia University Press.

———. 2013. "Chinese Youth: Hot Romance and Cold Calculation." In *Restless China*, edited by P. Link, R. P. Madsen, and P. G. Pickowicz. Lanham, MD: Rowman & Littlefield.

———. 2021. "The Chinese Proto Neo-Family Configuration: A Historical Ethnography." In *Chinese Families Upside Down: Intergenerational Dynamics and Neo-Familism in the Early 21st Century*, edited by Y. Yan. Leiden: Koninklijke Brill NV.

Jankowiak, W., and X. Li. 2017. "Emergent Conjugal Love, Mutual Affection, and Female Marital Power." In *Transforming Patriarchy: Chinese Families in the 21st Century*, edited by G. Santos and S. Harrell, 146–62. Seattle: University of Washington Press.

Jankowiak, W., and R. L. Moore. 2016. *Family Life in China.* Oxford: Polity Press.

Jeffreys, E., and H. Yu. 2015. *Sex in China.* Cambridge: Polity Press.

Ji, Y. 2017. "A Mosiac Temporality: New Dynamics of the Gender and Marriage System in Contemporary Urban China." *Temporalities* 26: http://doi.org/10.4000/Temporalities .3773.

Johnson, K. A. 2004. *Wanting a Daughter, Needing a Son. Abandonment, Adoption, and Orphanage Care in China*. St. Paul, MN: Yeong and Yeong.

Judd, E. 1994. *Gender and Power in Rural North China*. Stanford, CA: Stanford University Press.

Kagitcibasi, C. 2007. *Family, Self, and Human Development across Cultures Theory and Applications*. 2nd edition. New York: Routledge.

Kipnis, A. 1997. *Producing Guanxi: Sentiment, Self, and Subculture in a North China Village*. Durham, NC: Duke University Press.

———. 2011. *Governing Educational Desire: Culture, Politics and Schooling in China*. Chicago: University of Chicago Press.

———. 2017. "Urbanization and the Transformation of Kinship Practice in Shandong." In *Transforming Patriarchy: Chinese Families in the Twenty-First Century*, edited by G. Santos and S. Harrell. Seattle: University of Washington Press.

Ko, P. C., and K. Hank. 2014. "Grandparents Caring for Grandchildren in China and Korea: Findings from CHARLS and KLoSA." *Journals of Gerontology: Series B* 69, no, 4: 646–51.

Komter, A. 1989. "Hidden Power in Marriage." *Gender and Society* 3, no. 2.

Kuan, T. 2012. "The Horrific and the Exemplary: Public Stories and Education Reform in Late Socialist China." *Positions* 20, no. 4: 1095–1125.

———. 2015. *Love's Uncertainty: The Politics and Ethics of Child Rearing in Contemporary China*. Oakland: University of California Press.

Kurz, D. 2006. "Keeping Tabs on Teenagers." In *Couples, Kids and Family Life*, edited by J. F. Gubrium and J. A. Holstein. Oxford: Oxford University Press.

Labrecque, L., and M. Whisman. 2017. "Attitudes Toward and Prevalence of Extramarital Sex and Descriptions of Extramarital Partners in the 21st Century." *Journal of Family Psychology* 31: 952–57.

Lai, R.Y.S., and S.Y.P. Choi. 2021. "Premarital Sexuality, Abortion, and Intergenerational Dynamics in China." *Modern China* 47, no. 3: 239–65.

Lareau, A. 2003. *Unequal Childhoods: Class, Race and Family Life*. Berkeley: University of California Press.

Lesthaeghe, R. 2010. "The Unfolding Story of the Second Demographic Transition." *Population and Development Review* 36: 211–51.

Leung, J., and Y. Xu. 2016. *China's Social Welfare*. Cambridge, MA: Polity Press.

Li, J. 1998. "Nongcun ganqun guanxi jinzhang gengyuan zai tizhi" [The tension between rural cadres and villagers is rooted in the political system]. *Gaige neican* [Internal reference to reforms), no. 13: 30–33.

Li, K. 2022. *Marriage Unbound: State Law, Power and Inequality in Contemporary China*. Stanford, CA: Stanford University Press.

Li, M., and S. P. Hu. 2009. "Urban Care Institutions—A Case Study of Guangzhou." *Social Sciences in Nanjing* 1: 89–95. [In Chinese.]

Li, W. 2022. "Childcare Crganizations in Shanghai (1949–1959)." MA thesis, Shanghai Normal University.

Li, Y., W. Ma, and L. Wang. 2019. "A Study of Childcare Institutions for Infants 0–3 in China since 1949." *Education Development Studies* 24: 68–74. [In Chinese.]

Li, Y., Q. Wu, C. Łiu, Z. Kang, X. Xie, H. Yin, M. Jiao, G. Liu, Y. Hao, and N. Ning. 2014. "Catastrophic Health Expenditure and Rural Household Impoverishment in China: What Role

Does the New Cooperative Health Insurance Scheme Play?" *PLoS One* 9, no. 4: https://doi .org/10.1371/journal.pone.0093253.

Lin, A.-H. 1992. *Study of Filial Piety in Confucian Thought.* Taipei: Wen Jin.

Ling, M. 2020. *The Inconvenient Generation: Migrant Youth Coming of Age on Shanghai's Edge.* Stanford: Stanford University Press.

Liu, F. 2016. "The Rise of the 'Priceless' Child in China." *Comparative Education Review* 60, no. 1: 105–30.

Liu, J. 2007. *Gender and Work in Urban China: Women Workers of the Unlucky Generation.* London: Routledge.

———. 2017a. *Gender, Sexuality and Power in Chinese Companies: Beauties at Work.* London: Palgrave Macmillan.

———. 2017b. "Intimacy and Intergenerational Relations in Rural China." *Sociology* 51, no. 5, 1034–49.

———. 2022. "Childhood and Rural to Urban Migration in China: A Tale of Three Villages." *Children and Society*: 1–16. https://doi.org/10.1111/chso.12666.

Liu, J., E. Bell, and J. Zhang. 2019. "Conjugal Intimacy, Gender and Modernity in Contemporary China." *British Journal of Sociology* 70, no. 1: 283–305.

Liu, J., M. Cheng, X. Wei, et al. 2020. "The Internet-Driven Sexual Revolution in China." *Technological Forecasting and Social Change* 153: https://doi.org/10.1016/j.techfore.2020 .119911.

Liu, X. 2000. *In One's Own Shadow: An Ethnographic Account of the Condition of Post-Reform Rural China.* Berkeley: University of California Press.

Lu, J., and Q. Liu. 2019. "Four Decades of Studies on Population Aging in China." *China Population and Development Studies* 3: 24–36. https://doi.org/10.1007/s42379-019-00027-4.

Lu, M. 2020. "The Analysis and Recommendation of Grandparenting in the Cities." *Research on Transmission Competence* 21: 186–88. [In Chinese.]

Lu, W. 2013. "Abstaining from Sex: Mourning Ritual and the Confucian Elite." In "Sexuality in Chinese History," edited by Weijing Lu. Special issue, *Journal of the History of Sexuality* 22, no. 2: 230–52.

Lui, L. 2018. "Marital Power in Inter-Hukou Families in China: An Intersectionality Approach." *Journal of Family Issues* 39, no. 5: 1165–90.

———. 2021. "Filial Considerations in Mate Selection: Urban and Rural Guangdong in the Post-Mao Era." *Modern China* 47, no. 4: 383–411.

Lukes, S. 1974. *Power: A Radical View.* London: Macmillan.

Luo, W., and J. Yu. 2022. "Sexual Infidelity among the Married in China." *Chinese Journal of Sociology* 8, no. 3: 374–97.

Lutz, H., and E. Palenga-Mollenbeck. 2012. "Care Workers, Care Drain, and Care Chains: Reflections on Care, Migration, and Citizenship." *Social Politics* 19, no. 1: 15–37.

Lynch, R. A. 2010. "Foucault's Theory of Power." In *Michel Foucault: Key Concepts,* edited by Dianna Taylor, 13–26, Durham, UK: Acumen Publishing.

Lyu, J., X. Shen, and T. Hesketh. 2020. "Sexual Knowledge, Attitudes and Behaviours among Undergraduate Students in China—Implications for Sex Education." *Internal Journal of Environmental Research and Public Health* 17, no. 18: https://doi.org/10.3390/ijerph17186716.

Mann, S. 2011. *Under Confucian Eyes.* Berkeley: University of California Press.

Martin, F. 2022. *Dreams of Flight: The Lives of Chinese Women Students in the West*. Durham, NC: Duke University Press.

Mason, J. 2002. *Qualitative Interviewing*. London: Sage.

McCarthy, R. J., R. Edwards, and V. Gillies. 2003. *Making Families: Moral Tales of Parenting and Step-Parenting*. Durham, UK: Sociology Press.

McLanahan, S. 2004. "Diverging Destinies: How Children Are Faring under the Second Demographic Transition." *Demography* 41: 607–27.

Mead, G. H. 1967 [1934]. *Mind Self and Society*. Chicago: University of Chicago Press.

Medick, H., and D. W. Sabean, eds. 1984. *Interest and Emotion*. Cambridge: Cambridge University Press.

Ménard, A. D., P. J. Kleinplatz, L. Rosen, et al. 2015. "Individual and Relational Contributors to Optimal Sexual Experiences in Older Men and Women." *Sexual and Relationship Therapy* 30, no. 1: 78–93.

Mezzadri, A., S. Newman, and S. Stevano. 2021. "Feminist Global Political Economies of Work and Social Reproduction." *Review of International Political Economy*. https://doi.org/10.1080/09692290.2021.1957977.

Miller, E. T. 2004. "Filial Daughters, Filial Sons: Comparisons from North Rural China." In *Filial Piety: Practice and Discourse in Contemporary East Asia*, edited by C. Ikels, 34–52. Stanford, CA: Stanford University Press.

Moore, R., and L. Wei. 2012. "Modern Love in China." In *The Psychology of Love*, vol. 3, edited by Michele Paludi. Santa Barbara, CA: Praeger.

Murphy, R. 2020. *The Children of China's Great Migration*. Cambridge: Cambridge University Press.

Naftali, O. 2009. "Empowering the Child: Children's Rights, Citizenship and the State in Contemporary China." *China Journal* 61: 79–104.

———. 2014. *Children, Rights, and Modernity in China: Raising Self-Governing Citizens*. Basingstoke, UK: Palgrave Macmillan.

———. 2016. *Children in China*. Cambridge: Polity Press.

National Statistical Bureau. 2021. "Main Data on the Seventh Population Census." May 11, 2021. http://www.stats.gov.cn/english/PressRelease/202105/t20210510_1817185.html.

———. 2022. *China Statistical Abstract—2022*. China Statistics Press. [In Chinese.]

Nunn, A., and D. Tepe-Belfrage. 2019. "Social Reproduction Strategies: Understanding Compound Inequality in the Intergenerational Transfer of Capital, Assets and Resources." *Capital and Class* 43, no. 4: 617–35.

Ocko, Jonathan K. 1991. "Women, Property, and Law in the People's Republic of China." In *Marriage and Inequality in Chinese Society*, edited by R. S. Watson and P. B. Ebrey. California: University of California Press.

Okin, S. 1989. *Justice, Gender and the Family*. New York: Basic Books.

O'Rand, A. M. 1990. "Stratification and the Life Course." In *Handbook of Aging and the Social Sciences*, edited by R. H. Binstock and L. K. George. 3rd ed. San Diego, CA: Academic Press.

Palmer, M. 1995. "The Re-emergence of Family Law in Post-Mao China." *China Quarterly* 141: 110–34.

Pan, S. 2018. *Chinese Sexuality 2000–2015*. Hong Kong: 1908 Limited Company. [In Chinese.]

Pan, S., and Y. Huang. 2013. *The Transformation of Sexuality: Chinese People's Sex Life in the 21st Century*. Beijing: Renmin University of China Press. [In Chinese.]

Pan, S., W. Parish, A. Wang, and E. Laumann. 2004. *Sexual Behaviour and Relation in Contemporary China* Beijing: Social Science Documentation Publishing House. [In Chinese.]

Parish, W. L., and M. K. Whyte. 1978. *Village and Family in Contemporary China*. Chicago: University of Chicago Press.

Parish, W. L., E. O. Laumann, and S. A. Mojola. 2007. "Sexual Behavior in China: Trends and Comparisons." *Population and Development Review* 33, no. 4: 729–56.

Peng, Y. 2024. "Gendered Parenting and Conjugal Negotiation over Children's Organised Extracurricular Activities." *British Journal of Sociology* 45, no. 1: 23–40.

Phillips, M. S. 2004. "What Is Tradition When It Isn't 'Invented'? A Historiographical Introduction." In *Questions of Tradition*, edited by M. S. Phillips and G. Sochet. Toronto: University of Toronto Press.

Pimentel, E. E. 2000. "Just How Do I Love Thee? Marital Relations in Urban China." *Journal of Marriage and Family* 62, no. 1: 32–47.

Polanyi, K. 1944. *The Great Transformations*. New York: Rinehart and Co.

Postiglione, G. A. 2011. "Education." In *Understanding Chinese Society*, edited by X. Zang, 80–95. London: Routledge.

Potter, S. H., and J. M. Potter. 1990. *China's Peasants: The Anthropology of a Revolution*. Cambridge: Cambridge University Press.

Pyke, K. D. 1994. "Women's Employment as a Gift or Burden? Marital Power across Marriage, Divorce, and Remarriage." *Gender and Society* 8: 73–91.

Raymo, J. M., H. Park, and J. Yu. 2023. "Diverging Destinies in East Asia." *Annual Review of Sociology* 49: 443–63.

Rofel, L. 2007. *Desiring China: Experiments in Neoliberalism, Sexuality and Public Culture*. Durham, NC: Duke University Press.

Salaff, J. W. 1981. *Working Daughters of Hong Kong—Filial Piety or Power in the Family?* American Sociological Association Rose Monographs. Cambridge: Cambridge University Press.

Salaff, J., and J. Merkle. 1970. "Women in Revolution: The Lessons of the Soviet Union and China." *Berkeley Journal of Sociology* 15: 166–91.

Santos, G. and S. Harrell, eds. 2017. *Transforming Patriarchy: Chinese Families in the Twenty-First Century*. Seattle: University of Washington Press.

Scott, J. 1998. "Changing Attitudes to Sexual Morality: A Cross-National Comparison." *Sociology* 32, no. 4: 815–45.

Shang, X. Y., and X. M. Wu. 2011. "The Care Regime in China." *Journal of Comparative Social Welfare* 27, no. 2: 123–31.

Shen, Y. 2016. "Filial Daughters? Agency and Subjectivity of Rural Migrant Women in Shanghai." *China Quarterly* 226: 519–37.

Sheng, L. 2022. "Embodying Ageing: Middle-Aged and Older Women's Bodily Fitness and Aesthetics in Urban China." *Ageing and Society* 42, no. 8: 1844–62.

Silverstein, M., and Z. Cong. 2013. "Grandparenting in Rural China." *Generations—Journal of the American Society on Aging* 37, no. 1: 46–52.

Silverstein, M., Z. Cong, and S. Li. 2006. "Intergenerational Transfers and Living Arrangements of Older People in Rural China: Consequences for Psychological Well-Being." *Journals of Gerontology: Series B* 61, no. 5: S256–66. https://doi.org/10.1093/geronb/61.5.s256.

Silverstein, M., Y. Xu. 2022. "Older Grandparents Caring for Grandchildren in Rural China: Cohort Change in Resources and Deficits Across 17 Years." *Public Policy & Aging Report* 32, no. 3: 112–17. https://doi.org/10.1093/ppar/prac012.

Siu, H. 1989. *Agents and Victims in South China: Accomplices in Rural Revolution.* New Haven, CT: Yale University Press.

Skinner, W., ed. 1977. *The City in Late Imperial China.* Stanford, CA: Stanford University Press.

Skolnick, E. 1997. "The Triple Revolution: Social Sources of Family Change." In *The Family on the Threshold of the 21st Century: Trends and Implications,* edited by S. Dreman. Mahwah, NJ: Erlbaum.

Smart, C. 2007. *Personal Life.* Cambridge: Polity Press.

Smart, C., and B. Shipman. 2004. "Visions in Monochrome: Families, Marriage and the Individualization Thesis." *British Journal of Sociology* 55: 491–509.

Solinger, D. 2006. "The Creation of a New Underclass in China and Its Implications." *Environment and Urbanisation* 18: 177–93.

———. 2022. *Poverty and Pacification: The Chinese State Abandons the Old Working Class.* Lanham, MD: Rowman & Littlefield.

Steinmüller, H., and T. Tan. 2015. "Like a Virgin? Hymen Restoration Operations in Contemporary China." *Anthropology Today* 31, no. 2: 15–18.

Sun, W. 2023. *Love Troubles: Inequality in China and Its Intimate Consequences.* London: Bloomsbury Academic.

Tan, L. and J. Li. 2002. "What Do Marriage and Employment Mean to Women? An Analysis Based upon Theories on Gender and Social Capital." *Journal of Women's Studies* 7: 5–11. [In Chinese.]

Tan, Z. 2007. *Family Teachings of Yan Lineage.* Beijing: China Book Bureau.

Theiss, J. M. 2004. *Disgraceful Matters: The Politics of Chasity in Eighteenth-Century China.* Berkeley: University of California Press.

Thomas, C. 1993. "Deconstructing Concepts of Care." *Sociology* 27, no. 4: 649–69.

Tian, F. F., M. G. Merli, and Z. Qian. 2013. "Job Mobility and Extramarital Sex in Reform-Era Urban China." *Chinese Sociological Review* 46, no. 1: 60–82.

Tsui, M., and L. Rich. 2002. "The Only Child and Educational Opportunity for Girls in Urban China." *Gender and Society* 16, no. 1: 74–92.

Van de Kaa, D. J. 2001. "Postmodern Fertility Preferences: From Changing Value Orientation to New Behavior." *Population Development Review* 27: 290–331.

Van Gulik, R. H. 1961. *Sexual Life in Ancient China: A Preliminary Survey of Chinese Sex and Society from ca. 1500 B.C. Tile 1644 A.D.* Leiden: Brill.

Walder, A. 1986. *Communist Neo-Traditionalism: Work and Authority in Chinese Industry.* Berkeley: University of California Press.

Wall, G., and S. Arnold. 2007. "How Involved Is Involved Fathering? An Exploration of the Contemporary Culture of Fatherhood." *Gender & Society* 21, no. 4.

Wang, L. 2015. "Childcare Facilities in Tianjin in the 1950s." *Contemporary China History Studies* 22, no. 1: 77–87. [In Chinese.]

Wang, N., M. Evandrou, J. Falkingham, and M. Xu. 2022. "Typologies of Intergenerational Relations in Urban and Rural China: A Latent Class Analysis." *Journal of Applied Gerontology* 42, no. 2.

Wang, R. R. 2005. "Dong Zhongshu's Transformation of 'Yin-Yang' Theory and Contesting of Gender Identity." *Philosophy East and West* 55, no. 2: 209–31.

Wang, S., and Wang H. 2017. "Grandparents Caring for Grandchildren in the United States and China." *Innovation in Aging* 1, supplement 1: 804. https://doi.org/10.1093/geroni/igx004.2906.

Wang, X. 2017. *Gender, Dating and Violence in Urban China*. London: Routledge.

Wang, X., and S. Y. Ho. 2007. "My Sassy Girl: A Qualitative Study of Women's Aggression in Dating Relationships in Beijing." *Journal of Interpersonal Violence* 22, no. 5: 623–38.

Watson, R., and P. B. Ebrey, eds. 1991. *Marriage and Inequality in Chinese Society*. Berkeley: California University Press.

Wells, A. 2001. "Sun's Three Principles of the People: The Principle of Nationalism." In *The Political Thought of Sun Yat-sen*. London: Palgrave Macmillan. https://doi.org/10.1057/9781403919755_6.

Whyte, M. K. 1990. "Changes in Mate Choice in Chengdu." In *Chinese Society on the Eve of Tiananmen: The Impact of Reform*, edited by D. Davis and E. F. Vogel, 181–213. Cambridge, MA: Harvard University Press.

———. 1992. "Choosing Mates—The American Way." *Society* 29, no. 3: 71–77; 29, no. 3: 71–77.

———, ed. 2003. *China's Revolutions and Intergenerational Relations*. Ann Arbor: University of Michigan Press.

———. 2010. *Myth of the Social Volcano: Perceptions of Inequality and Distributive Injustice in Contemporary China*. Stanford, CA: Stanford University Press.

———. 2020. "Confronting Puzzles in Understanding Chinese Family Change: A Personal Reflection." *Chinese Journal of Sociology* 6: 339–63.

———. 2023. "Be Careful What You Wish For: China Confronts Population Decline." *China-US Focus*. https://www.chinausfocus.com/author/20592/martin-king-whyte.html.

———. 2024. "Xi Jinping Confronts Inequality: Bold Leadership or Modest Steps?" In *The Xi Jinping Effect*, edited by A. Esarey and R. Han. Seattle: University of Washington Press.

Whyte, M. K., and W. L. Parish. 1984. *Urban Life in Contemporary China*. Chicago: University of Chicago Press.

Whyte, M. K., F. Wang, and Y. Cai. 2015. "Challenging Myths about China's One-Child Policy." *China Journal*: 144–59.

Whyte, M. K., and Q. Xu. 2003. "Support for Aging Parents from Daughters versus Sons." In *China's Revolutions and Intergenerational Relations*, edited by M. K. Whyte, 167–96. Ann Arbor: University of Michigan Press.

Wile, D. 1992. *Art of the Bedchamber: The Chinese Sexual Yoga Classics Including Women's Solo Meditation Texts*. Albany: State University of New York Press.

Winders, J., and B. E. Smith. 2019. "Social Reproduction and Capitalist Production: A Genealogy of Dominant Imaginaries." *Progress in Human Geography* 43, no. 5: 871–89.

Wolf, M. 1972. *Women and the Family in Rural Taiwan*. Stanford, CA: Stanford University Press.

———. 1985. *Revolution Postponed: Women in Contemporary China*. Stanford, CA: Stanford University Press.

Woronov, T. E. 2008. "Raising Quality, Fostering 'Creativity': Ideologies and Practices of Education Reform in Beijing." *Anthropology & Education Quarterly* 39, no. 4: 401–22.

Wu, J. 1990. "The Current Condition of Chinese Children." *Sociological Studies* 3: 49–60. [In Chinese.]

Xiang, B. 2011. "Review of *The Individualization of Chinese Society*." *Journal of Biosocial Science* 43: 126–27.

Xiao, S. 2014. "Strict Mother and Kind Grandmother: Intergenerational Cooperation in Childcare." *Sociological Studies* 6: 148–71. [In Chinese.]

Xie, Y., J. Hu, and C. Zhang. 2014. "Chinese Family Panel Study: Ideals and Practice." *Society*, no. 2: 1–21. [In Chinese.]

Xiong, Y. 2015. "The Broken Ladder: Why Education Provides No Upward Mobility for Migrant Children in China." *China Quarterly* 221: 161–84.

Xu, A., and X. Yan. 2014. "The Changes in Mainland Chinese Families During the Social Transition: A Critical Analysis." *Journal of Comparative Family Studies* 45, no. 1: 31–53.

Xu, J. 2013. "The New Law for Protecting Older People's Rights Will Be Implemented from 1 July 2013." *Xinhua News Agency*. http://news.xinhuanet.com/photo/2013-07/02/c _124940503.htm. [In Chinese.]

Yan, Y. 2003. *Private Life under Socialism: Love, Intimacy, and Family Change in a Chinese Village, 1949–1999*. London: Stanford University Press.

———. 2009. *The Individualization of Chinese Society*. Oxford: Berg.

———. 2011. "The Changing Moral Landscape." In *Deep China*, edited by A. Kleinman. Berkeley: University of California Press.

———. 2016. "Intergenerational Intimacy and Descending Familism in Rural North China." *American Anthropologist* 118, no. 2: 244.

———. 2018. "Neo-Familism and the State in Contemporary China." *Urban Anthropology and the Studies of Cultural Systems and World Economic Development* 47, nos. 3/4: 181–224.

———, ed. 2021. *Chinese Families Upside Down: Intergenerational Dynamics and Neo-Familism in the Early 21st Century*. Leiden: Brill.

Yang, C. K. 1959. *The Chinese Family in the Communist Revolution*. Cambridge: MIT Press.

Yang, L. 2020. "Review of Urban Childcare Policies." *Theory Monthly* 12: 70–80. [In Chinese.]

Yang, M.M.H. 1994. *Gifts, Favors & Banquets: The Art of Social Relationships in China*. Ithaca, NY: Cornell University Press.

———. 2002. "The Resilience of Guanxi and Its New Deployments: A Critique of Some New Guanxi Scholarship." *China Quarterly* 170: 459–76.

Yi, H., L. Zhang, R. Luo, Y. Shi, D. Mo, X. Chen, C. Brinton, and S. Rozelle. 2012 "Dropping Out: Why Are Students Leaving Junior High in China's Poor Rural Areas?" *International Journal of Educational Development* 32: 555–63.

Yu, J. 2006. "Household Division Custom and Inheritance Law in Modern China." *China Social Science* 5: 119–30. [In Chinese.]

Yu, J., W. Luo, and Y. Xie. 2022. "Sexuality in China: A Review and New Findings." *Chinese Journal of Sociology* 8, no. 3: 293–329.

Yu, J., and Y. Xie. 2015. "Cohabitation in China: Trends and Determinants." *Population and Development Review* 41, no. 4: 607–28.

———. 2021. "Recent Trends in the Chinese Family." *Demographic Research* 44: 595–608.

Yue, J., and X. Fan. 2018. "Childcare Policies in China." *Social Sciences in China* 9: 92–111. [In Chinese.]

Zelizer, V. A. 1985. *Pricing the Priceless Child: The Changing Social Value of Children*. New York: Basic Books.

———. 2005. *The Purchase of Intimacy*. Princeton, NJ: Princeton University Press.

Zhan, H. J. 2004. "Willingness and Expectations: Intergenerational Differences in Attitudes toward Filial Responsibility in China." *Marriage and Family Review* 36: 175–200.

Zhang, D., and P. Unschuld. 2008. "China's Barefoot Doctor: Past, Present, and Future." *Lancet*, 327, no. 9653: 1865–67.

Zhang, E. Y. 2011. "China's Sexual Revolution." In *Deep China: The Moral Life of the Person*, edited by A. Kleinman, J. Jun, S. Lee, and Y. Yan, 106–51. Berkeley: University of California Press.

Zhang, H. 2017. "Recalibrating Filial Piety: Realigning the State, Family, and Market Interests in China." In *Transforming Patriarchy: Chinese Families in the Twenty-First Century*, edited by G. Santos and S. Harrell. Seattle: University of Washington Press.

Zhang, J[uan]. 2016. "Research on Transformation and Development of Rural Homes for the Elderly." *Scientific Research on Ageing* 8, no. 4: 42–51. [In Chinese.]

Zhang, J[unsen]. 2021. "A Survey on Income Inequality in China." *Journal of Economic Literature* 59, no. 4: 1191–1239.

Zhang, J., M. Cheng, X. Wei, and X. Gong. 2018. "Does Mobile Phone Penetration Affect Divorce Rate? Evidence from China." *Sustainability* 10, no. 10: 1–19.

Zhang, J., and Sun, P. 2014. "When Are You Going to Get Married?: Parental Matchmaking and Middle-Class Women in Contemporary Urban China." In *Wives, Husbands, and Lovers: Marriage and Sexuality in Hong Kong, Taiwan, and Urban China*, edited by Deborah S. Davis and Sara L. Friedman, 118–44. Redwood City: Stanford University Press.

Zhang, L. 2008. "Private Homes, Distinct Life Styles: Performing a New Middle Class." In *Privatizing China: Socialism from Afar*, edited by L. Zhang and A. Ong, 23–40. Ithaca, NY: Cornell University Press.

Zhang, N., W. L. Parish, Y. Huang, et al. 2012. "Sexual Infidelity in China: Prevalence and Gender-Specific Correlates." *Archives of Sexual Behaviour* 41, no. 4: 861–73.

Zhang, Y., X. Wang, and S. Pan. 2021. "Prevalence and Patterns of Extramarital Sex among Chinese Men and Women: 2000–2015." *Journal of Sex Research* 58, no. 1: 41–50.

Zheng, L., and Y. Wu. 2014. "Impact of Parental Migration on Educational Development of Left-Behind Children." *Journal of Beijing Normal University* 2, no. 2, 139–46. [In Chinese.]

Zheng, T. 2009. *Red Lights: The Lives of Sex Workers in Postsocialist China*. Minneapolis: University of Minnesota Press.

Zheng, Y., and S. Peng, eds. 2003. *Trust in Chinese Society*. Beijing: China City Publisher. [In Chinese.]

Zhong, X. 2019. "The Impact of Childcare Patterns upon the Implementation of Two-Child Policy." *Journal of Guangdong Institute of Public Administration* 31, no. 2: 21–27. [In Chinese.]

———. 2020. "Chinese Family Research under the Individualization Framework." *China Studies* 25: 5–23. [In Chinese.]

Zhong, X., and M. Peng. 2020. "Grandmothering and Its Departure under the Context of Two-Child Policy." *Chinese Women's Newspaper*, July 14. [In Chinese.]

Zhongguo Laoling Kexue Yanjiu Zhongxin [China Gerontology Research Centre]. 2003. *Zhongguo Cheng Xiang Laonian Renkou Zhuangkuang Yi Ci Xing Chouyang Diaocha Shuju*

Fenxi [Data analysis of the sampling survey of the situation of the aged population in China]. Beijing: China Official Publishing.

Zhou, S. 2015. "*Suku* and the Self-Valorization of Chinese Women Workers: Before, during, and after Enterprise Privatization." *Frontiers of History in China* 10, no. 1: 145–67.

Zhou, Y., M. Shao, and R. Liu. 2014. "67.7% Interviewees Agree that Adhering to the Principle of 'Matching Households' Would Benefit Marriage." *China Youth Daily*, May 20. [In Chinese.]

Zimmer, Z., M. Wen, and T. Kaneda. 2010. "A Multi-Level Analysis of Urban / Rural and Socio-economic Differences in Functional Health Status Transition among Older Chinese." *Social Science Medicine* 71: 559–67.

Zuo, J., and Y. Bian. 2004. "Gendered Resources, Division of Housework, and Perceived Fairness—A Case in Urban China." *Journal of Marriage and Family* 63, no. 4: 1122–33.

INDEX

agricultural collectivization, 157

agricultural de-collectivization, 35, 61, 144, 172

Beck-Gernsheim, Elisabeth, 7, 8, 9, 13, 18, 225n9, 236n26

Beck, Ulrich, 7, 8, 9, 13, 18, 225n9, 236n26

Bengston, Vern L., 8, 15, 225n16

Biblarz, Timothy J., 15, 225n16

biological time, 190–91

Bourdieu, Pierre, 39, 231n30, 233n65

bricolage, 19–20, 228n91

bride price, 12, 60, 107, 146, 161, 168, 234n7

care: capacity to, 160, 172, 197, 207; commercialization of, 176; community-based, 189, 251n62; familial, 42, 176; home-based, 189, 251n62; institutional, 43, 175, 189, 232n36, 249n21, 251n62; long-term, 191, 195, 252n67, 252n78; motivation to, 160, 177, 186, 205; naturalization of, 150; personal, 77, 166, 171, 173, 176, 190, 194, 196, 203

care drain, 198

care replacement, 198

Carter, Julia, 19, 20, 26, 225n12, 228n90, 228n92, 229n108

Cherlin, Andrew, 7, 208, 225nn6–7, 225n18, 254n15

childcare facilities, 11, 129, 136, 137, 138, 140, 142

childcare responsibilities, 112, 128, 136, 143, 144, 252n72

childhood: free-range, 33–34; regimented, 35, 56

childminder, 137, 138, 139, 246n32

Choi, Susanne, 227n64, 235n22, 237n48

communication, 48, 51–53, 59, 88, 117, 233n63, 240n24

Communist Party, 10, 11, 63, 71, 72, 83, 96, 136, 161

compound inequalities, 31, 37–40, 57, 190

concerted cultivation, 31, 37, 201, 229n5, 232n50

Confucianism, 9, 15, 47, 96

conjugal family, 7, 162, 164, 167, 186, 202. *See also* conjugal ties

conjugal ties, 60, 75, 77–81, 86; versus vertical ties, 75–81, 86, 91

consumerism, 10, 13, 60, 88, 92

convergence, 31, 72, 91, 197, 202, 206

courtship, 1, 4, 6, 26, 66, 71, 76, 98–99, 204

Davis, Deborah, 14, 225n25, 226n41, 227nn53–54, 230n14, 233n53, 235n8, 235n22, 236n35, 244n93, 250n41, 254n17

Davis-Friedmann, Deborah, 11, 16, 196, 200, 226n38, 226n39, 227n67, 252n71, 253n81, 253n86

deinstitutionalization, 7, 8, 14, 244n93

democratization thesis, 47, 91, 239n92

demographic family profile, 6, 46, 67, 80, 130, 197

demographic transformation, 28, 154

demographic transition, 7, 14, 45, 192, 196, 230n7

desiring subject, 120–23, 244n91

de-traditionalization, 7, 8

differential mode of association, 18–19, 50, 233n58

GPSR Authorized Representative: Easy Access System Europe - Mustamäe tee 50, 10621 Tallinn, Estonia, gpsr.requests@easproject.com

www.ingramcontent.com/pod-product-compliance
Lightning Source LLC
Chambersburg PA
CBHW020843270326
41928CB00006B/520

9 780691 258409